Maui

Sara Benson

LONELY PLANET PUBLICATIONS
Melbourne • Oakland • London • Paris

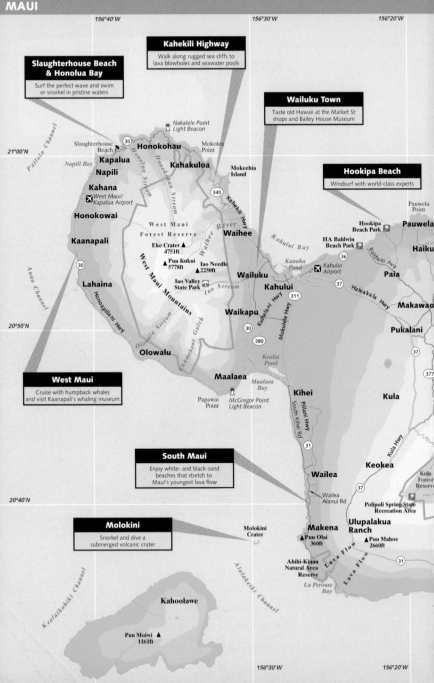

MAUI

Slaughterhouse Beach & Honolua Bay
Surf the perfect wave and swim or snorkel in pristine waters

Kahekili Highway
Walk along rugged sea cliffs to lava blowholes and seawater pools

Wailuku Town
Taste old Hawaii at the Market St shops and Bailey House Museum

Hookipa Beach
Windsurf with world-class experts

West Maui
Cruise with humpback whales and visit Kaanapali's whaling museum

South Maui
Enjoy white- and black-sand beaches that stretch to Maui's youngest lava flow

Molokini
Snorkel and dive a submerged volcanic crater

156°40'W
156°30'W
156°20'W

21°00'N
20°50'N
20°40'N

156°30'W
156°20'W

Patiolo Channel
Napili Bay
Auau Channel
Kealaikahiki Channel
Alalakeiki Channel

Nakalele Point
Light Beacon
Slaughterhouse Beach
Mokolea Point
Mokeehia Island
Pauwela Point

Honokohau
Kapalua
Napili
Kahana
West Maui/Kapalua Airport
Honokowai
Kaanapali
Lahaina

Kahakuloa

West Maui Forest Reserve
Eke Crater ▲ 4751ft
▲ Puu Kukui 5778ft
Iao Needle ▲ 2250ft
Iao Valley State Park

West Maui Mountains

Honoapiilani Hwy
Olowalu Stream
Ukumehame Gulch
Honokohau Stream
Kanaha Stream
Wailee River
Iao Stream

Waihee
Wailuku
Kahului
Kahului Airport
Kahului Bay
Kanaha Pond
Waikapu

HA Baldwin Beach Park
Hookipa Beach Park
Pauwela
Haiku
Paia
Makawao
Pukalani

Baldwin Ave
Haleakala Hwy
Kula Hwy

30
340
36
37
311
30
380
31
377
37

Olowalu

Maalaea
Maalaea Bay
Papawai Point
McGregor Point Light Beacon
Kealia Pond

Kihei

Piilani Hwy
South Kihei Rd
Kuihelani Hwy
Mokulele Hwy

Kula

Keokea

Wailea Alanui Rd
Wailea

Molokini Crater

Makena
▲ Puu Olai 360ft
Ahihi-Kinau Natural Area Reserve
La Perouse Bay
Lava Flow

Ulupalakua Ranch
▲ Puu Mahoe 2660ft

Polipoli Spring State Recreation Area
Kula Forest Reserve

Kahoolawe
▲ Puu Moiwi 1161ft

Puu Moiwi ▲

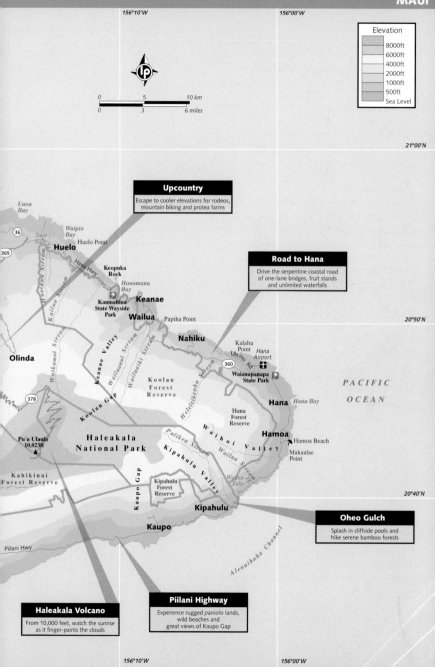

Maui
1st edition – July 2002

Published by
Lonely Planet Publications Pty Ltd ABN 36 005 607 983
90 Maribyrnong St, Footscray, Victoria 3011, Australia

Lonely Planet Offices
Australia Locked Bag 1, Footscray, Victoria 3011
USA 150 Linden St, Oakland, CA 94607
UK 10a Spring Place, London NW5 3BH
France 1 rue du Dahomey, 75011 Paris

Photographs
Many of the images in this guide are available for licensing from
Lonely Planet Images.
W www.lonelyplanetimages.com

Front cover photograph
Windsurfer turns board at speed (John Carter/Corbis)

ISBN 1 74059 271 9

Contents

Maui
1st edition – July 2002

Published by
Lonely Planet Publications Pty Ltd ABN 36 005 607 983
90 Maribyrnong St, Footscray, Victoria 3011, Australia

Lonely Planet Offices
Australia Locked Bag 1, Footscray, Victoria 3011
USA 150 Linden St, Oakland, CA 94607
UK 10a Spring Place, London NW5 3BH
France 1 rue du Dahomey, 75011 Paris

Photographs
Many of the images in this guide are available for licensing from
Lonely Planet Images.
w www.lonelyplanetimages.com

Front cover photograph
Windsurfer turns board at speed (John Carter/Corbis)

ISBN 1 74059 271 9

text & maps © Lonely Planet Publications Pty Ltd 2002
photos © photographers as indicated 2002

Printed by The Bookmaker International Ltd
Printed in China

Contents

MAUI MAP INDEX

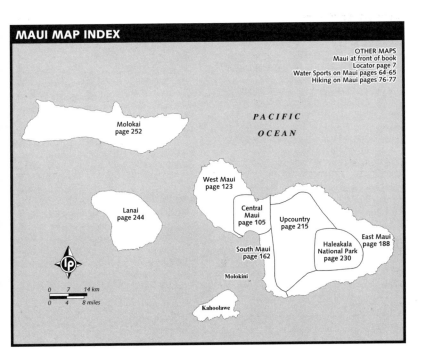

OTHER MAPS
Maui at front of book
Locator page 7
Water Sports on Maui pages 64-65
Hiking on Maui pages 76-77

PACIFIC

OCEAN

Molokai
page 252

West Maui
page 123

Lanai
page 244

Central
Maui
page 105

Upcountry
page 215

East Maui
page 188

South Maui
page 162

Haleakala
National Park
page 230

Molokini

0   7   14 km
0   4   8 miles

Kahoolawe

The Author

Sara 'Sam' Benson

Years ago Sara Benson graduated with a futile liberal arts degree from the University of Chicago. After spending one summer wandering the streets of San Francisco, she found herself swept away to Maui. That taste of wild guava and volcanic *mana* never left her, even as she later journeyed through the wilds of Asia, racking up thousands of kilometers on rickety Laos buses, broken Chinese bicycles, Japanese *shinkansen* and along all kinds of roads on foot.

At home and abroad, Sara ran through several jobs as an editor, high school teacher, journalist and corporate hack before signing on with Lonely Planet many moons ago. For the moment she pitches her tent on the Big Island of Hawaii, but still resides, at least a few months out of the year, in the Bay Area of Northern California. A writer by inclination and a traveler by trade, she has worked on nearly a dozen titles for Lonely Planet.

FROM THE AUTHOR

The foundations of this book were laid by Lonely Planet *Hawaii* authors Ned Friary and Glenda Bendure.

Big thanks to LP Oakland for lifting me on board this project, especially to the cartographers, editors and staff who armed me with anecdotes and professional advice. Without Maria Donohoe and Paul Sheridan, who both exhibited saintly patience and understanding, I might have gone mad, especially during the last days of manuscript tweaking. Special thanks to Melena McKaskill, Ryan Ver Berkmoes, David Zingarelli and everyone else who sprang to the virtual rescue when my laptop died.

Mahalo to da max to Lonely Planet author Conner Gorry, who saved my sanity with mid-morning smoothies and answers to obscure Hawaiiana questions after midnight. Wahine, this guidebook could not have come to life without your *makaku*! Big mahalo to all islanders who also showed me aloha, especially Lisa Davis and her cohorts for not laughing their heads off at my mountain-biking disaster.

Warmest thanks to my family and bicoastal tribe of friends for spare rooms in which to write and sometimes sleep. Half a decade ago, Blake Macurdy once hauled me up out of Haleakala crater by my backpack straps, and even forgave me for having made us almost miss our flight to Hawaii – thank you, and this book is all your fault.

This Book

This is the first edition of *Maui*. Portions of this book were taken from Lonely Planet's *Hawaii* book, which was written by Glenda Bendure and Ned Friary.

Like Maui himself pulling the island up from the sea with a fish hook, a talented team at Lonely Planet's Oakland, USA, office pulled the guidebook version through the production process with only slightly less impressive results.

FROM THE PUBLISHER

The book was edited by Paul Sheridan with the guidance of senior editor Maria Donohoe. The proofreading team comprised Bruce Evans, Anastasia Safioleas and Nancy Ianni in the Melbourne office and Oakland's own Stefani Barber and Kate Hoffman. Rachel Bernstein and Suki Gear kindly lent a hand at the layout stage. Kate Hoffman also stepped in as acting senior editor as the book went to press.

The lead cartographer was Anneka Imkamp, with David Ryder drawing the Excursions maps. Bart Wright took over as senior cartographer from Tracey Croom when she busted out of the Cartography corral and headed for the Design department. The basemap editors were Kat Smith, Narrinder Bansal, Rudie Watzig, Buck Cantwell, Rachel Jereb, John Culp, Patrick Huerta, Brad Lodge, Don Patterson and Terence Philippe. Kat and Buck proved their multitasking prowess by assisting with map proofing too. Source materials were collected by CDSs Molly Green and John Spelman. Technical support and expertise was lent by Chris Howard, Tim Lohnes and Patrick 'Peaches' Phelan. Cartography manager Alex Guilbert kept an eye on the whole darn lot of 'em.

Designer Henia Miedzinski expertly laid out the book and colorwraps, and Jennifer Steffey designed the cover with production and design help from Henia. The fabulous new illustrations, including the best ever chapter end, were created by Justin Marler, with other illustrations courtesy of Hugh D'Andrade, Hayden Foell, Rini Keagy, Jim Swanson and Wendy Yanagihara. Margaret Livingston indexed the book and art director Susan Rimerman led the design effort.

Phew! Now, where's that Mai Tai?

Foreword

ABOUT LONELY PLANET GUIDEBOOKS

The story begins with a classic travel adventure: Tony and Maureen Wheeler's 1972 journey across Europe and Asia to Australia. There was no useful information about the overland trail then, so Tony and Maureen published the first Lonely Planet guidebook to meet a growing need.

From a kitchen table, Lonely Planet has grown to become the largest independent travel publisher in the world, with offices in Melbourne (Australia), Oakland (USA), London (UK) and Paris (France).

Today Lonely Planet guidebooks cover the globe. There is an ever-growing list of books and information in a variety of media. Some things haven't changed. The main aim is still to make it possible for adventurous travelers to get out there – to explore and better understand the world.

At Lonely Planet we believe travelers can make a positive contribution to the countries they visit – if they respect their host communities and spend their money wisely. Since 1986 a percentage of the income from each book has been donated to aid projects and human rights campaigns, and, more recently, to wildlife conservation.

Although inclusion in a guidebook usually implies a recommendation, we cannot list every good place. Exclusion does not necessarily imply criticism. In fact, there are a number of reasons why we might exclude a place – sometimes it is simply inappropriate to encourage an influx of travelers.

UPDATES & READER FEEDBACK

Things change – prices go up, schedules change, good places go bad and bad places go bankrupt. Nothing stays the same. So, if you find things better or worse, recently opened or long-since closed, please tell us and help make the next edition even more accurate and useful.

Lonely Planet thoroughly updates each guidebook as often as possible – usually every two years, although for some destinations the gap can be longer. Between editions, up-to-date information is available in our free, quarterly *Planet Talk* newsletter and monthly email bulletin *Comet*. The *Upgrades* section of our website (**W** www.lonelyplanet.com) is also regularly updated by Lonely Planet authors, and the site's *Scoop* section covers news and current affairs relevant to travelers. Lastly, the *Thorn Tree* bulletin board and *Postcards* section carry unverified, but fascinating, reports from travelers.

Tell us about it! We genuinely value your feedback. A well-traveled team at Lonely Planet reads and acknowledges every email and letter we receive and ensures that every morsel of information finds its way to the relevant authors, editors and cartographers.

Everyone who writes to us will find their name listed in the next edition of the appropriate guidebook and will receive the latest issue of *Comet* or *Planet Talk*. The very best contributions will be rewarded with a free guidebook.

We may edit, reproduce and incorporate your comments in Lonely Planet products such as guidebooks, websites and digital products, so let us know if you don't want your comments reproduced or your name acknowledged.

How to contact Lonely Planet:
Online: **e** talk2us@lonelyplanet.com.au, **W** www.lonelyplanet.com
Australia: Locked Bag 1, Footscray, Victoria 3011
UK: 10a Spring Place, London NW5 3BH
USA: 150 Linden St, Oakland, CA 94607

Introduction

Maui, a demigod with Herculean strength and the trickster cunning of Odysseus, once yanked the Hawaiian islands up out of the sea with a fish hook. He climbed Haleakala volcano and lassoed the sun, refusing to let go until the islands had been rescued from ancient darkness. Today sun seekers still reap the fruits of Maui's mythical labors as they laze upon kaleidoscopically colored beaches and enjoy 120 miles of sunshine coast.

'Maui no ka Oi' – Maui is the best! – that's how the saying goes. Maui may not be the biggest island, or where the state capital stands, and it is far away from Waikiki. But if visitors can be judged to vote with their feet, then Maui is the favored son among all of the Hawaiian Neighbor Islands. Even endangered humpback whales prefer these warm coastal waters above all others during their winter migrations.

Honeymooners, surfers and hikers all find their own slice of paradise on Maui. And yet there is room for you to secret yourself away in natural ocean baths, secluded waterfalls or at royal volcanic heights. Even in the main tourist urban enclaves – the old whaling town of Lahaina, the Kaanapali-Kapalua resorts and the Kihei strip – there are no super-highrises as

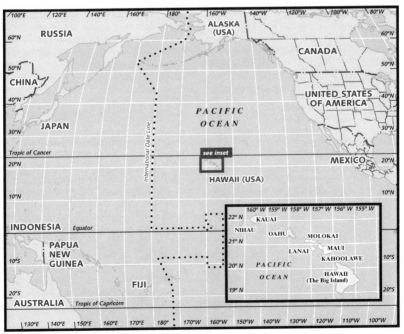

on Oahu. By law every beachfront remains open to the public. And some of the most beloved Hawaiian chefs practice their island culinary wizardry nearby.

Yet Maui has a more raw side. Escape is never far away when you realize that it takes only a couple of hours to circumnavigate the entire island. You are absolutely free to get as near to the *aina* (land) as you want: pitch your tent on the beach or pick fresh guava out of the jungle. Tomorrow you can get muddy all over again while mountain biking, or you can let the salt spray rub against your skin on a surfboard.

Staying in the small towns of Paia, Haiku or Hana is another experience altogether. These small settlements sit beneath Haleakala, the massive volcano that provides the backdrop to all of East Maui. Upcountry on the drier slopes of the volcano are pastures where Hawaiian cowboys still ride and fields where Kula truck farmers raise an abundance of flowers and vegetables. At 10,023 feet, the summit itself overlooks an extraordinary landscape of spewed red cinders and gray lava hills, all inside a crater basin that could engulf Manhattan. Magnificent hiking trails cross the crater floor, and at sunrise it seems like the gods are finger-painting the clouds.

Haleakala's windward side is lush, wet and rugged. The famed Hana Hwy runs down the full length of it, winding its way above the coast through tropical jungle and past roadside waterfalls. It's arguably the most beautiful coastal road in Hawaii. Past timeless Hana town, the Piilani Hwy takes over and passes by bamboo forests, waterfall pools and the cliffs of Oheo Gulch, then onward for jaw-dropping views up Kaupo Gap and solitary beaches where the ocean roars. Only the dramatic cliffs, lava blowholes and pristine bays of the Kahekili Hwy that snakes around West Maui's back side can compare.

Critics say that Maui is past its prime: overdeveloped, overtouristed, overpopulated and outdone. It's true that strong doses of imagination are required to see anything of Hawaii's early history here. The few *heiau* (temples) that exist are often overgrown and inaccessible. A few quaint historical museums and the antique shops in old Wailuku town only hint at what the island must have looked like before the 1960s resort boom and the birth of strip malls. Sigh.

Yet places where the heart of Hawaii still throbs are not far away, thanks to the last remaining interisland ferry services in the state, which both leave from Lahaina Harbor. One goes to Molokai, the birthplace of hula and a refuge of exiles, outcasts and *mana* (power) wielding priests since long ago. There isn't a single stoplight anywhere and wild beauty is never more than a mile down the road. Maui's closest Neighbor Island is Lanai, where Manele Bay offers beautiful snorkeling and camping. Solo adventurers can take on 4WD tracks and explore Lanai's ancient Hawaiian ruins, Shipwreck Beach or the challenging Munro Trail.

When all is said and *pau* (finished), there's no better place to first dip your toes into the waters of Polynesia than Maui. Whether you are diving among brilliant sea life in a submerged volcano crater, or stepping out above the clouds into rain forest, or even simply sunning yourself lizardlike on Big Beach, Maui no ka Oi indeed. Aloha.

Facts about Maui

HISTORY

As far as anyone can tell, the original settlers of Polynesia (literally, 'many islands') followed a long migratory path through Southeast Asia, down through Indonesia and across Melanesia, before settling Tonga and Samoa in about 1000 BC. Over the next 1500 years, they migrated to the more far-flung islands of the Pacific, with Hawaii being one of the last areas settled.

Archaeological evidence indicates the first Polynesians arrived in Hawaii from the Marquesas Islands between AD 500 and 700. As the Hawaiian islands are the most geographically isolated in the world, that was no small feat. They used double-hulled canoes loaded down with enough plant cuttings, stock animals, cooked food, fruit and water to last the journey. Their navigators, called 'wayfinders,' were astronomers, fishermen, boat builders, sailors and master decision makers. It was they who navigated vast stretches of open ocean by interpreting ocean swells, floating animal matter, the position of stars over known islands and even the colors of sunrises and sunsets to predict weather.

Ancient Hawaii

When the first wave of Tahitians arrived in Hawaii around AD 1000, they apparently fought and subjugated the Marquesans, who were forced to build temples, irrigation ditches and fishponds for the conquerors. Hawaiian legends about a tribe of little people called *menehune* may well refer to the Marquesans. Indeed, the word 'menehune' is very similar to the Tahitian word for 'outcast.'

Around the 12th century, a powerful Tahitian *kahuna* (priest), Paao, arrived on the Big Island of Hawaii. Convinced that the Hawaiians were too lax in their worship, Paao introduced the concept of offering human sacrifice to the gods and built the first *luakini* (sacrificial temples) on the islands. He also established the *kapu* system, a practice of taboos that strictly regulated all social interaction.

Kapu forbade commoners from eating the same food, walking the same ground or even crossing the shadow of the *ali'i*, or royalty. Women were forbidden from eating coconuts, bananas, pork and certain varieties of fish. The penalty for breaking kapu was death unless the offender could reach a place of refuge before being caught, in which case he or she would be pardoned.

Paao also summoned the chief Pili from Kahiki (Tahiti) to establish a new royal lineage. With Pili as chief and Paao as *kahuna nui* (high priest), their dynasty was to last 700 years, all the way down through King Kamehameha the Great.

Unification

Before western contact, the island of Maui had three major population centers: the lush southeast coast around Hana, the Wailuku area on the central plains and the district of Lele (present-day Lahaina) on the western shore.

In the 14th century, Piilani, the chief of the Hana district, conquered the entire island. During his reign, Piilani built Maui's largest temple, Piilanihale Heiau (which still stands today north of Hana town) as well as an extensive islandwide road system. Almost half of Maui's highways still bear his name.

The last of Maui's ruling chiefs was Kahekili. During the 1780s, he was the most powerful chief in Hawaii, bringing Oahu, Molokai and Lanai under Maui's rule.

At about the same time, the Hawaiian Islands were the last of the Polynesian islands to be 'discovered' by the West. There is speculation that Spanish sailors, whose galleons had been making annual runs between Mexico and the Philippines since 1565, may have stumbled upon Hawaii even earlier but kept the discovery a secret.

British explorer Captain James Cook spent the better part of a decade exploring and charting most of the South Pacific before chancing on Hawaii in 1778 as he sailed from Tahiti in search of a northwest passage to the Atlantic. Captain Cook named the Hawaiian archipelago the Sandwich Islands, in honor of the Earl of Sandwich. He and his crew returned home with charts and maps that would allow others to follow in their wake, and in Britain and Europe their stories and drawings were published, stirring the public's keen sense of adventure. What he and his crew left behind was also quite a legacy: iron that was turned into weapons, diseases that decimated the native population and the first children of mixed blood.

When Captain George Vancouver, one of the original crew members who sailed with Cook in 1778, landed on Maui at Kihei four years later he attempted to make peace between the warring chiefs. He eventually befriended an ambitious young royal from the Big Island, later known as Kamehameha the Great. In 1790, while old Kahekili was on Oahu, Kamehameha launched a bold naval attack on Maui. Using Western cannons and the aid of two captured foreign seamen, Isaac Davis and John Young, Kamehameha defeated Maui's warriors in a fierce battle at Iao Valley. Before he could take full command of the island, he was recalled to the Big Island by attacking rivals. After Kahekili died on Oahu in 1794 and his chiefdom was destroyed by squabbling heirs, Kamehameha quickly invaded Maui again and this time he conquered the entire island.

The New Religion

When Kamehameha the Great died in 1819, the crown of the Hawaiian monarchy was passed to his reluctant son, Liholiho, who was proclaimed Kamehameha II. In reality the power was passed to Queen Kaahumanu, who had been the favorite of the old king's wives. Kaahumanu was an ambitious woman who single-handedly brought down the kapu system, wiping out 600 years of taboos and restrictions. A frenzy of temple-smashing and idol-burning quickly spread across the islands, perfectly setting the stage for the arrival of Western missionaries.

Both whalers and missionaries arrived in Lahaina on Maui in the early 1820s, and they were soon at odds. Ready for grog and native women who freely associated with them, the sailors didn't take kindly to the puritanism of the New England missionaries. Queen Kaahumanu, however, did and she became a patron of the church in Hawaii.

Lahainaluna Seminary, the first school west of the Rockies in what would later become the USA, was established right above Lahaina harbor, and the first native Hawaiian to be ordained there was David Malo. With great foresight, Malo urged Kamehameha III, the last son of Kamehameha the Great, to adopt modern measures to protect Hawaii from being taken over by waves of invading foreigners. With his help, Kamehameha III penned a declaration of rights and the first constitution in 1840, which created a national assembly.

Hawaii's only 'invasion' by a foreign power took place in 1843 when George Paulet, an upstart British commander upset about a petty land deal, sailed into Honolulu and seized Oahu for six months. After catching wind of the incident, Queen Victoria dispatched Admiral Richard Thomas to restore Hawaiian independence. As the Hawaiian flag was raised, Kamehameha III uttered the now famous words '*Ua mau ke ea o ka aina i ka pono,*' meaning 'The life of the land is perpetuated in righteousness,' which remains Hawaii's official motto.

Robber Barons

What changed Hawaii forever was the Great Mahele of 1848. For the first time, land became a commodity that could be bought and sold. Although the missionaries persuaded Kamehameha III that the majority of Hawaiians would own small farms, it was in fact Westerners who profited by gobbling up huge tracts of land. By the time the native Hawaiians clearly grasped the concept of private land ownership, there was little land left to own. Many drifted into ghettoes in larger cities or tried working on the vast sugar plantations that eventually appeared.

Two of the first sugar planters were Samuel Alexander and Henry Baldwin, sons of prominent missionaries who founded what became Hawaii's biggest sugar company, starting with just a dozen acres of land in Haiku in 1870. To expand their operations, they and the other plantation owners on other islands began to look overseas for a labor supply. They needed immigrants accustomed to working long days in blisteringly hot weather, and for whom the low wages would still seem like an opportunity. Immigration from around Asia and parts of Europe brought a wealth of ethnic diversity to Maui, this in spite of plantation camps being strictly segregated to prevent unionized labor. A dozen languages filled the air, and a unique pidgin English developed as a means for the various groups to communicate with one another.

As the sugar industry boomed, Hawaii's native population declined, largely as the result of diseases introduced by foreigners. Leprosy was called *mai pake,* meaning the 'Chinese disease,' although no one knew exactly which immigrant groups brought the infection to Hawaii. Those who were infected were forcibly exiled to a leprosy colony on Molokai's Kalaupapa peninsula. In later decades bubonic plague swept the islands, and a fire burned Kahului to the ground.

As a means of eliminating the tariffs that ate up profit margins, most plantation owners favored the annexation of Hawaii to the USA, the islands' largest trading partner. In 1872, General John Schofield was sent by the USA to assess Pearl Harbor's strategic value. He was impressed with what he saw – the largest anchorage in the Pacific – and reported his enthusiasm back to Washington.

An End to Sovereignty

King David Kalakaua turned out to be Hawaii's last king. Although known as the 'Merrie Monarch,' he ruled in troubled times. The first challenge to his reign came on election day in 1874. His contender was the dowager Queen Emma, and when election results were announced, her followers rioted in the streets, requiring Kalakaua to request aid from US and British warships that happened to be in Honolulu Harbor at the time.

Amazingly Kalakaua went on to reign as a great Hawaiian revivalist. He brought back the hula, turning around decades of missionary repression against the 'heathen dance,' and worked to ensure some measure of self-rule for native Hawaiians, who had become a minority in their own land. His nationalism and the debts he incurred by gallivanting around the world made him increasingly unpopular with the sugar barons, whose business was now the backbone of the economy. In 1887 they formed the Hawaiian League. It presented the king with a list of demands and forced him to accept a new constitution strictly limiting his powers.

In 1891 Kalakaua was succeeded by his sister, Liliuokalani, wife of Oahu governor John O Dominis. Queen Liliuokalani was even more determined than Kalakaua to increase the power of the monarchy, charging that the 1887 constitution had illegally been forced upon King Kalakaua.

In January 1893, as Liliuokalani was preparing to proclaim a new constitution that restored sovereign royal powers, a group of armed *haole* (white) businessmen occupied the government building and declared the monarchy overthrown. They announced a provisional government, led by Sanford Dole, son of a pioneer missionary, and appealed to the US for annexation. President Grover Cleveland was sympathetic to the queen and refused to act.

The new government, with Dole as president, inaugurated itself as the Republic of Hawaii on July 4, 1894. Liliuokalani was forced to abdicate and was tried and placed under house arrest in her own palace. In 1896 her first act after being set free was to go to Washington to plead for help in restoring the Hawaiian monarchy. To most islanders, Liliuokalani was still their queen.

Until Kingdom Come

Over the past decade, a native Hawaiian sovereignty movement, intent on righting some of the wrongs of past centuries, has emerged. Although badly splintered into factions, all Hawaiian sovereignty groups would agree (as does the World Court at The Hague) that Hawaii is an independent, sovereign nation, that has been unlawfully occupied by the USA for more than 100 years.

In 1893 when Queen Liliuokalani was forced to abdicate from her throne, US President Grover Cleveland said that 'a substantial wrong has thus been done which a due regard for our national character as well as the rights of injured people requires that we should endeavor to repair.' Unfortunately, the next US president William McKinley did not agree; he sent the Hawaii annexation treaty to Congress in 1898.

In 1993 on the centennial of the monarchy's overthrow, US president Bill Clinton signed into law what became known as 'The Apology Bill,' acknowledging that native Hawaiians had an inherent right to self-determination and had in fact never relinquished their claims to their land.

Although this opened the floodgates for reconciliation, Hawaiian sovereignty groups have yet to agree, mostly because no consensus can be reached. Some groups favor the restoration of the monarchy, while others focus on monetary reparations. Another rallying point is the growing discontent over the mismanagement of Hawaiian Home Lands.

Many sovereignty groups have adopted their own constitutions, established pro-tem governing bodies and staged protests, but generally without paying much attention to one another or building public consensus. However, most sovereignty groups are looking at some form of the nation-within-a-nation model used by Native American tribal governments on the US mainland. Polls show that a significant majority of all Hawaii residents support the concept of Hawaiian sovereignty, if only someone could please come up with a plan.

By that time events had gone too far, and the annexation of Hawaii was passed in the US Congress on July 7, 1898. Hawaii entered the 20th century as a territory of the USA.

The Slow Boat to Statehood

In 1936, Pan American flew the first passenger flights from the US mainland to Hawaii, an aviation milestone that ushered in the transpacific air age. Hawaii was now only hours away from the US mainland, but it took decades for Congress to accept these far-flung islands as an official state.

On December 7, 1941, a wave of Japanese bombers attacked Pearl Harbor, forcing the USA into WWII. After the smoke cleared, Hawaii was placed under martial law and Oahu became the US military headquarters in the Pacific theater. While sheer numbers prevented the sort of racist practices that took place on the mainland, the Nisei, or second-generation Japanese, in Hawaii were subject to interrogation and

harassment. Their religious and civic leaders, specifically *kibei* who had been educated in Japan, were sent to mainland internment camps, while those who remained kept a low profile and took to calling themselves AJAs, or Americans of Japanese Ancestry, to emphasize their loyalty.

During the final stages of the war, when fighting was at its heaviest, AJAs leapt at the chance to form volunteer combat units. One of these, the 442nd Regimental Combat Team, which was sent into action on the European front, became the most decorated fighting unit in US history. Among the veterans of the 442nd is Hawaii's senior US senator, Daniel Inouye.

Overall, WWII brought Hawaii closer to the center stage of American culture and politics. The prospect of statehood had long been the central topic of Hawaiian politics. Almost thirty years had passed since Hawaii's first delegate to the US Congress, Prince Jonah Kuhio Kalanianaole, intro-

Until Kingdom Come

Even if they can't agree on how to move forward, sovereignty groups all know what they don't want. In 1996 the first referendum on Hawaiian sovereignty was boycotted because it was believed to have been co-opted by the state legislature. In January 1999, another election took place, with voters selecting 85 delegates to form a Hawaiian Convention aimed at charting the sovereignty course. Again, and for similar reasons, it too was boycotted by the sovereignty groups. Consequently, the voter turnout was only 8.7% – fewer than 9000 of the 102,000 eligible voters participated.

Enter US Senator Daniel Akaka, now notorious enough to be the target of the activist group **W** www.stopakaka.org. At first, things looked good when Akaka introduced Senate Bill 2899 to Congress in 2000, because it outlined a path for moving toward Hawaiian sovereignty and economic self-sufficiency. The bill was passed by both houses of Congress, but then mysteriously died. During the next legislative session, Senator Akaka replaced it with SB746, a watered-down version that would cut federal funding for the sovereignty process and again subject it to control by the state legislature.

No Hawaiian sovereignty group likes this bill, even if they can agree on little else, and efforts are already underway to defeat it. Meanwhile, on July 5, 2001, the Hawaiian Kingdom group filed a provocative complaint with the United Nations, asking it to investigate Hawaii's case against the US government. Peaceful sovereignty protests continue across the islands, many of them on Maui recently. One shut down Kahului Airport for hours while sovereignty groups in a rare show of unity clogged access roads with their pickup trucks, flying Hawaiian flags turned upside down (the symbol of a nation in distress) and shouting out *Ku'e!* (Resist!) to newly enlightened passersby.

duced the first statehood bill in 1919. But to the overwhelmingly white and conservative post-war Congress, Hawaii's multiethnic community seemed too exotic to be thought of as 'American.'

Years of tireless lobbying and the acceptance of an equally oddball state, Alaska, as the 49th state in the union paved the way for Hawaiian statehood. In March 1959, the US Congress passed legislation to make Hawaii a state and on June 27 a plebiscite was held in Hawaii, with more than 90% of the islanders voting for statehood. The island of Niihau was the only precinct to vote against it.

On August 21, 1959, after 61 years of territorial status, Hawaii became the 50th state of the USA.

GEOGRAPHY

The Hawaiian Islands chain is 2500 miles from the nearest continental land mass, and the most geographically isolated place in the world. The islands form the apex of the Polynesian triangle (with Easter Island and New Zealand as the other two vertices) and stretch from remote Kure Atoll in the northwest to the Big Island's Ka Lae, the southernmost point of the USA.

The total land mass (6432 sq miles) of all the Hawaiian Islands is slightly smaller than Fiji but a bit larger than the US state of Connecticut. The Northwestern Hawaiian Islands, which lie scattered across a thousand miles of ocean west of Kauai, contribute a total land mass of just under 5 sq miles. Meanwhile Maui is the second-largest Hawaiian Island, with about 728 sq miles of land. If you count the islands of Molokai, Lanai and Kahoolawe, all part of Maui County, that figure rises to 1162 sq miles.

The equator lies 1470 miles south of the state capital Honolulu, which puts all of the major Hawaiian islands south of the tropic of Cancer and inside the tropical zone. Hawaii shares approximately the same latitude as Hong Kong, Bombay, Mexico City and Cuba.

GEOLOGY

The island of Maui arose from the ocean floor as two distinct volcanoes. Haleakala, on Maui's eastern side, is the larger and younger of the two. It majestically rises to an elevation of 10,023 feet and measures five miles from sea floor to summit. The other more ancient volcano has been carved up into the West Maui Mountains, with Puu Kukui (5788 feet) as its highest peak. The eastern flanks of both volcanic masses are cut with deep ravines and valleys reaching downhill to windy stretches of coastline.

The valleylike isthmus between the two volcanoes was formed by later lava flows and soil erosion carried downstream from the mountains. Today this fertile isthmus provides a perfect setting for fields of sugarcane, and has given Maui the nickname 'The Valley Isle.'

CLIMATE

Obviously Hawaii has great weather. That's why you picked up this book, right? Most of the year it's balmy, with northeasterly trade winds prevailing. Temperatures and rainfall vary more with elevation and direction – whether *mauka* (toward the mountains) or *makai* (toward the sea) – than season.

Da Islands, Old & New

The Hawaiian Islands are the tips of massive shield volcanoes, created by a crack in the earth's mantle that has been spewing out molten rock for more than 25 million years. As weak spots in the earth's crust pass over this hot spot, molten lava rises and bursts through, slowly piling up and building underwater mountains. Some of these shield volcanoes finally emerge above the waterline as islands.

This hot spot is stationary, but the ocean floor is part of the Pacific Plate, which is moving northwest towards Japan at the rate of about 3 inches a year. (Californians will already know this plate by its eastern edge, which lies along the jumpy San Andreas Fault.) Every new shield volcano eventually creeps past the hot spot that created it. The farther from the source, the lower the volcanic activity, until the volcano is eventually cut off completely and turns cold. Haleakala last erupted in 1790, which on the geological clock means it could just be snoozing.

Once the lava stops, it's a downhill battle. The forces of erosion – wind, rain and waves – slowly wash the mountains away. The ocean floor settles, and the island essentially crushes itself under its own weight. Thus, the once mountainous Northwestern Hawaiian Islands, the oldest in the Hawaiian chain, are now low, flat atolls that in time will be totally submerged. Similarly, the islands of Maui County were once joined as a single land mass called Maui Nui ('Big Maui'), but their land links have already sunk back under the sea. Even the island of Maui will eventually be split into two islands, just like when it arose as two separate volcanoes from the ocean floor.

The Big Island, Hawaii's southernmost island, is still in the birthing process. Its most active volcano, Kilauea, is directly over the hot spot. In its latest eruptive phase, which began in 1983 and still continues, Kilauea has pumped out more than 2 billion cubic yards of lava, making this the largest known volcanic eruption in Hawaii's history.

Around 20 miles southeast of the Big Island, a new seamount named Loihi has already risen to within 1000 yards of the ocean surface and over 3000 yards from the ocean floor. The growing mounds of lava are expected to break the ocean surface in as little as 10,000 years – some like to say that if the volcano were to become hyperactive, it could emerge within a century or two. Not likely, but then again the 1996 earthquake swarms in the summit region returned with a vengeance starting in September 2001, so it's still anybody's game.

Like most Hawaiian islands, Maui has basically two kinds of weather, at least along the coast. The western *kona,* or leeward, side of the islands is dry and sunny year-round. Meanwhile on the *koolua,* or windward, side high volcanic mountains block trade winds and moisture-laden clouds coming from the northeast, bringing down abundant rainfall.

Likewise Maui has only two seasons, *kau* (summer) and *hooilo* (winter). Average temperatures differ only 8°F between summer and winter, and coastal waters are always warm. At the height of summer, the average daytime highs are 88°F in Lahaina, Kahului and Kihei, slightly less in Hana and Upcountry. The lowest temperature ever recorded on Maui was 14°F at the summit of Haleakala, although the average daytime high there is about 50°F. Overnight lows dip below freezing and the volcano even gets an occasional winter snowcap.

Maui gets most of its rain between December and March. The average annual rainfall is about 15 inches in Lahaina, Kahului or Kihei, and 69 inches in wet Hana on the rainy east coast. Rainfall within Haleakala crater ranges from desert conditions to rain forest, averaging 45 inches annually overall. Puu Kukui, which sits just five miles from the dry Wailuku plains, holds the US record for annual rainfall at an astoundingly soggy 739 inches.

Not only does winter have about twice the rainfall of summer, but winter storms can hang around for days. Kona weather sees the winds blow from the south, a shift from the typical northeast trades. The ocean swell pattern also changes at this time – snorkeling spots suddenly become surfing spots and vice versa. In summer, the rain is more likely to fall as brief tradewind showers. This doesn't mean winter is a bad time to go to Hawaii; it just means the weather is slightly more of a gamble.

The hurricane season is June to November, and although these storms usually bypass Maui, strong winds and flash flooding do cause some injury and property damage. For the National Weather Service's recorded forecast of weather conditions on

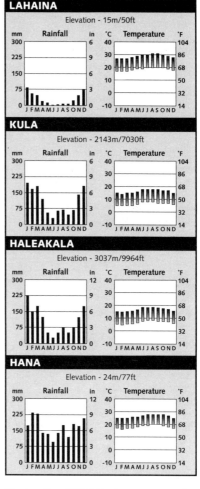

Maui, call ☎ 877-5111. A more extensive marine forecast, including surf conditions, winds and tides, is available by dialing ☎ 877-3477. Several local radio stations broadcast weather, surf and traffic reports throughout the day.

ECOLOGY & ENVIRONMENT

Hawaii's native ecosystems have been greatly stressed by the introduction of exotic flora and fauna species. Erosion caused by free-ranging cattle, goats and pigs, and the monocrop cultures of sugarcane and pineapple have destroyed native ground covers, resulting in washouts that sweep prime topsoil into the sea and choke nearshore reefs. In the past few decades tourism development has certainly taken its toll, especially the proliferation of megaresorts and golf courses built on fragile coastal lands.

Amazingly the islands have no polluting heavy industry and not a single roadside billboard to blight natural vistas. Hawaii has virtually all of the world's ecological zones represented and some of the only tropical rain forest in the USA. Haleakala National Park itself was named an International Biosphere Reserve in 1980. The movement to turn the preserve along the Keoneoio coastline at La Perouse Bay into another national park is gaining momentum. In the meantime volunteer docents are monitoring the area to educate visitors about sensitive archaeological, geological and biological features.

Among the hot environmental issues on Maui is a proposed 'dolphinarium' inside a new Kihei shopping complex. Activists are pushing the county government to make keeping any cetacean species in captivity illegal. Other eternally, and fiercely, debated issues include the expansion of Kahului airport, resort development and water rights. The resorts around Wailea and Makena want to expand, but they already cannot supply their own water needs, and a new resort at Spreckelsville near Paia will further divert much needed water from East Maui and Upcountry farmers. Last, the US military wants to blast a new channel to protect Maalaea harbor from southern swells, but the plan is widely criticized for its potential to cause siltation and destroy the harbor reef, beach, sea turtle habitats and the Maalaea Pipeline, a premier surfing spot.

Currently there are more than 150 environmental groups in Hawaii, ranging from chapters of international organizations to neighborhood groups defending local beaches from encroaching development.

One of the broadest-based groups is the Hawaii chapter of the Sierra Club, which has its own Maui group (Ⓦ www.hi.sierraclub.org/maui) engaging in local environmental activism and organizing outings aimed at eradicating invasive plants from native forests. Formerly directed by the Sierra Club, the nonprofit Earthjustice Legal Defense Fund (☎ 808-599-2436, Ⓦ www.earthjustice.org) plays a leading role in protecting Hawaii's environment and endangered species through court action.

The Nature Conservancy of Hawaii (Ⓦ http://nature.org) has opted for a different approach; it protects Hawaii's rarest ecosystems by buying up vast tracts of land and working out long-term stewardships with some of Hawaii's biggest landholders. One project included purchasing the Kipahulu Valley on Maui in conjunction with the state and turning the 11,000 acres over to the federal government to become part of Haleakala National Park. The adjoining rain forest of Waikamoi Preserve is still managed by the Nature Conservancy, as is 8000 acres of the West Maui Mountains surrounding Puu Kukui and an undisclosed spot that harbors a unique lava tube ecosystem found only at that site. On Molokai, the nature conservancy protects the rain forest at Kamakou Preserve and the windswept Moomomi dunes, along with some dryland forest on Lanai. The conservancy strictly limits the number of hikers granted access to its lands, but you can catch a glimpse by viewing its Hawaii slide show over the Web.

FLORA & FAUNA

It is estimated that before any human contact a new species managed to take hold in Hawaii only once every 35,000 years. Probably the first life forms to arrive on these volcanic islands were fern and moss spores, able to drift thousands of miles in the air.

All living things that reached Hawaii's shores were carried across the ocean on wing, wind or by waves – seeds clinging to a bird's feather, a floating hala plant, or insect eggs in a piece of driftwood. When the first Polynesian settlers arrived, they brought chickens, dogs and pigs, as well as medicinal plants and fruit. They cleared swathes of lowland forest for planting *ko* (sugarcane), breadfruit, taro, coconut and banana trees. Each species evolved to fit a specific niche in its new environment. Today the majority of Hawaii's more than 10,000 native flora and fauna species are found nowhere else on earth.

The legacy of Western contact has been the destruction of much of Hawaii's fragile ecosystems, starting with Captain Cook, who dropped off goats and left melon and pumpkin seeds. In fact, many of the flora and fauna we think of as Hawaiian today are later imports, for example, pineapples from Brazil or macadamia nuts from Australia. Hawaii didn't even have mosquitoes before water casks unloaded from whaling ships brought them – imagine: paradise without skeeters!

Having few predators and limited defenses, native plants and animals have slowly been choked out, consumed and otherwise decimated by introduced species, even though not all of the latter are pests. Exotic songbirds and game birds spread avian diseases to which native Hawaiian birds had no immunity. Introduced pigs, goats and cattle, which all grazed and foraged at will, spelled extinction for many Hawaiian plants, which were compromised by erosion and deforestation, too.

Hawaii accounts for 75% of extinct species in the USA and one-third of its endangered flora and fauna, even though the islands make up only 1% of the total US land mass. Some species are slowly making a comeback, like the silversword plant and nene (Hawaiian goose) and are easily found in Haleakala National Park. But twenty new exotic species arrive on Hawaiian soil each year, the worst threats now being noisy Caribbean frogs and miconia, a tenacious South American plant that has taken over 70% of Tahiti's rain forests.

Flora

Because climate zones vary from dry alpine desert to lush tropical rain forest in Hawaii, you'll find a wide variety of flora. Of course, less than half of the islands' original forest cover remains today.

The most bewitching of native Hawaiian forest trees is koa, nowadays found only at higher elevations and even then rarely. It grows up to 100 feet high. The young saplings have fernlike compound leaves that are an evolutionary throwback to its African origins. Hawaiians traditionally used this rich hardwood for making canoes, surfboards and ukulele and more recently, high-quality furniture and woodcarvings.

The versatile ohia lehua was one of the first plants to colonize old lava flows. It grows in barren areas as a shrub and on more fertile land as a tree. Found everywhere, it is easily recognized by its

Ohia lehua

tufted flowers that reveal themselves to be groups of red, orange, yellow or rare white stamens with no petals.

Brought by early Polynesian settlers, the *kukui* (literally 'candlenut tree') has oily nuts used for making lei, dyes and candles. The kukui has light silver-tinged foliage that stands out brightly in the forest. Another early Polynesian gift was bamboo, now found in tall forest groves and growing sometimes six inches in a single day. It has a sweet edible root and its stalk is used for furniture and Japanese *shakuhachi* (bamboo flutes).

Two coastal trees that proved useful in old Hawaii are the *hala* (pandanus or screw pine), whose spiny leaves were used for thatching and weaving, and the *niu* (coconut palm), which thrives in coral sands and produces about 50 to 75 coconuts a year.

Common native coastal plants include pohuehue, a beach morning glory with leathery green leaves and pale pink flowers, and the delicate orange-yellow flowers of the ilima, which has adapted to harsh winds by growing as a ground cover. A member of the alien mesquite family, kiawe is useful for making charcoal but is a nuisance for beachgoers, as its sharp thorns easily pierce soft sandals.

More than 5000 varieties of hibiscus bushes grow in Hawaii; on most, the colorful flowers bloom only for a day. There are a number of native hibiscus, including the hau tree, whose flowers open as yellow and change to dark orange and red as the day moves into the night. The kokio keokeo, a native Hawaiian white hibiscus tree that grows up to 40 feet high, is the only Hawaiian hibiscus with a fragrance. The yellow mauihauhele is the state flower.

Hawaii, of course, is abloom with scores of other tropical flowers, most introduced, including blood-red anthuriums, brilliant orange or blue birds of paradise, bougainvilleas, red torch ginger, white and yellow fragrant ginger, and various heliconias. There are also hundreds of varieties of orchid and protea grown mostly Upcountry.

Fauna

Native Hawaiian bird life is so varied, it deserves a book of its own; so do reef fish and whale and dolphin species. For recommended field guides, see also Books in the Facts for the Visitor chapter.

On a side note, geckos not only eat pesky mosquitoes but are a sign of good luck!

Birds Many of Hawaii's birds may have evolved from a single species, as is thought to have been the case with more than 50 species of native honeycreeper. The majority have evolved so thoroughly, however, that it's not possible to trace them to any continental ancestors. Sadly over half of Hawaii's native species are already extinct, and over 30 of those remaining species are still under threat.

One of the most critically endangered is the *alala* (Hawaiian crow), of which only a handful of birds remain in captive breeding programs on Maui and the Big Island. At least six birds native to Maui (mostly honeycreepers) are found almost nowhere else in the world and all are endangered, including the Maui parrotbill and the cinnamon-colored poouli, which quite amazingly wasn't discovered until 1973, when it was

sighted by a group of University of Hawaii students working in Hana rain forest. Thriving native Hawaiian species that you stand a good chance of seeing include the yellow-green amakihi and black-tailed iiwi, recognized by its vermilion feathers and salmon-colored bill. Both are common rain forest honeycreepers with curved bills to suck nectar from Hawaiian flowers.

Hawaiians believe that the *pueo,* or Hawaiian short-eared owl, has protective powers and represents a physical manifestation of ancestors' spirits. Seeing one is a good omen and most likely atop Haleakala where it soars at high altitudes. From a distance some mistake it for the *io* (Hawaiian hawk), a symbol of royalty.

Many long-distance migratory waterfowl use Maui as a stopping-off point; see Kanaha Pond and Kealia Pond in the Central Maui chapter.

Hawaiian Monk Seals Prior to human contact, Hawaii had no native land mammals save for monk seals and hoary bats. Both are now endangered.

The Hawaiian monk seal, so named for its solitary habits or the cowl-like fold of skin at its neck, exists only in the Hawaiian islands. The species has remained nearly unchanged for 15 million years, though in the past century it was nearly wiped out. Conservation efforts, including the translocation of some seals to create better breeding ratios (males will 'mob' and kill adult females if there are not enough breeding partners to go around), appear to be bringing the seals back from the edge of extinction.

Hawaiian monk seals, which are extremely sensitive to human disruption, breed and give birth primarily in the remote Northwestern Hawaiian Islands. Adults can grow up to 7 feet in length, weighing between 400lb and 600lb. The annual birth rate for monk seal pups is between 150 and

175 a year, though because of shark attacks and other predators, the majority fail to reach maturity. The total population now is estimated at 1500 to 2500 seals. Of the world's two other monk seal species, the Caribbean monk seal is believed extinct and the Mediterranean monk seal numbers only in the hundreds.

In recent years, sightings of Hawaiian monk seals hauling themselves onto beaches on the main islands have increased. It is illegal to approach one since mothers will abandon their pups at the slightest disturbance. Report any sightings to the National Marine Fisheries Service (☎ 808-973-2987 on Oahu) as soon as possible.

Whales Basically there are two types of whale: toothed whales, which use their teeth to catch prey, and baleen whales, which have rows of a horny elastic material, called baleen or whalebone, that hangs from the upper jaw and acts as a filter to extract food (normally krill and small fish) from the water. Both species are warm-blooded, air-breathing mammals. Hawaii has several species of toothed whales residing here year-round, plus a few migrating baleen species. It is the islands' most frequent visitor – the migrating North Pacific humpback whale – that everyone wants to see.

Once one of the most abundant of the great whales, humpbacks were hunted almost to extinction, and they are now an endangered species. Around the turn of the 19th century, an estimated 15,000 humpbacks remained. They were still being hunted as late as the 1960s, when an international ban on their slaughter came into force. The entire population of North Pacific humpbacks is now thought to be around 4000. About two-thirds of those winter in Hawaii, while others migrate to Mexico or the southern islands of Japan.

As the fifth largest of the great whales, the humpback can reach lengths of 45 feet and weigh up to 45 tons. The scientific name for humpback whales, *Megaptera novaengliae*, means 'Great Wings of New England.' Humpbacks have long white flippers, a knobby head and tail flukes with distinctive individual white markings, making them easy to identify. They spend the summer feeding in the plankton-rich waters off Alaska, developing a layer of blubber that sustains them through the winter. Each whale can eat close to a ton of food a day, but then fast for six months during the winter migration and breeding period.

Come November, humpbacks begin filtering into Hawaii. The largest numbers are found in the shallow waters between Maui, Lanai and Kahoolawe, now declared a national marine sanctuary. During their winter sojourn in the warm tropical waters, the whales mate and give birth to young that were conceived the year before. Mothers stay in shallow waters once their calves are born, apparently to protect them from shark attacks. At birth, calves are already about 12 feet long and weigh 3000lb.

Despite their size, humpbacks often put on an amazing acrobatic show, which includes arching dives, breaching and fin splashing. In breaching, humpbacks jump almost clear out of the water and then splash down with tremendous force. At breeding time sometimes several bull whales will do a series of crashing breaches to gain the favor of a cow, often bashing into one another, even drawing blood.

For whale-watching cruises and more background information see Whale Watching in the Activities chapter.

Dolphins Spinner dolphins are nocturnal feeders that often come into calm bays during the day to rest. If you are lucky enough to see them, perhaps off La Perouse Bay or during the ride over to Molokini, do not swim out and join them (an illegal act that is subject to a hefty fine). These wild, intelligent dolphins are easily disturbed by noise, so enjoy their acrobatics from at least 50 yards away. Bottlenose and spotted dolphins are also common in Hawaiian waters.

Sea Turtles Three species of sea turtle are endemic to the waters of Hawaii: the leatherback, *honu* (green sea turtle) and *honuea* (Hawksbill sea turtle). The latter weigh up to 200lbs when mature, while the soft-shelled leatherback can weigh 10 times that amount and grow up to 8 feet long. In Hawaiian mythology, sea turtles were *aumakua* (family gods and guardians), and their form appears often in ancient Hawaiian petroglyphs.

All three Hawaiian sea turtle species are protected by the Endangered Species Act, with the most threatened being the Hawksbill. It nests on only a few sand beaches on Oahu, Molokai, Maui and the Big Island and human disturbance to nesting grounds and poaching have killed uncountable numbers. The green sea turtles migrate hundreds of miles every few years to breed and nest in the remote Northwest Hawaiian Islands but are not uncommonly seen in Maui waters.

Reef Fish Maui also has over 400 species of reef fish. The most common are myriad species of butterfly fish, while other colorful specimens include the Picasso triggerfish and peacock flounder. The Maui Ocean Center in Maalaea is the best place to view and learn about reef fish; the free visitor guide includes a fold-out fish identification color map. *The Many-Splendored Fishes of Hawaii* by Gar Goodson is a handy, inexpensive fish identification book; it has lucid descriptions and 170 color drawings. Many dive shops sell plasticized fish identification charts designed for divers and snorkelers.

GOVERNMENT & POLITICS

Hawaii has no presidential primaries and no city government. Local politics are master-minded by individual mayors and their county councils, while the Hawaii state legislature and governor look on from over in Honolulu. While the colony of Kalaupapa on Molokai is called the 'county' of Kalawao, in actuality it has no county government and is under the jurisdiction of the Hawaii State Department of Health.

Maui County is comprised of the islands of Maui, Lanai, Molokai (except Kalaupapa) and Kahoolawe, which is presently uninhabited. The mayor is elected to a four-year term and the nine Maui County council members are elected at large to two-year terms. With its seat in Wailuku, the county provides all the services, such as police and fire protection, that on the mainland are usually assigned to cities. Currently the mayor is James 'Kimo' Apana, Jr, a fairly progressive Democrat. Both he and all nine council members are up for re-election in 2003. Expect debates over development issues to be central during the campaigns because Maui County is radically split between Hawaiian homeland activists found mostly on Molokai and some of the wealthiest neighborhoods in the state.

The state of Hawaii's lawmaking body is a bicameral legislature that has long been dominated by the Democratic party. Exhibiting a Hawaiian-style casualness, the regular legislative session convenes on the third Wednesday of January and meets for a mere 60 days a year. Executive power is vested in the governor, who is elected to a four-year term. Hawaii's governor currently is the controversial Benjamin Cayetano, who has been in office since 1994. Likely gubernatorial candidates running in the next election in 2002 include Maui's ex-mayor Linda Lingle, who narrowly lost to Cayetano in 1998, and the mayor of Honolulu, Jeremy Harris. Talk about in-bred politics.

For a discussion of the native sovereignty movement, see 'Until Kingdom Come,' earlier.

ECONOMY

Maui's biggest cash crop is tourists. After Oahu, the island captures the lion's share of Hawaii's tourist industry, receiving over two million visitors each year who collectively spend billions of dollars annually. Most visitors are from the US mainland, with Canadians and Japanese next in line. Although Maui has over half of the accommodations on all the Neighbor Islands, room rates are 25% higher than the state average, or $192 per night. The state spends a whopping $60 million per year to promote tourism, but then makes most of that money back by gouging tourists with an exorbitant room tax of 11.41%.

The Hawaii tourist industry was suffering from stagnation even before the terrorist attacks of September 11, 2001, which caused visitor statistics to drop through the floor. On Maui, room occupancy dropped to its lowest point in decades, and the unemployment rate quadrupled to 16%. Many considered it a wake-up call for what visionaries had been urging all along, namely economic diversification.

Hawaii is the most militarized state in the USA, but the military presence on Maui is far less evident than on Oahu. If the state-managed Kahului Airport were a private business, however, it would be the island's largest employer. Other employers include the wealth of scientific research conducted in Maui's national park, tropical rain forest preserves and various marine and wildlife sanctuaries. Elsewhere Maui is growing its high-tech industry and already boasts one of the world's thirty fastest supercomputers.

In official estimates, agriculture ranks far behind tourism and government jobs in terms of earnings. Unofficially, the cultivation of *pakalolo* (marijuana) is a multibillion dollar statewide industry even though aggressive law enforcement aimed at wiping out 'Maui Wowie' has partly hindered the harvests. Sugar and pineapple, which once formed the backbone of Hawaii's economy, have been scaled back dramatically in recent years. Pineapple production has ceased entirely on Lanai, which until the early 1990s was nicknamed the 'Pineapple Island,' and sugar has come close to entirely disappearing from the landscape across the state. The Big Five companies – Amfac, Castle & Cooke, C Brewer, Theo Davies and Alexander & Baldwin – hold onto their plantations not so much for what's being produced on them, but for the potential they hold as future golf courses and condo developments.

Diversified crops, defined as all crops except sugar and pineapple, have increased more than twofold over the past decade and have a combined sales value of nearly $350 million. Surprisingly, more land on Maui is used for grazing dairy and beef cattle than for any other purpose, while Kula is one of the state's major flower- and vegetable-producing regions. Many Upcountry truck farmers sell their cabbage, lettuce, Maui onions and potatoes to the island's hotel resorts and restaurants.

Overall the cost of living is 25% higher on Maui than in the average US mainland city, while wages are at least 10% lower. For those stuck in service jobs, which is the most rapidly growing sector of the economy, it's tough to get by. Native Hawaiians have the lowest median family income and are found at the bottom of most health and welfare indicators.

POPULATION & PEOPLE

Maui County has about 128,000 residents and accounts for just over 10% of the people living in the state. The population of Maui is about 118,000, but every month visitor arrivals more than triple this figure. Maui's central district, which includes the sister towns of Wailuku and Kahului, is home to just under half of the island's permanent residents.

During the 1980s, the major ethnic populations were pretty evenly balanced between native Hawaiians, Caucasians and those of Japanese descent. In the next decade Caucasians jumped into the majority position mostly because of excessive migration from the US mainland. Maui's population alone grew by 30% during those years, with most of the new arrivals either retirees or alternative types, such as surfers, artists and organic farmers. A quarter of Maui's residents still consider themselves to be predominantly of Hawaiian ancestry, although it is estimated that less than 2% are full-blooded Hawaiian.

The 2000 national census found that 26% of people on Maui identify as Caucasian, 16% Filipino and 11% Japanese, followed by less than 1% each for Chinese, Tongans, Koreans, African Americans and Samoans. The fastest growing immigrant groups are Mexicans, Guatemalans and South Americans, but their often undocumented status makes exact counts impossible. It is interesting to note the rapid rise and success of Hawaii's Filipino community, as evidenced in part by such famous figures as Angela Perez Baraquio, the Catholic schoolteacher who became Miss America 2001, and Governor Ben Cayetano, the first governor of Filipino descent in US history.

Hawaii's people are known for their racial harmony that goes hand-in-hand with the spirit of aloha. Half of islanders marry someone of a race different from their own, and the majority of children born in Hawaii are *hapa,* or mixed-blood. Some even say that there is no real ethnic majority in Hawaii because everyone belongs to some minority. Ethnic tension, particularly between haole and native Hawaiians, is not unheard of but short-term visitors are usually given a free pass out of any such conflicts.

EDUCATION
Unlike anywhere else in the USA, Hawaii's public school system is run by the state, not by the city or county. Hawaiian students rank nationally anywhere from the middle of the bell curve to below average. Supporters of public education point out that Hawaii struggles with a higher percentage of foreign-born students (at 15%, it's twice the national average) and a functional English literacy rate of 70% to 85% among parents. They also say that the state lacks sufficient funds to retain skilled teachers or develop a curriculum that addresses Hawaiian culture and language in meaningful ways.

Of course, it doesn't help that student drug and alcohol abuse is rampant in public schools. Hawaiian students drink at three times the national average and often get their liquor or home-grown pakalolo from a family member. The killer street drug is 'ice,' a highly addictive pure form of crystal meth that costs only $25 for a cocaine-like rush that lasts four days. Maui has few community centers or youth programs to offer a drug-free alternative like on Oahu.

It's not surprising that a fifth of parents enroll their students in special charter schools or private academies. The most esteemed college prep school is Seabury Hall, set on an impressive estate north of Makawao, where annual tuition costs a cool $11,000. Maui also has one of Hawaii's

Kamehameha schools, which are financed largely by a charitable trust from the estate of Bernice Pauahi Bishop, the last member of the Kamehameha royal dynasty. Established specifically to empower native Hawaiian students, the school system was recently accused of violating federal anti-discrimination statutes with race-based admissions policies.

There is a community college on Maui, but no university.

ARTS
The tourist resort boom of the 1970s and the beginning of the modern Hawaiian Renaissance are inextricably linked. Tourist enclaves have long been overrun with packaged Hawaiiana, from plastic lei to theme-park luaus that practically parody island culture, but tourism dollars have also built museums, supported traditional hula schools and led to the restoration of historic and natural sites.

In other respects, the Hawaiian Renaissance of the 1970s was a reaction against tourism and an explicit rejection of island development motivated by the almighty dollar in favor of traditional Hawaiian values. There has been a conscious effort to reintroduce Hawaiian words into everyday speech, and many artists and craftspeople are taking traditional media and themes and infusing them with new life. Hula performances are again focusing on the sacred nuances of hand movements and facial expressions, instead of the hip-shaking that sells luaus. Others combine artistic traditions brought by missionaries or plantation immigrants with Hawaii's Polynesian roots to make hybrid art found nowhere else in the world, for example Jawaiian, a uniquely Hawaiian form of reggae, or those contemporary potters using Japanese-inspired *raku* techniques with volcano ash glazes.

One word of warning about galleries first, however. About half of the art for sale on Maui is excruciatingly pedestrian, and you'll know it as soon as you see it. The most beautiful and authentic pieces are not only hard to find, but prohibitively expensive.

Hula

Perhaps nothing is more uniquely Hawaiian than the sacred hula dance. Students would study for years under *kumu hula* (hula masters), sometimes even moving to other islands to do so.

Most ancient hula dances expressed historical events, legendary tales and the accomplishments of the great ali'i. Facial expressions, hand gestures, hip sway and dance steps all conveyed the story, as did rhythmic chants called *mele,* some of which were prayers and others epic narratives. Dancers were also accompanied by drum beatings on a gourd.

There are countless schools of hula. One type is performed entirely seated. Perhaps the most notorious is the *hula ohelo,* named for Hawaii's indigenous red berries (think cherry here) and suggesting sex in every sinuous movement. The Christian missionaries thought it all too licentious for their liking and suppressed it. The hula might have been lost forever if not for King Kalakaua, the 'Merrie Monarch,' who revived it in the latter half of the 19th century.

Unlike what most people think, Hawaiian hula dancers traditionally wore skirts made from tapa cloth or ti leaves; grass skirts were introduced from Micronesia only a hundred years ago. Some modern hula dancers, of which there are increasing numbers every year, prefer them because they are long-lasting and lend themselves well to certain styles.

Some *hula halau* (hula schools) practice in public places or give free performances at shopping malls where visitors are welcome to watch. Hawaiian hula gained even more publicity in 1995 when PBS broadcast Hawaii's first hula opera, called 'Holo Maui Pele,' written by two kumu hula sisters from the Big Island, which retold the ancient saga of the goddess Pele and her sister Hi'iaka.

Traditional Crafts

Cloth & Weaving The goddess Hina spent much of her time beating *kapa* (tapa cloth), as did many Hawaiian women in earlier times. Tapa cloth, which was traditionally used not only for clothing but also kites, is made from the *wauke* (paper mulberry tree). First the bark was carefully stripped, then pounded with wooden beaters carved with geometric and floral patterns, which then became the imprint pattern of the tapa. Dyes were made from anything at hand, including charcoal, flower essences and even sea urchins. These days, the tapa for sale in Hawaii is usually Samoan or Fijian tapa, which can be identified by its bolder designs and coarse texture. The finer Hawaiian tapa of the quality so prized by museums requires soaking the mulberry bark in water for days first.

Hawaiian women also spent much of their time on lauhala weaving, which utilized the *lau* (leaves) of the *hala* (pandanus tree). Preparing the leaves for weaving was hard, messy work because of their razor-sharp spines. In old Hawaii the leaves were woven into mats and floor coverings, but smaller items like hats and baskets make up today's cottage industry.

Featherwork & Lei The Hawaiians were known for their elaborate featherwork. The most impressive pieces were the helmets and capes worn by chiefs and kings. The longer the cape, the higher the rank. Those made of the yellow feathers of the now-extinct mamo bird were the most desired. It's said that bird catchers would capture the birds, pluck the desired feathers and release them unharmed.

The ancient Hawaiians also sometimes used feathers when making lei (garlands). Although the lei most widely worn by visitors to Hawaii are made of fragrant flowers such as plumeria and tuberose, traditional lei of mokihana berries and maile leaves were more common in old Hawaii. Other lei were made out of shells, seeds, nuts and even carved fruit. The only lei no longer made is the *lei palaoa,* which was traditionally worn by royalty and made of finely braided human hair hung with smooth pendants of whale tooth or bone.

Nowadays cheaper plastic lei are often hung over car rearview mirrors and *haku lei,* once worn on the head, appear tied around hats.

Woodcarving The ancient Hawaiians had no pottery and made their containers using either gourds or wood. Wooden food bowls were mostly of kou or milo, two native woods that didn't leave unpleasant tastes. Bowls used for other purposes were sometimes made of koa, a beautifully grained reddish hardwood.

Ornamentation played no role in traditional Hawaiian bowls, which were free of designs and carvings. Their beauty lay in the natural qualities of the wood and in the shape of the bowl alone. Cracked bowls were often expertly patched with dovetailed pieces of wood. Rather than decrease the value of the bowl, patching suggested heirloom status, and such bowls were among the most highly prized.

Quilting

The concept of patchwork quilting was introduced by the early missionaries, but the Hawaiians, who had only recently taken to Western cotton clothing, didn't have a surplus of cloth scraps – and the idea of cutting up new lengths of fabric simply to sew them back together again in small squares seemed absurd. So Hawaiian women created their own designs adapted from tapa patterns, and reproduced images of native flora and fruit. They also used images from local legends.

You can see many of these quilts from yesteryear in historical museums across all the Hawaiian Islands and also in quilting shops (see Shopping in the Facts for the Visitor chapter), some of which also teach lessons to visitors.

Music

Contemporary Hawaiian music gives center stage to the guitar, which was first introduced to the islands by Mexican cowboys in the 1830s. The Hawaiians quickly made it their own.

Around 1889, Joseph Kekuku, a native Hawaiian and Honolulu college student, designed the steel guitar, the only major musical instrument invented in what is now the USA (contrary to popular belief, the banjo was invented in Africa).

Slack-key guitar is also a 19th-century Hawaiian creation that has come back into the spotlight. Slack-key is a type of tuning in which some guitar strings are slackened from the conventional tuning to produce soulful folk harmonies. It has been described even by people who love it as having been dreamt up by people who loved to play guitar, but didn't really know how. Some of Hawaii's more renowned slack-key guitar players are Cyril Pahinui, Keola Beamer, Atta Isaacs, Raymond Kane and the late Gabby Pahinui and Sonny Chillingworth.

The ukulele, so strongly identified with Hawaiian music, was actually derived from the braguinha, an instrument from Portugal introduced to Hawaii in the 19th century. In the Hawaiian language, the word 'ukulele' means 'jumping flea.' It's said to be the easiest instrument in the world to learn.

Both the ukulele and the steel guitar were essential to the lighthearted, romantic music popularized in Hawaii from the 1930s to the 1950s. 'Lovely Hula Hands' and 'Sweet Leilani' are classic examples. The 'Hawaii Calls' radio show, which for more than 30 years was broadcast from the Moana Hotel in Waikiki, made these tunes instantly recognizable worldwide as Hawaiian, conjuring up images of beautiful hula dancers swaying under palm trees in a tropical paradise.

Among the current-day masters of the ukulele revival are Troy Fernandez and Ledward Kaapana. Israel Kamakawiwo'ole, known affectionately as Bruddah Iz, was a soft-style ukulele player with a big heart and a phenomenal amount of Hawaiian pride that made him universally loved. When he died in 1997, he became one of only a few Hawaiians ever given a memorial in the state capital rotunda and over 20,000 people came to grieve.

The newest sound in Hawaii is Jawaiian, a blending of Hawaiian music and Jamaican reggae started in the early 1990s. A lot of well-known musicians do their own takes on elements of Jawaiian, including Kulana, Bruddah Waltah, Fiji, the Kaau Crater Boys and Hoaikane. Other contemporary Hawaiian musicians fuse folk, rock and traditional Hawaiian influences, for instance local Maui legend Willie K who still performs weekly at Hapa's Brew House in Kihei.

If you want to get the latest tips, tune into the annual Na Hoku Hanohano, which are like the Hawaiian Grammy awards.

Architecture

In the early 20th century, Hawaiian Regional Architecture came to be vaguely defined as a mishmash design of traditional Hawaiian *hale* (grass-roofed houses), California mission style and Spanish and Italian Mediterranean villas. It is also sometimes called Mediterranean Revival architecture and is often marked by a distinctive double-hipped roof. The leading architect of the early 20th century was CW Dickey, who kept offices in both Honolulu and the San Francisco Bay area. Among his many projects on Maui are the Wailuku County Courthouse (1907), which exhibits Beaux Arts stylings, the Wailuku Public Library (1928), now on the National Register of Historic Places, the Makawao Union Church and the Hu'i No'eau Visual Arts Center.

SOCIETY & CONDUCT

In many ways, Hawaii shares the same pop culture found on the US mainland. On Maui you can find hip-hop nightclubs and swing dancing, junk food and nouvelle fusion cuisine, NFL Monday night football and the most recent Hollywood releases.

But the radical thing is that mainland influences largely stand beside, rather than engulf, the culture of the islands. Radio stations play just as much Hawaiian slack-key guitar and Jawaiian as they do Top 40. Local TV news affiliates often cover late-breaking island developments before even world headlines.

On a deeper level, aloha is much more than a simple greeting, but a way of life that unites islanders of whatever ethnic background in an everyday philosophy of tolerance, hospitality and generosity of spirit. Its various shades of meaning work together beautifully and are reminiscent of the rainbows that appear on every Hawaii license plate, often alongside the popular bumper sticker 'Live Aloha.'

'*Ua mau ke ea o ka aina i ka pono,*' meaning 'The life of the land is perpetuated in righteousness,' is Hawaii's state motto and one that people act upon. Unlike the rampant consumerism on the mainland, locals choose to focus on *ohana* (family) and *aina* (land). You will see this in everything from the fact that there are no billboards cluttering up the landscape to the way Hawaiians will spend every chance they get outside, often spending the entire weekend camping and barbecuing at the beach instead of being holed up inside yet another shopping mall.

Not only is traditional Hawaiian culture an integral part of the social fabric, but so are the customs of the ethnically diverse immigrants who have made Hawaii their home. Hawaii is more than just a meeting place of East and West; it's also a place where these cultures flow together like lava to create new landscapes of the soul. And also the palate, when one considers the riot of tastes presented in a typical Hawaiian mixed plate lunch.

Dos & Don'ts

Genuinely interested travelers will find open attitudes and hearts in Hawaii, whether it is locals helping you fix your car when it breaks down on the side of some remote road or anyone else who goes the extra mile. Your only obligation, other than to say *mahalo* (thank you) and smile, is to repay that kindness by helping out someone else down the line. Hawaii often seems like the one place left where the golden rule still works.

In the words of late musical phenomenon Bruddah Iz, 'Hawaiian to me is a way of getting somewhere without stepping on anybody's toes.' Remember to slow down, especially since nothing more clearly sets you apart as *malihini* (someone fresh off da airplane, as it were) than being in a hurry. It's even easier to learn to say aloha and wave

Hawaiian Deities

Traditional Hawaiian religious ways are based on both older Polynesian gods and an animism unique to these islands.

Ku is the ancestor god for all generations of humankind, past, present and future. He presides over all male gods while his wife, Hina, reigns over the female gods. When the sun rose in the morning, it was said to be Ku; when it set in the evening, it was Hina. Like yin and yang, they were responsible for heaven and earth.

Ku had many manifestations, one as the benevolent god of fishing, *Ku-ula* (Ku of the abundant seas), and others as the god of forests and the god of farming. One of the most fearful of Ku's manifestations was Kukailimoku (Ku, the snatcher of land), the war god whom Kamehameha the Great worshipped. At the *luakini* temples built for the worship of Kukailimoku, the sacrificial offerings included the blood of humans.

Lono was the god in charge of the elements, bringing rain and an abundant harvest. He was also the god of fertility and peace. The ancient Hawaiians remembered Lono each year with a harvest festival, called the *makahiki,* which took place on Maui in the Iao Valley.

It was from Kane (the word also means 'man' in Hawaiian) that all humans were said to have descended. Each family worshipped Kane under the image of its personal *auamakua* (family guardian spirit). Worship was simple, everyday rituals, requiring no fresh blood or intensive supplication.

Kanaloa, the fourth major god, was often pitted in struggles against the other three gods, especially Kane. It was also Kanaloa who seduced the wife of the first man. When heaven and earth separated, Kanaloa was placed in charge of the spirits on earth. Forbidden from drinking the intoxicating beverage *kava,* these spirits revolted and were driven to the underworld, where Kanaloa became the ruler of the dead.

There was also a pantheon of at least a few dozen lesser gods. The best known was Pele, goddess of volcanoes. Her sister Laka was goddess of the hula, and another sister, Poliahu, was the goddess of snow and Pele's archrival. The Hawaiians also had gods for all occupations and natural phenomena.

Worship at heiau was abandoned in the late 19th century, when the temples were burned and idols smashed. Most heiau are in ruins today. A few of the old ways survive, mostly as folk superstitions about the wrath of Pele or the good luck of seeing a *pueo* (Hawaiian owl) ancestor spirit.

the shaka sign around, especially when driving (see 'The Shaka Sign'). Respect what is kapu and don't trespass. Walk with care in fragile natural areas and archaeological sites and always take off your shoes before entering someone's home.

RELIGION

Ever since the first missionaries and plantation workers arrived in the 19th century, Hawaii's population has been religiously diverse.

Although half of all Hawaii residents today say they are unaffiliated with any religion, Christianity has the largest following. The United Church of Christ, which includes the Congregationalists who initially converted the islands, claims only one-half as many members as Mormons and one-tenth the number of Catholics, who are the dominant denomination now. After that, Buddhism has the most adherents.

You'll find many old-fashioned mission temples scattered around the island, along with a Tibetan-style stupa and the original *zendo* of Maui's Diamond Sangha. There are also smaller Shinto and Taoist shrines, and Jewish and Muslim houses of worship.

For information on the island's historic Hawaiian churches, see Places of Worship in the Facts for the Visitor chapter.

LANGUAGE

Hawaii is the only state in the union to have two official languages, Hawaiian and English.

In everyday life the unifying language is English, but it's liberally peppered with Hawaiian phrases, pidgin slang and loan words from various immigrant tongues. It's not uncommon to hear islanders speaking in these other mother tongues as well, since the main language spoken in one out of every four homes is something other than English.

As for the Hawaiian language, it is most closely related to the other Polynesian languages of Tahitian, Maori and Indonesia-Malay. It is melodic and phonetically simple, full of vowels and repeated syllables. It is still spoken at home by about 9000 people. In recent years, however, speaking and studying the Hawaiian language has become a meaningful and sometimes political act for many islanders.

Pronunciation

The Hawaiians had no written language until the 1820s, when Christian missionaries arrived and wrote down the spoken language in just 12 roman letters and first printed primers and bibles in Hawaiian.

Pronunciation is easy, often just how the word looks on paper, and there are few consonant clusters.

Vowel sounds are about the same as in Spanish or Japanese, more or less like this:

a	ah, as in 'father,' or uh, as in 'above'
e	ay, as in 'gay' or eh, as in 'pet'
i	ee, as in 'see'
o	oh, as in 'go'
u	oo, as in 'noon'

Hawaiian also has diphthongs, created when two vowels join together to form a single sound. The stress is on the first vowel, although if you pronounce each vowel separately, you'll generally be understood.

The Shaka Sign

Islanders greet each other with the shaka sign, which is made by folding down the three middle fingers to the palm and extending the thumb and little finger. The hand is then held out, usually palm facing inside toward you, and shaken (hence the word 'shaka,' some say). On the highway, the shaka sign is an all-purpose solution to road rage, used to say 'I'm sorry, brah' if you cut someone off or 'mahalo' when someone yields to you.

Where this humble and sweet little gesture came from, no one really knows. One apocryphal story claims that it originated in the early 1900s when a sugar plantation worker named Hamana Kalili, who had lost his middle three fingers in a mill accident (or gotten them bitten off by a shark) waved his hand to say hello (or to warn local kids against trespassing) – or any other willy-nilly explanation thought up by the person telling the story. Others say it originated with an exclamation used by kids who played marbles. When one of them made a great shot, he would wave his hand in the follow-through position and shout 'Shaka!' meaning 'Right on!'

Wherever it started, the shaka sign became the trademark of the King of Pidgin, Lippy Espinda, a used-car salesman from Honolulu who was also a brilliant TV entertainer, appearing as the emcee of *Lanai Theater* as well as on *Hawaii 5-0* and *The Brady Bunch*. Lippy called himself the 'poor man's friend,' and his well-known salutation of 'Shaka, brah!' popularized forever the shaka sign as a symbol of aloha for island people. **The sign as seen by the person making it.**

The consonant *w* is usually pronounced like a soft English *v* when it follows the letters *i* and *e* (the town Haleiwa is pronounced

Hawaiian Pidgin

Hawaii's early immigrants communicated with *luna* (plantation foremen) and each other in pidgin, a simplified, broken form of English mixed with Japanese, Hawaiian, Portuguese and anything else at hand. It was a creole language born of necessity, stripped of all but the most needed words.

Modern pidgin equals local slang. Often speakers will drop just a word or two of pidgin into a standard English sentence, but lengthy conversations can also take place in pidgin. Shakespeare's *Twelfth Night* has been translated (by local comedian James Grant Benton) to *Twelf Nite O Wateva*. Malvolio's line 'My masters, are you mad?' becomes 'You buggahs crazy, o wat?' Now there's even *Da Jesus Book: Hawaii Pidgin New Testament,* published by the Pidgin Bible Translation Group (**w** www.pidginbible.org) for reading 'how plenny love en aloha God get fo you.'

Visitors won't make any friends by trying to speak pidgin. It's more of an insider's code that you're allowed to use only after you've lived in Hawaii long enough to understand the nuances. Some characteristics of pidgin include: a fast staccato rhythm, two-word sentences, dropping the soft 'h' sound from words that start with 'th' (the number three becomes 'tree'), loan words taken from various mother tongues and double meanings that trip up the uninitiated.

aiyah – Oh wow! Oh my goodness!
'ass right – you're right; that's correct
brah – brother, friend; also used for 'hey you'
broke da mouf – delicious
buggah – guy, friend; a pest
chicken skin – goose bumps
chance em – go for it
choke – lots, a vast amount
coconut wireless – word of mouth
cockaroach – to steal
da kine – that kind of thing, whatchamacallit, thingamajig
eat it – to fall down, wipe out or get totaled in an accident
geevum – go for it, beat them
grinds – food, eat; ono grinds is good food
hana hou – once more, do it again, encore
howzit? – hi, how's it going?
how you figga – how's that, why do you think that
how you stay? – how are you?
humbug – a real hassle

jam up – messed up; traffic jam
like beef? – wanna fight?
mo' bettah – much better, the best; as in Molokai mo' bettah!
moke – a very big local guy
nevah – didn't, don't
no can – I can't do it; cannot
no laugh me – don't tease or make fun of me
no 'nuff – not enough
ono – number one, the best; delicious
rubbah slippah – flip-flops, thongs
shahkbait – very pale, untanned people
stick – surfboard
stink eye – dirty look, evil eye
talk story – to strike up a conversation, make small talk or gossip
tanks – thanks; more commonly, tanks brah or tanks eh?
tita – very big, tough local girl
you go, I go stay come – you go on ahead, I'll meet up with you soon

Haleiva) and like the English *w* when it follows *u* or *o*. When *w* follows *a*, it can be pronounced either *v* or *w* – thus you will hear both Hawaii and Havaii.

The other consonants – h, k, l, m, n, p – are pronounced approximately the same as in English.

Glottal Stops & Macrons Written Hawaiian uses both glottal stops and macrons, although in modern print they are often omitted.

The glottal stop (') indicates a break between two vowels, which produces an effect similar to saying 'oh-oh' in English.

A macron, a short straight line over a vowel, stresses the vowel.

Glottal stops and macrons not only affect pronunciation, but can give a word a completely different meaning. For example, *ai* can mean 'sexual intercourse' or 'to eat,' depending on the pronunciation.

All this takes on greater significance if you learn to speak Hawaiian in depth. When you're using Hawaiian words in an English-language context (this *poi* is *ono*), there shouldn't be much of a problem.

Compounds Hawaiian may seem more difficult than it is because many proper names are long and look similar. Many begin with ka, meaning 'the,' which over time simply became attached to the beginning of the word.

When you break each word down into its composite parts, some of which are repeated, it all becomes much easier. For example: *Kamehameha* consists of the three compounds Ka-meha-meha. Every syllable ends with a vowel and the next-to-last sylla-ble is usually accented. *Humuhumunu-kunukuapuaa,* which is Hawaii's unofficial state fish, is broken down into humu-humu-nuku-nuku-a-pu-a-a. Talk about a tongue-twister!

Some words are doubled to emphasize their meaning. For example: *wiki* means 'quick,' while *wikiwiki* means 'very quick.'

Common Hawaiian Words

Learn these words first: aloha (welcome), *kokua* (please) and mahalo (thank you), which are everyday pleasantries; *kane* and *wahine,* often on bathroom doors; and makai and mauka, commonly used in giving directions.

Remember that in Hawaiian a noun can be singular or plural. Thus *keiki* can mean child or children. It isn't technically correct to add an 's' to indicate the plural tense, but you'll often hear it done, for example when bars and restaurants call their appetizers *pupus,* not *pupu.*

For more basic Hawaiian vocabulary, see the Glossary near the back of this book.

Facts for the Visitor

HIGHLIGHTS

Vibrant Maui can thrill you from the depths of underwater Molokini crater, which is brimming with rainbow-colored sea life, up through tropical rain forests into an alpine cinder desert inside Haleakala volcano, Maui's 'House of the Sun.' After all, Maui is small enough for anyone simply to see and do it all.

In West Maui, Lahaina town is the island's hottest – and most humid – tourist spot. Migrating humpback whales cruise off Maalaea Bay. During the winter season whales also favor the quieter waters off the coast of South Maui, which is entirely laden with white-, golden- and black-sand beaches stretching to La Perouse Bay.

Just a few miles from Kahului airport, old Wailuku town holds true to its vintage Hawaii atmosphere. It is also the gateway to the Iao Needle and narrow Kahekili Hwy that winds past *heiau* (temples), lava blow-holes and the Hawaiian village of Kahakuloa with its working taro patches. The Kahekili Hwy ends on the North Shore, where pristine bays and crescent beaches mesmerize surfers, snorkelers and spectators alike.

Paia is just a few miles east of the airport, but a world away from West Maui. Here alternative lifestylers make their homes and windsurfers make pilgrimages to nearby Hookipa Beach. Above Paia rises the Upcountry, which stretches from rural Haiku past the rodeo town of Makawao up to Haleakala. Kula, at a cool 3000-foot elevation on the volcano's western slopes, is Maui's garden land.

Back down on the coast, the Hana Hwy is famous for its abundant waterfalls, one-lane bridges and sweeping coastal views. Timeless Hana town is followed by the whispering bamboo forests and cliff-side pools of Oheo Gulch. Venturing farther around the island rewards travelers with a pick of off-the-beaten-path treks near Kaupo and the wild and beautiful Piilani Hwy.

PLANNING

If you have only a few days, base yourself nearby Maui's prime beaches. West and South Maui resorts both lay claim to stunning waterfront, famous Pacific Rim restaurants and the lion's share of island nightlife. Budget travelers mix with the local scene in Wailuku town or take in the alternative groove of Paia, either of which is convenient for islandwide excursions.

If you have a week or more, you might start off near the beach and then move Upcountry or down to East Maui to enjoy the cooler temperatures and rural aloha. No matter how cramped your schedule, make room for an overnight or day trek into Haleakala volcano – the extra planning and effort are immeasurably rewarded.

When to Go

Is there ever a wrong time to go to Maui?

Essentially the weather is agreeable all year round. It's a bit rainier in the winter and a bit hotter in the summer, but there are no extremes, and cooling trade winds modify the heat throughout the year.

Peak tourist season is from December to mid-April, but that has more to do with snowbirds escaping cold winters back home than island weather. Scores of families take summer vacations on Maui during July and August.

Keep in mind that many accommodations drop their prices around April 1 and most don't climb back up until mid-December. In terms of cost, the real bargains are found September to mid-November.

Naturally, various activities have their own peak seasons. If you're a board surfer, you'll find the biggest waves in winter, whereas if you're a windsurfer, you'll find the best wind conditions in summer.

Maps

The best selection of maps on Maui is at Borders Books & Music Café in Kahului. The *Ready Mapbook of Maui County*

($9.95), which includes coverage of Molokai and Lanai, is an invaluable resource for explorers. Admittedly, it's bulky. A more lightweight fold-out map with good street detail is Nelles' *Maui, Molokai & Lanai* ($5.95). Water sports fans can pick up the colorful Franko's Map *Maui, The Valley Isle* ($6.95) at dive shops and bookstores or order it over the Web from W www.frankosmaps.com. It is waterproof and rip-resistant.

The United States Geological Survey (USGS) publishes topographical maps of Maui. Both full-island and detailed sectional maps are available, including ones for Haleakala National Park. Maps have to be ordered in advance from the US Geological Survey (☎ 888-275-8747, fax 303-202-4693, W www.usgs.gov), PO Box 25286, Denver, CO 80225. Maps cost $4 per sheet, plus a $5 mailing fee per order.

What to Bring

Hawaii has balmy weather and a laid-back attitude, so pack light. You can always pick up some vintage aloha wear after arrival.

Shorts, sandals and a cotton T-shirt, with a long-sleeved shirt or lightweight jacket for after dark, will be the warmest clothing

Responsible Tourism

Hawaii's natural ecosystem has been ravaged by non-native plants and animals ever since the first contact with foreign ships. Seeds caught in the soles of your shoes or bugs left hiding out in the bottom of your backpack can potentially be a threat, as much as anything that the US Department of Agriculture specifically forbids and confiscates from travelers during airport inspections. Thoroughly clean all your gear before landing in Hawaii and cooperate with agricultural inspectors upon departure. There are legitimate ways of shipping pineapples, protea and other bounty home that won't harm the environment.

You'll see countless 'No Trespassing – Kapu' signs on Maui. Although you may be tempted to push on through that closed gate just to see what's beyond it, don't – unless, of course, a trustworthy local says it's actually OK. Respect the privacy of Maui residents, whose quality of life is continually being encroached upon by tourist development.

Practice respect for the *aina* (land). Leave nothing but footprints when walking through the rain forest or along beaches (snorkelers and divers shouldn't leave so much as a single toe print on fragile coral). Pack out all your garbage – if we can carry cockroach-infested trash bags out of Haleakala crater, then so can you dammit.

Don't take cuttings of native plants, stuff your shoes full of pretty black sand or steal lava rock for souvenirs. Unless you'd like to feel the wrath of Pele, the mythical creator-destroyer goddess of the Hawaiian islands, that is. (Remember what happened to *The Brady Bunch* when they took the idol from the *heiau* (temple) in the epic three-part 'Hawaii Bound' episode? Tarantulas in their hotel beds were the least of their troubles.)

In fact, every year Hawaii national parks staff receive hundreds of letters from visitors bemoaning the bad luck they've had after taking a hunk of lava home, and pleading for the lava (enclosed) to be returned to placate the goddess. After some friends of ours playfully threw lava rocks into a prehistoric lake on the Big Island, their car suddenly quit working. Eventually when they got home, their other car wouldn't start either. It wasn't vapor lock (we checked). It was Madam Pele.

Equally common are stories of those who treat Pele with kindness being rewarded. She often appears as a mysterious woman traveling alone on the Big Island. When the 1960 lava flow destroyed the village of Kapoho, the flow parted around both sides of the lighthouse to save it. Stories later circulated about how the lightkeeper had offered a meal to a wizened old woman who showed up at his house on the very eve of the eruption.

you'll need along the coast. Lightweight pants will afford added mosquito protection. Donning a tropical print shirt, dress or sarong usually suffices for 'dressing up,' island-style.

Elevated highland regions (called 'Upcountry') can be a good 20°F cooler than the coast. When the mist settles in and the wind picks up, it warrants an extra layer of clothing. At the summit of Haleakala, overnight temperatures can dip below freezing and most people come utterly unprepared for the bone-chilling sunrise experience. A hat, sweater, long pants, gloves and a warm jacket, preferably something waterproof, are advisable.

You won't regret bringing binoculars for watching whales and birds, and a flashlight is useful for exploring caves. For hiking, bring footwear with good traction. Many people hike with sport sandals or sneakers, but walking over lava can be brutal on your ankles (not to mention shoe soles). If you intend to camp or pursue outdoor sports extensively, it pays to bring your own gear.

TOURIST OFFICES
Local Tourist Offices
The Maui Visitors Bureau (☎ 244-3530, 800-525-6284, fax 244-1337, Ⓦ www.visitmaui.com), 1727 Wili Pa Loop in Wailuku, is open 8am to 4:30pm weekdays, but it's essentially an administrative office with a rack of brochures in the lobby; the same brochures are available at the visitor information booth at the airport.

The Lahaina Arts Society has a volunteer-staffed information desk (☎ 667-9193, 866-511-9193, events hotline ☎ 667-9194, 888-310-1117, Ⓦ www.visitlahaina.com), 648 Wharf St, inside the old courthouse in Banyan Tree Square. Volunteers can answer basic questions and make activities bookings for you.

When all else fails, rely on local word-of-mouth rather than biased advice from activity desk operators and hotel concierges.

Tourist Offices Abroad
The Hawaii Visitors and Convention Bureau (on the US mainland ☎ 800-464-2924, 800-648-2441) frequently changes its overseas agents. The following are the current addresses for HVCB representatives abroad.

Australia
(☎ 02-9955 2619, fax 9955 2171, Ⓔ rlane@thesalesteam.com.au) c/o The Sales Team, Suite 2, Level 2, 34 Burton St, Milsons Point, NSW 2061

Canada
(☎ 604-669-6691, fax 669-6075, Ⓔ compre@intergate.bc.ca) c/o Comprehensive Travel Industry Services, 1260 Hornby St, Suite 104, Vancouver, BC V6Z 1W2

Japan
(☎ 03-3201 0430, fax 3201 0433, Ⓔ mukumoto@hvcb.org) c/o Kokusai Building, 2nd floor, 1-1 Marunouchi 3-chome, Chiyoda-ku, Tokyo 100-8330

New Zealand
(☎ 09-379 3708, fax 309 0725, Ⓔ darragh@walwor.co.nz) c/o Walshes World, 11 Shortland Street, level 6, Auckland

UK
(☎ 020-8941 4009, fax 8941 4001) c/o Box 208, Sunbury-on-Thames, Middlesex TW16 5RJ

VISAS & DOCUMENTS
The requirements for entering Hawaii are the same as those for entering any state in the USA.

Passports & Visas
At the time of writing, Canadians were required to show proper proof of Canadian citizenship, such as a governmental photo ID card or a passport. The latter is required for Canadians arriving in Hawaii from anywhere outside the western hemisphere. Visitors from all other countries must have a valid passport, and most visitors also need a US visa.

However, a reciprocal visa-waiver program allows citizens of certain countries to enter the USA for stays of 90 days or less without first obtaining a US visa. Currently these countries are: Andorra, Argentina, Australia, Austria, Belgium, Brunei, Denmark, Finland, France, Germany, Iceland, Ireland, Italy, Japan, Liechtenstein, Luxembourg, Monaco, the Netherlands, New

Zealand, Norway, Portugal, San Marino, Singapore, Slovenia, Spain, Sweden, Switzerland, the UK and Uruguay. Under this program, you must have a roundtrip ticket, and you will not be allowed to extend your stay beyond the 90 days.

Other travelers will need to obtain a visa from a US consulate or embassy. In most countries the process can be done by mail.

Your passport should be valid for at least six months longer than your intended stay in the USA, and you'll need to submit two recent photos (37mm x 37mm) with the application. There is a nonrefundable US$45 application fee. Documents of financial stability and/or guarantees from a US resident are sometimes required, particularly for visitors from developing countries.

Visa applicants may also be required to 'demonstrate binding obligations' that will ensure their return home. Because of this requirement, those planning to travel through other countries before arriving in the USA are generally better off applying for their US visas while they are still in their home countries rather than applying for them while you're on the road.

The validity period for US visitor visas depends on which country you're from. The length of time you'll be allowed to stay in the USA is ultimately determined by US immigration authorities at the port of entry. Answering yes to the question on the non-immigrant visa application form, 'Have you ever been afflicted with a communicable disease of public health significance?' or carrying HIV-related medication in clearly marked prescription bottles can be grounds for exclusion. Waivers of inadmissibility for HIV-positive travelers are available from the Immigration & Naturalization Service (INS), but should only be applied for with the help of an experienced immigration lawyer.

If you want to stay in the USA longer than the date stamped on your passport, only certain classes of visa can be extended. You can apply for an extension by contacting the Honolulu INS office (☎ 808-532-2701, ⓦ www.insusdoj.gov), 595 Ala Moana Blvd, before the stamped date.

Travel Insurance

Foreign visitors should be aware that health care in the USA is expensive. It's a good idea to take out a travel insurance policy, which usually covers medical expenses, luggage theft or loss, and cancellation or delays in your travel arrangements. Policies vary widely in coverage, so get your insurer or travel agent to explain the details.

Check the small print because some policies exclude 'dangerous activities,' which can include scuba diving, motorcycling, anything to do with parachutes and even hiking.

While you may find a policy that pays doctors or hospitals directly, be aware that many practioners will demand payment at the time of service. If you have to make a claim later, keep all documentation.

It's best to purchase travel insurance as early as possible. If you buy it the week before you fly, you might find, for instance, that you're not covered for delays to your flight caused by a strike that may have been in force before you took out the insurance. International policies, including medical benefits, handled by STA Travel, Council Travel, Travel CUTS (Voyages Campus in Québec) and other discount travel agencies are reasonably priced.

Paying for your ticket with a credit card often provides travel accident insurance and may also give you the right to reclaim your payment if the operator doesn't deliver. Ask your credit card company, or the issuing bank, for details.

Documents & Cards

Visitors should keep in mind that all US airlines, including Hawaii's interisland carriers, now require passengers to present a photo ID during airport check-in. All foreign visitors (other than Canadians) must bring their passports. Everyone should bring along their driver's license and any health insurance or travel insurance documents. Divers, don't forget those certification cards.

Although Maui doesn't offer a lot of discounts, members of the American Automobile Association (AAA) or affiliated automobile clubs can get discounts on car rental, airfare and some activities, as can members of the American Association of Retired Persons (AARP) and its affiliates.

Photocopies

Before you leave home, you should photocopy all important documents (passport data and visa pages, credit cards, travel insurance policy, air/bus/train tickets, driver's license etc). Leave one copy with someone at home and keep another with you, separate from the originals.

It's also a good idea to store details of your vital travel documents in Lonely Planet's free online Travel Vault in case you lose the photocopies or can't be bothered with them. Your password-protected Travel Vault is accessible online anywhere in the world – create it at **w** www.ekno.lonely planet.com.

EMBASSIES & CONSULATES
Your Own Embassy

Generally speaking, your own embassy won't be much help in emergencies if the trouble you're in is remotely your own fault. You are bound by the laws of the country you are in, and your embassy will not be sympathetic if you end up in jail after committing a crime locally, even if such actions are legal in your own country.

In genuine emergencies, you might get some assistance, but only if other channels have been exhausted. If all your money and documents are stolen, it might assist you with getting a new passport, but a loan for onward travel is out of the question – the embassy would expect you to have insurance for that.

US Embassies & Consulates

For other US diplomatic representation abroad, try the Web links at **w** www.us embassy.state.gov.

Australia
  (☎ 02-6214 5600, **w** www.usembassy-australia
  .state.gov/index.html) 21 Moonah Place,
  Yarralumla, ACT 2600

Canada
  (☎ 613-238-5335, **w** www.usembassycanada.gov)
  490 Sussex Dr, PO Box 866, Station B, Ottawa,
  Ontario K1P 5T1

France
  (☎ 01 43 12 22 22, **w** www.amb-usa.fr)
  2 avenue Gabriel, 75382 Paris

Germany
  (☎ 030-8305-0, **w** www.usembassy.de)
  Neustädtische Kirchstrasse 4-5,10117 Berlin

Hong Kong
  (☎ 2523 9011) 26 Garden Rd, Hong Kong

Italy
  (☎ 06-4674-1, **w** www.usembassy.it)
  via Vittorio Veneto 119/A, 00187 Roma

Japan
  (☎ 03-3224 5000,
  w www.ebusembassy.state.gov/tokyo)
  10-5 Akasaka 1-chome, Minato-ku, Tokyo

New Zealand
  (☎ 04-462 6000, **w** www.ebusembassy.state.gov/
  wellington) 29 Fitzherbert Terrace, PO Box
  1190, Thorndon, Wellington

Spain
  (☎ 91-587 22 00, **w** www.embusa.es)
  Calle Serrano 75, 28006 Madrid

UK
  (☎ 020-7499 9000, **w** www.usembassy.org.uk)
  24 Grosvenor Square, London W1A 1AE

Foreign Consulates in Hawaii

The following consulates and government liaison offices are hosted in Honolulu, except where noted.

Australia
  (☎ 808-524-5050) 1000 Bishop St

Germany
  (☎ 808-946-3819) 2003 Kalia Rd

Japan
  (☎ 808-543-3111, fax 808-543-3170)
  1742 Nuuanu Ave

CUSTOMS

Each visitor is allowed to bring one liter of liquor and 200 cigarettes into the USA, but you must be at least 21 years old to possess the former and 18 years old to possess the latter. In addition, each traveler is permitted to bring up to $100 worth of gift merchandise into the United States without incurring any duty.

Most fresh fruits and plants are restricted from entry into Hawaii, and customs officials are militant. Because Hawaii is a rabies-free state, the pet quarantine laws are Draconian, but you can slice the time and expense to 30 days for $655 with a pre-arrival battery of shots and an exhaustive physical examination. For complete quarantine information, visit the Hawaiian Department of Agriculture Web site at W www .hawaiiag.org or call ☎ 808-483-7151 in Oahu for a free brochure.

MONEY
Currency
US paper currency comes in $1, $5, $10, $20 and $50 denominations. The $50 and larger bills are less common and can prove difficult to cash, while $2 bills are so rare that people collect them.

Some denominations have two styles as older versions in fair condition continue to circulate. The newer bills look a bit drunk with an asymmetrical design and gigantic head shots of US presidents.

Coins usually come in 1¢ (penny), 5¢ (nickel), 10¢ (dime), 25¢ (quarter) and rare 50¢ pieces. The new $1 gold-colored coins feature an image of Sacagawea, but aren't common yet.

Exchange Rates

country	unit		dollars
Australia	A$1	=	$0.52
European Union	€1	=	$0.88
Hong Kong	HK$1	=	$0.13
Japan	¥100	=	$0.77
New Zealand	NZ$1	=	$0.43
UK	UK£1	=	$1.42

Exchanging Money
It's best to change your money or traveler's checks at a recognized bank or other financial institution. Some hotels and souvenir shops exchange money, but rates aren't likely to be good. Automated teller machine (ATM) transactions at banks usually offer the best exchange rates.

There are a few foreign exchange offices at Kahului airport, as well as the main tourist areas. You can save yourself the hassle and fees involved by purchasing traveler's checks in US currency before departure. Then you can use them just like cash almost anywhere on the island.

Cash & Personal Checks Most Americans do not carry large amounts of cash for everyday use, relying instead on a mix of credit cards, ATMs and direct debit cards. Personal checks are rarely accepted here unless they are drawn on a Hawaiian bank account.

Traveler's Checks American Express, Thomas Cook and Visa traveler's checks in US dollars are the best; they are accepted as cash at many hotels, restaurants and stores.

American Express and Thomas Cook offices cash their own traveler's checks fee-free. American Express has a branch office (☎ 661-7155) inside the Westin Maui resort in Kaanapali that is open 8am to 4:30pm daily. Banks usually offer better rates than currency exchange booths, but keep in mind that all will charge transaction fees of up to 3% of the total amount, with $2 minimum. If it's a flat fee and not a percentage, be sure to cash several checks at once.

The main benefit of traveler's checks is theft protection. If you keep records and can supply a list of which are missing, a prompt refund should be forthcoming with minimal inconvenience. For stolen or lost traveler's checks, call American Express (☎ 800-992-3404), Thomas Cook (☎ 800-287-7362) or Citicorp Visa (☎ 800-541-8882).

ATMs ATMs often offer superior exchange rates, and most give cash advances using Visa, American Express or MasterCard (see Credit & Debit Cards, below). There are plenty of ATMs in Hawaii linked to the international Cirrus, Plus and Maestro networks. ATMs are found in convenience stores, gas stations, shopping centers, bus and train stations, airports etc.

A bit of savvy is needed to make the best of surcharges and fees. Most Hawaiian banks tack a surcharge of $1 to $2.50 per transaction, so make sure you take out enough money each time to beat the 1% commission fee you would otherwise be paying on traveler's checks. Ask your home bank about added fees and daily withdrawal limits before leaving home.

Credit & Debit Cards Visa, MasterCard, American Express and JTB cards are all widely accepted in Hawaii. Credit cards also get you cash advances at bank ATMs, generally adding a 3% or minimum $5 transaction fee.

Credit cards are more or less essential for deposits when booking accommodations, purchasing tickets or renting cars. At other times, paying by credit card for accommodations or car rental actually incurs a surcharge. Go figure.

Debit cards can be handy as they act as both an ATM card and a credit card. You can skip ATM fees entirely if you get cash back when making a purchase at a grocery store using your debit card.

Costs

Hawaii is not exactly a bargain travel destination, and prices are usually highest on Maui. The most expensive everyday item is food, with grocery store prices 25% higher than on the US mainland. Usually the rental, tour and accommodations rates you see advertised do not include taxes either. Because there is no public transit system, most people end up renting a car, which adds a minimum of $25 per day to any budget.

If you are on a strict budget (ie, staying in hostels, self-catering and limiting your explorations to free hostel tours), you could scrape by on $40 a day. Staying in a modest vacation rental or B&B, eating in budget restaurants and allowing yourself more freedom runs $60 if you share expenses with someone, closer to $90 if you are going solo. After that, the sky is the limit where luxury is concerned.

Tipping & Bargaining

The average tip left in restaurants is 15% to 20% minimum. Poor service merits slightly less, but there has to be real cause not to tip at all.

Smaller tips of at least 10% are also given to taxi drivers, hairdressers and barbers. Hotel bellhops and porters are tipped a dollar or two per item.

During off-peak season, you may save some money on walk-in accommodations, bicycle rentals or flying stand-by on helicopter tours if you care to bargain. It never hurts to ask.

Taxes

Hawaii is tax-hungry, especially for tourist money. The state attaches a 4.17% sales tax to virtually everything, including food, car rental and accommodations. There is another 7.24% room tax, which pushes the total surcharge on most accommodations to almost 11.5%. Last, a $3-a-day 'road use' tax is imposed upon all car rentals.

POST & COMMUNICATIONS

The US postal service (☎ 800-275-8777, Ⓦ www.usps.gov) is inexpensive and reliable. That said, mail delivery to and from the Hawaiian Islands usually takes a little longer than the US mainland.

Post offices are generally open 8am to 4:30pm weekdays. Main post offices may stay open later weekdays and open Saturday from 9am until noon. Even the smallest local branches offer a full range of services and packing materials.

Postal Rates

Postage rates for 1st-class mail sent and delivered within the USA are 34¢ for letters up to 1oz (23¢ for each additional ounce) and 21¢ for standard-size postcards. First-class mail between Hawaii and the mainland usually goes by air and takes under a week. For faster delivery, Priority Mail letters cost $3.95 and parcels start at $3.50 for 1lb. Express Mail costs from $12.45 and guarantees two-day delivery.

International airmail rates are 80¢ for a 1oz letter and 70¢ for a postcard to any foreign country, with the exceptions of Canada and Mexico (60¢ for a 1oz letter and 50¢ for a postcard).

It's cheaper to send parcels internationally via surface (sea) mail, but it takes longer and might be a bit rougher on the contents.

Receiving Mail

You can have poste restante mail sent to you c/o General Delivery at almost any post office in Hawaii. General delivery mail is usually held for up to 30 days.

To pick up mail at the main post office in Kahului (see the Central Maui chapter), have it addressed as follows:

YOUR FAMILY NAME, First Name
c/o General Delivery, Main Post Office
Kahului, HI 96732

Some hotels and condo complexes will also hold mail for incoming guests.

Telephone

The telephone area code for all of Hawaii is ☎ 808.

All seven-digit telephone numbers listed in this book are local Maui numbers. Only dial the area code when calling from one island to another or when calling Hawaii from outside the state. Toll-free phone numbers (those that begin ☎ 800, 877 or 888) work from the US mainland and sometimes Canada, unless otherwise noted.

Public pay phones can be found throughout Hawaii at beaches, gas stations, shopping malls and in hotel lobbies. You can pump in coins, use a phone card or make collect calls. Emergency 911 calls and toll-free numbers can be dialed from pay phones without inserting any money.

Rates at pay phones vary depending on the company. From a GTE pay phone (usually the cheapest), local calls cost 35¢ for unlimited talk time. Long-distance calls anywhere within the USA are 25¢ per minute with a $1 minimum charge. Any calls made with operator assistance will be more expensive.

Be aware that many hotels add a service charge of 25¢ to $1 for each local call made from room phones, and most impose hefty surcharges on long-distance calls.

International Calls When calling Hawaii from overseas, you must precede the 808 area code with 1, the international country code for the USA.

To make an international call direct from Hawaii, dial ☎ 011 + country code + area code + number. An exception is Canada, where you just have to dial ☎ 1 + area code + number (but beware international rates still apply!). For international operator assistance and information on the cheapest times to call, dial ☎ 0. However, it's almost always better to use a phone card (see below).

Phonecards Lonely Planet's eKno Communication Card is aimed specifically at travelers and provides cheap international calls, a range of messaging services and free email. For local calls, you're usually better off with a local card. You can join online at ⓦ www.ekno.lonelyplanet.com, or by phone from Hawaii by dialing ☎ 800-527-6786. To place calls from Hawaii with eKno once you have joined, call ☎ 800-527-6786.

There's a wide range of private prepaid phone cards that work for local and international calls. Cards sold by major telecommunication companies like AT&T at Wal-Mart compete with small upstart companies whose cards have catchy names like Islander or Beautiful Hawaii, often sold at small grocery stores. The key is to read all of the fine print *before* buying any card. Which card is best depends on where in the world you're dialing, and if you usually make short or long calls. Cards that advertise the cheapest per-minute rates may charge hefty connection fees for each call (especially from pay phones) and hide miscellaneous bogus surcharges.

Cell Phones The North American GSM1900 cell phone standard is not compatible with the GSM 900/1800 standard used throughout most of Europe, Asia and Africa. If you have a GSM phone from abroad, check with your service provider about using it in Hawaii and beware of calls being routed internationally (it is very expensive for a 'local' call).

Similarly, visitors from the US mainland and Canada should ask if their cell phone service providers add exorbitant long-distance or roaming surcharges on calls made from Hawaii.

The major provider of cell phone products and services in Hawaii is Verizon (W www.verizonwireless.com). Renting a cell phone is very expensive (minimum $15 per day) here, so you're probably better off with a phonecard.

Fax, Photocopy & Shipping

There are many business centers around Maui. The most convenient is the 24-hour Kinko's (☎ 871-2000, fax 871-2854, W www .kinkos.com), 395 Dairy Rd, at the Dairy Center in Kahului. Mail Boxes Etc has branches in Kahului (☎ 877-0333), 415 Dairy Rd, and at Longs Center in Kihei (☎ 874-5556), 1215 S Kihei Rd. Both offer reasonably priced photocopy and fax services, as well as shipping via FedEx or UPS, respectively.

Email & Internet Access

If you usually access your email through your office or school network, you'll find it easier to open a free Web-based email account such as Yahoo! (W www.yahoo .com) or Hotmail (W www.hotmail.com) before you leave home.

If you plan to carry your notebook or palmtop computer with you, remember that the power supply in the US may be of different voltage (see Electricity, later). Invest in a universal AC and plug adapter, which will enable you to plug in these devices anywhere without frying their innards. Also your PC-card modem may not work once you leave your home country – but you won't know for sure until you try. The safest option is to buy a reputable 'global' modem before you leave home. For more technical help, visit W www.teleadapt.com or W www .igoproducts.com.

Cybercafés Maui cybercafés come and go, but they're always pricey. Kinko's (see Fax, Photocopy & Shipping, earlier), offers computers with Internet access from 20¢ a minute, with no minimum charge. Most cybercafés charge less, hopefully around $6 per hour if you're lucky.

Cafés may offer free Internet access to customers, but these schemes are usually short-lived. At the time of writing, McDonald's in Kahului had a free Internet kiosk with a cup holder and minitray for your french fries. Wailuku hostels and a few B&Bs also offered Internet access free for guests.

Many public library branches have computers that are online. Although a few librarians will sometimes bend the rules, officially you need a Hawaii library card to use the computers (see Libraries, later). Each patron is limited to one 50-minute session per week. You should sign up in advance, as walk-in patrons are subject to computer availability.

INTERNET RESOURCES

There's no better place to start your Web explorations than the Lonely Planet Web site (W www.lonelyplanet.com). Here you'll find succinct summaries on traveling to most places on earth, postcards from other travelers and the Thorn Tree bulletin board, where you can ask questions before you go or dispense advice when you get back. You can also find travel news and updates to many of our most popular guidebooks, and the subWWWay section links you to the most useful travel resources elsewhere on the Web.

W **www.extreme-hawaii.com/pidgin**
Dis going buss you up, brah! It's the one and only 'Full On Pidgin' site, with e-postcards, daily talk lessons and a parody of a Hawaiian drivers license application – all in pidgin, of course.

W **www.hawaii-nation.org**
Hawaii, Independent and Proud, is one of many Hawaiian sovereignty Web sites for updates on local activism and political news archives.

W **www.molokai.com**
For an instant induction into Molokai's 'local waze,' here are pages on the great traffic light

debate (so far, the island doesn't have one) and lots of *ono* photos.

W banana.ifa.hawaii.edu
The real-time Haleakala volcano crater cam. 'Nuff said.

W www.aloha-hawaii.com
This award-winning Hawaii Webzine offers you the Dead Gecko of the Day cartoon, plus features on Hawaiian culture with a pop twist and e-postcards that'll make your buddies jealous.

W www.geocities.com/~olelo/hula.html
Nâ 'Ao 'ao Hula (The Hula Pages) will dispel all your hula misconceptions. Dive into the sacred heart of the dance, from hula proverbs to arranging greenery on the hula altar, and even find a hula *halau* (school) back home.

W www.mele.com
Hawaiian Music Island sells hard-to-find recordings of slack-key guitar, traditional *mele* (chants) and Jawaiian tunes. It keeps links to Hawaiian concert calendars and Na Hoku awards, Hawaiian Internet radio stations and star musicians.

In addition, **W** www.hawaii.com, **W** www .planet-hawaii.com and **W** www .alternative-hawaii.com have truly useful links to a wealth of Hawaii information. For the lowdown on Maui only, visit **W** www.info maui .com or **W** www.mauivisitor.com. Other Web sites are given throughout this book under specific topics.

BOOKS
There are so many outstanding books about Hawaii and its people, it would be Sisyphian to try and list them all here. These days every little tourist convenience shop on Maui stocks enough Hawaiiana titles to keep anyone reading straight through their vacation (as if!). The best bookstores are Borders Books & Music Café, in Maui Marketplace mall in Kahului, and the independent Lahaina Book Emporium; meanwhile the Maui Friends of the Library shop in Puunene sells excellent used books for just 10¢ each.

Most books are published in different editions by different publishers in different countries. As a result, a book that's a hardcover rarity in one country may be readily available in paperback in another. The following publishers – many of which special-ize in Hawaiian titles – have mail order catalogs or allow you to shop online.

Bamboo Ridge Press
(**W** www.bambooridge.com)
PO Box 61781, Honolulu, HI 96839

Bess Press
(☎ 808-734-7159, fax 808-732-3627,
W www.besspress.com) 3565 Harding Ave,
Honolulu, HI 96816

Island Bookshelf
(☎ 503-297-4324, 800-967-5944, fax 503-297-1702,
W www.islandbookshelf.com)
PO Box 91003, Portland, OR 97291

University of Hawaii Press
(☎ 808-956-8255, 888-847-7377, fax 808-988-6052, **W** www.uhpress.hawaii.edu/index.html)
2840 Kolowalu St, Honolulu, HI 96822

Lonely Planet
Captain Cook made a fatal mistake when visiting the Big Island of Hawaii, but you don't have to do the same if you have our *Hawaii: The Big Island* guide in hand when you go exploring. You can also discover *Oahu* or go merrily island-hopping with *Hawaii*. Divers should check out Lonely Planet's Pisces guide *Diving and Snorkeling Hawaii* by Casey & Astrid Witte Mahaney.

Outdoors Guides
Hawaii: The Islands of Life has strikingly beautiful photos of the flora, fauna and landscapes that are protected by the Nature Conservancy of Hawaii. Text is by Gavan Daws.

Mammals in Hawaii by P Quentin Tomich is an authoritative book that also covers all whale and dolphin species visiting the islands. *Hawaii's Birds* (Hawaii Audubon Society) is the best pocket-size field guide to the birds of Hawaii.

A brilliantly photographed and annotated guide for anything dwelling in Poseidon's realm is Ann Fielding and Ed Robinson's *An Underwater Guide to Hawaii*. Both authors lead their own underwater tour companies on Maui (see the Activities chapter).

Wahine (women) surfers will be inspired to wax up the deck by Andrea Gabbard's

Girl in the Curl: A Century of Women in Surfing.

History & Politics

The perennial favorite *Shoal of Time* by Gavan Daws is a comprehensive, no-holds-barred history covering the period from Captain Cook's 'discovery' of the islands to statehood.

Fragments of Hawaiian History by John Papa Ii, translated by Mary Kawena Pukui, is a firsthand account of old Hawaii under the *kapu* (taboo) system.

Hawaii's Story by Hawaii's Queen by Queen Liliuokalani, is an autobiographical account of Liliuokalani's life and the dastardly circumstances surrounding her 1893 overthrow and US annexation. Michael Dougherty's *To Steal a Hawaiian Kingdom* is a forceful indictment of western intrusion over the centuries.

Father Damien, the priest who worked in the leper colony on Molokai, is the subject of many books, including *Holy Man: Father Damien of Molokai* by Gavan Daws and *Damien the Leper* by John Farrow and others.

Culture

The Kumulipo by Martha Beckwith is a translation of the Hawaiian creation chant. Also see Beckwith's comprehensive *Hawaiian Mythology.*

Legacy of the Landscape by Patrick Vinton Kirch is a detailed treatment of 50 of the most important Hawaiian archaeological sites, including heiau, fishponds and petroglyphs with dramatic photos.

When it comes to pop culture, *The Hawaiian Shirt* by Thomas H Steele and *The Aloha Shirt: Spirit of the Islands* by Dale Hope are both treatises on the evolution of aloha wear.

Made in Paradise: Hollywood's Films of Hawaii and the South Seas by Luis Reyes delves into the history of the Hawaiian film industry while poking fun at its kitsch and misrepresentation.

By the way, did you know the annual per capita consumption of Spam in Hawaii hovers around a porky three pounds? Read

Spam: A Biography by Carolyn Wyman, which includes the full script for Monty Python's Spam skit, and John Nagamichi Cho's *Spam-Ku: Tranquil Reflections on Luncheon Loaf.*

Travelogues & Novels

Among the famed literary travelers who have visited the Hawaiian Islands are Mark Twain, Jack London and the gallivanting Isabella Bird. An excellent anthology with selections by all these authors, Captain Cook, Somerset Maugham, David Malo and others is *A Hawaiian Reader,* edited by A Grove Day and Carl Stroven.

Perhaps the best-known contemporary Hawaiian novel is Kiana Davenport's *Shark Dialogues,* which is part historical novel, part love story and part creation myth. Davenport writes the story in melodic, transfixing prose.

FILMS

Innumerable films have been shot in Hawaii and scores of others have used island footage for backdrops. Far fewer storylines are actually set here.

One of the few movies to insightfully delve into island life is *Molokai: The Story of Father Damien* (1999), which was filmed on Molokai, starring Peter O'Toole and Sir Derek Jacobi with a riveting performance by Belgian actor David Wenham.

If you've already got your *mai tai* in hand, some vintage Hawaii movies include: *From Here to Eternity* (1953), a romance filmed in Oahu about Hawaii before the outbreak of WWII, starring Burt Lancaster and Deborah Kerr; *South Pacific* (1958), with Mitzi Gaynor and Rossano Brazzi; *Blue Hawaii* (1961), starring Elvis Presley and Angela Lansbury; *The Devil at 4 O'Clock* (1961), with Spencer Tracy and Frank Sinatra, featuring a volcanic eruption and a party scene filmed at Lahaina's historic Pioneer Inn; and *Raiders of the Lost Ark* (1981) with Harrison Ford.

Starting in the early '80s, most movies have been filmed on Kauai, which receives the bulk of Hollywood dollars. Steven Spielberg's *Jurassic Park III* (2001) showcases a few of Molokai's remote valleys, too. Disney's *George of the Jungle* (1997) and scenes from *Baraka* (1992) were partly filmed at locations around Maui County.

NEWSPAPERS & MAGAZINES

The state's main daily newspaper is the *Honolulu Advertiser,* while the *Maui News* (☎ 244-3981, 800-827-0347, Ⓦ www.mauinews .com) provides decent coverage of local and mainland events and comes out every day except Saturday.

The alternative free weekly *Maui Time* (☎ 661-3678, Ⓦ www.mauitime.com) gives the lowdown on local activism, surfing and sports, and entertainment around the island. You can pick it up almost anywhere. There are several smaller community newspapers that focus on local issues, including *Lahaina News* and *Haleakala Times.*

In Kahului, Borders Books & Music Café has racks upon racks of newspapers and magazines from all over the USA and abroad. Newspapers tend to be a bit out-of-date, however, and enjoy a pricey mark-up. Look for these Hawaiian magazines, *MAUI no ka oi* and islandwide *Aloha.* At least a dozen other surfing and sports magazines serve more niche markets, notably *Wahine* for women surfers and *Hawaii Fishing News,* a paragon of entertaining journalism and local talk story.

Free tourist magazines such as *This Week Maui* (actually published monthly) and *101 Things to Do: Maui* are full of ads, discount coupons, maps and general sightseeing information. They're worth picking up at the airport or island resorts and restaurants.

RADIO & TV

Hawaii Public Radio (HPR) broadcasts at 90.7FM. If you're looking for Hawaiian music with surf reports, try KPOA 93.5 FM (for Internet broadcasts, click to Ⓦ www .kpoa.com). Wild 105.5FM plays hip-hop, dance and some Filipino music, while The Point 101.1FM covers modern rock. All of the island sounds of aloha are played continuously at KNUI (literally, 'The Big One') at 900AM. News, talk and sports fans should tune to KAOI 1110 AM.

On Hawaiian TV channels you'll find affiliates of all the major US networks. For fine local flavor, the evening news on Channel 2 (KHON-NBC) ends with slack-key guitar music and island residents waving the *shaka* sign.

Most island residents, as well as condos and hotels, have either cable or satellite TV. Sports programs either have tape delays or are broadcast on pay-per-view. Maui's cable channel 7, The Visitor Channel, runs advertorial programs geared for visitors. While flipping through, you might catch interviews with famous Hawaii Regional chefs or sneak previews of island attractions.

In decades past, two of TV's top-drawing police detective series were Hawaiian home-growns, *Hawaii Five-O* and *Magnum PI.* Yet TV's heyday in Hawaii was a fading memory until the 1999 arrival of *Baywatch Hawaii,* lured by a cool $3 million in state-sponsored incentives. Even with a new theme song by Jawaiian star Fiji and Pat Morita playing a cranky island patriarch with some excellent aloha shirts, *Baywatch Hawaii* was canceled after just two seasons.

PHOTOGRAPHY & VIDEO
Film & Equipment

Both print and slide film are readily available on Maui. Throw-away underwater cameras costing about $10 are widely available at discount tourist stores and dive shops.

If you're going to be in Hawaii for any length of time, consider having your film developed here, as the high temperature and humidity of the tropics greatly accelerates the deterioration of exposed film. The sooner it's developed, the better the results.

Longs Drugs is one of the cheapest places for both purchasing film and having it developed. All the main tourist enclaves have one-hour print processing shops, including Wolf Camera and Fox 1-Hour Photo.

Videotapes can be readily purchased throughout Hawaii. North America uses the NTSC system, which is incompatible with the PAL system used in Europe or French SECAM standards.

Technical Tips

Now with the implementation of high-powered X-ray scanning machines that detect explosive materials at many international airports, do not pack unexposed film into either checked luggage or carry-on bags. Instead pack your film in a transparent plastic bag to show separately to airport security officials. Remember to finish off the roll in your camera, rewind it and take it out, too, or else your photos will end up looking fogged after being developed.

Don't leave your camera in direct sun or a locked car any longer than necessary as film can be damaged by excessive heat. Sand and water are intense reflectors, and in bright light they'll often leave foreground subjects shadowy. You can try compensating by adjusting your f-stop or attaching a polarizing filter, or both, but the most effective technique is to take all of your beach photos in the gentler light of early morning and late afternoon.

TIME

Hawaii does not observe daylight saving time. When it's noon in Hawaii, it's 1pm in Anchorage, 2pm in Los Angeles, 5pm in New York, 10pm in London, 11pm in Bonn, 7am the next day in Tokyo, 8am the next day in Melbourne and 10am the next day in Auckland. The time difference is one hour greater during those months when other countries *are* observing daylight saving time, for example, from the first Sunday in April to the last Sunday in October in the rest of North America.

Of course, there's always 'Island Time,' which means that everything happens a little bit more slowly here; it's also a handy excuse for being late.

ELECTRICITY

The USA, like Canada, operates on 110V, 60-cycle electric power. US electrical goods have a plug with two flat, vertical prongs (the same as for Canada and Mexico) or sometimes a three-pronger with the added ground. Note that gadgets built for higher voltage and cycles (such as 220/240V, 50-cycle appliances from Europe) will function poorly. Visitors from outside North America should bring a universal plug adapter.

WEIGHTS & MEASURES

Hawaii uses the US version of the imperial system of measurement. Distances are measured in feet, yards and miles; weights are tallied in ounces, pounds and tons. Those unaccustomed to the US system can consult the metric conversion table on the inside back cover of this book.

TOILETS

That dirty word, 'toilet,' is rarely used in the USA. Americans refer to it as the bathroom, the men's or women's room, the restroom or the washroom. Almost all bathroom facilities are sex-segregated. When the signs are in Hawaiian, *wahine* is for women and *kane* is for men.

Unlike on the mainland, gas stations generally don't have public restrooms, but virtually every beach park does have them. Restaurants also have bathrooms supposedly for their customers. Otherwise stride right into a luxury hotel resort and revel in the fine linens, air-con and commodious commodes.

HEALTH

Hawaii has the greatest life expectancy, currently about 76 years for men and 81 years for women, of anywhere in the USA. The longer you stay, the healthier you'll feel and look. No immunizations are required to enter Hawaii or any other port in the USA, but you should have adequate health insurance before setting out (see Visas & Documents, earlier).

Heat and humidity can rapidly take their toll on newcomers, especially by making them more susceptible to minor ailments. Let yourself acclimatize to the tropics slowly and keep drinking plenty of water. Just because water comes out of a tap doesn't make it safe to drink, however. Rural areas of East Maui, Upcountry and Haleakala National Park take their water supply from unfiltered rain catchments. Purified water is also dispensed at grocery stores for about 50¢ a gallon.

There are many poisonous plants in Hawaii, and only an idiot would sample a plant they couldn't positively identify as edible. On the other hand, natural herbal extracts and preparations certainly contribute to overall rosy health. Among those that travelers might find useful are ginkgo biloba for altitude sickness, melatonin for jet lag, lavender essence for preventing insect bites and tiger balm to soothe them, Echinacea to ward off colds and flu, acidophilus for yeast infections and ginger tea for upset stomachs.

Unparalleled among traditional Hawaiian restoratives is *noni* (Indian Mulberry), which is effective against everything from diarrhea to diabetes, impotence to immunodeficiency, and tastes bad enough to prove it. Noni preparations are sold in health food stores. Some other traditional Hawaiian remedies include *awa* (kava), good for hypertension, anxiety and headaches; guava for deep cuts and sprains; breadfruit sap for minor scratches; and *kukui* (candlenut) as a laxative and for ulcers or skin sores.

Hospitals, Clinics & Pharmacies

Maui Memorial Hospital (☎ 244-9056), 221 Mahalani St, Kahului, is one of the largest hospital facilities in the state with 24-hour emergency services.

For nonemergencies there are several hospitals and clinics with outpatient services. Kihei Physicians Urgent Care (☎ 879-7781), 1325 S Kihei Rd, is open 6am to midnight daily and accepts walk-in customers. Inside Whalers Village mall at Kaanapali, West Maui Healthcare Center (☎ 667-9721), 2435 Kaanapali Pkwy, stays open 8am to 10pm daily.

Maui Medical Group (☎ 249-8080) has three locations in Wailuku (2180 Main Street), Lahaina (130 Prison St) and the Pukalani Shopping Center (Haleakala Hwy). Planned Parenthood of Hawaii (☎ 871-1176), 140 Hoohana St, suite 303, in Kahului, offers low-cost sexual and reproductive health treatment.

You can have prescriptions filled quickly and cheaply at some Safeway stores, Longs Drugs outlets or local pharmacies.

Medical Problems & Treatment

Dengue Fever In 2001 an outbreak of dengue fever (called 'break bone fever' for how it wracks your body) all over East Maui required calling in the Centers for Disease Control, whose teams supervised the spraying of pesticides and other eradication offensives. Although the dengue fever strain found was the relatively benign Type I spread by the Asian tiger mosquito *Aedes albopictus,* over 80 people were stricken statewide.

Signs and symptoms of dengue fever include a sudden onset of high fever, intense headache, joint and muscle pains, nausea and vomiting; sometimes a rash of small red spots appears three to four days after the onset of fever. Aspirin should be avoided, as it increases the risk of hemorrhaging. In the early phase, dengue may be mistaken for other diseases, including malaria and influenza. A blood test is the only way to know and seeking medical help will speed recovery, which left alone may take weeks. There is no vaccine or cure for dengue.

Visitors will want to take precautions against mosquito bites, especially between July and September. Wear light-colored clothing, including long-sleeved shirts and long pants, especially during the early morning and before dusk. Avoid perfumed soaps and deodorants. Use mosquito repellents with DEET on exposed areas and a mosquito net or tent if you're camping. Regularly empty all receptacles containing standing water as mosquitoes need only a teaspoon of stagnant water to breed.

Leptospirosis Hawaii's feral animals such as rats, mongooses and wild pigs carry leptospirosis, a nasty disease caused by bacteria found in freshwater streams and ponds. Humans can contract leptospirosis by swimming or wading in idyllic-looking waterfalls or rain forest streams that have washed down through habitats contaminated by animal urine.

The bacteria enter the body through the nose, eyes, mouth or cuts in the skin. Symptoms can occur within two to 20 days after exposure and may include fever, chills, sweating, headaches, muscle pains, vomiting and diarrhea. More severe symptoms include blood in the urine and jaundice. Symptoms may last from a few days to several weeks.

Because symptoms of leptospirosis resemble the flu and hepatitis, only a few dozen cases are confirmed each year. Although deaths have been attributed to the disease, they are relatively rare. Some sensible precautions include wearing waterproof *tabi* (reef walkers) when hiking and avoiding unnecessary freshwater crossings, especially if you have open cuts.

Sunburn Sunburn is always a concern in the tropics, as the closer you get to the equator, the fewer of the sun's rays are blocked out by the atmosphere. The most severe sunshine is between 10am and 2pm. Don't be fooled by what appears to be a hazy, overcast day – you can get sunburned surprisingly quickly, even through clouds. This is especially true at high altitudes.

Sharkbait (very pale or untanned folks) should use sunscreen with an SPF rating of 30 or higher. Wearing a hat and lip balm containing sunblock affords added protection. Swimmers, snorkelers and surfers should use water-resistant sunscreen and consider throwing on a T-shirt during long aquatic adventures.

Prickly Heat Prickly heat is an itchy rash caused by excessive perspiration trapped under the skin. It usually strikes people who have just arrived in a hot climate and whose pores have not yet opened sufficiently to cope with greater sweating. Keep cool by bathing often or indulging in air-con until you acclimatize.

Heat Exhaustion Dehydration or salt deficiency can cause heat exhaustion. Take time to acclimatize to high temperatures and make sure you get sufficient liquids. Don't rely on being thirsty as a gauge for when to hit the water bottle: by the time your body registers thirst, you're already about two quarts dehydrated. Passing very dark urine or not needing to urinate are danger signs.

Salt deficiency is characterized by fatigue, lethargy, headaches, giddiness and muscle cramps. Salt tablets may help, but adding salt to your food is a better preliminary step. Vomiting or diarrhea can deplete both your liquid and salt levels, when fluid replacement becomes imperative. Be sure to drink at least the volume of fluids being lost and watch closely for signs of dehydration, particularly in older travelers and children.

Heat Stroke Heat stroke is a serious, sometimes fatal condition that occurs when the body's heat-regulating mechanism breaks down. Long, continuous periods of exposure to high temperatures can leave you vulnerable to heat stroke. Avoid strenuous activity in open sun, especially when you first arrive.

The symptoms of heat stroke include very little perspiration and a high body temperature (102°F to 106°F). Where sweating has ceased, the skin becomes flushed and red. Severe, throbbing headaches and lack of coordination will also occur, and the sufferer may be confused or aggressive. Eventually the victim may become delirious or convulse. Hospitalization is essential, but you can help by getting heat stroke sufferers out of the sun, removing their clothing, covering them with a wet sheet or towel and fanning them continuously.

Fungal Infections That same tropical climate that produces lush rain forests, fruits and fantasies also promotes prolific growth of skin fungi and bacteria. Hot-weather fungal infections are most likely to occur between the toes or fingers or in the groin.

To prevent fungal infections, it's essential to keep your skin dry and cool and allow air to circulate. Choose loose cotton clothing rather than artificial fibers, and sandals rather than shoes. If you do get an infection, wash the infected area daily with a disinfectant or medicated soap. Rinse and dry well and then apply an antifungal powder.

Pesky Creatures Maui has no snakes, but makes up for it with more than a fair share of mosquitoes (see Dengue Fever, earlier), stinging centipedes, bees and ground-nesting wasps. The last three generally pose danger only to those who are allergic to their stings. For information on stinging sea creatures and coral cuts, see Dangers & Annoyances, later.

Black Widow Spiders Black widows are glossy black, with bodies a half-inch in diameter with a characteristic red hourglass mark on the abdomen. They spin low-lying webs close to the ground and inhabit brush piles, sheds and outdoor privies. Bites are not terribly common in Hawaii, but they do happen.

Black widow bites, which resemble a pin prick, can be barely noticeable, but within 30 minutes, you'll experience severe cramping in which the abdominal muscles become boardlike and breathing becomes difficult. Other reactions will include vomiting, headaches, sweating, shaking and a tingling sensation in the fingers. In severe cases, the bite can be fatal. Seek immediate medical help if you think you've been bitten.

Scorpions The scorpion, which is confined principally to warm and dry regions, is capable of inflicting a painful sting with its caudal fang. Like the black widow, the venom contains neurotoxins. The severity of the symptoms (shortness of breath, swelling or vomiting) generally depends on the age of the victim, and stings can be fatal for very young children. Apply diluted household ammonia and cold compresses to the stung area and seek immediate medical help.

While the odds of encountering a scorpion are quite low in Hawaii, campers should always check inside their hiking boots before putting them on.

Ciguatera Poisoning Ciguatera is a serious and possibly fatal illness caused by eating mostly reef fish (raw or cooked, it doesn't matter) affected by ciguatoxin, which herbivorous fish can pick up from marine algae. Symptoms similar to food poisoning usually occur a few hours after ingestion. Vomit until your stomach is empty and seek medical attention immediately.

Although this disease does not pose a danger with any of the fish served in Hawaii's restaurants, fisherpeople and foragers should get a hold of the free brochure published by the Department of Land and Natural Resources. It's available from the Division of Aquatic Resources office (☎ 243-5294), 130 Mahalani Street, Wailuku, HI 96793. It lists potentially affected fish and where they are found.

WOMEN TRAVELERS
Hawaii presents few unique problems for women travelers and may even be more relaxed and comfortable than many popular destinations on the mainland. The one area women – especially solo travelers – may feel ill at ease is in local watering holes, which are often the domain solely of men. In any culture the world over, groups of men knocking back liquor with abandon can get dicey, so keep your wits fully about you or go in groups.

If you're camping, opt for well-used, secure campgrounds (like Camp Pecusa in Olowalu) rather than isolated locales where you might be the only camper (Polipoli Springs). County parks and campgrounds, notably Kahana Beach Park near the airport, are notorious for late-night beer binges, and some are known for long-term squatting and may be less than copacetic for solo travelers. Women walking alone on beaches after dark should stay alert to any nefarious, drunken vibes floating their way.

GAY & LESBIAN TRAVELERS
Gay marriages aside, Hawaii is as popular a vacation spot for gay men and lesbians as it is for straights. The state has strong minority protections and a constitutional guarantee of privacy that extends to sexual behavior between consenting adults. What's more, traditional Polynesian acceptance of homosexuality and the spirit of aloha encourage widespread tolerance.

Certainly in terms of nightlife, the main gay club scene is centered on Waikiki on Oahu. Most of the gay scene on the Neighbor Islands is low-key, with grassroots community groups creating a sense of *ohana*

Tying the Knot in a Pink Paradise

Gay marriages in Hawaii? In recent years, it had looked as if travelers of all persuasions might soon be able to legally tie the knot in Hawaii, as the state moved center stage in the movement to legalize same-gender marriages. Then the activism fizzled out, leaving most of us wondering why.

In December 1996, a state circuit court judge ruled that Hawaii's prohibition of same-sex marriage violated the equal protection clause of the state constitution, which explicitly bans gender discrimination. Implementation of the ruling, however, was given a stay pending appeal to the Hawaii Supreme Court.

In the meantime, Hawaii became the first US state to extend broad rights to domestic partners in 1997. To appease the vocal conservatives who oppose gay marriages, the domestic partnership laws were written to cover any two adults who cannot legally marry, including a range of pairings beyond same-sex couples, such as a mother and adult child or two siblings living together. Those who register are covered on an umbrella of items ranging from medical insurance to survivorship rights. New laws are expected to extend these rights in the near future.

For many Hawaii legislators, the original reciprocal beneficiary legislation was a compromise, meant to quiet both the pro and con voices in the controversy over gay marriages. As it was being established, the state legislature proceeded to put forth an amendment to Hawaii's state constitution allowing the legislature 'to reserve marriage to opposite-sex couples' only. This amendment was overwhelmingly passed by Hawaii voters in a November 1998 referendum. One year later the Hawaii Supreme Court voted to dismiss the original gay-marriage appeal, calling the case moot in light of the new constitutional amendment.

And that, as they say, was that. It's a testament to the spirit of aloha that the movement for gay marriage got as far as it did in Hawaii. Dozens of wedding planners still happily provide services in paradise for gay and lesbian couples, who are not deterred from saying their not quite legal vows on Maui's beautiful beaches.

(family) by throwing beach picnics and potluck brunches and organizing sports teams and outdoor adventures. Maui also boasts Hawaii's only lesbian-owned surfing school (see the Activities chapter). Interestingly the island of Molokai, long an ancient place of refuge for Hawaiians who broke kapu or were somehow outside the mainstream, has a long tradition of transvestitism still continuing today. Transvestites are generally treated with respect and affection by the greater community. They are traditionally called *mahu*, but nowadays this word can refer to any gay man; whether it's an insult or term of endearment depends on who is saying it, and why.

Public displays of affection are not commonplace on Maui, but then again neither do they cause too much excitement. Clothing-optional Little Beach in Makena is a perennially popular daytime meeting spot. Although Maui has no gay bars, Casanova in Makawao and Hapa's and Maui Pizza Café in Kihei have gay-friendly nightlife. The Hawaii-wide Island Lesbian Connection (☎ 573-3077) newsletter is published right here in Haiku. Lesbians may also want to keep an eye open for the Wyld Womyn's Weekend, an extravaganza of live entertainment, workshops and beachfront camping that moves from island to island each year.

The *Rainbow Handbook Hawaii*, by Matthew Link, is your best resource; you can check it out on the Web at ⓦ www.rain bowhandbook.com. The all-islands gay magazine is called *Odyssey*, while *Out on Maui* (ⓦ www.pride maui.com) is a free monthly newspaper published by the Gay/Lesbian Ohana Maui (GLOM; ☎ 572-5013). It has a great entertainment calendar and is usually available at Wild Banana Gallery in Wailuku.

Pacific Ocean Holidays (☎ 923-2400, 800-735-6600, fax 923-2499), PO Box 88245, Honolulu, HI 96830, arranges vacation packages for gay men and women. The company also produces a booklet called *Pocket Guide to Hawaii,* which is geared to the gay community and costs $5 by mail.

For links to a variety of gay and lesbian sites that cover items from travel and entertainment to politics and wedding ceremonies, browse ⓦ www.gayhawaii.com or the adults-only ⓦ www.hawaiiscene.com/gayscene. Purple Roofs (ⓦ www.purpleroofs .com) has a fantastic online directory of queer-friendly accommodations.

DISABLED TRAVELERS

Many of the major resort hotels and tourist areas have elevators, TTD-capable phones, wheelchair-accessible rooms, and other features to smooth the way.

Elsewhere around the island, the lack of tourist traffic means that infrastructure for the disabled is often missing. 'The Aloha Guide to Accessibility' published by the Commission on Persons with Disabilities (in Honolulu ☎ 808-586-8121), 919 Ala Moana Blvd, room 101, has three parts, the most general being free and the most detailed $15.

Seeing-eye and guide dogs are not subject to the same quarantine laws as other pets, provided they meet the Department of Agriculture's minimum requirements. Travelers should also remember to pack their disabled parking placard or apply for a new one upon arrival. Placards are available with a doctor's note from the Maui mayor's office (☎ 270-7855, fax 270-7870), 200 South High Street, in Wailuku. Some car rental companies also have hand-controlled cars available as long as you make reservations in advance.

Accessible Vans of Hawaii (☎ 871-7785, 800-303-3750, fax 871-7536, ⓦ www.accessible vanshawaii.com), 296 Alamaha St, suite C, Kahului, HI 96732, is a well-regarded organization that books accommodations and personal assistants, rents accessible vans and arranges various activities for disabled travelers. Call HandiVan (☎ 456-5555) paratransit to make taxi reservations.

SENIOR TRAVELERS

Kupuna (elders) are accorded much respect, and the average life expectancy for Hawaii's residents is four years higher than anywhere on the mainland.

In Hawaii, senior travelers often are the norm, not the exception. Generally visitors over the age of 65 can qualify for big discounts on transportation and entry to attractions, historic sites, museums and cinemas. You may be asked to show proof of age, so carry photo ID with you. Some hotels and motels may also offer reductions – it's always worth asking.

Elderhostel (☎ 978-323-4141, 877-426-8056, ⓦ www.elderhostel.org), 11 Avenue de Lafayette, Boston, MA 02111-1746, is a nonprofit organization offering study vacations for those aged 55 or older. It offers a range of ongoing programs, some on the Big Island and educational island-hopping tours affiliated with the University of Hawaii at Hilo and Honolulu. Many programs focus on Hawaii's people and culture, while others explore the natural environment. The fee is about $700 for one-week programs and $1400 for two weeks, including accommodations, meals and classes but excluding airfare.

For those over 50 years, the American Association of Retired Persons (AARP; ☎ 800-424-3410, ⓦ www.aarp.org), PO Box 199, Long Beach, CA 90801, offers travel information and substantial savings on auto and medical travel insurance. The annual membership costs $10, but the Web site resources are free. Members of the Canadian Association of Retired Persons (CARP; ☎ 800-363-9736, W www.50plus.com) can take advantage of similar savings.

TRAVEL WITH KEIKI (CHILDREN)

Hawaii has adventure activities galore and all the necessary perks to stave off kiddie crankiness: splashy beaches, food for the finicky, video arcades, fruit falling from trees and loads of bugs to mess around with. Nevertheless, enjoyable family travel entails some logical gymnastics and juggling of activities to keep kids from getting bored. When the going gets tough, bust out the chocolate-covered macadamia nuts or stop for shave ice. Don't forget to pack extra sunscreen, either.

For those vacationing with children, Lonely Planet's *Travel with Children* by Cathy Lanigan has lots of valuable tips and anecdotes. Maui attractions aimed at younger minds include the Hawai'i Nature Center in Iao Valley, Keiki Zoo outside Kula and junior ranger activity books at Haleakala National Park.

Many hotels and condos offer free rollaway cots or sofa beds and let children stay free, but many B&Bs do not. If you're traveling with infants and come up short, Baby's Away (☎ 800-942-9030, W www.babysaway.com) rents cribs, strollers, playpens, high chairs and more.

USEFUL ORGANIZATIONS

The American Automobile Association (AAA; on Oahu ☎ 808-593-2221, 800-736-2886, W www.aaa-hawaii.com), 1270 Ala Moana Blvd in Honolulu, can provide members with information and maps for driving in Hawaii and roadside assistance (☎ 800-222-4357). AAA members are also entitled to receive discounts on car rentals, hotel rooms and some sightseeing attractions, as well as cheaper Aloha Airlines tickets and Wolf Camera print processing. A first-time AAA annual membership costs from $75.

Entertainment (☎ 800-374-4464) travel club publishes an annual membership book good for 50% discounts at participating

hotels and resorts and coupons for sightseeing activities and two-for-one meals. Entertainment books are sold by mail-order or at various outlets in Hawaii, including Borders bookstore. The coupons are good for one calendar year starting November 1. Another travel club, Encore (☎ 800-638-0930) offers 50% off accommodations at member hotels and resorts. An annual membership costs $70 to $100 and is valid for 12 months from the date of enrollment. Keep in mind that many businesses refuse to honor travel club discounts during peak season, and some hotels may not accept reservations more than 30 days in advance, so you'll have to be flexible.

LIBRARIES

Hawaii has a statewide system of public libraries, with nearly 50 branches. Visitors can check out books only after applying for a Hawaii library card; a visitor's card valid for three months costs $10 but cannot be renewed. A nonresident library card ($25) is valid for five years and is renewable. Not only is the same library card good at all branches, but you can borrow a book at one branch and return it at another branch – even on another island.

Maui has public libraries in Lahaina, Kahului, Wailuku, Kihei, Makawao and Hana. They have excellent Hawaiiana sections, with stacks of books on culture, history, flora and fauna. Most libraries also subscribe to Hawaii's daily newspapers and a few mainland newspapers and magazines. For information on Internet access through Hawaii's public libraries, see Internet Resources, earlier.

PLACES OF WORSHIP

If you're looking for a spiritual home away from home, you don't have to go far. Don't miss attending a church service with hymns sung in the melodious Hawaiian language at Keawalai Congregational Church, built from coral rock and nestled on Makena Bay, or the queen's Kaahumanu Church in Wailuku. Also memorable among Maui's historic Christian churches are David Malo's open-air church in Kihei and the

Portuguese-style Holy Ghost Church in· Waiakoa.

Equally historic Buddhist mission temples are scattered across the island. Zen meditation retreats are periodically held at the Bamboo Sanctuary (see Places to Stay under Haiku in the Upcountry chapter) on the original site of Maui's Diamond Sangha where Robert Aitkin Roshi once taught.

As you drive north out of Lahaina along Front St, look for the neon 'JESUS COMING SOON' sign above a church that was made famous by The Eagles' song *The Last Resort,* spotlighting the down-and-out drugs and rock & roll culture of 1970s Lahaina.

DANGERS & ANNOYANCES
Theft & Violence
For the most part, Hawaii is a relatively safe place. Crime is lower here than in most of the US mainland. That said, break-ins and car theft are quite common and tourist rental cars are most often targeted. Don't leave anything of value in your car or at least put things well out of sight (preferably locked in the trunk) before you pull into any likely parking lot. Many locals leave their car doors unlocked all the time to avoid paying for broken windows.

Except for activity-desk rip-offs and time-share scams, the most hassles encountered by visitors take place in locals-only zones at beach parks or in residential neighborhoods. Pockets of resentment do exist against the excessive influx of mainlanders and tourists here on Maui, but most visitors see little of it. Local surfers and windsurfers can be fiercely territorial, and have been known to break boards or otherwise drive newcomers off the waves. Thankfully, these things are the exception rather than the rule. Act courteously and when in doubt, ask permission to go where you want to go.

Tsunami
Tsunami (literally 'harbor wave' in Japanese) are caused by earthquakes, typhoons or volcanic eruptions. They are incorrectly called tidal waves, when those are instead big waves caused by the gravitational pull of the sun and moon on the sea. Hawaii has installed a modern tsunami warning system, which is aired through speakers around the islands, although there may often be scant warning that a tsunami is approaching. If you're in a low-lying coastal area when one occurs, head for higher ground immediately. On all islands the tsunami speakers are tested on the first working day of each month at 11:45am and the front sections of telephone books show maps of areas susceptible to tsunami and safety evacuation zones.

Although Hawaii has had a tsunami every 10 years or so over the past century, killing more people statewide than all other natural disasters combined and causing millions of dollars in property damage, Maui has just missed most of them.

Ocean Safety
Drowning is the leading cause of accidental death in Hawaii, with an average of 60 people (visitors and residents inclusive) drowning each year.

It's best not to swim alone in any unknown place. If you're not familiar with local water conditions, ask someone who knows. If there's no lifeguard around, surfers are generally helpful – they'd rather give you the lowdown on water conditions than pull you out later.

Shorebreaks Shorebreaks – waves that break close to or directly on shore – form when ocean swells pass abruptly from deep to shallow waters. If only a couple of feet high, they're generally fine for novice bodysurfers to try their hand, but otherwise they're for experts only.

Large shorebreaks can hit hard with a slamming downward force. Broken bones, neck injuries, dislocated shoulders and loss of wind are the most common injuries, although anyone wiped out in the water is a potential drowning victim as well.

Rip Currents Rip currents, or rips, are fast-flowing ocean currents and are most common in conditions of high surf. Essentially the waves are coming in faster than they can flow back out, so the water then runs along the shoreline until it finds an escape route out to sea, usually through a channel or out along a point.

Swimmers caught up in these invisible currents can be ripped out to deeper water. Anyone caught in one should either go with the flow until it loses power, even if that means going farther out to sea, or swim parallel to the shore to slip out of it. Trying to swim directly against a rip current and back toward shore can drown even the strongest of swimmers.

Undertows Undertows are common along steeply sloped beaches when large waves backwash directly into incoming surf. The outflowing water picks up speed as it flows down the slopes. When it hits an incoming wave it pulls under it, creating an undertow. Swimmers caught up in an undertow can be pulled beneath the surface. The most important thing is not to panic. Go with the current until you get beyond the wave.

Rogue Waves Never turn your back on the ocean. Waves don't all come in with equal height or strength. An abnormally high 'rogue wave' can sweep over shoreline ledges or tear up onto beaches. Over the years, numerous people have been swept into the ocean from both. You need to be particularly cautious during high tide and in conditions of stormy weather or high surf.

Some people think rogue waves don't exist because they've never seen one. But that's the point – you don't always see them.

Coral Cuts Most coral cuts occur when swimmers are pushed onto a reef by rough waves or surges. It's a good idea to wear diving gloves when snorkeling over shallow reefs. Avoid walking on coral, which can not only cut your feet but also damage the coral.

Because living animal matter gets left behind in any coral cut, they can take a painfully long time to heal. If you do get cut, wash the wound thoroughly with soap and water, then a half-water solution of hydrogen peroxide. Then apply an antibacterial topical gel and cover the wound with a dry, nonadhesive dressing. Repeat cleaning and dressing twice daily until healed. (Would you rather have a nasty infection? We didn't think so.)

Jellyfish Take a peek into the water before you plunge in to make sure it's not jellyfish territory. These gelatinous creatures, with saclike bodies and stinging tentacles, are fairly common around Hawaii. They're most apt to be seen eight to 10 days after the full moon, when they come into shallow nearshore waters starting in the morning.

The pain from a sting varies from mild to severe, depending on the variety of jellyfish. Unless you have an allergic reaction to their venom, though, the stings are not dangerous. Douse in vinegar and apply ice.

Portuguese Man-of-Wars The body of a Portuguese man-of-war consists of a translucent, bluish, bladder-like float, which in Hawaii generally grows to four or five inches long. Known locally as 'bluebottles,' they're most often found on the windward coasts, particularly after storms.

The sting of a Portuguese man-of-war is very painful, and you're likely to get stung more than once, seeing as they have clusters of long tentacles containing hundreds of stinging cells that can be up to 75% as toxic as cobra venom. Even touching a bluebottle a few hours after it's washed up onshore can result in burning stings.

If you do get stung, quickly remove the tentacles and thoroughly wash the area with seawater or fresh water (do not use vinegar or urine). Apply ice. For serious reactions, including chest pains or difficulty in breathing, seek medical attention immediately.

Sharks Unpleasant encounters with sharks are unlikely, but not unheard of in Hawaii. About 40 varieties of shark are endemic to Hawaiian waters, including the nonaggressive whale shark, which can reach lengths of 50 feet. Nevertheless, in recent years, increasing numbers of shark attacks have been reported in Hawaii, with serious attacks now occurring on average two or three times a year.

Outside of the rarely encountered great white shark, the most dangerous specimens are the tiger and Galapagos sharks. The tiger shark, which averages 12 to 18 feet in length, is identified by its blunt nose and vertical bars along its side. It is not terribly particular about what it eats and has been known to chomp down on pieces of wood (including surfboards) floating on the ocean surface. The Galapagos shark is harder to identify, but in shallow water any large grey shark over six feet long probably qualifies.

Primarily, sharks follow blood in the water, anything from an open cut on a diver's hand to the catch being dragged by a spearfisher. Most recently they have been known to frequent offshore waters during winter when pods of whales are birthing or just cruising around. After heavy rains, sharks sometimes come in around river mouths and so murky waters should be avoided.

Should you come face to face with a shark, the best thing to do is move casually and quietly away. Don't panic, as sharks are attracted by things that thrash around. They are also attracted to anything shiny or by brightly-colored, especially high-contrast, swimwear. In general sharks are curious creatures and will sometimes investigate divers, although they generally just check things out and continue on their way. If they start to hang around, however, it's time for you to go.

Some aquatic safety officials suggest thumping or kicking an attacking shark on the nose or sticking your fingers into its eyes, which may confuse it long enough to give you time to escape. Indeed, some divers who dive in shark waters carry a billy club or bang stick.

Other Sea Creatures Encounters with venomous sea creatures in Hawaiian waters are rather rare.

You should, however, learn to recognize scorpion fish and lionfish, two related species that can inject venom through their dorsal spines if touched. Both are sometimes found in quite shallow water.

The Hawaiian lionfish, which grows up to 10 inches long, is strikingly attractive with vertical orange and white stripes and feathery appendages that contain poisonous spines. It likes to drift along reefs, particularly at night.

The scorpion fish is more drab in appearance, has shorter and less obvious spines, is about six inches in length, and tends to sit immobile on the ocean bottom or on ledges.

The sting from either can cause a sharp burning pain, followed by numbness around the area, nausea and headaches. Immediately stick the affected area in water that is as hot as bearable (but take care not to unintentionally scald the area due to numbness) and go for medical treatment.

The *wana,* or spiny sea urchin, has long brittle spines that can puncture the skin and break off, causing burning, possible numbness and infection. The spines sometimes inflict a toxin and can cause extreme muscle spasms, difficulty in breathing and even collapse. You can try to remove the spines with tweezers or by soaking them in hot water, but be careful not to break them off or push them deeper beneath the skin. More serious cases may require surgical removal.

Cone shells should be left alone unless you're sure they're empty. There's no safe way of picking up a live cone shell, as the animal inside has a long harpoon-like tail that can dart out and reach anywhere on its shell to deliver a painful or even fatally venomous sting. The wound should be soaked in hot water and medical attention sought immediately.

The *puhi,* or moray eel, is often spotted by snorkelers around reefs and coral heads. The eels constantly open and close their mouths to pump water across their gills, which makes them look far more menacing than they actually are. Eels don't attack, but will protect themselves by clamping down with razor-sharp teeth (and a strong jaw) if someone sticks a hand in their door while poking around reef crevices or holes.

EMERGENCIES

Dial ☎ 911 for police, ambulance and fire emergencies. For late-night clinics and 24-hour emergency rooms at hospitals, see Health, earlier. The inside front covers of island phone books also list vital service agencies, such as poison control, Coast Guard rescue and various crisis lines. On Maui the 24-hour sexual assault hotline can be reached by dialing ☎ 242-4357.

If you lose your passport, contact your consulate in Honolulu; a complete list of consulate phone numbers can be found in the yellow pages.

For refunds on lost or stolen American Express traveler's checks, call ☎ 800-221-7282; for MasterCard traveler's checks, dial ☎ 800-223-9920. For other types of theft, if you plan to make an insurance claim you should contact the nearest police station immediately for an incident report.

LEGAL MATTERS

Anyone arrested on Maui is (theoretically) innocent until proven guilty and has the right to a lawyer, from the time of their arrest to their trial. The Hawaii State Bar Association (☎ 888-808-4722) can make referrals; foreign visitors may want to call their consulate for advice.

In Hawaii, anyone driving with a blood alcohol level of 0.08% or higher is guilty of driving 'under the influence,' which carries severe penalties. Operating a motor vehicle under the influence of any substance, be it beer, buds or barbiturates, is decidedly dangerous (and stupid). According to the letter of the law, hitchhiking is also illegal.

As with most places in the world, the possession of marijuana and nonprescription narcotics is illegal in Hawaii. Be aware that US Customs has a zero-tolerance policy for drugs; federal authorities have seized boats after finding even minute quantities of marijuana onboard.

Hawaii's Department of Commerce & Consumer Affairs offers a handy recorded information line for consumer issues. Dial ☎ 808-587-1234 for information on your rights regarding refunds and exchanges, time-share contracts, car rentals and similar topics.

BUSINESS HOURS

Typical office hours in Hawaii are 8:30am to 4:30pm Monday to Friday. Shops in urban areas stay open later into the evening and on weekends. Some gas stations, pharmacies, grocery and convenience stores are open 24 hours, but those that sell liquor may only legally do so between 6am and 11pm daily.

Banks are usually open 8:30am to 4pm Monday to Thursday, staying open until around 6pm on Friday. However, bank branches inside grocery stores keep longer hours, typically 10am to 7pm weekdays and 10am to 4pm weekends.

PUBLIC HOLIDAYS

On national public holidays, all banks, schools and government offices (including post offices) are closed and transportation services, museums and historic sites are on a Sunday schedule. Holidays falling on a weekend are usually observed the following Monday.

Major 2003 public holidays in Hawaii are:

New Year's Day	January 1
Dr Martin Luther King, Jr Day	January 20
Presidents' Day	February 17
Prince Jonah Kuhio Kalanianole Day	March 26
Good Friday	April 20
Memorial Day	May 26
King Kamehameha Day	June 11
Independence Day	July 4
Statehood Day	August 15
Labor Day	September 1
Veterans Day	November 11
Thanksgiving	November 27
Christmas Day	December 25

SPECIAL EVENTS

With its multitude of cultures and summer weather year-round, Maui has an incredible number and variety of holidays, festivals and events. Many dates vary a bit from year to year, so check local newspapers or inquire at tourist offices for exact schedules. Water-sport events are particularly reliant on the weather and the surf, so any schedule is tentative and competition venues tend to hop between (and around) all of the Hawaiian Islands.

January

New Year's Eve Fireworks displays and arts festivals take place in some of the larger towns and resorts to ring in the new year.

Mercedes Championship The PGA tour kicks off at Kapalua's Plantation Golf Course (☎ 669-2440) in early January.

Ka Molokai Makahiki A modern-day version of the ancient *makahiki* festival takes place in Kaunakakai, Molokai, near the middle of the month. The weeklong celebration features a tournament of traditional Hawaiian games and sporting events, an outrigger-canoe fishing contest, Hawaiian music performances and sacred hula.

Annual Festival of Hula All of Maui's hula halau (schools) perform together at the Lahaina Cannery Mall (☎ 661-5304).

Chinese New Year Festivities begin at the second new moon after the winter solstice (mid-January to mid-February) with lion dances and thousands of firecrackers at Wing Ho Temple in Lahaina.

Hula Bowl All-Star Classic The all-stars of American college football compete in mid-January or early February at War Memorial Stadium. For details, see ⓦ www.hulabowlmaui.com.

February

Whale Month February is a busy month of whale parades, whale regattas, storytelling and special whale-watching programs in Lahaina and South Maui, sponsored in part by the Pacific Whale Foundation (☎ 879-8660, 800-942-5311).

March

East Maui Taro Festival On the last weekend in March, this festival (☎ 248-8972) held near Hana town features *poi*-making demonstrations, a taro pancake breakfast, traditional hula and outrigger canoes.

April

Banyan Tree Birthday Lahaina (☎ 667-9175) celebrates the history of its almost 130-year-old banyan tree near the end of the month.

Kapalua Celebration of the Arts The Ritz-Carlton Kapalua (☎ 669-6200, ⓦ www.celebrationof thearts.org) hosts this hands-on arts and cultural festival every year with traditional hula and Hawaiian chants, nose flutes, shell lei-making and other workshops for residents and visitors.

The Ulupalakua Thing Held on a Saturday in late April, the Maui County Agricultural Trade Show & Sampling fair at Ulupalakua Ranch has live entertainment, local product exhibits and sampling food prepared by Maui's top chefs.

May

May Day Known as Lei Day in Hawaii, the first day of May finds everyone wearing lei. Festivities include lei-making competitions and Hawaiian entertainment.

Da Kine Classic One of the world's top international windsurfing racing series takes place at Hookipa Beach in early May.

Molokai Ka Hula Piko This weeklong Molokai festival celebrates the birth of the hula, with traditional dance performances, Hawaiian food, cultural demonstrations and visits to sacred sites in mid-May.

Seabury Hall Craft Fair This prestigious college preparatory school (☎ 572-7235) on Olinda Rd in Makawao opens its doors for an annual craft fair.

June

Ki Ho'alu This Hawaiian slack-key guitar festival takes place in mid-June at the Maui Arts & Cultural Center (☎ 242-7469).

Upcountry Fair At the Eddie Tam complex in Makawao, this traditional agricultural fair has livestock auctions, live entertainment and local food.

July

Independence Day Fireworks and festivities mark this national holiday on July 4. Makawao holds its traditional rodeo parade and other *paniolo* events at the Oski Rice Arena.

Kapalua Wine & Food Festival In early July, international winemakers and chefs gather for a culinary extravaganza (☎ 800-527-2582, ⓦ www .kapaluamaui.com).

August

Obon Celebrated around the islands in July and August, traditional Japanese dances are performed at Buddhist mission temples to honor deceased ancestors.

Maui Onion & Pineapple Festivals The annual Maui Onion cook-off heats up with raw onion-eating contests, live music and a farmers market at Kaanapali's Whalers Village (☎ 661-4567) shopping complex in early August. The Queen Kaahumanu Mall (☎ 877-3369) hosts similar celebrations for pineapple lovers near the middle of the month.

Ole Longboard Classic This is Maui's premier longboarding event, which takes place off Launiopoko Beach Park in mid-August.

September

A Taste of Lahaina Everyone comes out for Lahaina's signature food competition (☎ 667-9194) in early September, featuring cooking demonstrations by top Maui chefs, various tasting booths and a beer garden. Admission costs $2 (kids under 12 free) at the Lahaina Special Events Arena.

Aloha Festivals This celebration of all things Hawaiian involves parades, cultural events, contests, canoe races and Hawaiian music. Celebrations (☎ 879-1866) are staggered from mid-September to early October, depending on the island.

Red Bull King of the Air This professional kiteboarding competition happens at Hookipa Beach in mid-September.

Na Wahine o Ke Kai In late September, Hawaii's major women's outrigger canoe race (W www.holoholo.org) starts around sunrise at Kaluakoi on Molokai, and ends 40 miles later at Waikiki Beach on Oahu.

The Haleakala Run to the Sun Maui's 36.2-mile ultramarathon (☎ 871-6441) begins at dawn at sea-level Paia and climbs 10,000 feet to the top of Haleakala. The best finishers usually hit the summit in an exhausting six hours.

October

Maui County Fair This 80-year-old country fair (☎ 242-2721), held at the War Memorial Complex, has agricultural exhibits, multicultural food, live music and carnival rides in early October.

Na Molokai Hoe In early October, teams from around the Pacific Rim and North America compete in this major annual men's outrigger canoe race. The route is the same used for the Na Wahine o Ke Kai in September.

Xterra World Championship This off-road triathlon (W www.xterraplanet.com) includes a 30km bike ride up the slopes of Haleakala, an 11km trail run and a 1.5km ocean swim. It's held in mid- to late October.

Aloha Classic World Windsurfing Championship The final event of the Pro Boardsailing Association's world tour invites top international competitors to Maui's Hookipa Beach in late October or early November.

Halloween Lahaina's grand 'Mardi Gras of the Pacific' (☎ 888-310-1117) attracts over 20,000 revelers to downtown Front Street for music, dancing, food and costume competitions.

November

Aloha Classic The Maui racing series for the Windsurfing World Cup takes place at Hookipa Beach.

Hawaii International Film Festival About 150 independent films from Pacific Rim and Asian nations are screened in theaters throughout the islands. Festival (☎ 528-FILM, W www.hiff.org) venues on Maui include Iao Theatre in Wailuku and the Maui Arts & Cultural Center in Kahului.

Hula o Na Keiki Young hula dancers perform solo and *palua* (partnered) along with food & arts festivities at the Kaanapali Beach Hotel (☎ 661-0101). Tickets cost $5-10.

Ice Carving Exhibition & Competition Master chefs and ice carvers from Japan and Hawaii create impressive speed sculptures out of 300-pound ice blocks at the Lahaina Cannery Mall (☎ 661-5304).

WORK

US citizens can pursue work in Hawaii as they would in any other state – the problem is actually finding a decent job. Foreign visitors who are in the USA for tourist purposes are not legally allowed to take up employment. Many of the jobs that are available pay minimum wage. You can look over the *Maui News* classifieds or apply on-the-spot at restaurants, hotel resorts and shops.

Folks with language, scuba, fishing or guiding skills could investigate employment with resorts, the National Park Service, fishing charter companies and whatever outfit fits your experience. It's an even tighter labor market for professionals, but teachers and nurses are in chronically short supply.

Volunteer Work

Haleakala National Park participates in the national Volunteers in Parks program (☎ 572-4487, Ⓦ www.nps.gov/volunteer), PO Box 369, Makawao, HI 96768. Duties may be as varied as staffing information desks, leading hikes, trapping predatory animals or controlling invasive plants. Some positions are quite competitive and candidates with a background in natural sciences or any practical knowledge like first aid are preferred. Volunteers receive no salary or help with airfare, though for longer-term assignments barracks-style housing and a food stipend of about $10 a day are provided. There are other ongoing projects, for example, the Adopt-a-Trail program, that almost anyone is qualified for.

The Hawaii chapter of the Sierra Club coordinates service trips doing backcountry trail work, fence building and noxious plant control. These trips are usually one to two weeks in length with groups of up to 20 people. Participants pay to cover their own administrative costs, usually from $100. For information, call ☎ 808-538-6616 on Oahu or write to: Hawaii Service Trip Program, PO Box 2577, Honolulu, HI 96803. Check the Web site (Ⓦ www.hi.sierraclub.org) for current service trips and armchair volunteerism ideas for those not already in Hawaii.

Another group, the Student Conservation Association (☎ 603-543-1828), PO Box 550, Charlestown, NH 03603, sends a handful of people each year to work for three months as volunteers at Haleakala National Park. Positions range from interpretive assistants to habitat restoration aides. Roundtrip airfare to Hawaii, a biweekly stipend of about $100 and accommodations are provided, as well as AmeriCorps education benefits. Anyone over 18 with a high school diploma may apply. Browse the current volunteer database at Ⓦ www.sca-inc.org.

Other environmental groups like the Nature Conservancy (Ⓦ nature.org) and the Pacific Whale Foundation (Ⓦ www.pacificwhale.org) advertise volunteer openings with the online volunteer database at Ⓦ www.malamahawaii.org, as well as on their own Web sites.

ACCOMMODATIONS

Unless otherwise noted, accommodation rates given throughout this book don't include the painful 11.41% room tax. Rates are substantially lower outside of peak season (mid-December to mid-April), but you'll need reservations almost any time of year to lock in the best deals.

Campgrounds on Maui have been recently expanded and upgraded. The next cheapest places to stay on Maui are hostels in Wailuku or Aloha Windsurfers Hostel in Paia, each charging around $20 per night. There are some studio-style cottages that rent from about $60, with most of these found around Haiku-Paia area. Other tropical hideaway B&Bs are spread over East Maui, while those B&Bs found along the western shore are mostly plain homes adrift in residential subdivisions. Expect to pay at least $75 a night at either. Wailuku and Lahaina also have excellent historic inns worth a romantic splurge, costing from around $100 per night.

Condos make up the bulk of mid-range accommodations in Kihei and along the West Maui shore. The lower end of this price range is around $75, but it's easy to spend over $100 a night for nothing special. Maui's two biggest resort developments are Kaanapali Beach Resort and Wailea Resort, both of which have luxury hotels and condos.

Camping

In addition to the state and county campgrounds following, there's also church-sponsored tenting on the beach at Olowalu, about five miles south of Lahaina, and beautiful campgrounds in Haleakala National Park. Many Hawaiian families informally camp out at different beaches, but this is illegal.

If you're going to be camping at high elevations, bring a waterproof tent, winter-rated sleeping bag, rain gear and layers of warm clothing. Camping on the beach is another matter entirely. A very lightweight cotton bag is the most you'll need. Public campgrounds require campers to use tents – a good idea anyway because of mosquitoes.

There are no camping supply stores worthy of the name on Maui. A pathetically limited array of camping supplies are sold at the Sports Authority in the Maui Marketplace and at other discount stores in Kahului. Try to bring everything from home instead, but remember that camp stove fuel canisters are not allowed on flights (you can buy them on Maui).

State Parks Maui has state campgrounds and cabins at Polipoli Spring Recreation Area in the cool Upcountry and Waianapanapa State Park off the Hana Hwy. Polipoli is in a coniferous highland forest, and often strangely deserted. The extremely popular Waianapanapa campground is set on a black-sand beach near Hana on Maui's rainy side.

Each park has a maximum stay of five consecutive nights per month and permits are required. Tent camping is free while cabins cost $45/50/55 for up to four/five/six people. For camping permits or cabin reservations, contact the Division of State Parks (☎ 984-8109), State Office Building, 54 S High St, Wailuku, HI 96793, which also has a free brochure to all of Hawaii's state parks. Office hours are 8am to 3:30pm weekdays.

County Parks Maui is in the midst of upgrading and expanding its county campgrounds. The first to reopen was Kanaha Beach Park, just north of the airport, but safety and noise pollution are both problematic. Better options will someday be the proposed campgrounds at Papalaua Wayside Park, Waihee Beach Park and Honomanu Beach.

Permits cost $3 per day (50¢ for children under 18), and camping is limited to three consecutive nights. Permits are available by mail or in person from the Department of Parks & Recreation (☎ 243-7389), 1580 Kaahumanu Ave, Wailuku, HI 96793. The office is in the War Memorial Complex at Baldwin High School in Wailuku, which is actually closer to Kahului than Wailuku, despite its address (see the Kahului map in the Central Maui chapter).

B&Bs

In addition to the organizations listed here, you should also try Web search engines or sites such as W www.alternative-hawaii.com to find smaller, often cheaper B&Bs. Those single-family operations with one or maybe two properties often offer the most seclusion and budget deals.

Ho'okipa Haven (☎ 579-8282, 800-398-6284, fax 579-9953, W www.hookipa.com), 62 Baldwin Ave No 2A, Paia, HI 96779. Vacation rental houses, studios and rooms from $60 a night, mostly in and around the Paia-Haiku area. More expensive luxury properties are kept in West Maui and on the North Shore.

Bed & Breakfast Hawaii (☎ 808-822-7771, 800-733-1632, fax 808-822-2723, W www.bandbhawaii.com), PO Box 449, Kapaa, HI 96746. This long-running Kauai-based service has many listings on Maui and a few on Molokai. Rates are from $65 per night.

Hawaii's Best B&Bs (☎ 808-885-4550, 800-262-9912, fax 808-885-0559, W www.bestbnb.com), PO Box 563, Kamuela, HI 96743. The two ladies who own this business get rave reviews for their high standards and for picking hidden-away properties, including some on Maui, Molokai and Lanai.

Condos

Maui has many more condominium units than hotel rooms. Some condo complexes are booked only through rental agents. Others operate more like a hotel with a front desk, though even in those places some units are usually handled by rental agents.

Most condos require deposits within one to two weeks of booking, with full payment due 30 days prior to arrival. The minimum stay is usually three to seven days, depending on the place and season. In some cases you might have to pay security deposits and cleaning fees, especially for shorter stays. Cancellation policies vary, but expect a hefty charge (or no refund at all) for canceling within the last month.

Each agent listed in the regional chapters handles a number of condo complexes and will send listings with rates, making it possible for you to compare values. Sometimes they are more expensive than booking with the condo complex directly, but you never know. Both will advertise special promotional discounts on their own Web sites.

FOOD

In Hawaii you'll find the pork and taro of the original Polynesian settlers mingling with the staples of all the immigrant groups that arrived later, for example Japanese sashimi or Portuguese sausage. Seafood abounds but it can be surprisingly expensive, as can most anything else you buy at the grocery stores since most of it must be imported from the mainland. Short-term visitors qualify for free discount membership cards simply by asking; of the two biggest grocery store chains, Foodland issues its Makai Card right at the checkout counter without paperwork, while Safeway requires you to visit the customer service desk first. For even fresher, cheaper seafood and produce, go to the source and purchase from fisherman hauling their catch at harborside or visit a farmers market in Kihei or Honokowai.

Many island chefs specialize in what's loosely called Hawaii Regional or Pacific Rim cuisine. Either way this style incorporates fresh local ingredients and borrows liberally from the islands' various ethnic groups, so expect exotic fusion dishes. Roy Yamaguchi, Peter Merriman, Bev Gannon, David Paul Johnson and Gerard Reversade are just a few of the more renowned chefs owning and operating restaurants on Maui. You can often watch famous chefs at work on the cooking show *Hawaii's Kitchen*, which broadcasts at 5:30pm on Sunday on channel 2 (KHON-NBC). Alternately, you can visit the recipe archives at W www .khon.com.

For island visitors, the free *Maui Menus* magazine comes out quarterly and is available everywhere. It is of refreshingly high quality, coming complete with chef interviews, dining news and recipes. For scores of discount dining coupons, check the Thursday edition of *Maui News* and the free alternative weekly *Maui Time*.

Hawaiian Cuisine

The traditional Hawaiian feast celebrating special events is the *luau*. Nowadays they're mostly family affairs thrown in honor of say, a baby's first birthday, and short-stay visitors would be lucky indeed to get invited to one. Many Maui resorts also throw what they call 'luaus,' but with few exceptions all this means is a Las Vegas–style Polynesian dance review and a hotel-style buffet.

The traditional luau centers around a *kalua* pig (roasted in a pitlike earthen oven known as an *imu*). The imu is readied by building a fire and heating rocks in the pit. When the rocks glow red, layers of damp banana trunks and ti leaves are placed over the stones. A pig is split open, stuffed with some of the hot rocks and laid atop the bed. Other foods wrapped in ti and banana leaves are placed around it. It's all covered again with more ti leaves and a layer of mats and topped with dirt to seal in the heat, which then bakes and steams the food.

Anything cooked in this style is called kalua, not just pig. It all takes about four to eight hours, depending on the size of the swine or whatever else is being cooked. A few of the resort luau still bake their pigs outdoors in the traditional manner, and you can often go in the morning and watch them prepare and bury the pig. Considering the work involved, most home chefs favor a conventional oven instead.

Wetland taro is one of the world's few purple foods and is used to make poi, a paste pounded from cooked taro corms. Water is added to make it pudding-like, and its consistency is measured by how many fingers you'll need to transport it from dish to mouth, hence one-, two- and three-finger poi. It is sometimes fermented for a few days to give it more zing. Poi is highly nutritious and easily digestible, but it's an acquired taste. It was designed to highlight and balance the flavor of stronger-flavored

Tropical Trail Mix

Coconut palms drop their nuts on beaches, while wild fruits grow with abandon alongside hiking trails and rural roadsides. Only pick what you can personally consume and never violate the *kapu* on someone's private orchard.

Pineapple Hawaii's number-one fruit crop is the pineapple. Most Hawaiian pineapples weigh a solid 5lb and are of the Smooth Cayenne or new Sugarloaf type. Although they're harvested year-round, the long sunny days of summer produce the sweetest pineapples.

Papaya The ubiquitous papaya comes in several varieties. One of the best is the smallish Solo, with pale strawberry-colored flesh; its name stems from the fact that it's good eating for one person. Papayas, which are a good source of calcium and vitamins A and C, are harvested year-round.

Guava Nothing falls off trees faster in Maui than guavas. This yellow, lime-shaped fruit is a few inches in diameter. It has a moist, pink, seedy flesh, all of which is edible. Young guavas are a little tart but sweeten as they ripen. They're a richer source of vitamin C than oranges. Pick as many as you want, as they are considered an invasive pest.

Lilikoi Passion fruit is a vine with beautiful flowers that grow into small round fruits. The thick skin of the fruit is generally purple or yellow and wrinkles as it ripens. The pulp inside is juicy, seedy and slightly tart; once you taste it you'll be hooked.

Mango Big old mango trees are abundant in Hawaii, even in remote valleys. These juicy palm-sized fruits change as they ripen from green to blush red and finally orange and are edible at any stage. Two popular varieties, Pirie and Haden, are less stringy than those usually found in the wild. Mangoes are mainly a summer fruit.

Avocado Hawaii has three main types of avocado: the West Indian, a smooth-skinned variety that matures in summer and autumn; the rough-skinned Guatemalan, which matures in winter and spring; and the Mexican variety, which has a small fruit and smooth skin. Many of the avocados now in Hawaii are a hybrid of the three.

Breadfruit The Hawaiian breadfruit is a large, round, green fruit. It's comparable to potatoes in carbohydrates and is prepared much the same way. In old Hawaii, as in much of the Pacific, breadfruit was one of the traditional staples.

Star Fruit The carambola, or star fruit, is a translucent yellow-green fruit with five ribs like the points of a star. It has a crisp, juicy pulp and can be eaten without being peeled.

Ohelo These berries grow on low shrubs common in lava areas. The ohelo is a relative of the cranberry, similar in tartness and size, with the sweet overtones of a kiwi. The fruit is red or yellow and is used in jellies and pies. Several other berries that are poisonous resemble the ohelo, so don't pick them unless you are sure.

Watermelon The watermelons grown on Molokai are so famous throughout the islands that airlines had to create special regulations for passengers transporting them, ostensibly to prevent loose melons from cannonballing down the aisles.

Hawaii also has a bewildering variety of hybrid fruit shown off at farmers markets, including apple-bananas, pluots (plum-apricots) and the strawberry papaya developed by the University of Hawaii on Kauai.

foods like kalua (or Spam!) with its steady, flat salinity and a fingerful eaten alone is sure to turn you off.

Another food to accompany poi is *laulau*, fish, pork and taro wrapped in a ti leaf bundle and steamed. *Lomi* salmon (sometimes called *lomilomi* salmon) is made by massaging and marinating thin slices of raw salmon with diced tomatoes and green onions. Other Hawaiian foods include baked *ulu* (breadfruit), *opihi* (tiny limpet shells picked off the reef at low tide) and *pipikaula* (beef jerky). *Haupia,* the standard dessert, is a stiff pudding made of coconut cream thickened traditionally with arrowroot but more commonly nowadays with cornstarch.

Spices particular to Hawaiian cooking and available everywhere include *alaea* (an iron-rich, red salt), *limu* (the generic term for a variety of edible seaweeds) and chili pepper water. Ti leaves are indispensable: food is wrapped in them, cooked in them and served upon them.

Local Food 'Local food' refers to all the poi, laulau, lomi salmon or anything else still eaten in modern Hawaii and almost nowhere else in the world. Basically, it's Hawaiian soul food.

Saimin is the local version of ramen noodle soup and *loco moco* is a morning wake-up call for the strong-stomached, with a bed of rice topped by a fried egg, hamburger patty and rivulets of brown gravy.

Local plate lunches are available everywhere, especially at drive-ins and *kaukau* wagons, basically a kitchen on wheels. Typically, a plate lunch averages 1400 calories and consists of 'two scoop rice,' a helping of macaroni salad and protein in whatever ethnic flavor the cook favors, be that beef stew, Korean BBQ, Japanese *katsu,* Filipino adobo or Hawaiian-style mahimahi.

Snacks

Pupu is the word for all kinds of munchies or appetizers. Boiled peanuts (a popular, soggy bar snack), soy-flavored rice crackers and sashimi are common choices. Another local favorite pupu is *poke,* pronounced 'POH-kay,'' which is cubed, raw fish marinated in salt, soy sauce, chili peppers and seaweed, though nontraditional marinade possibilities are endless. You'll come across tofu poke, escargot poke and oyster poke.

Crack seed is a Chinese snack food that can be sweet, sour, salty or some combination of the three. It's often made from dried fruits, such as plums and apricots; more exotic ones include pickled mangoes, lemon strips and *li hing mui,* one of the most assaulting for uninitiated taste buds.

The idea of shave ice resembles mainland snow cones, but taken to the next heavenly level. Here, the ice is shaved fine like powdered snow and drenched with sweet fruit-flavored syrups in psychedelic hues. Get wild and request sweet *azuki* beans in the bottom or ice cream on top.

DRINKS

Only a fool would bypass Maui's tropical elixirs for a Pepsi. Coconut water straight from the nut, guava nectar, fresh papaya juice or addictive, cures-what-ails-you smoothies with lilikoi, banana, pineapple, star fruit, guava or papaya are only some of the delights. If it's caffeine you crave, try 100% Maui coffee grown on the Upcountry slopes of Haleakala instead.

Hawaii is also one of the main *awa* (kava) growing regions in the United States. This root has a long history in Polynesia, and when steeped with water and extracted through a fine cloth, makes a pleasing, mildly narcotic drink.

For all other intoxicants, the drinking age in the USA is a retrograde 21 years. Baby faces will be asked to produce photo ID when purchasing alcohol. It's illegal to have open containers of alcohol in motor vehicles and, although it's commonplace, drinking in public parks or on the beaches is also technically illegal. Most of Hawaii's microbrews come from the Big Island, although a few bars on Maui are trying their own hand at it. The island's Upcountry winery is pretty disappointing, but the pineapple dessert wine is worth a free tipple.

All of Hawaii has become synonymous with those rum-defiling tropical cocktails dolled up with paper umbrellas, cherries and the odd plastic monkey. The classic favorite is a mai tai, mixing rum, grenadine and lemon and pineapple juices, while a lava flow throws together cream of coconut, strawberries, banana and pineapple juice. For natural flavor and subtlety, however,

A Glossary from under the Sea

Debates rage about which of Maui's restaurants has the best market-fresh fish, and somehow Mama's Fish House at Paia always comes out on top.

Yet eating fresh fish just about anywhere on the island is going to be a pricey experience, so you should know what you're ordering, right? Some of the most popular locally caught fish and other seafood are as follows (a few are better known by their Japanese names than traditional Hawaiian terms):

ahi	yellowfin tuna; a mild-tasting fish, often served as sashimi or poke
aku	bonito or skipjack tuna (called *katsuo* in Japanese); a fish with firm wine-red flesh and a stronger flavor than ahi, usually served broiled or grilled
akule	big-eyed scad; often eaten smoked or salted in Hawaii
au	any species of marlin (mostly Pacific Blue in Hawaii); a lean and extremely tender fish
enenue	rudderfish or chub (also known as *nenue*); favored locally for its strong seaweed aroma
kaku	barracuda
mahimahi	a fish called 'dolphin' (not the mammal) with white, fairly sweet flesh
mano	shark
onaga	red snapper (called *ulaula* in Hawaiian): a tender, moist fish that is especially popular for making sushi for New Year celebrations and weddings
ono	wahoo; a fish similar to mackerel, with white, flaky, delicate flesh
opah	moonfish; a versatile, fatty fish considered lucky by old-fashioned Hawaiian fishermen, who would rather give it away than sell it
opakapaka	Hawaiian pink snapper; similar to onaga, the flesh is firmest and fattiest in winter, when it is used for sashimi
opelu	mackerel scad; best eaten dried or broiled with poi
tako	Japanese for octopus (*he'e* in Hawaiian); often eaten as poke or sushi
uku	gray snapper; delicate, moist pink meat and a pronounced fishy taste
ula	Hawaiian lobster (clawless); ula are smaller and reputedly sweeter then mainland lobsters
wana	sea urchin; the gonads are eaten as *haute* sushi

nothing beats a coconut fresh from the palm, whacked open, and the water spiked with rum.

ENTERTAINMENT

The best sources of up-to-date entertainment information are 'Maui Scene' published in the Thursday edition of *Maui News* and covering arts, music and special events, or *Maui Time,* a free alternative weekly with extensive bar and club listings.

Maui's nightlife scene lags far behind Oahu's. Most of what action there is exists in Lahaina, Kihei and Casanova in Makawao. All over the island, happy hour starts as early as 2pm and can last until 7pm, with possibly another late-night happy hour from 10pm to midnight.

The Maui Arts & Cultural Center (see the Central Maui chapter) in Kahului is the venue for performances by the Maui Symphony Orchestra, loads of community theater and cultural groups, film festivals and concerts by big-name musicians.

Luau are held regularly in Lahaina, Kaanapali and Wailea, with varying degrees of authenticity (often nil). All include a buffet dinner with a flashy Polynesian dance revue and cost around $60 before discounts. The Old Lahaina Luau foregoes the fire sticks and Tahitian drums in favor of something more traditionally Hawaiian (see the West Maui chapter).

The Napili Kai Beach Club (see the West Maui chapter) in Napili has Friday dinner shows that feature hula dancing by local children. Free hula shows are offered at many shopping centers, especially in Lahaina, Kaanapali and Wailea, and these performances all go to support real hula halau.

SPECTATOR SPORTS

Maui's deeply rooted paniolo (Hawaiian cowboy) culture shows off its colors at Upcountry rodeos near Makawao. Maui is also host to several major sports events like the Hula Bowl All-Star Classic, PGA golf championships, world-class surfing and windsurfing competitions and all sorts of extreme sports craziness. Drag races are held at the Mokulele Hwy racetrack on weekends and over on Molokai, you can also see traditional outrigger canoe races. See Special Events, earlier, for details on all of these happenings.

In ancient Hawaii *he'e holua* (sled racing) was the premier spectator sport. Racers would ride prone on narrow wooden sleds (called *papa holua*) lashed together with coconut fibers, racing at high speeds down steep hills along furrows that had been covered with cinders and *pili* grass or ti leaves to make the surface smooth. Many of the holua slide paths were a mile or two long and were constructed near heiau (temples). Sledders often bloodied themselves in the races, but that only heightened their *mana* (spiritual power). Holua sledding is now making a fledgling comeback on the Big Island of Hawaii.

Ancient Hawaiians were also heavy risk-takers and often wagered on the holua races, as well as on foot races, surfing competitions and many other sports. Other popular ancient Hawaiian games included *ulu maika*, in which rounded stone discs were rolled between two stakes, resembling

modern bowling (interestingly, the distance between stakes was 60 feet, which is exactly the length of a modern ten-pin lane). Another ancient game was *oa pahee*, like ula maika but using a large wooden torpedo slide. For the more passive, there was *konane*, a strategy game similar to checkers; indentations were carved into a stone board to hold the pebbles of white coral and black lava that were used as playing pieces.

SHOPPING

Maui residents shop for everyday items in Kahului, where discount stores include Costco and Wal-Mart. It's worth stopping off here for supplies after exiting the airport but before going anywhere else on the island.

Found islandwide wherever tourists are, *ABC Store* has cheap beach essentials, plus Kona coffee and macadamia nuts, cheap clothes and liquor. *Crazy Shirts* outlets sell quality T-shirts with home-grown Hawaiian designs, some tongue-in-cheek or dyed with hemp or beer. Local *Maui Tropix* sells Maui Built surf gear and accessories, but you'd better hope its surfboards last a lot longer than its T-shirts!

Local arts and crafts are booming on Maui, but sometimes it's hard to sort out the dross. Reliable galleries are the *Lahaina Arts Society* in Banyan Tree Square, *Maui Crafts Guild* in Paia, *Hu'i No'eau Visual Arts Center* and downtown shops in Makawao. In West Maui, the *Hawaiian Quilt Collection* (☎ 800-367-9987, **W** www .hawaiian-quilts.com) has stores at the Hyatt Regency in Kaanapali and the Kapalua Shops. Both offer three-hour introductory Hawaiian quilting classes for about $50, including a starter quilted pillow kit.

Several businesses sell food and flowers, including lei, protea, papayas, pineapples, Maui onions and husked coconuts, which are agriculturally preinspected and delivered to the airport for you to pick up on your way out. Two such places are *Take Home Maui* (☎ 661-8067, 800-545-6284, 121 Dickenson St, Lahaina) and *Airport Flower & Fruit* (☎ 243-9367, 800-922-9352, **W** www .mauiexpress.com) in Kahului. You can also buy direct from Upcountry farms.

Activities

Congratulations. You've made it to Hawaii. Now what? The sky – or the sea – is the limit. The islands of Maui, Molokai and Lanai run wild with outdoor activities, and there's something about paradise that spurs people to take risks, whether that's scuba diving for the first time or tackling the most extreme of sports.

Admittedly, most people come to Maui for the warm, tropical beaches. But the island is also one of the premier windsurfing spots in the world, so good that it overshadows some excellent surfing, which includes one of Hawaii's fastest breaks. Snorkelers and scuba divers dig the added bonus of exploring an ancient underwater volcano, Molokini. Kayakers carve out their own niches in Maui's quieter coastal regions, and during winter the whale watching here is unsurpassed.

What most travelers don't realize is that Maui and its neighboring islands offer excellent land-based adventures. You can hike inside the Haleakala volcanic cinder desert or make your way through prize rain forests, then hang glide off into an ocean sunset. Maui's long history of *paniolo* (Hawaiian cowboy) ranching makes for unusually scenic horseback riding, too. Back in the modern world, championship golf courses and tennis clubs are easily found. You can also take an interisland ferry to Lanai where 4WD tracks lead to ancient Hawaiian petroglyphs, or ride the slow boat to Molokai and kayak forgotten coasts, hike to remote valleys and mountain bike along the tallest *pali* (sea cliffs) in the world.

Details of activity tours, rental equipment and activity lessons are found later under the relevant activity headings. Most of the reputable sports-equipment shops are located in Kahului near the airport, including the all-purpose **Extreme Sports Maui** (☎ 871-7954, 800-328-8877, Ⓦ *www.extremesportsmaui.com, Dairy Center, 397 Dairy Rd*). They have got just about everything you need.

Molokai and Lanai are covered in more depth in the Excursions chapter.

Activity Desks & Discounts

The number of activity desks and tour operators can be bewildering if you don't know what you're looking for.

The key is simply do your own research *before* going price shopping. Often high-quality tour operators are not the ones suggested by activity desk booking agents, since their commissions generally aren't as good. Even if agents will give you big discounts on the tour you really want, there may be other drawbacks (for instance, you have to listen to a time-share presentation first).

If you're looking for someone honest, drop by **Tom Barefoot's Cashback Tours** (☎ 888-222-3601, Ⓦ *www.tombarefoot.com, 834 Front St, Lahaina*). Here you can read through extensive files kept on every imaginable Maui tour operator. The other Front St activity desks and those around Lahaina and major resorts may offer better deals, but don't come with the same guarantees.

Often the tour companies offer equal or better discounts if you contact them directly instead of going through an agent. Most will advertise with discount coupons in all of the free tourist magazines; *101 Things to Do: Maui* has the most comprehensive ads.

Note that advance reservations are usually only necessary if you plan to visit Maui over Christmas and New Year's or at the height of summer.

Water Sports on Maui

BOOGIE BOARDING

Those who can't surf boogie board. No, we're just kidding about that. Expert boogie boarders can ride the waves of the northern coast of West Maui with as much dazzling acrobatics as true surfers.

Beginners, you're looking for gentler shorebreaks (not big whomping waves), usually found along Maui's leeward (western) side. The most popular places for boogie boarding are beaches in the Kihei and Wailea area, DT Fleming Beach Park near Kapalua and HA Baldwin Beach Park north of Paia.

Special boogie boarding flippers, which are smaller than snorkel fins, will help you paddle out. Remember to wear reef shoes or other protective footwear. Boogie boards can be rented for around $8/45 per day/week at numerous locations around Maui, including many of the surfing and windsurfing shops (see those sections later). You can buy your own board for less than a week's rental from discount stores in Kahului.

CANOEING & KAYAKING

The first Polynesian settlers in Hawaii arrived by outrigger canoe, and racing clubs still practice at Hanakaoo Beach (also known as 'Canoe Beach') near Kaanapali in the early morning. Of all the kayaking tour companies, only Big Kahuna Adventures (see Rentals & Tours, below) offers outrigger canoe trips, costing $60 from Kihei Cove.

Many people kayak along the shores of South Maui, either near Kihei or from Ahihi- Kinau Natural Area Reserve toward La Perouse Bay. Both are extraspecial during the winter whale-watching season. Other favorite spots are near Olowalu or farther north at Kapalua or Honolua-Mokuleia Bay Marine Life Conservation District near Honolua Bay in West Maui. Maalaea Bay and the Hana coast are workable when weather conditions are not at their windiest.

Speaking of wind, that will be your biggest challenge on Maui. Don't let yourself get blown down the coast farther than you can paddle back. If you're concerned, rent a kayak with a rudder. Weather conditions on Maui are usually clearest and calmest early in the morning.

Molokai offers expert-level kayaking along its remote northeast shore. *Paddling Hawaii* by Audrey Sutherland is an indispensable guide for everything from cleaning

your fresh octopus dinner to making safe surf landings.

Rentals & Tours

South Pacific Kayaks & Outfitters (☎ 875-4848, 800-776-2326, **w** www.mauikayak.com, *Rainbow Mall, 2439 S Kihei Rd, lower Kihei*) Tours $55-90. Daily rental single/double kayaks $30/45. Three- to five-hour guided kayak tours visit La Perouse Bay or West Maui and include snorkeling and lunch.

Kelii's Kayak Tours (☎ 888-874-7652, **e** kelii@maui.net, *Kihei*) Tours $59-85. Kelii's offers guided ocean kayak tours, with stops for snorkeling. The five-hour trip includes lunch and visits Honolua Bay (summer only).

Big Kahuna Adventures (☎ 875-6395, **w** www.bigkahunaadventures.com, *Island Surf Bldg, 1993 S Kihei Rd*) Tours $60-85. Kayak trips mostly around Makena.

Other tour operators include **Tradewind Kayak Maui** (☎ 879-2247) and **Hana Bay Kayaks & Outfitters** (☎ 264-9566). For kayak scuba-diving trips see Snorkel Tours, later.

Duke's Surf & Rental Shop (☎ 661-1970, *602 Front St, Lahaina*) rents kayaks starting at $20.

KITEBOARDING

As if the waves and wind were already not powerful enough, somebody decided to get out there and popularize the extreme sport of kiteboarding. Proponents say the sport's history stretches all the way back to Ben Franklin, who once dragged himself across a pond using kite power.

Basically, kiteboarding involves maneuvering a modified surfboard using gigantic U-shaped kites to pull yourself up into the air. Kiteboarding moves remind spectators of skateboarding or snowboarding. But it is actually surfing, wakeboarding or windsurfing experience that helps.

Kiteboarding is impressive to watch, *!$£ing hard to master. All instructors follow a three-step curriculum, with each lesson lasting one to two hours. First you learn how to fly the kite, then you practice bodydragging (letting the kite pull you across the water) and finally you step on board.

WATER SPORTS ON MAUI

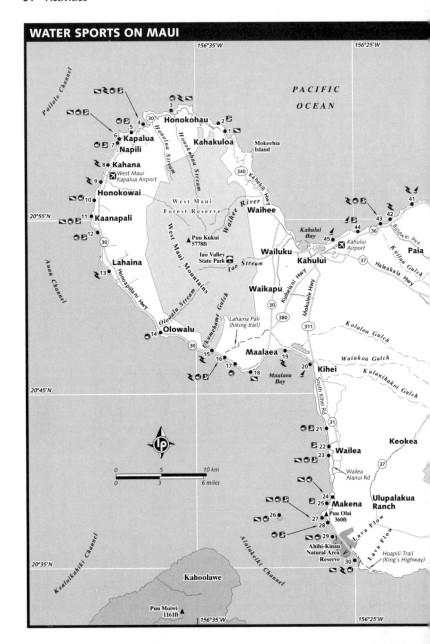

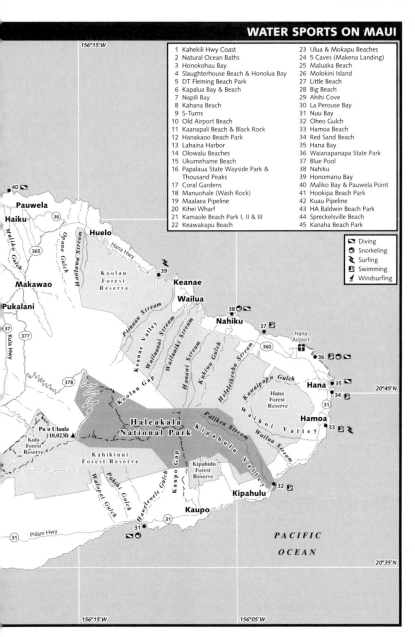

WATER SPORTS ON MAUI

1 Kahekili Hwy Coast
2 Natural Ocean Baths
3 Honokohau Bay
4 Slaughterhouse Beach & Honolua Bay
5 DT Fleming Beach Park
6 Kapalua Bay & Beach
7 Napili Bay
8 Kahana Beach
9 S-Turns
10 Old Airport Beach
11 Kaanapali Beach & Black Rock
12 Hanakaoo Beach Park
13 Lahaina Harbor
14 Olowalu Beaches
15 Ukumehame Beach
16 Papalaua State Wayside Park & Thousand Peaks
17 Coral Gardens
18 Manuohale (Wash Rock)
19 Maalaea Pipeline
20 Kihei Wharf
21 Kamaole Beach Park I, II & III
22 Keawakapu Beach
23 Ulua & Mokapu Beaches
24 5 Caves (Makena Landing)
25 Maluaka Beach
26 Molokini Island
27 Little Beach
28 Big Beach
29 Ahihi Cove
30 La Perouse Bay
31 Nuu Bay
32 Oheo Gulch
33 Hamoa Beach
34 Red Sand Beach
35 Hana Bay
36 Waianapanapa State Park
37 Blue Pool
38 Nahiku
39 Honomanu Bay
40 Maliko Bay & Pauwela Point
41 Hookipa Beach Park
42 Kuau Pipeline
43 HA Baldwin Beach Park
44 Spreckelsville Beach
45 Kanaha Beach Park

Diving
Snorkeling
Surfing
Swimming
Windsurfing

On Maui all the action centers on Kite Beach, which is the western end of Kanaha Beach Park in Kahului (not to be confused with Kahana Beach in West Maui). Check the Maui Kiteboarding Association Web site at Ⓦ www.mauikiteboardingassociation .org for the latest guidelines.

Maui Kiteboarding (☎ 873-0015, Ⓦ www .ksmaui.com, 111 Hana Hwy, Kahului) Beginners course $240, advanced lessons $90/ hour. Some of the island's original kiteboarders teach private lessons here. Some speak multiple languages or specialize in kids lessons, but all are pros.

Windsurfing schools (see Windsurfing, later) may also give kiteboarding lessons.

PARASAILING

Parasailing is basically parachuting skyward behind a speedboat that is towing you along. On Maui parasailing is only allowed between May 16 and December 14, outside of whale breeding season. Flights are usually short, no more than fifteen minutes (which can be an eternity) and most take place at Kaanapali.

Prices vary depending on flight height and duration, averaging $40 for seven minutes at 400 feet or $52 for ten minutes up to 800 feet, maybe with some simulated freefall thrown in. Ask about tandem rides and half-price early-bird specials.

UFO Parasail (☎ 661-7836, 800-359-4836, fax 667-0373, Ⓦ www.ufoparasail.com) Fly direct with this on-the-beach place, by Whalers Village in Kaanapali.

Parasail Kaanapali (☎ 669-6555) Boats depart for Kaanapali from Lahaina Harbor every 30 minutes from around 8am daily.

SCUBA & SNORKELING

Some dive and snorkel boat tours go along the Maui shoreline, but the main destinations are the sunken volcanic crater of Molokini and the island of Lanai.

Although a few dive boats take snorkelers, and some snorkeling tours take divers, as a rule you'll be better off going out on a tour that's geared for the activity you're doing.

Maui's most popular dive spots are the 5 Caves (also known as the 5 Graves), near Makena Landing, for sea turtles, or the live coral along Black Rock in Kaanapali. Beginners may favor easier beach dives off Wailea, while expert divers can plumb the depths of Manuohale (Wash Rock), pristine Honolua-Mokuleia Bay Marine Life Conservation District or La Perouse Bay.

Some of Maui's best snorkeling is right off the beach, too. Areas include Black Rock, Wailea-Makena beaches and reefs south of Lahaina. Kapalua usually has calm waters for snorkeling year-round. If you are up for some hiking, try snorkeling the isolated pools in Ahihi-Kinau Natural Area Reserve near La Perouse Bay.

Lanai also has clear snorkeling waters, but without the crowds. The most common destination is Manele Bay off Hulopoe Beach, although a few boats go around to a private beach on the northern side of the island. For divers, the Cathedrals offer intriguing geological formations, including caves, arches and connecting passageways.

Generally, water conditions are calmest and clearest in the morning because afternoon winds pick up surges and often make waters murky. Maui Dive Shop (see Dive Operators, later) has a good free map that details the island's best diving and snorkeling spots, as well as waterproof maps and plasticized reef fish identification cards for sale.

Molokini

Crescent-shaped Molokini, a submerged volcanic crater only a few miles off Maui's southwest coast, is Maui's most popular snorkeling tour site. The fish are tame and numerous, and the water is clear.

Morning is the best time to snorkel Molokini, as winds pick up in the afternoon. However, inside the crater wall is often protected from the wind and currents and may be OK even late in the day.

For divers, Molokini has walls, ledges, white-tipped reef sharks, manta rays, turtles and a wide variety of other marine life. Novice divers should stay inside the crater, while intermediate divers can head toward the north point of the crescent (lots of rudderfish there) or the south point (antler

Responsible Diving

The popularity of diving is placing immense pressure on many sites. Please consider the following tips when diving and help preserve the ecology and beauty of reefs.

• Do not use anchors on the reef and take care not to ground boats on coral. Encourage dive operators and regulatory bodies to establish permanent moorings at popular dive sites.

• Avoid touching living marine organisms with your body or dragging equipment across the reef. Polyps can be damaged by even the gentlest contact. Never stand on coral, even if they look solid and robust. If you must hold on to the reef, only touch exposed rock or dead coral.

• Be conscious of your fins. Even without contact, the surge from heavy fin strokes near the reef can damage delicate organisms. When treading water in shallow reef areas, take care not to kick up clouds of sand. Settling sand can easily smother the delicate organisms of the reef.

• Practice and maintain proper buoyancy control. Major damage can be done by divers descending too fast and colliding with the reef. Make sure you are correctly weighted and that your weight belt is positioned so that you stay horizontal. If you have not dived for a while, have a practice dive in a pool before taking to the reef. Be aware that buoyancy can change over the period of an extended trip: initially you may breathe harder and need more weight; a few days later you may breathe more easily and need less weight.

• Take great care in underwater caves. Spend as little time within them as possible, as your air bubbles may be caught within the roof and thereby leave previously submerged organisms high and dry. Taking turns to inspect the interior of a small cave will lessen the chances of damaging contact.

• Resist the temptation to collect or buy coral or shells. Aside from the ecological damage, taking home marine souvenirs depletes the beauty of a site and spoils the enjoyment of others. The same goes for marine archaeological sites (mainly shipwrecks). Respect their integrity; some sites are protected from looting by law.

• Ensure that you take home all your rubbish and any litter you may find as well. Plastics in particular are a serious threat to marine life. Turtles can mistake plastic for jellyfish and eat it.

• Resist the temptation to feed fish. You may disturb their normal eating habits, encourage aggressive behavior or feed them food that is detrimental to their health.

• Minimize your disturbance of marine animals. It is illegal to approach endangered marine species too closely; these include many whales, dolphins, sea turtles and the Hawaiian monk seal. In particular, do not ride on the backs of turtles, as this causes them great anxiety.

coral and butterfly fish galore). The outside of the crater presents a sheer black-lava wall with brilliant sponges and schools of fish, but it is only for advanced divers.

Although the snorkeling and diving is good, don't expect pristine conditions – dozens of tour boats crowd the islet every day, and all of the activity has taken a toll on the reef. The fish are given their breakfast call by boat captains who drop in loaves of bread to start the action. Some reef sections have been permanently damaged, largely from dropped and dragged anchors that have carved swaths in the coral.

See 'Molokini' in the South Maui chapter.

Dive Operators

Most dive schools offer a full range of refresher and advanced certification courses. Be sure to go straight to the source and don't monkey around with activity-desk bookings or shops that are just a front for booking you with someone else. Those aiming for certification should look for a small class and expect to spend up to four days studying and learning the ropes.

Maui Dive Shop (☎ 800-542-3483, W www .mauidiveshop.com) 1-tank/2-tank dives from $70/100, 3½ day certification course $355. This five-star PADI operation offers one-tank introductory dives in shallow water for beginners, two-tank boat dives at Molokini and night dives in South Maui, to name just a few options. However, its dive boats take up to 18 divers at a time (talk about a cattle call). Maui Dive Shop has several branches around the island, with its head office in lower Kihei *(☎ 879-3388, 1455 S Kihei Rd)*.

Maui Dreams Dive Co (☎ 874-5332, 888-921-3483, W www.mauidreamsdiveco.com, Island Surf Bldg, 1993 S Kihei Rd) Dives $60-110, certification course $225. This family-run five-star PADI outfit gets enthusiastic reviews for personal attention (boats limited to four or six divers). Discount specials might include a night dive for $50 or one-tank underwater scooter dive for $90.

Ed Robinson's Diving Adventures (☎ 879-3584, 800-635-1273, W www.maui scuba.com) 2-tank boat dive $105, 2-tank night or Lanai dive $125. Operated by underwater photographer Ed Robinson, this small company caters to certified divers looking for site variety and environmental background talks. Three-tank dives are available.

Mike Severns (☎ 879-6596, fax 874-6428, W www.mikesevernsdiving.com) 2-tank dive $120. Mike Severns literally wrote the book (well, one book anyway) on diving Molokini. Certified divers appreciate the thorough pre-trip briefings on marine life and charters are possible for night dives and to see coral spawning.

Kapalua Dive Company (☎ 662-0872, 877-669-3448, fax 662-0692, W www.kapalua dive.com) Tours from $90; full certification available. Using a specially-designed kayak, divers paddle for about 20 minutes from Kapalua Beach out to Hawea Point where sea turtles are numerous. There are lots of 'mixed plate' dive packages available, too.

Snorkel Tours

Countless snorkeling cruises leave for Molokini daily from Maalaea and Lahaina Harbor. Boats are usually out from about 7am to noon and cost $40 to $60 per person, including snacks and snorkeling gear. Competition is heavy, so deals and discount coupons are easy to come by.

Pacific Whale Foundation (☎ 879-8811, 800-942-5311, W www.pacificwhale.org) Molokini/Lanai tours $55-75. Reef tours with this nonprofit foundation are led by experienced marine naturalists, and their 65-foot ecoboats are powered by recycled cooking oil! Special deals often lower the price or let kids go free. The organization has many offices around the island but not necessarily designed for walk-ins; it's best to call. The foundation also staffs a few beach snorkel sites around the island where volunteers answer questions and give free reef tours (bring your own mask, snorkel and fins) at around 9am; call for details.

Trilogy (☎ 661-4743, 888-628-4800, fax 667-7766, W www.sailtrilogy.com) Lanai/ Molokini tours $170/95, kids half price. Trilogy consistently gets rave reviews year after year, which means crowded, busy boats. High-tech ocean catamarans leave early from Lahaina Harbor with an onboard naturalist and homemade cinnamon rolls. The Lanai trips anchor off Manele Bay with a big lunch before you actually get to Hulopoe Beach. Online discounts and free daily pool dive classes are available.

Ann Fielding's Snorkel Maui (☎ 572-8437, W www.maui.net/~annf) Adult/child $85/75. This marine biologist, formerly associated with the Waikiki Aquarium, leads nature-oriented half-day shoreline trips that are both educational and personalized.

Kapalua Dive Company (see Dive Operators, earlier) Kayak snorkel tours around Kapalua $60/35 per adult/child.

SeaView Adventure Cruises (☎ 661-5550, W www.seaview-maui.com) Adult/child $44/25. It doesn't get much cheaper than this. Two-hour narrated trips in a 128-passenger glass-sided semisubmersible leave from Lahaina Harbor for West Maui reefs daily; 'sunset splash' tours happen on select weekdays. Optional snorkel lesson and floaters are available on board, plus TV monitors for nonsnorkeling passengers.

Snorkel Rentals

Snorkeling gear can be rented at reasonable prices from most dive shops and at inflated prices from hotel beach huts. Many condo owners provide free snorkel gear to guests.

Maui Dive Shop (*see Dive Operators, earlier*) Snorkel-set rental with silicone mask $8/25 per day/week.

A few high-profile chains have come-on rates for cheaper snorkel gear, but you'll probably want better quality, and prices will rise accordingly.

Snorkel Bob's (☎ 661-4421, Ⓦ www.snorkelbob.com, 1217 Front St, Lahaina) Snorkel Bob has branch shops in Kihei and Napili. Also, you can get your gear on one island and return it on another (if you like).

If you're snorkeling often, think about buying your own snorkel set from dive shops or discount stores in Kahului.

SNUBA

SNUBA is a snorkel-scuba diving hybrid. Divers wear a snorkel mask and stay connected by an air hose to the oxygen tank floating a maximum of 20 feet above. No certification is needed, but a 20-minute introductory lesson is a good idea.

Snuba Tours of Maui (☎ 879-8410, Ⓦ www.geocities.com/snuba_maui, Island Surf Bldg, 1993 S Kihei Rd) First/each additional dive $60/40. One of the only SNUBA operators on Maui takes boats out to Olowalu and Makena Beach.

Some snorkel boats offer SNUBA as part of their regular cruises for about the same price and go to far more fascinating places.

SURFING

Maui has some unbeatable surfing spots, with peak surfing conditions in winter, from November to March. *Surfer's Guide to Hawaii: Hawaii Gets All the Breaks* by Greg Ambrose gives the skinny on six top Maui breaks. Always ask local surfers for updates and advice before paddling out.

When conditions are right, **Honolua Bay** on the northern coast of West Maui has the island's top action with swells up to 15 feet. Observers often pull off the highway just above the beach to get a little vicarious thrill. The **Maalaea Pipeline**, at the south side of Maalaea Bay, has a very fast break, best during south swells. However, this break, which *Surfer* magazine has described as one of the world's 10 best, could be seriously altered if a proposed expansion of Maalaea Harbor is allowed to go through. Experienced surfers are also seen toting their surfboards along hiking trails near La Perouse Bay.

Hookipa Beach near Paia supports challenging surfing year-round, but the waves are shared (ie, crowded) with windsurfers. For beginners, there are a number of places near **Lahaina Harbor** and along the breakwall, especially before the 505 Front St shopping center. Other places are strung out along the coast south past Olowalu or off the Hana Hwy.

Instruction

Surfing lessons typically last 1½ to two hours and cost $50 to $75. Most places guarantee that students of all ages will be surfing at the end of the lesson. Beware that the cheapest lesson deals are usually for impersonal large-group classes.

Nancy Emerson's School of Surfing (☎ 873-0264, Ⓦ www.surfclinics.com, Lahaina) This stunt woman even taught her dog to surf, so you shouldn't present much of a challenge to her staff. Ask about advanced surf clinics and adventures.

Goofy Foot Surf School (☎ 244-9283, Ⓦ www.goofyfootsurfschool.com, 505 Front St, Lahaina) Goofy Foot has all-day surf camps and lessons at all levels of experience, including for kids.

Maui Surfing School (☎ 875-0625, 800-851-0543, Ⓦ www.maui.net/~mol/activitysea/surfsch.html) Everyone knows this famously womyn-friendly surfing school.

Surf Dog (☎ 250-7873, Ⓦ www.surfdog maui.com, Lahaina) Lots of aloha is given out by a local Maui boy who gets rave reviews for his one-man surfing school.

Royal Surfing

Surfing is a purely Hawaiian creation that has its roots in royalty and religion. Religious chants mentioning *he'e nalu* (surfing) date back over five centuries, and Hawaiian petroglyphs depicting surfing figures are perhaps even older.

When the waves were up in ancient Hawaii, the *kapu* (taboo) system still carried its weight. Commoners were restricted from using royal surfing grounds, and only *ali'i* (nobles) were free to use the long *olo* boards. The boards were up to 16 feet in length and made of *wiliwili*, the lightest of native woods (yet they still weighed up to 175lb!). Commoners made do with truncated boards made of heavy breadfruit or koa wood.

Religious ceremony enveloped ancient surfing. Before chopping down any tree to make a surfboard, craftsmen would leave a fish ceremonially in the roots. After roughly carving the board with bone or an adze, they were planed with coral or lava rock, then blackened with ti leaf root and polished with kukui nut oil.

Kahuna (priests) blessed the new boards, which were highly prized possessions kept carefully wrapped in coconut oil and tapa (pounded bark cloth).

If you aren't fussy, you could take a cheap surf lesson from ***Duke's Surf & Rental Shop*** (☎ 661-1970, 602 Front St) in Lahaina.

Rentals & Equipment

Surfboards can be rented everywhere around Maui, including at many of the windsurfing shops. If you're going bodysurfing, look at buying special webbed gloves that will help your endurance.

Extreme Sports (☎ 871-7954, 800-328-8877, Ⓦ www.extremesportsmaui.com, Dairy Center, 397 Dairy Rd, Kahului) Rental surfboards from $20/112/279 per day/week/month. Extreme Sports also sells used surfboards.

Hi-Tech Surf Sports (☎ 877-2111, 425 Koloa St, Kahului) Rental per day/week; entry-level surfboards $14/80, custom boards $20/112.

Second Wind (☎ 877-7467, 800-936-7787, Ⓦ www.secondwindmaui.com, 111 Hana Hwy, Kahului) Rental surfboards $18/90 per day/week. You can apply 50% of the week's rental toward the purchase of new equipment.

Locally owned ***Maui Tropix*** (☎ 871-8726, 261 Dairy Rd, Kahului) sells Maui Built surfboards and paraphernalia, with several other outlets around the island. ***Ono Surf***

Supply (☎ 579-6444, 120 Hana Hwy, Paia) also has reputable gear.

SWIMMING

Maui has endlessly fine beaches, with plenty of good swimming spots. The northwest coast from Kaanapali up to Honolua Bay and the southwest coast from Maalaea down to Makena are largely fringed with white-sand beaches. This western side is dry and sunny, and water conditions are generally calmer than on the windward northern and eastern coasts.

Most of the west coast's best beaches are backed by hotel and condo developments – good if you're looking to stay right at the beach, not so good if you prefer seclusion. Still, the west coast does have some gorgeous undeveloped strands, the most notable being Makena's Big and Little Beaches, a short drive south of Kihei.

Those looking for more waters in their pristine natural state should visit the waterfalls and hidden pools along the Hana Hwy, the Oheo Gulch sector of Haleakala National Park and the natural ocean baths around the Kahekili Hwy.

Maui County maintains several heated swimming pools open to the public. These include: Kahului Pool (☎ 270-7410); Kihei Aquatic Center (☎ 874-8137); Lahaina

Royal Surfing

The missionaries who came to Hawaii in the early 19th century hated surfing almost as much as they hated hula. Were it not for King David Kalakaua, 'The Merrie Monarch,' they would've driven both to extinction. But it wasn't until a high school dropout named Duke Kahanamoku and his friends founded Hui Nalu ('Club of the Waves') in 1905 under a hau tree on Waikiki Beach that the surf revival was on. A couple of years later, the writer Jack London showed up here and was taught to surf by George Freeth, who later was the first person to bring surfing to California.

Freeth also revolutionized surf board design simply by cutting one in half, but it was the Duke who became the aloha ambassdor of surfing around the world. After winning Olympic gold in swimming at Stockholm in 1912, Duke toured internationally and gave public demonstrations of Hawaii's little secret sport. It was even he who showed up on Australia's shores in 1915, where he took a local girl on a tandem ride.

Duke rode the waves for the rest of his life, and when he died in 1968, thousands of devotees attended the beachboy funeral procession to Waikiki Beach, where his ashes were taken by canoe and cast into the sea. One of his regal surfboards still hangs outside the Bailey House Museum in Wailuku.

Aquatic Center (☎ 661-7611); Pukalani's Upcountry Pool (☎ 572-1479) and Wailuku New Pool (☎ 270-7411). Call first for directions and open-swim schedule information.

WHALE WATCHING

The western coastline of Maui from Olowalu to Makena and the eastern shore of Lanai are the chief birthing and nursing grounds for wintering North Pacific humpbacks. Luckily for whale watchers, humpbacks are coast-huggers.

Peak whale-watching season is from January to the end of March. Maui's finest shoreline whale-watching spots are the stretches from Olowalu to Maalaea Bay and from Keawakapu Beach to Makena Beach. Humpbacks are highly sensitive to human disturbance and noise, and seem to have a particular distaste for jet skis. Coming within 100 yards of a humpback (300 yards in 'cow/calf waters') is prohibited by federal law and can result in a $25,000 fine.

Whale-watching cruises are heavily advertised, and you'll have no trouble finding one. Boats range from catamaran sailboats to large cruise vessels. Some companies even have hydrophones to hear whale songs, which change from year to year.

Most cruises depart from Maalaea or Lahaina Harbors, although a few leave from Kihei or Kaanapali. A two- to three-hour tour usually costs $25 to $40 for adults, half price for children.

Pacific Whale Foundation *(see Snorkel Tours, earlier)* Adult/child $21/15. Throw your dollars at this nonprofit foundation and get enlightening commentary from on-board naturalists. You can take a 50-foot

'Don't know about you, but I come here just for the people watching.'

sailboat that leaves in the morning from Lahaina or either a 36-foot motorboat or a 65-foot sailing catamaran from Maalaea in the afternoon. Some proceeds go to the foundation's marine conservation projects.

WINDSURFING

Maui is a mecca for windsurfers. Some of the world's best windsurfing is at **Hookipa Beach** in Paia, although it's only suitable for experts. Trade winds could blow at any time of the year, just as flat spells could also hit anytime, but as a rule expect the windiest time to be from June to September and the flattest from December to February.

Those who aren't ready for Hookipa often head to nearby Spreckelsville Beach or Kanaha Beach Park in Kahului, where kiteboarders also practice. Kihei Beach offers slalom sailing in summer. In Maalaea Bay, the winds are usually strong enough for advanced speed sailing and blow offshore toward the island of Kahoolawe (don't wipe out, or that's where you'll end up). During the winter when kona winds blow, the Maalaea-Kihei area is often the only place windy enough to sail and becomes the main scene for all windsurfers.

The Maui Boardsailing Association has developed a 'sail safe' program with windsurfing guidelines; brochures with the guidelines are available at windsurfing shops. For an excellent full-color guide, buy the *Hawaiian Windsurfing Guide* published by Printech Hawaii.

Rentals & Instruction

Most windsurfing shops are based in Kahului. Daily rental rates for two sails and a board start around $45.

The business is very competitive, so if you ask about discounts and say you're getting price quotes with more than one company, you may be offered a better deal.

Some places will let you use a weekly rental rate on nonconsecutive days. You could sail for three days, take a couple of days off and then sail four more days for the price it would cost to rent for a week straight.

Hawaiian Island Surf & Sport (☎ 871-4981, 800-231-6958, fax 871-4624, W *www .hawaiianisland.com, 415 Dairy Rd, Kahului*) These folks also sell used windsurfing equipment.

Hi-Tech Surf Sports (☎ 871-7766, fax 871-6943, 425 Koloa St, Kahului*) Hi-Tech has 5000 sq ft of new, used and rental equipment for surf sports.

Maui Windsurf Co (☎ 877-4816, 800-872-0999, fax 877-4696, W *www.mauiwindsurf co.com, 22 Hana Hwy, Kahului*) Near Maui Mall, this shop boasts a 'drive-thru rental' service.

Second Wind (☎ 877-7467, 800-936-7787, fax 877-0091, W *www.secondwindmaui.com, 111 Hana Hwy, Kahului*) This place rents gear that is a maximum of three months old.

Most of the Kahului shops also sell windsurfing equipment and can book package tours that include accommodations and windsurfing gear. Some can book used vehicles, including older vans or station wagons for schlepping gear around.

Land Adventures on Maui

For spelunking in lava caves near Hana, see the East Maui chapter. Helicopter and walking tours are listed in the Getting Around chapter. For adventures on Lanai and Molokai, see also the Excursions chapter.

CYCLING & MOUNTAIN BIKING

Each morning before dawn, groups of cyclists gather at the top of Haleakala for the thrill of coasting 38 miles down the mountain, with a 10,000-foot drop in elevation. It's an all-day affair, starting with hotel pick-up bright and early around 2:30am, then a van ride up the mountain for the sunrise and 3½ hours of maneuvering back down.

It's not a nonstop cruise, as cyclists must periodically pull over for cars following behind, and the primary exercise is squeezing the brakes – you'll need to pedal only about 400 yards on the entire trip! The road is narrow and winding, with plenty of dastardly blind curves. Don't forget to bring sunglasses and warm clothes for the sunrise.

For real single-track mountain biking, take the rough Skyline Trail instead from Haleakala summit down into Polipoli Springs and Kula Forest Reserve, where several more trails lead through upland redwood forests. It's also possible to bike near Kahakuloa on the Kahekili Hwy or the Kaupo section of the Piilani Hwy if you're fit. The island of Molokai has superb single-track courses above sea cliffs and through forests, but unfortunately most land is privately owned by the Molokai Ranch and its mountain-bike tours are expensive unless you are a guest. Lanai's 4WD roads are open to mountain bikers free of charge. On any island, John Alford's *Mountain Biking the Hawaiian Islands* should be your bible.

Tours & Rentals

The major downhill volcano tour companies (did someone say cattle call?) are *Maui Downhill* (☎ 871-2155, 800-535-2453), *Maui Mountain Cruisers* (☎ 871-6014, 800-232-6284) and *Maui Mountain Riders* (☎ 877-4944, 800-706-7700). The going rate before any discounts is $115, which includes your bike, helmet, transportation, rain gear and continental breakfast. Daytime or afternoon rides are usually cheaper than sunrise tours.

Haleakala Bike Company (☎ 575-9575, 888-922-4453, w *www.bikemaui.com, 810 Haiku Rd*) From a legit bike shop in scenic Haiku, these folks give you a lift up the volcano and then you bike back down on your own. The sunrise special ($75) includes a minitour of the national park sights, while the Haleakala Express ($55) shuttle leaves a bit later. If you have your own transport, you can just rent a bike with car rack for $35.

Cruiser Phil's Volcano Riders (☎ 893-2332, 877-764-2453, w *www.cruiserphil.com*) Tours from $70. This family-run tour company provides all the expected perks, along with specially designed mountain bikes and racing jackets.

Aloha Bicycle Tours (☎ 249-0911, 800-749-1564, w *www.maui.net/~bikemaui*) Tour $95. Aloha offers a 33-mile nonsunrise tour that begins with breakfast in Kula followed by a glide down the Haleakala Crater Rd,

but instead of continuing downhill to the coast, it takes in various Upcountry sights. The tours are selfpaced and led by a championship rider.

For more bicycle rental shops, see the Getting Around and Excursions chapters.

FISHING & HUNTING

Spearfishing and hunting are both traditional Hawaiian activities. The latter now serves to kill off feral goats, pigs and other animals that are decimating the island's fragile ecosystem. Hunting is strictly controlled, so going on a hunting charter will cost hundreds of dollars. Nonresidents also need a $100 license.

Maui has some of the finest deep-sea fishing in the world, with gigantic tuna and marlin aplenty. Licenses aren't required, and charter boats are available right on the pier in Lahaina Harbor, as well as a few in Maalaea. Sharing a boat costs around $130 to $190 per person. Many boats let you keep only a small fillet from your catch; see w www.mauifishing.com for reasons why.

GOLF

Maui boasts high-end resorts designed almost exclusively for golfers, as does Lanai. The resorts at Kapalua and Wailea are both pricey and prestigious. Slightly less expensive are the championship courses found nearby at Kaanapali and Makena. Pick up the free tourist magazine *Maui Golf Review* for in-depth profiles of all courses open to the public.

Rates for pro courses average $100 to $200, about half that everywhere else. For discount rental equipment and tee time bookings, visit *Maui Golf Shop* (☎ 875-4653, 357 Huku Liu Pl, upper Kihei), behind Tesoro gas station.

HANG GLIDING

Hang Gliding Maui (☎ 893-0750, ☎/fax 572-6557, w *www.hangglidingmaui.com*) Powered tandem flight per half-hour/hour $95/165. Armin Engert offers instructional flights over the Hana coast. The outing starts from Hana Airport in East Maui (transportation not included).

Salmon Massage & Seaweed Wraps?

Spa tourism is hot in Hawaii – as in *ilili* (lava hot stone) therapy, that is. Other tropical treatments available here sound good enough to eat: *lomi lomi,* which is also the name of a way to prepare salmon, is traditional Hawaiian massage. Then there are coconut milk baths, Kona coffee scrubs, kukui nut reflexology and *awapuhi* (wild ginger) or *limu* (seaweed) body wraps.

Grand Wailea Spa *(Grand Wailea Resort Hotel & Spa; see Wailea in the South Maui chapter)* The queen of Maui spas is famous for its hydrotherapy circuit of mineral baths, tropical essences and hot and cold plunge pools.

Spa Moana *(Hyatt Regency Maui Resort & Spa; see Kaanapali in the West Maui chapter)* A suite of massage and therapy rooms on the oceanfront, exuding all the calm of a Japanese tearoom.

Spa at Kea Lani *(Fairmont Kea Lani Hotel; see Wailea in the South Maui chapter)* Soak in 75-gallon tubs filled with seaweed, mud, aromatherapy oils or a 'tropical fizzy,' each $60 per half-hour.

The Spa at 505 *(505 Front Street Shopping Center;* ☎ *661-1178, 505 Front St)* Lomi lomi from $35 per half-hour, facials $70. For an inexpensive spa experience or sunset massage on the beach, try this hideaway in busy Lahaina.

Third Heaven Spa & Massage *(*☎ *665-0087, locations in Napili, Lahaina & Kihei)* Lomi lomi $75. Another local spa, but this one also offers sea salt or sugar body scrubs with aromatic tropical essences. Deluxe packages include pineapple enzyme rub, seaweed mask, aromatherapy and lomi lomi.

HIKING

At Haleakala National Park, some extraordinary trails – from half-day walks to overnight treks – cross the moonscapelike crater. Elsewhere around the island, trails vary from historic routes to rain forest preserve hikes to blistering walks along Maui's youngest lava flow. See the Hiking special section at the end of this chapter for details.

HORSEBACK RIDING

Maui has lots of ranch land and some of Hawaii's best opportunities for trail rides. The settings are unusual, anywhere from inside a volcano crater to waterfalls and open ranch land. You should choose one based on your ability and the setting that appeals, since all are friendly, reputable outfitters. All of this is thanks to paniolo culture, probably not something you were expecting of a tropical island in Polynesia.

Only **Pony Express** (see the Upcountry chapter) leads trips inside Haleakala crater and on nearby Haleakala Ranch. **Oheo Stables** (see the East Maui chapter), near Kipahulu, offers rain-forest rides in the southern sector of Haleakala National Park.

Makena Stables (see the South Maui chapter) takes riders along the volcanic slopes that overlook pristine La Perouse Bay, while **Mendes Ranch** (see the West Maui chapter) rides high atop the cliffs of the Kahekili Hwy. Beginners will like the easy, low-cost rides at **Thompson Ranch** (see the Upcountry chapter) in Keokea.

TENNIS

Public tennis courts are found at: Lahaina Civic Center, Lahaina; Maluuluolele Park, Lahaina; Wells Park, Wailuku; War Memorial Complex, Wailuku; Kahului Community Center, Kahului; Kalama Park, Kihei; Hana Ball Park, Hana; Kula Community Center, Waiakoa; Eddie Tam Memorial Center, Makawao; and Pukalani Community Center.

Some hotels and condos are open to the public on a fee-for-play basis. The most prestigious tennis clubs are in the Wailea-Makena area and at Kapalua. Several of the Kaanapali hotels also have well-kept courts.

Rates are around $15 per person 'per day' or $55 'per week.' Rackets can be rented at all tennis clubs for around $5 a day; some clubs also rent shoes.

HIKING ON MAUI

Tracing the Valley Isle of Maui is a spider's web of hiking trails. Some follow the ancient footsteps of *ali'i* (chiefs) along rocky, sunburned coast. Others snake their way through dripping wet jungle, or groves of bamboo stalks played like xylophones by the wind.

At Haleakala National Park, some extraordinary trails (see that chapter, later) cross the moonscape-like Haleakala crater from half-day walks to overnight treks. In the Oheo Gulch section of the park, which is south of Hana, muddy trails lead to cascading waterfall pools. Several pull-offs along the Hana Hwy also lead to waterfalls, while others are simply nature walks offering basketfuls of fresh air.

In Maui's Upcountry, Polipoli Spring State Recreation Area has an extensive trail system in cloud forest. One route, the Skyline Trail, leads down from Haleakala summit. An equally rugged trail exits the crater by picking its way down through Kaupo Gap and out to sea.

The Kahekili Hwy in West Maui provides unlimited cliff walks above crashing surf, while two inland Waihee trails give hikers valley overlooks and swinging-rope bridges. On the dry side of the island, Lahaina Pali is one of only a few routes into the West Maui Mountains, finishing up a few miles from the Olowalu petroglyphs.

And, of course, Maui has endless black-, white- and red-sand beaches for sunset (and sunrise) strolls.

On Lanai, ambitious hikers can tackle the Munro Trail or scramble along old fishing trails and shipwrecked beaches. Molokai offers unique hikes through rain forest and wild beach dunes, while the mule trail to Kalaupapa peninsula switchbacks down the world's tallest *pali* (sea cliffs). See the Excursions chapter.

Directions to the trailheads mentioned in this special section are generally given in the relevant regional chapters.

Right: It's downhill from here, Haleakala National Park

SHANNON NACE

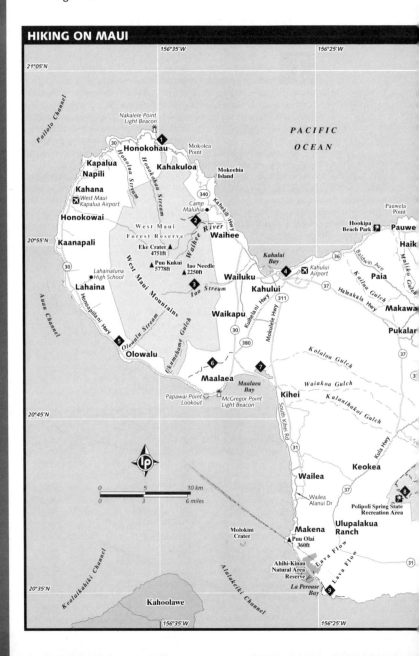

HIKING ON MAUI

HIKING ON MAUI

1. Kahekili Hwy [moderate]:
Easy scramble to dramatic sea cliffs, lava pools and blowholes

2. Waihee Ridge & Valley Trails [moderate, horseback riding]:
Misty rain forest, swinging-rope bridges and staggering canyon overlooks

3. Iao Valley State Park [easy]:
As close as you can get to Maui's lush landmark, the Iao Needle

4. Kanaha Pond [easy, birdwatching]:
Short jaunt ideal for viewing vibrant migratory and native Hawaiian birds

5. Olowalu Petroglyphs [easy]:
Short trek through sugarcane fields to ancient Hawaiian petroglyphs

6. Lahaina Pali Trail [challenging]:
A historic way into the West Maui Mountains for Neighbor Island panoramas

7. Kealia Pond National Wildlife Refuge [easy, birdwatching]:
A quick trail among native and migratory birds

8. Polipoli Spring & Skyline Trails [strenuous, mountain biking]:
Rugged paths, eucalyptus groves and Hawaiian redwoods all to yourself

9. King's Hwy Coastal Trail (Hoapili) [strenuous]:
Aquamarine waters meet the jet-black lava of Maui's youngest volcanic flow.

10. Hana Hwy [moderate]:
Waterfalls, hidden pools and ocean vistas around every bend

11. Waikamoi Ridge Trail [easy]:
Casual stroll amid eucalyptus and ferns

12. Waihou Springs Trail [easy]:
Cool Upcountry wandering on forest paths carpeted with pine needles

13. King's Hwy Coastal Trail (Waianapanapa) [moderate, horseback riding]:
Beachside lava trails lead to legendary caves and ancient Hawaiian ruins.

14. Haleakala Crater [strenuous, horseback riding]:
The ultimate adventure - kaleidoscopic cinder cones and rain-forest ridges in Maui's House of the Sun

15. Oheo Gulch Pools [moderate, horseback riding]:
Rustling bamboo forests, waterfalls and freshwater pools hang above the sea.

PRACTICAL INFORMATION

What makes Maui such a hiker's delight is that most trails are do-it-yourselfers (only the Waihee Valley Trail currently requires a permit). Basically, just pull on your hiking shoes and go.

Try to wake up early to avoid hiking in the midday heat and check the weather forecast first. Tropical showers can turn into flash floods quite suddenly. For the latest weather conditions, call ☎ 877-5111 or click on W www.nws.noaa.gov/pr/hnl/index.shtml.

If you're not being doused from above, you can count on the sun burning any tender exposed skin. Hiking atop lava, which reflects and intensifies the sun's radiation, increases your risk of heat exhaustion, heat stroke and dehydration (see Health in the Facts for the Visitor chapter). Double your intake of water and wear a high-SPF sunscreen.

Also, see Responsible Tourism in the Facts for the Visitor chapter for information on hiking among flora and fauna.

Na Ala Hele *(☎ 873-2508, W www.hawaiitrails.org, 54 S High St, room 101, Wailuku)*, a group affiliated with Hawaii's Division of Forestry & Wildlife, has negotiated with other private landowners and the military to gain access to previously restricted areas and re-establish abandoned trails. Look for brown Na Ala Hele signs that sport a yellow hiking petroglyph figure to mark an increasing number of open island trails.

GUIDED & VOLUNTEER HIKES

If you'd like to know Hawaiian terrain more deeply, hike in the company of experts in ecology and natural history, some of whom share their knowledge free of charge.

Rangers in Haleakala National Park lead free hikes mostly on public trails through the volcano crater and Kipahulu rain forest (see Activities in the Haleakala National Park chapter and Beyond Hana in the East Maui chapter).

Nonprofit environmental groups lead organized hikes on private lands and nature reserves not otherwise open to the public. Hike guides are often scientists or trained naturalists, and advance reservations are required. On work service trips, hikers can volunteer to help with trail maintenance and the eradication of harmful exotic plants by bagging fruit and seedlings, pulling up vines and spraying herbicide on the roots.

The Sierra Club *(☎ 579-9802, W www.hi.sierraclub.org/maui, PO Box 791180, Paia, HI 96779)* outings include hikes on private ranch lands and clean-up days at coastal beaches. Nonmembers usually pay $5 each, and carpooling to trailheads may be available.

The Nature Conservancy *(☎ 572-7849, on Molokai 808-553-5236, fax 572-1375, W www.tnc.org/hawaii, PO Box 1716, Makawao, HI 96768; suggested donation for nonmembers/members around $25/10)* leads hikes in its exclusive preserves around Haleakala and the West Maui Mountains, as well at Kamakou rain forest and Moomomi Beach on Molokai. Each site usually hosts one or two trips per month.

The Hawai'i Nature Center organizes family-oriented rain-forest walks in the Iao Valley (see the Central Maui chapter).

Also, see Organized Tours in the Getting Around chapter for hiking and walking tours.

STARTER TRAILS

These modest trails are the ones you're likely to skip over without realizing that they're there.

There is a multitude of short nature walks, especially in **Haleakala National Park** or off East Maui's **Hana Hwy** and West Maui's remote **Kahekili Hwy**. The wildlife sanctuaries of **Kanaha and Kealia ponds** in Central Maui are made for bird watching but also for peaceful strolling. See the relevant chapters for details on these areas.

Waihou Springs Trail
Rating: Easy
One-way Contour: Downhill
Location: Olinda Rd, Upcountry
Roundtrip Distance/Time: 1 to 1½ miles, 30 minutes to one hour

Sometimes mean-looking dogs seemingly straight out of *The Hound of the Baskervilles* abound by the forest entrance, but don't be discouraged. Press on through the gate onto a wide trail softly carpeted with pine needles. It slopes downhill through an early 20th-century experimental forest – note how the tree plantings are evenly spaced and staggered. Midway along, a short half-mile spur leads off to the left over a fallen log and loops around back to the main trail before its final, steep descent to the springs. The springs may be dry except after heavy rains, since the experimental tree plantings failed to restore the damaged watershed. However, the forest surroundings are still beautiful and serene.

Waikamoi Ridge Trail
Rating: Easy
One-way Contour: Uphill
Location: Hana Hwy, East Maui
Roundtrip Distance/Time: 1 mile, 30 minutes

This trail loops through tall trees with wonderful fresh scents, providing a quick respite from the Hana Hwy traffic. The path straight up from the parking lot welcomes you with a sign reading: 'Quiet. Trees at Work.' The longer trailhead is up on the left beyond the picnic table. Both meet farther uphill before emptying out onto a 4WD road, an alternate return route past some abandoned irrigation equipment. From the ridge at the very top, there's a good view of the winding Hana Hwy.

Especially if you're walking with children, keep an eye out for occasional metal spikes and tree roots that protrude along the path. Those grand reddish trees you see are *Eucalyptus robusta*. Note the huge climbing philodendron vines wrapped around them – the vines provide an apt illustration of the etymology of 'philodendron,' a Greek word meaning 'lover of trees.' Both trails also pass *hala* (pandanus), ferns and paper-bark eucalyptus.

HALF-DAY OUTINGS

If you have an appetite for hiking, but need other rewards like nearby snorkeling, natural swimming holes, archeological ruins or swinging-rope bridges, do we have hikes for you! Also, don't forget the waterfall trails of Oheo Gulch (see Beyond Hana in the East Maui chapter).

Waihee Valley (Swinging Bridges) Trail
Rating: Easy to moderate
One-way Contour: Slightly Uphill
Location: Kahekili Hwy, West Maui
Roundtrip Distance/Time: 3½ to 4 miles, under two hours
Permit: Available after 7am, weather permitting, from Wailuku Agribusiness (☎ 244-9570), Waikapu

From the Kahekili Hwy, follow Waihee Valley Rd inland and turn right at the T-intersection past a few homes and junk cars. When the road becomes rough, park somewhere out of the way and continue walking along, always keeping to the right. When you enter the forest, do not stray uphill onto one of the access roads, but instead take the flat trail alongside the irrigation ditch.

Squeeze past the gate for an easy walk underneath fruit trees. After the first half mile, banyan trees begin to take over and a stream comes into view off to the right below you. Soon you come to two swinging-rope bridges, complete with groaning cables and cracked wooden planks – fun!

After that, the trail dips down through a stream favored by picnickers and swimmers. Linger here or follow the final overgrown trail section for another 15 minutes uphill to an old dam, where a rickety metal ladder leads down into an artificial pool.

Note that permits are required for this hike because of the danger of flash flooding. If it starts to rain, turn back. Hikers who failed to do so have been injured or even killed on this otherwise gentle trail.

Waihee Ridge Trail
Rating: Moderate
One-way Contour: Uphill
Location: Kahekili Hwy, West Maui
Roundtrip Distance/Time: 4½ miles, two hours

Be prepared to stop for cattle crossing the pavement on the access road (gate open 7am to 6pm daily). The trailhead is a mile up from the highway, on the left just before Camp Maluhia. It's marked with a brown Na Ala Hele sign and a squeeze-through 'turnstile' fence.

It's a bit steep, if fairly steady climb up a private 4WD road and not overly strenuous. Look for a well-defined path heading off across forest-reserve land on your left – that's the trail. Starting at an elevation of 1000 feet, the trail climbs a ridge, passing from pasture into cool forest. Guava trees and groves of rainbow eucalyptus predominate, and if you look closely, you can usually find thimbleberries.

From the ¾-mile post, sweeping panoramas open up interior valleys all

Left: Lush vegetation along the Waihee Ridge Trail atop Mt Lanilili in the West Maui Mountains

KARL LEHMANN

the way down Waihee gorge to the churning ocean. The trail finishes $1\frac{1}{2}$ miles later after passing through a muddy field at the 2563-foot peak of Lanilili. The ridgetop views from the humble picnic table are similar to those you'd get from a helicopter, although the stillness along this route can only be appreciated by those on foot. If the sky is cloudy when you arrive, wait a few minutes and it usually clears.

King's Highway Coastal Trail
Only a few sections of the old King's Hwy exist today. Once this ancient trail system ringed the entire island, connecting remote fishing villages, fields and *heiau* (temples). It followed the coastline across jagged barren lava flows and Hawaiians used to bring along three pairs of woven bark or leaf sandals for a single journey. In modern times, the chunky terrain remains relentless in both its beauty and its rigor, so hiking boots are a good idea. Following are two sections of the trail:

Waianapanapa State Park
Rating: Moderate
Contour: Mostly Level
Location: Hana Hwy, East Maui
Roundtrip Distance/Time: 6 miles, $2\frac{1}{2}$ hours

Some of the original smooth lava stepping stones are still in place along this part of the trail. Gorgeous coastal views take in endless expanses of cobalt-blue water below craggy black lava outcrops. Hala and beach *naupaka* are the predominant flora along the trail; the naupaka has delicate white flowers that look as if they've been torn in half.

Marked by stepping stones, the trail heads south, passing the housekeeping cabins, a few lava blowholes, and over a bridge before reaching the ruins of a heiau at the $\frac{3}{4}$-mile marker, and just beyond that a small fishing shack with folding chairs perched on the cliff. From here if the trail fades, just keep following the coast over fields of *a'a* and *pahoehoe* lava toward Kauiki Head. Once you reach the boulder-strewn beach at Kainalimu Bay, it's only another half mile to Hana Bay and a mile into the center of town.

A shorter trip would be to head north from the end of Waianapanapa's black-sand beach for about 30 minutes along the rocky lava coast. At one time this trail went all the way to Piilanihale Heiau, but nowadays hikers are forced to turn around after about a mile at the Hana airport fence.

Hoapili Trail
Rating: Moderate
One-way Contour: Level to Hilly
Location: La Perouse Bay, South Maui
Roundtrip Distance/Time: 4 to 6 miles, over two hours

This trail section offers a study in contrasts. To begin, walk down from La Perouse Monument to the bay's edge and head south along the coastline. After about 15 minutes the trail then ducks under the cover of native foliage beside a sandy beach.

Twenty minutes later as the trail emerges onto spiky lava fields, it's possible to take a spur trail for $\frac{3}{4}$ mile down to the light beacon at the tip of Cape Hanamanioa. Otherwise walk *mauka* (inland) toward the Na Ala Hele sign and turn right onto the hilly King's Hwy, constructed in its present form by Governor Hoapili in the 19th century.

It's a dry area with no water and little vegetation, so it can get very hot. Plan to hike early in the morning or around sunset. Two miles from where you started, the trail runs back to the coast at Kanaio Beach. You'll see a number of old Hawaiian house foundations, pebble and coral beaches and heiau. After another mile or so, the trail peters out onto private land.

CHALLENGING TREKS

Of course, the most exhilarating hikes are right inside the belly of the beast, Haleakala volcano (see the Haleakala National Park chapter).

Lahaina Pali
Rating: Strenuous
Contour: Steep Hills
Location: Central & West Maui
One-way Distance/Time: $5\frac{1}{2}$ miles, $3\frac{1}{2}$ hours

From nearby Maalaea this historic 19th-century route zigzags steeply through kiawe and native dryland sandalwood trees and past old military installations. After the first mile it passes into open sun-baked scrub, from where you can see Haleakala and the fertile central plains. Ironwood trees precede the crossing of Kealaoloa Ridge (elevation 1600 feet), after which you descend through Ukumehame Gulch. Keep your eyes open for postcard views of Kahoolawe and Lanai, stray petroglyphs and *paniolo* graffiti. Stay on the footpath all the way down to Papalaua Beach – don't detour onto 4WD roads.

If you haven't arranged to be picked up here, you'll have to hitchhike back to your car (not an easy task, considering that cars often pass by too quickly to stop). You can hike the trail in either direction, but by starting off early from the east side of the mountains as described here, you'll keep ahead of the blistering sun.

Take Hwy 30 to just south of the intersection of Hwy 380 near Maalaea. Look for a trailhead access road around the 5-mile marker and the posted Na Ala Hele sign; note that parking any further inland on this private road is technically illegal.

Polipoli Spring State Recreation Area
Rating: Strenuous
Contour: Steep Hills
Location: Upcountry
Roundtrip Distance/Time: Varying

All of these trails require making your way along the park's 4WD access road, perhaps on foot or by bicycle. For hikes nearer to the recreation area's entrance, see the Upcountry chapter.

It's only fair to warn prospective hikers that some people find these trails gloomy, especially if they become a bit lost in the forest during the cold afternoon fog. Others love the haunting solitude. In recent years the trails have been improved.

The 4-mile **Boundary Trail** is a marked and maintained trail that begins about 200 yards beyond the end of the paved road. Park to the right of the cattle grate that marks the boundary of the Kula Forest Reserve. This is a steep downhill walk that crosses gulches and drops deep into woods of eucalyptus, pine and cedar, as well as a bit of native forest. In the afternoon, the fog generally rolls in and visibility fades.

About halfway down, the trail intersects with the **Waiohuli Trail**. A crude shelter marks the junction. If you insist on taking the rough Waiohuli Trail back up, expect to climb over 1000 feet before reaching the dirt access road. From there it's about two miles back to the paved road.

Otherwise continue downhill to the main network of paths hidden deep inside the forest. A profusion of fuchsia plants marks your arrival near the old Civilian Conservation Corp bunkhouse, where the **Redwood Trail** is the first spur trail leading off to the left. Farther along, the second spur that appears is the **Tie Trail**. Both spurs lead to the state housekeeping cabin, from where it's an easy walk to the campground.

Back at the Tie Trail junction, the Boundary Trail turns into the **Plum Trail** for vistas of ranch lands and neighboring islands. After approximately 1½ miles the Plum Trail links up with the **Haleakala Ridge Trail** which leads uphill back to the dirt access road, passing the **Polipoli Loop**, a trail back to the campground.

If you follow the dirt access road even deeper inside the forest preserve, you'll come to 'Ballpark Junction.' The path to your left is the terminus of the **Skyline Trail** (see below). Over to your right lies **Kahua Road**, a 4-mile dirt road mainly used by hunters that winds around the side of Haleakala volcano, passing unique views of cinder cones and Science City.

Skyline Trail
Rating: Strenuous
Contour: Steep Downhill
Location: Haleakala National Park to Upcountry
One-way Distance/Time: 6½ miles, three hours

The otherworldly Skyline Trail is the major link in a hiking route that begins near Science City at 9750 feet near the summit of Haleakala and leads down to Polipoli campground at 6200 feet. That makes for a total of 8½ trail miles in about four hours, but only if you go all the way.

The Skyline Trail, actually a dirt road used to maintain the state park, starts in open terrain made up of cinder, lava bombs and vents. After three crunchy miles it reaches the tree line (at an elevation of 8500 feet) and enters native mamane forest. In winter, mamane is heavy with clusters of delicate yellow flowers that look like sweet pea blossoms.

There's solitude on this walk. And if the clouds treat you kindly between the barren summit and the dense cloud forest, you'll sometimes have broad views of neighboring islands. Keep your ears open for the occasional mountain biker behind you.

Eventually the trail meets the Polipoli access road, where you can either walk to the paved road in about four miles, or continue via the Haleakala Ridge Trail and Polipoli Loop to the campground. Either way you should arrange for someone to meet you.

Getting There & Away

AIR

All taxes for US airports are normally included in the price of tickets when you buy them, whether they're purchased in the USA or abroad. There are no additional departure taxes to pay when leaving Hawaii.

At the time of writing, airport security was tight after the September 11, 2001 terrorist attacks on the USA. Only ticketed passengers were being allowed beyond the airline check-in counters. All luggage was subject to random search for potential weapons and even small items, such as pocket knives, staplers and matches, were being confiscated from carry-on bags. If possible, you should check all of your luggage at the front counter. Arrive at the airport at least 2½ hours before international departures, or 90 minutes for interisland flights.

Airports

Most domestic and international travelers deplane at Kahului Airport (OGG; ☎ 872-3830). Even though the main terminal is modern, the open-air plan with a sprinkling of lei and pineapple stands, palm trees waving outside and Hawaiian art make it feel immediately tropical.

There's a small information desk (☎ 872-2893) in baggage claim. It is open 6:30am to 10pm daily. Nearby are free courtesy phones for contacting accommodations and transportation. There are racks of free tourist magazines and brochures here, as well as scattered throughout the terminal.

Near the gates are a couple of newsstands, snack bars, gift shops, overpriced restaurants and a cocktail lounge. Only a few automated teller machines (ATMs) and foreign exchange counters are available. There is no baggage storage service, but the lost and found office (☎ 872-3821) is located on the ground level corridor between the ticket counters and baggage claim area.

Airport parking is a fairly reasonable $7 per day, or $1 for the first half-hour and $1 for each additional hour.

Kapalua/West Maui Airport (JHM; ☎ 669-0623) is a small airport with a 3000-foot runway that's serviced by prop planes and commuter aircraft from other Hawaiian Islands. The terminal is off Hwy 30 about midway between Kapalua and Kaanapali, and within easy reach of Lahaina.

Hana Airport (HNM; ☎ 248-8208) has a single terminal and passenger runway mainly used for island-hopping commuter flights. It's off the Hana Hwy about three miles north of Hana town in East Maui.

Buying Tickets

Airfares are constantly in flux. Usually the cheapest fares are for flying midweek during low season with added restrictions. These tickets may have advance purchase requirements or be nonrefundable or non-changeable.

Last-minute fares and special promotions can offer big savings, but are usually

---

Warning

The information in this chapter is particularly vulnerable to change: prices for international travel are volatile, routes are introduced and canceled, schedules change, special deals come and go, and rules and visa requirements are amended. Airlines and governments seem to take a perverse pleasure in making price structures and regulations as complicated as possible. You should check directly with the airline or a travel agent to make sure you understand how a fare (and any ticket you may buy) works. In addition, the travel industry is highly competitive, and there are many lurks and perks.

The upshot of this is that you should get opinions, quotes and advice from as many airlines and travel agents as possible before you part with your hard-earned cash. The details given in this chapter should be regarded as pointers and are not a substitute for your own careful, up-to-date research.

Instant Aloha O'Lei

OK, it's cheesy, but we all dream of it – stepping off a plane in tropical Hawaii and having brilliant flower lei laid around our necks. In Polynesian legends the giving of lei was practiced even by gods as an expression of aloha (love and good wishes). However, the Hawaiian custom of gifting visitors with lei probably dates back only to WWII, when, some say, a female USO entertainer gave one (and a kiss) to a lonely-looking serviceman.

What better way to surprise, and possibly embarrass your own *ipo* (sweetheart) under a new hula moon? Here's where to start:

Greeters of Hawai'i (☎ 808-836-0161, 800-366-8559, fax 800-926-2644, **w** www.holoholo.com/greethi) Lei $21–31 (add $10 for last-minute orders). Made by an exotic flower company, their deluxe lei can have up to 2000 flowers, while looser strands have about 30 tropical blooms.

Kenui Aloha Lei Greeters (☎ 800-969-9904, fax 808-239-1310, **w** www.leigreeters.com) Lei $15–30. You can also add on a traditional hula dancer or Hawaiian musician for $75 per hour.

Mango Rose (☎ 800-645-3753, fax 879-9100, **e** mauimangorose@aol.com, **w** www.maui411.com/greet.html) Lei $25–50. This award-winning Maui lei maker even offers special *haku lei*, which are worn around the head (or a hat), and traditional green *maile lei*.

Most airport lei greeters will meet you right at the gate and require only 48 hours advance notice.

only valid for one to two weeks. Know that the longer you intend to stay in Hawaii, the more expensive your ticket will be. With few exceptions, one-way tickets to the islands are just as expensive as return fares.

Many airlines offer Internet-only special fares for passengers who book online via their Web site. Much-touted travel sites like Travelocity and Expedia are useful for giving you ballpark fare estimates, but don't often secure you the best deal. Instead look for travel discounters who specialize in Hawaii flights. Some places to start searching are **w** www.smarterliving.com, **w** www.travelzoo.com, **w** www.air-fare.com and **w** www.flyaow.com. Ticket consolidators who advertise in the travel sections of major newspapers, free alternative weeklies and magazines also offer cut-rate tickets, as do student and youth travel agencies.

If you are planning on redeeming your frequent flyer miles for a ticket to Hawaii, think again. Hundreds of other people try doing the same thing every year, so frequent flyer award seats can be nearly impossible to come by, especially if your airline has to arrange a connecting flight from Honolulu to Maui with a Hawaii-based airline.

Whether you intend to use frequent flier miles or pay for your ticket yourself, remember that it may be easier and cheaper to book your flight only as far as Honolulu and then hop on an inexpensive interisland flight to Maui that you book yourself (see Within Hawaii, later). You could save hundreds of dollars this way!

Round-the-World Tickets Round-the-World (RTW) tickets allow you to circumnavigate the globe by flying on the combined routes of two or more airlines. Usually the maximum ticket validity is 12 months, and you must travel in one general direction without backtracking. This means you can't fly in and out of the same airport twice, sometimes effectively putting half the world out of reach. For example, most airlines don't fly direct to Maui and you are not allowed to fly Honolulu-Maui-Honolulu by RTW rules. Also note that a few heavily traveled routes (such as Honolulu-Tokyo) are sometimes blocked out.

Depending on which countries and therefore airlines you select, as well as the season in which you start traveling, the price of the fare will change, with an absolute minimum of UK£600, A$2200 or US$1300. A 28-day advance purchase is usually required. As a general rule, travel solely in the Northern Hemisphere is cheaper than travel that includes Southern Hemisphere destinations.

Major international airlines and partnerships, such as the Star Alliance and OneWorld, all offer RTW tickets through code-sharing flights on different routes and continents. It may be quicker and cheaper to price all the possible variations of your trip with a travel agent who specializes in RTW tickets rather than calling the airlines directly. US-based Air Treks (☎ 415-912-5600, 800-350-0612, ⓦ www.airtreks.com) and multilingual Air Brokers (☎ 415-397-1383, 800-883-3273, ⓦ www.airbrokers.com) have Web sites with helpful itinerary builders to get you started.

Circle Pacific Tickets

If you only intend to visit Hawaii, Polynesia and the Pacific Rim, look at Circle Pacific fares. Rather than simply flying between Point A and Point B, Circle Pacific itineraries allow you to swing through parts of Asia and the Pacific, making several stops along the way. The only catch is that you must travel in the same circular direction with the same partnered airlines.

Circle Pacific routes are essentially the same price regardless of your origin point. At the time of research, the standard fare for a One World ticket from Los Angeles to Honolulu, on to Tokyo, over to Bangkok, down to Sydney and back to LA, cost $2656. After the first four free stopovers you have the option of adding additional stops at $50 each. There's typically a seven-day advance purchase requirement and a maximum stay of six months.

Air New Zealand's Pacific Escapade fare, offered in conjunction with Singapore Airlines, costs US$2600 and allows unlimited stops as long as you don't travel more than 22,000 miles. If you already know your itinerary and dates, Air New Zealand can offer you even better deals.

Air New Zealand also offers an amazing Coral Explorer fare that allows travel from Los Angeles to New Zealand, Australia and a number of South Pacific islands with a return via Honolulu. Fares start at $1180 including one free stopover and a maximum three-month stay. Three additional stops can be added for $150 each. The priciest fare for a one-year ticket with four stopovers is $2220.

Discount Fares from Honolulu Honolulu is a good place to get discount fares to virtually any place around the Pacific or North American mainland. For cheap flights to Neighbor Islands, see Within Hawaii, later.

Check the travel pages of the Sunday *Honolulu Advertiser* for currently advertised fares and discount travel agencies. Often you can find a roundtrip ticket to Los Angeles, San Francisco or Vancouver for around $300; to Tokyo for $400; to Toronto for $450; to Hong Kong or Seoul for $500; to Bangkok or Singapore for $550; to Auckland or Sydney for $625; and to Bali for $700.

Also try these Honolulu-based travel agents: Cheap Tickets (☎ 800-652-4327, 888-922-8849, ⓦ www.cheaptickets.com); King's Travel (on Maui ☎ 270-8088, on Oahu ☎ 808-593-4481, 800-801-4481, ⓦ www.kingstravel .com) Imperial Plaza Bldg, 725 Kapiolani Blvd, suite C-103.

US Mainland & Canada

Only a few international airlines and charter-flight companies fly direct to Maui, and at any given time any of them could be offering the cheapest fares. Package tour companies sometimes offer the best airfare deals, even if you don't want to buy the whole 'package' (see Organized Tours, later).

Competition is much higher among airlines flying to Honolulu, from where you could easily hop on an interisland flight (see Within Hawaii, later), thereby saving yourself some money. Typically the lowest roundtrip fares from the US mainland to Honolulu are $300 to $450 from the West Coast, or $600 to $850 from the East Coast. Then add at least $100 for a ticket all the way to Maui. For those flying from other parts of the USA, it may be cheaper to buy two separate tickets – one to the West Coast with a low-fare carrier such as Southwest Airlines, and then another ticket to Hawaii. A few charter airlines, such as American Trans Air (ATA; ☎ 800-435-9282, **w** www.ata.com), fly direct from the West Coast to Maui or Honolulu. Their fares are competitive, but they only schedule a few flights per week.

Hawaiian Airlines (see Within Hawaii, later) has nonstop flights to Honolulu. If you're lucky, a direct flight to Maui will cost only $90 more. Typical discount fares to Honolulu include Los Angeles $320, San Francisco $410, and Portland, Seattle or San Diego $450. Hawaiian Airlines also has flights from Washington, DC, and Juneau, Alaska. If you end up paying the standard fare, direct flights to Maui cost the same as to Honolulu, between $500 and $700.

The other interisland carrier, Aloha Airlines (also see Within Hawaii, later), has daily nonstop flights between California (Oakland or Orange County airports) and Maui. Typical fares hover around $700, or connecting from Las Vegas $900. Flights from these West Coast cities to Honolulu only cost about $50 to $150 less, so you may as well go straight to Maui. Members of the American Automobile Association (AAA) may be eligible for discounts of 15% off standard fares.

At $119 each way, Air Tech's Space-Available FlightPass is surely the cheapest way to fly between the US West Coast and Maui. Air Tech (☎ 212-219-7000, **w** www.airtech.com) can offer these super deals by selling standby seats. If you provide them with a two- to four-day travel window, they guarantee you a seat. Currently, flights depart only from San Francisco.

From Canada, the cheapest roundtrip Air Canada (☎ 888-247-2262) fares to Honolulu are C$585 from Vancouver, C$665 from Calgary, C$700 from Toronto and C$1000 from Montréal. Many of these low fares are only available for online bookings at **w** www.aircanada.com. Canadian charter flight companies and ticket consolidators offer competitive deals, especially for discount flights from Montréal. If you want to fly direct to Maui, your ticket may be up to twice as expensive no matter where you buy it.

Travel agencies specializing in student and under-26 youth discount airfares, such as Council Travel (☎ 800-226-8624, **w** www.counciltravel.com) and STA Travel (☎ 800-781-4040, **w** www.sta-travel.com), have offices in major cities across the USA. In Canada, try Travel CUTS/Voyages Campus (☎ 866-246-9762, **w** www.travelcuts.com). Cut-rate travel agents (also known as ticket consolidators) often advertise discount fares in major newspapers and alternative weeklies. In New York, try the *Village Voice* and *New York Press;* on the West Coast try the *San Francisco Bay Guardian, San Francisco Chronicle* and *Los Angeles Times.* In Canada, there's the *Globe & Mail,* Toronto's *Now* and Vancouver's *Georgia Straight.*

Europe

From Europe, most travelers to Hawaii fly west via New York, Chicago or Los Angeles. If you'd like to stop off in Asia along the way, consider going in the reverse direction with an RTW ticket (see Round-the-World Tickets, earlier).

United offers a roundtrip fare from London to Maui for £610, allowing a maximum stay of 90 days. The cheapest one-month return ticket from Paris via London and LA costs around €1050, while from Frankfurt the fare is €980. With any of these tickets, it may be cheaper to fly direct to Honolulu and then pick up an interisland flight to Maui (see Within Hawaii, later).

Also try discount 'student' travel agencies, such as STA Travel (in the UK ☎ 0870-160 0599, **w** www.sta-travel.com). Advertisements appear in the travel pages of weekend newspapers as well as in London's *Time Out, Evening Standard* and *TNT.* Also in London, Trailfinders (☎ 020-7938 3939, **w** www.trailfinders.co.uk), 194 Kensington High St, is a reliable ticket agent.

Australia & New Zealand

Qantas flies to Maui via Honolulu from Sydney or Melbourne from A$1780 return, valid for up to 60 days. Other international carriers serving this route include Air Canada, American Airlines and United Airlines.

No airline offers attractive fares between Auckland and Maui, or even Auckland and Honolulu for that matter. At the time of research, the cheapest roundtrip fares were NZ$2573 with one free stopover and a maximum one-year stay; each additional stop costs NZ$150. At this price, you'd probably be better off with a Circle Pacific fare (see Circle Pacific Tickets, earlier).

These fares are only the airlines' official fares. You will find the best deals by shopping around the travel agencies, classified ads in the *Sydney Morning Herald* or Melbourne's *The Age* and over the Internet. In Australia, Flight Centre (☎ 13 31 33, W www.flightcentre.com.au) and STA travel (☎ 1300 733 035, W www.statravel.com.au) agencies in Melbourne and Sydney have competitively priced tickets. STA also operates an office in Auckland, New Zealand (☎ 0508 782 872, W www.statravel.co.nz).

South Pacific Islands & Micronesia

Air New Zealand flies to Honolulu from Tonga, the Cook Islands and Western Samoa. The lowest roundtrip fare from Tonga to Honolulu costs T$1756.

Polynesian Airlines flies to Honolulu from Tonga, Tahiti and American Samoa. Roundtrip tickets from Pago Pago in American Samoa cost US$732 and are good for one year, while a 90-day return ticket from Western Samoa costs WS$2807. From Tahiti the standard roundtrip fare is a steep US$1442, but you may be able to corral a special fare off the Internet.

From Rarotonga on the Cook Islands, Air New Zealand's cheapest roundtrip fare to Honolulu is NZ$1549 and allows stays of up to six months. Air Pacific offers a roundtrip fare from Fiji to Honolulu for F$1520.

Island addicts should look into Continental's Circle Micronesia Fare, which takes in several of the Federated States of Micronesia. Flights only originate in the USA

(either Honolulu or the mainland), and take one of two routes: Guam-Yap-Palau or Guam-Truk-Pohnpei-Majuro. Departing from Los Angeles or San Francisco, the first option costs US$1230, while the second is US$1650. Leaving from Honolulu, fares are US$300 to US$400 less. Unlimited stops are permitted, as long as you continue traveling in the same circular direction.

Eastern Asia

Many flights from Asia to the US mainland allow a stopover in Honolulu for little or no extra charge. Not only that, but these tickets are only slightly more expensive than typical roundtrip fares to Hawaii only. From Honolulu to Maui, you can easily catch an inexpensive interisland flight (see Within Hawaii, later).

. Hawaii is a top destination for Japanese tourists. Japan Airlines (JAL; ☎ 0120-25-5971, W www.jal.com) flies direct to Maui via Honolulu from Tokyo, Osaka, Fukuoka and Sapporo. Excursion fares vary with the departing city and the season, but they can dip as low as ¥75,000. Discount fares to Honolulu with All Nippon Airways (ANA; in Osaka ☎ 0120-029-006, W www.ana.co.jp) can beat that by almost half, matching the best fares offered by US-based competitors Northwest and United Airlines of ¥44,500. Add the equivalent of at least another US$100 for flights to Maui.

Remember that during Japanese holiday periods, particularly New Year, Golden Week in May and Ōbon in August, these fares instantly triple or even quadruple, that is if you can even get any seats. Deregulation of the travel industry in Japan has been slow in coming. A few discount travel agencies, which are found mainly in Tokyo, Osaka and Kyoto, offer unbeatable multistop USA tickets for less than ¥100,000 return.

From elsewhere around Northeast and Southeast Asia, the major international carriers are Northwest Airlines, Cathay Pacific, Singapore Air, Korean Air, China Airlines and Thai Airways. Although seasonal variations exist, the lowest published roundtrip fares to Honolulu average B31,000 from

Bangkok; 1,155,000 won from Seoul; HK$7800 from Hong Kong; S$1850 from Singapore; and about P57,500 from Manila. Again, add the equivalent of at least US$100 for flights direct to Maui.

Many discount travel agencies in Bangkok, Hong Kong and Singapore sell cut-rate tickets for less than half the major airline fares. As an example, a one-way ticket from Bangkok to Hawaii may go for as little as B6400. A few such discount agencies are of the cut-and-run variety, so ask around before you buy.

In Singapore, try STA Travel (☎ 737 7188, W www.statravel.com.sg), 33A Cuppage Rd, Cuppage Terrace, or the travel agencies at Chinatown Point shopping center, New Bridge Rd. Bangkok and Hong Kong each have a number of excellent, reliable travel agencies, and some not-so-reliable ones. The greatest number are found along Bangkok's Khao San Rd, or in Hong Kong on Nathan Rd in Tsimshatsui. A good way to check on a travel agent is to look it up in the phone book: Fly-by-night operators don't usually stay around long enough to get listed.

Latin America

Most flights to Hawaii from Central and South America go via Mexico City or a major US gateway city. To Honolulu, United Airlines offers flights from Mexico and Central America, including gateways like Mexico City, Guadalajara and Cancún, San José and Guatemala City. United's lowest roundtrip fare from Mexico City to Honolulu is 7300 pesos.

Within Hawaii

Interisland air travel is competitive in Hawaii. The two major interisland carriers are Hawaiian Airlines (on Oahu ☎ 808-838-1555, Neighbor Islands ☎ 800-882-8811, US mainland and Canada ☎ 800-367-5320, W www.hawaiianair.com) and Aloha Airlines (☎ 244-9071, on Oahu ☎ 808-484-1111, US mainland and Canada ☎ 800-367-5250, W www.alohaairlines.com). Both offer frequent flights in full-bodied jet aircraft between the major island airports, but often involving stops or transfers in Honolulu.

Airlines Merger

As this book went to press, Hawaiian Airlines and Aloha Airlines announced that they would merge operations starting in 2002. Airline representatives say that fares for interisland flights will not change for the next two years, after which fares will jump based on inflation. In the long run, the merger will mean higher prices and route cutbacks across the board, including fewer flights from Hawaii to the mainland and around the Islands. Even the airline names themselves are subject to change. Contact Hawaiian or Aloha directly for updates on the merger situation when making your travel plans.

Island Air, an affiliate of Aloha Airlines, offers the most extensive schedule of commuter flights (see Commuter Airlines, later).

Oddly enough, interisland flights often have many empty seats. If your original flight arrives at Honolulu early, ask the ticket agent at the gate if you may fly standby on the next available flight to Maui. Chances are you'll get a seat. The flip side of this phenomenon is that a few interisland flights each day end up being canceled, so stay flexible.

The highest standard fare for any interisland flight on Hawaiian Airlines, Aloha Airlines or Island Air is $104. Roundtrips cost exactly twice the one-way fare. However, almost no one ends up paying that standard fare. When you call to make a reservation, always ask what promotions are being offered and don't be surprised if you receive a discount of 50%. All three airlines also offer steep discounts on interisland flights via their respective Web sites. For AAA members, Aloha Airlines and Island Air automatically knock 10% off standard coach seats.

Because interisland flights can work out to be so inexpensive, travelers might save hundreds of dollars by booking their flight from home only as far as Honolulu and then taking an interisland flight for the final leg of their trip to Maui. The only trick is to secure a great interisland fare either directly from the airline or by picking up a discount flight coupon in Honolulu (see below).

Flight Coupons Unless you received a super-duper promotional fare from the airline, you can usually save money by buying discount flight coupons. These cost between $60 and $75, depending on the airline and the agent.

Using interisland flight coupons couldn't be more straightforward. Just make your flight reservations as you normally would and inform the airline representative that you'll be paying with a coupon. One of the many advantages of using flight coupons is that there are no penalties for changing the date or time of your flight reservation, as long as seats are still available. You can even make your booking before buying the coupon, and since there are no advance purchase requirements, you could theoretically put off buying it until the very last minute. When making connections in Honolulu, there are no additional fees for layovers of less than four hours, if you'd like to get out and look around.

Many island residents and travelers buy flight coupons for interisland flights from the discount travel agencies in Kahului, a five-minute drive from the airport. Cheap Tickets (☎ 242-8094, 800-594-8247) is in the Dairy Center at 395 Dairy Rd, while Cut Rate Tickets (☎ 871-7300, 800-297-5093), 333 Dairy Rd, is on the next block west. The latter is open seven days a week, 7am to 7pm weekdays, 9am to 5pm Saturday and 9am to 2pm Sunday. Cut Rate Tickets also has a branch in Lahaina (☎ 661-5800), 222 Papalaua St, open 7am to 7pm daily. Coupons are also sold at Star Market and other grocery or convenience stores.

Hawaiian Airlines sells its coupons for $65.25 per ticket from Bank of Hawaii ATMs, one of which can be found inside the interisland terminal at Honolulu Airport. You will need to use your PIN number along with your credit card (Visa or MasterCard). To check on the going rate for interisland coupons, visit W www.cutratetickets.com.

Hawaiian and Aloha each sells coupon booklets containing six interisland flight tickets at all of their airport ticket counters in Hawaii. Usually these can be used by any number of people on any flight without restrictions. At the time of writing, Aloha was charging $375 per booklet and Hawaiian Airlines $390. A similar book of six coupons good for flights on both Aloha Airlines and its affiliate Island Air costs $475. During special promotions, Hawaiian Airlines periodically allows passengers to exchange all six coupons for one roundtrip ticket to the US West Coast from Kahului or Honolulu.

Air Passes Air passes offer unlimited travel within a specified time period, from five consecutive days up to one month. Reservations can be made in advance, and you can revise your itinerary at will. The drawback is that air pass prices within Hawaii have skyrocketed and for most people the aforementioned coupons will work out better.

With Hawaiian Airlines, an interisland air pass costs $324 for five days, $345 for seven days, $410 for 10 days and $470 for two weeks. Aloha Airlines charges $321 for a seven-day Visitor Pass valid on both Aloha and Island Air flights. The same pass costs commuters $999 for one calendar month.

Commuter Airlines An affiliate of Aloha Airlines, Island Air (on Oahu ☎ 808-484-2222; Neighbor Islands ☎ 800-652-6541; US mainland ☎ 800-323-3345, W www.island air.com) serves Hawaii's smaller airports using prop planes. Since they fly lower than jet aircraft, you often get better views en route. Island Air is the only scheduled carrier flying into Kapalua/West Maui Airport, with four flights a day from Honolulu; the first leaves Honolulu at 8am, the last at 4:50pm. Book flights either directly or through Aloha Airlines. Island Air also flies to Molokai and Lanai a few times a day, but only after connecting through Honolulu.

Other commuter airlines, sometimes consisting of just a single plane, frequently come and go in Hawaii. Keep in mind that schedules are a bit elastic – if there aren't advance bookings for a flight, the flight is often canceled. Call in advance before making any plans.

Pacific Wings (☎ 873-0877, 888-575-4546; on Molokai ☎ 808-567-6814) has flights from Kahului to: Molokai (three per day), Honolulu (six per day), Hana (at least daily) and Waimea on the Big Island (at least daily). Its flights typically depart early in the morning and again in mid-afternoon. Fares vary, but special promotions and newspaper coupons offer $50 each way to Honolulu, or $50 roundtrip to Molokai. If you have a small group, ask Pacific Wings about its three-passenger plane, which can sometimes be chartered for even less. Hawaii residents are also entitled to receive discounts.

Paragon Air (on Maui ☎ 800-244-3356, 800-428-1231, W www.paragon-air.com) flies six-seater prop planes (every seat is a window seat!) from Kahului to Molokai, Lanai and the Big Island. The flights typically head out in the morning and back in the afternoon, but there's no regular schedule and you may have to be flexible. There is limited luggage space and reservations are necessary. Special roundtrip fares can dip as low as $65 to Molokai, $88 to Lanai and $110 to Kona or Hana.

Molokai Air Shuttle (on Oahu ☎ 808-545-4988; on Molokai ☎ 808-567-6847) flies a five-passenger Piper between Honolulu and Molokai; the flights are on demand, leaving when enough passengers arrive at the airport. Unlike other airlines, the company charges tourists the same as locals, and offers a roundtrip fare of just $65, almost half of any competitor's prices.

SEA

Most private yachts visiting the South Pacific weigh anchor in Honolulu beforehand. Experienced crew looking to sail between Hawaii and the US mainland or the South Pacific can try one of the following Web sites:

W www.boatcrew.net
This well-organized site has a database of boats

leaving from various mainland ports, and membership was free at the time of research.

W www.sfsailing.com
The San Francisco Sailing site lists skippers leaving from the San Francisco Bay Area, including a few long-distance ocean cruisers.

W www.latitude38.com
Latitude 38 skippers are heading for exotic destinations and seeking particular crew types, eg, 'have more desire than experience' and 'be willing to bust butt preparing the boat.'

Interisland Ferries

The only passenger ferry services between the Hawaiian Islands leave from Maui's Lahaina Harbor. Advance reservations are usually required. There are also sightseeing cruises and snorkel trips to Molokai and Lanai (see the Activities and Excursions chapters).

The privately owned *Expeditions* (☎ 661-3756, 800-695-2624, W www.go-lanai.com) ferry to Lanai deposits passengers at Manele Bay, a stone's throw from Hulopoe Beach. Not only is taking the ferry easy and cheap when compared to flying, but if you take it in winter, you'll have a fair chance of seeing whales along the way. The 24-passenger boats leave Lahaina Harbor at 6:45am and 9:15am and 12:45pm, 3:15pm and 5:45pm, taking about an hour for the often smooth-as-silk crossing. Return boats leave Manele Harbor on Lanai at 8am and 10:30am and 2pm, 4:30pm and 6:45pm. The one-way adult/child fare for nonresidents is $26/20. You can purchase tickets in Lahaina from the ticket booth at the public pier or from Lanai on the boat.

The commuter ferry *Molokai Princess* (☎ 667-6165, 800-275-6969, W www .molokaiferry.com) sails at least once daily between Lahaina and Kaunakakai, Molokai, taking about 1½ hours. A trip on this 100-foot rollicking ship includes all the thrills of a rough channel crossing for no extra fee. Once the boat gets into the open waters of what locals call the Pakalolo Channel, anyone up on the sundeck will get drenched. Departures from Lahaina are at 5:15pm daily and 7:30am Monday, Wednesday, Friday and Saturday. The boat leaves

Kaunakakai at 5:45am Monday to Saturday and 3:30pm daily except Tuesday and Thursday. The simple one-way fare is $42.40/21.20 per adult/child, while a book of six one-way tickets will set you back $185. Granted some commuter flights cost less, but that's missing the whole point. You can pay in advance by credit card or bring exact cash with you on the boat.

ORGANIZED TOURS
For those with limited time, package tours can be the cheapest way to go. The basic ones cover just airfare and accommodations (or airfare only), while deluxe packages include car rental, island-hopping and all sorts of recreational activities. If you're interested, travel agents can help you sort through the various options.

Costs vary, but one-week tours with airfare and no-frills hotel accommodations start as low as $500 from the US West Coast, or $800 from the US East Coast, based on double occupancy. Special sales may include car rental for the same rates. Sun Trips (☎ 800-786-8747, ⓦ www.suntrips .com) offers airfare-only or other packages from San Francisco or Los Angeles airports. Airfare-only specials to Maui can dip as low as $289 roundtrip, but departures are limited to a few flights per week. Pleasant Hawaiian Holidays (☎ 800-742-9244, ⓦ www.2hawaii.com) has departures from the US West Coast, Midwest and East Coast.

Cruises
Hefty state-government–sponsored incentives have enabled a handful of cruise ships to offer tours that include Hawaii, typically stopping off at Oahu, Maui, Kauai and the Big Island. Many of these trips are referred to as 'repositioning tours,' since they visit Hawaii during spring and fall on ships that are otherwise used in Alaska during the summer and in the Caribbean during the winter. A few of the larger cruise lines operate in Hawaiian waters from September through May without taking any winter breaks.

Most of these cruises last 10 to 12 days, although some go for up to a month. The best way to get a deal is to go through a cruise specialist travel agent. Fares start at around $150 a day per person, based on double occupancy, but discounts and promotions can drop that price under $100 a day.

If you've never been on a cruise before, some things to ask about when shopping for one include: How much time is spent off-ship in Hawaii? What is the passenger-to-crew ratio? How big is the ship, what is the size of my own room and where exactly is it located? What kind of extra activities and perks, such as free babysitting, are available?

Princess Cruises (☎ 800-774-6237, ⓦ www .princesscruises.com) offers the longest Hawaii cruising season and the most varied trips. Shorter cruises depart from Vancouver or Los Angeles via Ensenada, Mexico. Longer Tahiti cruises stop over at Bora Bora and Easter Island, while the 25-day sailing between Tokyo and San Francisco includes Midway Island, the Marianas and Marshall Islands.

Royal Caribbean Cruise Lines (☎ 800-307-8413, ⓦ www.rccl.com) has Hawaii cruises typically departing from Ensenada, Mexico or Vancouver.

Most cruises with Norwegian Cruise Lines (☎ 800-327-7030, ⓦ www.ncl.com) sail between Honolulu and Kiribati. Others depart from Vancouver or Ensenada, Mexico.

Holland America (☎ 877-932-4259, ⓦ www.hollandamerica.com) has cruises leaving from San Diego, Vancouver or Ensenada, Mexico.

Norwegian Cruise Lines is the only company currently offering cruises between the Hawaiian Islands. Its brand-spanking-new cruise ship operates year-round. Week-long cruises stop at Kiribatil Lahaina, Maui; Nawiliwili, Kauai; and Kona on the Big Island, while shorter trips skip Kauai. State-rooms for the 7-day route start at $900 and top out at $25,000 for an on-board villa.

Getting Around

Maui is not an easy island to get around without your own transportation. Taxis and airport shuttles are expensive by US mainland standards. Public buses are almost nonexistent, except for a few run by private companies along the western shore. Cycling is a possibility, but only if you're really fit. Many islanders without their own cars hitch, but that's illegal and not always easy or safe. The hostels in Wailuku offer free tours around the island, but to really explore you'll have to rent your own wheels.

Once you've sorted that out, however, anywhere on Maui is within a couple of hours' driving time for less than a full tank of gas. Distances are relatively short and traffic conditions quite manageable, especially when traffic proceeds apace of 'island time.' Morning and afternoon rush hours start fairly early (around 6am and 3pm), and you can expect to sit in traffic jams on major cross-island highways, especially around the Kahului-Wailuku area, Lahaina and Upcountry.

Most visitors to Maui land at the main airport in Kahului. Here you'll find most of the island's shopping malls and discount stores. Traffic moves slowly west through the three-mile corridor to Wailuku town, where the government offices and medical facilities stand.

Several of the major cross-island highways intersect in the Kahului-Wailuku area. The quickest route to Lahaina from Kahului is diagonal Hwy 380, which meets Hwy 30 from Wailuku. To get to South Maui, take the Mokulele Hwy (Hwy 311) past the sugar mill from the airport.

It's just a few miles from Kahului to Paia, but even before that you'll see the Haleakala Hwy (Hwy 37) branching off and heading Upcountry, finishing off 33 miles later at Haleakala summit. Back on the coast it's a 45-mile, two-hour drive to Hana. The rough but passable Piilani Hwy (Hwy 31) continues around the island to Oheo Gulch, Kipahulu and Kaupo on its way back

into Upcountry. Note that this highway is not the same as the one that connects Kihei with Wailea, even though they share the same name.

Be aware that most main roads are called 'highways' whether they're busy four-lane thoroughfares or just quiet country roads. What's more, islanders refer to highways by name, rarely by number. If you ask someone how to find Hwy 36, chances are they aren't going to know. Ask for the Hana Hwy instead.

TO/FROM THE AIRPORT

Outrageously, getting to and from the airport on Maui can cost as much as taking an interisland flight. If you plan to rent a car, doing so immediately when you arrive will save you money. Otherwise your only option is an expensive airport shuttle or taxi.

At Kahului Airport, car rentals are outside the baggage claim area, past the taxi dispatchers at the exit. Approximate taxi fares from Kahului Airport are: Wailuku ($13), Kihei ($25), Haiku area ($25 to $30), Lahaina ($45), Kaanapali ($50) and Kapalua ($60).

Speedi Shuttle (☎ 661-6667, 800-977-2605, w www.speedishuttle.com) operates charter transportation to most island locations, as well as airport transfers. Advance reservations are a good idea. Rates depend on the destination and group size, but are marginally cheaper than taking a taxi. From Kahului Airport a shuttle costs $16 to Wailuku, $25 to Kihei and $46 to Lahaina for two passengers, while a single person pays $13, $22 and $35, respectively. There's a courtesy phone in the baggage claim area – just dial ☎ 65.

At Kapalua/West Maui Airport, there are courtesy phones to contact nearby car rental agencies in Kaanapali. Most of West Maui's resort hotels (but not condos) offer airport shuttle services for guests, often for a fee. Taxi fares average $15 to Kaanapali resorts, and at least $20 to anywhere farther north along the coast or Lahaina.

From Hana Airport, the Hotel Hana-Maui provides a complimentary shuttle service for guests. Many B&Bs and inns also pick up guests by prior arrangement.

As a last resort, some travelers may try hitching, although that's technically illegal (see Hitchhiking, later). From Kahului Airport it's a long two-mile walk along the airport access road out to the main highway intersection. Theoretically, you could catch a ride to anywhere on the island from here, but drivers may not pick you up when traffic conditions are crowded, especially since most are only going short distances. From Kapalua/West Maui or Hana Airports, you can walk out to the highway in about 20 minutes *sans* luggage. Although passing traffic is mostly tourists in rental cars, an obliging local may stop for you.

BUS

At the time of writing only one company, Akina Aloha Tours (☎ 879-2828, 800-845-4890, 800-800-3989, w www.akinatours.com), operates 'Shopping Shuttle' bus routes connecting West Maui coastal points between Kapalua and Maalaea, then all the way south to Kihei and Makena. Note that these schedules are subject to change.

Along Route 1, buses travel an hour-long loop between Kapalua and Kaanapali, stopping at several resorts and condo complexes along the way. The first southbound bus leaves the Ritz-Carlton Kapalua at 9am, arriving at the Whalers Village shopping center half an hour later. The same bus departs at 9:40am and returns along the same route to Kapalua. Service is pretty much hourly throughout the day. The last southbound bus from Kapalua is at 8:20pm, while the last northbound bus leaves Whalers Village at 8:55pm.

Route 2 connects the Kaanapali resorts with Lahaina Harbor via the Lahaina Cannery Mall; Route 2B also stops at the tourist Sugar Cane Train stations. The first bus along Route 2 leaves the Royal Lahaina Resort in Kaanapali at 8:45am, stopping at Whalers Village ten minutes later and arriving at the Lahaina Harbor flagpole around 9:30am. Buses immediately return to the Royal Lahaina Resort, without making any stops along the way. Service is hourly throughout the day, with the last bus southbound to Lahaina Harbor at 8:45pm. Buses running on Route 2B leave Whalers Village every 1½ hours between 8:45am and 3:50pm, arriving in Lahaina Harbor about an hour later after making a few extra stops.

Buses on Route 3 link Kaanapali and Lahaina with Maalaea Bay, stopping at Olowalu Beach and Ukumehame Beach State Park en route. The first bus leaves Whalers Village at 7:50am, picking up at Lahaina Harbor at 8:20am and arriving at Maalaea Harbor Village shopping center around 8:50am. These buses promptly turn around and follow the same one-hour route back to Lahaina. Service is every two hours, with the last southbound bus leaving Whalers Village at 7:50pm (or 9:50pm for passengers to Kihei only) and the last northbound bus from Maalaea at 6:50pm (8:50pm for passengers to Lahaina and stops farther north only).

Buses along Route 4 pick up where Route 3 leaves off at Maalaea Bay for points farther south, namely Kihei, Wailea and Makena. The first bus southbound from Maalaea Harbor Village leaves at 8:55am and arrives one hour later at the Maui Prince Hotel in Makena. These buses stop at several shopping centers along S Kihei Rd directly opposite the beach parks as well as The Shops at Wailea. From the Maui Prince, the first bus northbound is at 7:50am. Route 4 buses leave every two hours throughout the day, with the last northbound bus at 7:50pm and the last southbound bus at 8:55pm.

Akina Tours also offers 'early bird' express shuttles from the Kamaole Shopping Center in Kihei, leaving at 6:45am for Lahaina Harbor (45 minutes) and Whalers Village (one hour) or 7:45am for stops all the way to Kapalua (1¼ hours).

All single point-to-point trips on Route 2 cost $1; $2 on Route 1 or 4; and $5 on Route 3. An all-day system-wide pass costs $10. Monthly passes vary from $25 to $65.

Say What?

Some 85% of all place names on Maui are in Hawaiian, and as often as not their meanings are enlightening, or at the very least amusing.

Some names state the obvious to those who've already visited, for example Lahaina ('cruel sun'), Olowalu ('many hills'), Makawao ('forest beginning'), Kula ('open country') and Kaanapali ('land divided by cliffs'). Other names may seem oddly prescient, considering they were given decades, if not centuries, ago: Paia is just as 'noisy' today as it was during the sugar plantation camp days. Still other meanings have become ironically twisted over the years, for example Hookipa, whose name means 'welcoming,' even when relations between surfers and windsurfers nowadays are anything but friendly.

Many Maui place names are composed of easily recognizable Hawaiian compounds. *Wai* means 'freshwater,' and it appears in almost every one of the names of the 54 Hana Hwy bridges. *Wailea* means 'the waters of Lea,' the Hawaiian goddess of canoe-making. Meanwhile *Wailuku* (probably 'waters of slaughter') takes its name from its bloody war history, and beautiful *Waianapanapa* means 'glistening waters,' with the last syllable repeated for special emphasis. Another common compound is *pu'u*, which means 'hill' or 'peak'. Puunene, then, means 'hill of the *nene*' (Hawaiian goose), and at one time geese really did make their home there. All of the cinder cones atop Haleakala, literally 'house *(hale)* of the sun *(la)*' have names beginning with pu'u, too.

Some names defy all of your attempts to puzzle them out. For example, Iao could mean 'cloud supreme,' which would be an appropriate name for this rain-soaked valley. But Iao is also the name of the morning star (Venus) and one of the first legendary Polynesian wayfinders to reach the Hawaiian islands. Another bizarre name is Ulupalakua, which may refer to 'breadfruit ripened on the back,' since resident chiefs would send runners all the way to Hana for fresh breadfruit, hoping it would nicely ripen on the return trip.

Akina Tours also runs a free resort-wide shuttle around Wailea between 6:30am and 8pm daily, which stops at resorts, golf courses, the shopping center and tennis club. In addition, the hotels and condos of Kaanapali and Kapalua have their own free resort-wide shuttle services.

For information on island bus and van sightseeing tours, see Organized Tours, later.

CAR & MOTORCYCLE

Although demand is high, car rental agencies remain competitive on Maui. You won't use much gas either, since distances are relatively short. Parking is generally not a problem, except in downtown Lahaina and at some beaches where only a few parking spaces are meant for the general public. Parking regulations are enforced, so expect a ticket if you park in the wrong zone or don't move your vehicle in a timely manner.

A few resorts and condo complexes charge their own guests for parking (the nerve!), so ask before making reservations.

Gas in Hawaii is more expensive than on the US mainland, with regular unleaded gasoline averaging $2.10 per US gallon for now. Usually the cheapest places to fuel up are local Tesoro gas stations, but Costco in Kahului may offer steeply discounted gas to its wholesale club members soon.

The minimum age for driving in Hawaii is 18 years. If you're under age 25, you should call the car rental agencies in advance to check their policies regarding age restrictions and surcharges.

Hawaii requires the use of seat belts for drivers and front-seat passengers. Heed this, as the ticket is a stiff one. State law also strictly requires the use of child-safety seats for children aged three and under, while four-year-olds must either be in a safety seat or secured by a seat belt. Most of the car rental companies rent child-safety seats for around $5 a day, but they don't always have them on hand so reserve one in advance if you can.

Car break-ins and theft regularly happen at remote parking lots, even during daylight hours. The worst hit are those lots at beaches, parks and other sightseeing spots. Do not leave any valuables in your car and keep any possessions you must leave behind in the trunk. Many locals just leave their cars unlocked so that break-in artists don't damage them further by busting the windows or locks.

For specific motorcycle information, see Motorcycle & Moped, later.

Road Rules & Safety

With very few exceptions, you can legally drive a car in the state of Hawaii as long as you have a valid driver's license issued by your home country. If your license is not in English, you may be required to show an international driver's license as well.

A popular bumper sticker here reads: 'Slow down. This is not da mainland.' Locals will tell you there are three golden rules for driving on Maui: don't honk your horn, don't follow too closely and let people pass whenever it's safe to do so. Any cool moves like this are acknowledged by waving the shaka sign. Horn honking is considered rude unless required for safety, or for urging complacent cattle off the road.

As with the rest of the USA, driving is – mostly – on the right-hand side of the road. If it's an unpaved or poorly paved road, locals tend to hog the middle stripe until an oncoming car approaches. Drivers at a red light can turn right after coming to a full stop and yielding to oncoming traffic, unless there's a sign at the intersection prohibiting the turn. Island drivers usually just wait for the next green light.

Stay alert for one-lane bridge crossings: one direction of traffic usually has the right of way while the other must obey the posted yield sign. Downhill traffic must yield to uphill traffic where there is no sign, which is often on the Kahekili or Hana Hwys.

Speed limits are posted *and* enforced. If you're stopped for speeding, expect a ticket, as the police rarely just give warnings. Cruising unmarked police cars come in hot makes and models on Maui, so they're not always easy to spy. Most accidents are caused by speed demons on the Haleakala and Mokulele Hwys. Unfortunately, drivers under the influence are also a hazard to be aware of, no matter if it's 11am or 11pm, or if marijuana, beer or ice is the vice. The crime of driving while intoxicated (DWI) is legally defined as having a blood alcohol level of greater than 0.08%.

Driving Times

Average driving times and distances from Kahului are as follows. Naturally these get longer during rush hours and on weekends.

Destination	Mileage	Duration
Haleakala Summit	36 miles	90 minutes
Hana	51 miles	125 minutes
Honolua Bay (via Kahekili Hwy)	26 miles	90 minutes
Kaanapali	26 miles	50 minutes
Kaupo (via Kula)	45 miles	120 minutes
Kihei	12 miles	25 minutes
La Perouse Bay	21 miles	50 minutes
Lahaina	23 miles	40 minutes
Maalaea	8 miles	20 minutes
Makawao	14 miles	30 minutes
Oheo Gulch	61 miles	160 minutes
Paia	7 miles	15 minutes
Polipoli Springs Campground	24 miles	100 minutes
Wailuku	3 miles	15 minutes

Car Rental

Rental cars are available all over the island, with most agencies having branches in the Kahului-Wailuku area near the main airport.

Rates vary from company to company depending on season, time of booking and current promotions. Be sure to ask the agent for the cheapest rate, as the first quote given is not always the lowest. If you belong to a travel or automobile club, a frequent-flier program or even have a youth hostel card, you'll often be eligible for some sort of discount. You'll often need to get that discount code from your own organization before making any bookings. Sometimes Internet specials offered directly by the agency for online bookings beat these other discounts.

Walking up to the counter without a reservation will not only subject you to higher rates, but during busy periods, which can include weekends year-round, it's not uncommon for all cars to be booked out. For daily rentals, most cars are rented on a 24-hour basis, so you could get two days' use by renting at midday and driving around all afternoon, then heading out to explore somewhere else the next morning before the car is due back.

For a small car, the daily rate ranges from $25 to $45, while typical weekly rates are $150 to $200. Monthly rates can work out to be as little as $500 from local agencies. When you're asking for price quotes, make sure they includes all surcharges and taxes. In Hawaii rental cars usually enjoy unlimited mileage, but there's a $3-a-day state road tax.

Having a major credit card greatly simplifies the rental process. Without one, some agents simply will not rent vehicles, while others will require prepayment by cash or traveler's checks, as well as a hefty deposit of a few hundred dollars. Be aware that many car rental companies are loathe to rent to people who list a campground as their address on the island, and a few specifically add 'No Camping Permitted' to their rental contracts. Most officially prohibit use of their cars on dirt roads. If you plan on camping or driving your economy compact like a 4WD monster, make sure to have it thoroughly washed and/or detailed before returning it to the rental agency. Gas stations in Kahului have heavy-duty automatic car washes with self-serve vacuums outside.

A word about specialty rentals: blame it on *Baywatch,* but it's true that many visitors to Hawaii suddenly become enamored of renting a cherry-red Mustang convertible or 4WD Jeep. Either is pointless on Maui for the simple reason that the island isn't big or rugged enough to have any real fun. Remember that the flashier your vehicle looks, the more of an instant target you are for thieves, break-in artists and of course, general local derision. Only on Lanai, where terrific off-roading necessitates a 4WD vehicle, does renting a Jeep make any practical sense (see the Excursions chapter, later). If you simply must drive a Mustang convertible or a dune buggy around, Wheels USA (see Local Agencies, later) probably has the cheapest rates.

Insurance Rental companies in Hawaii have liability insurance, which covers injury to people that you might hit with their vehicles, but not property damage to either rental vehicle or anything else that crossed your accidental path. For this, a collision damage waiver (CDW) is available from car rental agencies, typically for an additional $10 to $15 a day.

The CDW is not really insurance per se, but rather a guarantee that the rental company won't hold you liable for any damages to its car (although even here there are exceptions). If you decline the CDW, you are usually held liable for any damage up to the full value of the car. Remember that the littlest thing – someone scraping against the car door in a parking lot – can cost hundreds of dollars to fix.

If you have collision coverage on your vehicle at home, it might cover damages to vacation car rentals. Some credit cards, including most 'gold cards' issued by Visa and MasterCard, offer reimbursement coverage for collision damages if you rent the car with that credit card and decline the CDW. Check before leaving on your trip.

If damages do occur and you find yourself in a dispute with the rental company, call the state Department of Commerce & Consumer Affairs at ☎ 808-587-1234 and then key in 1, then 1 again, and finally 7220 for recorded information on your legal rights. Document any alleged damage by taking photographs before surrendering the vehicle and keep copies of any incident reports filled out by agency representatives.

International Agencies All of the following operate out of Kahului Airport. Alamo, Avis, Budget, Dollar and National have offices on Hwy 30 in Kaanapali and will do courtesy pick-ups at Kapalua/West Maui Airport. Dollar is the only rental agency at Hana Airport and is one of the more liberal agencies renting to people under the age of 25. Alamo often gives the best rates on compact cars.

Alamo (☎ 871-6235, 800-327-963
  W www.goalamo.com)

Avis (☎ 871-7575, 800-321-3712
  W www.avis.com)

Budget (☎ 871-8811, 800-527-0700
  W www.budget.com)

Dollar (☎ 877-6526, 800-800-4000
  W www.dollarcar.com)

Hertz (☎ 877-5167, 800-654-3131
  W www.hertz.com)

National (☎ 871-8851, 800-227-7368
  W www.nationalcar.com)

All agencies expect you to return the car with a full tank of gas. If you forget, they'll happily charge you double or triple the usual price of gas to fill up your tank for you. Some agencies now offer a new scam called 'pre-paid gas,' where you pay them to fill up your car at the regular price, no matter how much gas you return it with. The problem is that you can only pre-pay for a *full* tank of gas. So unless you return the car precisely on empty, you're actually losing money!

Local Agencies What is the number-one benefit of renting from a local agency? Well, it makes you look local. Driving around in a beat-up Toyota Tercel or Nissan Sentra will discourage break-ins and help you blend in a little. Minor scratches and bumps aren't disasters with older cars, and if you don't mind driving without air-con or a stereo, then you can save plenty of money.

However, not all agencies rent reliable cars, so if you're planning on heading up the Haleakala Hwy or around Kaupo Gap, tell them what you need. Many agencies based near Kahului will pick you up free of charge

from the airport if you phone in advance, but sometimes only if you're renting the car for longer than a few days. Drivers under age 25 and those without credit cards should expect to pay more, unless otherwise stated.

Maui Cruisers (☎ 249-2319, 877-749-7889, in Canada ☎ 800-488-9083, W www.mauicruisers.net), 1270 Piihana Rd, in Wailuku, rents reliable, used compact cars from $30/150/500 per day/week/month. Personable service goes hand-in-hand with honest deals, plus free racks for surfers. Rates include absolutely everything, and there are no surcharges as long as you pay with cash or traveler's checks.

Word of Mouth (☎ 877-2436, 800-533-5929, fax 877-2439, W www.maui.net/~word), 150 Hana Hwy, in Kahului, rents old cars by the week for around $110 and newer used cars for $125. Daily rates start from $25 depending on the season, the model of car, your age and how the manager is feeling.

Wheels USA (☎ 667-7751, fax 661-8940), 741 Wainee St, in Lahaina, rents used compact cars from $25/130 per day/week and jeeps or dune buggies from $50/250. Add $6 per day for younger drivers. There is another branch (☎ 871-6858) at 75 Kaahumanu Ave in Kahului.

Kihei Rent-a-Car (☎ 879-7257, 800-251-5288, W www.kiheirentacar.com), 96 Kio Loop, is family-owned and offers 24-hour roadside assistance. Rates start at $25/150 per day/week, not including tax. Drivers must be 21 years old (but there are no surcharges for those under 25), and rates are higher during peak season.

Good Kar-Ma Cars (☎ 871-2911, 243-0126 recorded information, fax 871-4696, W maui2000.com/carrental), 536 Keolani Pl, Kahului, has really old cars. Vehicles range from compacts for $30/130 per day/week to windsurfing vans for $45/170.

Some of the windsurf shops can arrange reasonably priced car and van rentals for their customers.

Accessible Vans of Hawaii (see Disabled Travelers in the Facts for the Visitor chapter) is a well-regarded Kahului organization that rents accessible vans.

Motorcycle & Moped

You can legally drive a motorcycle or moped in the state of Hawaii as long as you have a valid driver's license issued by your home country.

Many Harley-Davidson fanatics come over to Maui, rent hogs and zoom around the island – but since that only takes about three hours, it's more than a little like overkill. Still, there are no helmet laws in the state of Hawaii and even cautious riders will likely seize the opportunity to be swaddled in tropical breezes as they cruise along the Hana Hwy; please be careful and remember rental agencies often provide free helmets.

Motorcycle & Moped Rental The minimum age to rent a bike at most places is 21, and you'll need to show a valid motorcycle license. Riding on the eastern side of the island may require foul weather gear. Snug cuffs and waterproof seams are essential and a stash of double-sided Velcro and seam sealer will work wonders for your riding disposition. Some rental agencies also supply rain gear; ask.

The minimum age for renting a scooter or moped (the former can go highway speeds, while the latter is for around town) is 16 years. Bizarrely, they are more expensive to rent than cars and are really only useful for scooting around limited urban or resort areas, such as Kihei-Wailea and Kaanapali-Kapalua.

Aloha Toy Store (☎ 662-0888, fax 661-7909, W www.alohatoystore.com), 640 Front St, in Lahaina, rents Harley-Davidsons from $100 per day. It also offers an electric car package with snorkel sets, lunch and ice chest for $120/155 for two/four people. There's another branch (☎ 891-0888) in The Shops at Wailea.

Duke's Surf & Rental Shop (☎ 661-1970), 602 Front St, in Lahaina, rents Harleys from $135 per day and mopeds from $50/192 per day/week.

Hawaii Island Cruzers (☎ 879-0956, W www.vrmaui.com/cruzers), 2395 S Kihei Rd, in Dolphin Plaza in lower Kihei, rents high-performance Italian scooters only to experienced riders for $50/280 per day/week, with free helmets and locks.

Hula Hogs (☎ 875-7433, 877-464-7433, W www.hulahogs.com), 1279 S Kihei Rd, in Azeka Place II in upper Kihei, rents Harley-Davidsons from $80 to $110 per day, or $180 to $230 per weekend. Helmets, rain gear and accessories are available for no extra charge.

Ride Maui (☎ 242-1015, W www.ride-maui .com), 509 Kainula Place, in Wailuku, rents mostly Honda motorcycles for $70 to $130 per day, depending on the type and length of rental.

Wheels USA (see Car Rental, earlier) rents motorcycles from $60/300 per day/week. Its mopeds cost $36/180 per day/week, or $26 for rentals from 8am to 4:30pm only.

Buying a Vehicle

If you're staying on Maui for more than a month, consider buying a used car. If you're lucky, you can resell it later. Start by looking at the *Maui News* classified ads and notice boards outside cafés, grocery stores, shopping malls and other community centers. You may find OK deals at used car dealerships in Kahului, too.

Island cars don't suffer as much from rust and freezing cold weather as on the mainland, so any used car might look good at first. However, since many locals live on unpaved roads, the whole undercarriage of the car may be wrecked and the steering will most likely be shot, if not the brakes. Also check for blown gaskets that could cause the car to overheat.

To be legal, all vehicles in Hawaii must have a safety inspection sticker (available at most gas stations) and carry no-fault insurance. If you're buying from a used-car lot, the car should already be 'legal,' ie, safety-checked. After you purchase the vehicle, you then have 10 days to change the title and 30 days to register the car with the Department of Motor Vehicles in Wailuku, Lahaina, Kihei or Makawao. The average wait time is 47 minutes per customer, so enjoy. Maui DMV is a privately owned business that will take care of all this paperwork for you (for a fee, of course), but its sage advice for used car buyers is free at www.mauidmv.com.

Shipping Vehicles from the Mainland

If you're thinking of staying a couple of months, it might behoove you and your wallet to ship your vehicle from the US mainland instead of renting a car. Note, however, that prices from the West Coast are much more palatable than from the East Coast (did someone say road trip?!). If your ride isn't a total junker, you'll probably be able to sell it when you leave; Toyotas, Fords, pickup trucks and 4WDs are particularly coveted and provide attractive resale value.

Matson Navigation (☎ 800-462-8766, www.matson.com) ships passenger vehicles to Kahului from Oakland, Los Angeles and Seattle for $880 and its service is speedy and reliable. It usually takes one to three weeks for cars to arrive. For an exhaustive list of worldwide shippers, see MoveCars.com (www.movecars.com).

TAXI

Taxi fares are regulated by the county with fares based on mileage regardless of the number of passengers. The minimum flag-down fare is $2.50, and each additional mile is about $2.

Taxi companies include: Maui Central Cab (☎ 244-7278, 877-244-7279) in Kahului; Alii Taxi (☎ 661-3688) in Lahaina; Island-wide Taxi (☎ 874-8294); and Kihei Taxi (☎ 879-3000).

Based in Kaanapali, Classy Taxi (☎ 665-0003) has 1920s gangster-era limos and a 1933 Rolls Royce. It charges the same rates as a regular taxi. Reservations are advisable.

Disabled travelers call HandiVan (☎ 456-5555) paratransit to make a reservation.

BICYCLE

It's possible to cycle all around all the Hawaiian Islands – if you don't mind blistering heat, strong crosswinds and crowded traffic conditions, that is.

Cyclists on Maui face a number of challenges: narrow one-lane highways, traffic jams along the coast, inland mountains and the same persistent winds that so delight windsurfers. While the island's stunning scenery may entice hard-core cyclists, casual riders hoping to use a bike as a primary source of transportation may find it feasible only within the major resort areas or around Paia, especially once the ecofriendly greenway between Kanaha and Spreckelsville is completed.

Although Maui has been slow to adopt cycle-friendly traits, a few roads now include bike lanes. Serious cyclists should pick up the *Maui County Bicycle Map* ($6) available at some bicycle rental and repair shops. This full-color map outlines bike lanes, mountain biking trails and recommends highway routes, including helpful elevation, wind and distance charts.

For more information on mountain biking, see the Activities chapter, later.

Bicycle Rental & Sales

Rental rates vary from $10 to $45 per day, depending on the quality and type of bike. Helmet and locks are usually free, and car racks are available. If you're planning to stay on Maui for more than a week, consider buying a bike and then reselling it. Some rental shops even offer buy-back plans for this very purpose.

Island Biker (☎ 877-7744), 415 Hana Hwy, in Kahului, rents quality front-shock and road bikes for $29/95 per day/week and stocks bicycle maps and trail books.

Haleakala Bike Co (☎ 575-9575, 888-922-2453, www.bikemaui.com), Haiku Marketplace, 810 Haiku Rd, Haiku, has rental mountain bikes from $35/80 per day/week, with long-term rentals negotiable. It also sells used bikes from $125.

Hawaii Island Cruzers (☎ 879-0956), 2395 S Kihei Rd, in Dolphin Plaza, Kihei, rents Schwinn cruisers from $7/67 per half-day/week; mountain bikes cost $10/100. Deposit is required.

South Maui Bicycles (☎ 874-0068), Island Surf Bldg, 1993 S Kihei Rd, rents mountain bikes for $19/89 and has a few serious off-road bikes.

West Maui Cycles (☎ 661-9005, www .westmauicycles.com), 840 Wainee St, in

Lahaina, rents cruiser road bikes for $10/50 per day/week, hybrids for $20/80 and front-suspension mountain bikes for $25/110.

Wheels USA, Kihei Rent-a-Car and other car rental agencies (see Car Rental, earlier) may also rent older mountain bikes for around $15/60 per day/week.

HITCHHIKING

Hitching is never entirely safe in any country in the world, and we don't recommend it. Travelers who decide to hitch should understand that they are taking a small but potentially serious risk. People who do choose to hitch will be safer if they travel in pairs and let someone know where they are planning to go.

Hitchhiking is illegal in Hawaii, yet that hardly stops anyone. Considering how limited other transportation options are, many locals and travelers have no other choice. The police will generally look the other way if you do them the courtesy of hiding your thumb until they drive past.

You should size up each situation carefully before getting inside a car. One trick is to ask drivers where they are going before revealing your own destination. That way, if your gut gives you a bad feeling, you can always make up an excuse like 'Oh, I'm hitching on the wrong side of the road!' Better to sound stupid than be sorry later.

Hitching around the major resort areas can be painfully slow, especially since tourists driving rental cars can be reluctant to pick up hitchhikers. It's easier to get cars to stop along the major island highways when traffic isn't too heavy, so walk as far out of town as possible and try your luck there. Quiet back roads in Upcountry and around East Maui have far less traffic, but a local will usually pick you up eventually.

ORGANIZED TOURS

All of these sightseeing tours can be booked after arrival in Hawaii. The only time you may need to make advance reservations is in December or July and August. For organized tours geared toward activities, such as whale watching, snorkeling and downhill volcano cycling, see the Activities chapter.

Bus & Van Tours

A number of companies operate half-day and full-day sightseeing bus tours on Maui. Most of these climb Haleakala to see the sunrise, or rush down the Hana Hwy, passing Oheo Gulch, and around the island in just a few hours.

Roberts Hawaii (☎ 800-831-5411, Ⓦ www .roberts-hawaii.com) has tours starting from $40. This giant among Hawaiian tour companies offers an 11-hour 'Heavenly Hana' itinerary ($75).

Polynesian Adventures (☎ 877-4242, 800-622-3011, fax 871-7262, Ⓦ www.polyad.com) offers cheaper rates for the Haleakala sunrise tour and discounts for online bookings.

Local outfits offer the same trips with less canned commentary, as well as more out-of-the-way spots. Ekahi Tours (☎ 877-9775, 888-292-2242, fax 877-9776, Ⓦ www.ekahi.com) runs tours from $65/50 per adult/child. The family-run tour company offers free pick-ups around the island. Its six-hour cultural tour of Kahakuloa village includes visiting a working taro patch. Incidentally, the company's e-newsletter archives make fascinating reading.

Rent-a-Local Tours (☎ 877-4042, 800-228-6284, fax 661-9698, Ⓦ www.rentalocal.com) has eight-hour tours for up to eight people for $235. If you provide the car, they'll arrange for a knowledgeable local to show you around. Award-winning guides have been known to detour to the houses of friends and family to show visitors some real aloha hospitality. Discounts are available for online bookings.

The cultural nonprofit organization Maui Nei (see Walking & Hiking Tours, later) can also arrange outings for small groups to Kahakuloa village or the Iao Valley.

Helicopter Tours

Helicopter tours go to some amazing places, such as inaccessible waterfalls in the West Maui Mountains or across the channel to view Molokai's towering coastal *pali* (sea cliffs). Note that helicopters are prohibited from flying directly over Haleakala volcano, so don't expect much more than a peek from the crater rim.

Most helicopter tour companies are based at the Kahului heliport and prices are competitive. Prices vary depending on the destination and the length of the flight but average from about $115 per passenger for a 30-minute tour to $215 for an hour-long tour with a side trip to Molokai. You often get better discounts by dealing with the company directly instead of booking through tourist activity desks. Many companies advertise perennial specials in the free tourist magazines or offer discounts via their own Web sites.

Be aware that not every seat in all helicopters is a window seat. A common configuration is two passengers up front with the pilot, and four people sitting across the back. The two back middle seats simply don't give the photo opportunities proclaimed in the brochures. People are usually seated according to weight with the lightest passengers, or those traveling solo, enjoying the greatest views up front. Morning flights often have the clearest and smoothest weather, but cloudy conditions could obscure viewing at any time.

With veteran helicopter pilots and the best safety record, Blue Hawaiian (☎ 871-8844, 800-745-2583, W www.bluehawaiian.com) was the company chosen to help film the *Jurassic Park* series. Its multimillion heliport lounge has an atrium and a reef aquarium.

Alexair (☎ 877-4354, 888-418-8457, W www.helitour.com) is the only company that offers an East Maui tour including a ground stop at Waianapanapa black-sand beach ($215). All passengers get headset mikes so they can ask the pilot questions.

Sunshine Helicopters (☎ 871-0722, 800-544-2520, W www.sunshinehelicopters.com) are equipped with a Skycam video system and state-of-the-art audio equipment.

Cruises & Underwater Tours

Maui has enough dinner cruises, sunset sails, deep-sea fishing boats and charter sailboats to fill a book. Most of them leave from crowded Lahaina Harbor, although a few also use Maalaea Harbor and South Maui landings. You can get current rates and information from activity booths all around Maui or from the tourist magazines. Or just go down to Lahaina Harbor, where the booths and the boats are lined up, and check out the scene for yourself.

Atlantis Submarines (☎ 667-2224, 800-548-6262, W www.goatlantis.com), at the Wharf Cinema Center, Lahaina, runs tours from 9am to 1pm daily for $79/39 per adult/child. Atlantis whisks passengers by catamaran from Lahaina Harbor out to its 65-foot submarine, which dives up to 130 feet for viewing coral and reef fish. The actual time spent in the submarine is about 40 minutes. Discounts are available for online bookings.

For snorkeling and diving tours, see the Activities chapter.

Walking & Hiking Tours

Maui Nei (☎ 661-9494, W www.mauinei.com), 505 Front St, suite 234, runs tours for $34. Most of Lahaina's historic sites don't look like much until someone explains their significance, so consider joining one of the walking tours offered by this nonprofit cultural group. Morning walking tours start from the Old Lahaina Courthouse and advance reservations are required. All proceeds benefit the Friends of Moku'ula restoration fund in Lahaina.

Low-cost hiking tours offered by environmental groups are listed in the Hiking special section at the end of the Activities chapter. Private hiking guides usually stick to well-trodden trails that you can get to on your own, but the knowledgeable ones give you natural and cultural commentary as well.

Hike Maui (☎ 879-5270, fax 893-2515, ⓦ www.hikemaui.com) runs half/full-day hikes from $85/100. The founder of this, Maui's longest-running hike company, used to live in the island's jungles and has been described as 'an encyclopedia in hiking boots.' All of his nature hiking guides are well-qualified in their own fields of expertise.

Maui Hiking Safaris (☎ 573-0168, 888-445-3963, fax 572-3037, ⓦ www.maui.net/~mhs) runs tours for $50 to $90. Its small group hiking tours of the rain forest, valley and coastal areas cost a bit less. Discounts are given for *keiki* (child) hikers and online bookings.

Neighbor Islands Tours

If you want to visit another island while you're in Hawaii and only have a day or two to spare, it might be worth looking into 'overnighters,' which are mini–package tours to the Neighbor Islands.

Rates include roundtrip airfare, car rental and hotel accommodations, with a one-night package at a no-frills hotel starting around $150 per person, based on double occupancy. Last-minute specials may drop this price even further. Rates rise for better-quality accommodations, and extra days can be added for $75 to $100 per person. Companies that organize these minipackages also sell room/car packages, but their prices are not always cheaper than similar packages offered by hotels and car rental agencies.

One more caveat: if you read the fine print, you'll find that package tours often don't apply to Molokai or Lanai. Check with the ferry companies instead about accommodations/car rental discounts (see Interisland Ferries in the Getting There & Away Chapter).

Two of the biggest agents for Neighbor Island package tours are Roberts Hawaii (☎ 523-9323, 800-899-9323, fax 808-522-7870, ⓦ www.robertsovernighters.com) and Pleasant Island Holidays (on Oahu ☎ 808-922-1515, 800-654-4386, ⓦ www.gtesupersite.com/pih). Pleasant Island Holidays offers discounts to seniors, military personnel and Hawaii residents. Also check with Hawaiian Airlines (☎ 800-882-8811) about all-inclusive getaway packages.

Central Maui

Kahului and Wailuku, Maui's two largest communities, flow together to form a single urban sprawl, where half of the island's locals live, work and shop. Several major highways crisscross the island's central plains, past waving fields of sugarcane. The historic town of Puunene has Maui's last working sugar mill and a tidy little museum of early plantation life and immigration. On the western coast is Maalaea Bay, good for surfing, eating fresh seafood or dropping by the Maui Ocean Center.

The commercial center in Kahului is near Maui's international airport. After landing, most people drive right out of town and don't come back until they're ready to leave. Apart from discount shopping and sports stores, there's really not much in Kahului for visitors. Kahului Harbor, Maui's deepwater commercial port, services barges, cargo ships and the occasional cruise liner. This one's geared for work – there are no charming wharves or sailboats. Toward the airport you'll find Kanaha Pond and Kanaha Beach Park, known for windsurfing and kiteboarding.

Wailuku, the county seat, is the more distinctive and less hurried end of it all. It is a vintage Hawaiian town with backstreets of curio shops, mom-and-pop stores and hole-in-the-wall ethnic restaurants. Wailuku has an excellent historical museum and some of Maui's cheapest places to stay. You'll probably find yourself passing through on the way to Iao Valley State Park. North of both Wailuku and Kahului are two ancient *heiau* (temple) sites, where Maui's last human sacrifices took place.

KAHULUI

In the early 1880s, Kahului became the headquarters of Hawaii's first railroad, which was built to haul sugar from the fields around Paia to the refinery and harbor. When an outbreak of the bubonic plague hit in 1900, the settlement that had grown up around Kahului Harbor was deliberately

Highlights

- Surfing the Maalaea Pipeline, Hawaii's fastest break

- Watching rain clouds break over the verdant pinnacle of the Iao Needle

- Dipping into old Hawaii at Market Street shops in Wailuku

- Paying your respects to the Duke's surfboard at the Bailey House Museum

- Spying on rare native birds and migratory waterfowl at Kanaha and Kealia Ponds

- Loading up on two-scoop plate lunches and fiery ethnic eats, for only a few bucks

- Delving into the past and the present at the sugar museum and Maui Ocean Center

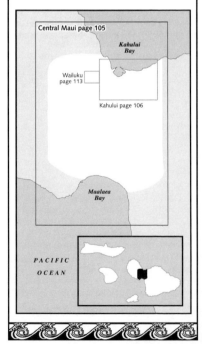

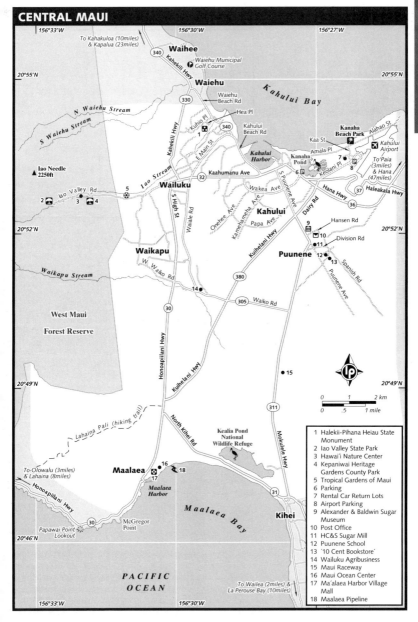

CENTRAL MAUI

156°33'W · 156°30'W · 156°27'W

20°55'N · 20°52'N · 20°49'N · 20°46'N

To Kahakuloa (10miles) & Kapalua (23miles)

Waihee

Waihee

Waiehu Municipal Golf Course

Waiehu Beach Rd

Hea Pl

Kuhio Pl

Kahului Beach Rd

Kahului Bay

Kanaha Beach Park

Kaa St

Amala Pl

Kahului Harbor

Kanaha Pond

Alahao St

Kahului Airport

To Pa'ia (3miles) & Hana (47miles)

Keolani Pl

N Waiehu Stream

S Waiehu Stream

Iao Stream

Iao Needle 2250ft

Iao Valley Rd

Wailuku

Kaahumanu Ave

Wakea Ave

S Puunene Ave

Hana Hwy

Haleakala Hwy

E Main St

Kahekili Hwy

Onehee Ave

Kamehameha Ave

Papa Ave

Kahului

Dairy Rd

Hansen Rd

S High St

Walale Rd

Kuihelani Hwy

Waikapu

W Waiko Rd

Puunene

Division Rd

Spanish Rd

Puunene Ave

Waikapu Stream

West Maui Forest Reserve

Waiko Rd

Honoapiilani Hwy

Kuihelani Hwy

North Kihei Rd

Lahaina Pali (hiking trail)

To 'Olowalu (3miles) & Lahaina (8miles)

Honoapiilani Hwy

Papawai Point Lookout

McGregor Point

Maalaea

Maalaea Harbor

Kealia Pond National Wildlife Refuge

Mokulele Hwy

Kihei

Maalaea Bay

PACIFIC OCEAN

To Wailea (2miles) & La Perouse Bay (10miles)

0   1   2 km
0   .5   1 mile

1 Halekii-Pihana Heiau State Monument
2 Iao Valley State Park
3 Hawai'i Nature Center
4 Kepaniwai Heritage Gardens County Park
5 Tropical Gardens of Maui
6 Parking
7 Rental Car Return Lots
8 Airport Parking
9 Alexander & Baldwin Sugar Museum
10 Post Office
11 HC&S Sugar Mill
12 Puunene School
13 '10 Cent Bookstore'
14 Wailuku Agribusiness
15 Maui Raceway
16 Maui Ocean Center
17 Ma'alaea Harbor Village Mall
18 Maalaea Pipeline

KAHULUI

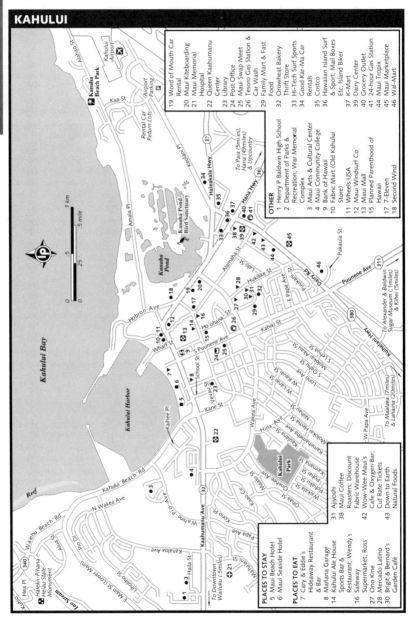

19 Word of Mouth Car Rental
20 Maui Kiteboarding
21 Maui Memorial Hospital
22 Queen Kaahumanu Center
23 Library
24 Post Office
25 Maui Swap Meet
26 Tesoro Gas Station & Car Wash
29 Family Mart & Fast Food
32 Orowheat Bakery Thrift Store
33 Hi-Tech Surf Sports
34 Good Kar-Ma Car Rentals
35 Costco
36 Hawaiian Island Surf & Sport; Mail Boxes Etc; Island Biker
37 K-Mart
39 Dairy Center
40 Grocery Outlet
41 24-hour Gas Station
44 Maui Tropix
45 Maui Marketplace
46 Wal-Mart

OTHER
1 Henry P Baldwin High School
2 Department of Parks & Recreation; War Memorial Complex
3 Maui Arts & Cultural Center
4 Maui Community College
9 Bank of Hawaii
10 Fabric Mart (Old Kahului Store)
11 Wheels USA
12 Maui Windsurf Co
13 Maui Mall
15 Planned Parenthood of Hawaii
17 7-Eleven
18 Second Wind

PLACES TO STAY
5 Maui Beach Hotel
6 Maui Seaside Hotel

PLACES TO EAT
7 Cary & Eddie's Hideaway Restaurant & Bar
8 Mañana Garage
14 Kahului Ale House Sports Bar & Restaurant; Wendy's
16 Safeway Supermarket; Ross
27 Ono Kine
28 Mercado Latino
30 Brigit & Bernard's Garden Café
31 Aiyoshi
38 Maui Coffee Roasters; Discount Fabric Warehouse
42 Wow-Wee Maui's Cafe & Oxygen Bar; Cut Rate Tickets
43 Down to Earth Natural Foods

burned to the ground in an attempt to eradicate the disease.

The present-day Kahului has its roots in a planned community developed in the 1950s by the Alexander & Baldwin (A&B) sugar company. It was nicknamed 'Dream City' by cane workers, who had long dreamed of moving away from the dusty mill camps to a home of their own. The post-WWII housing shortage meant that A&B could more profitably use some of its lands to build and sell houses, rather than raise sugar. Dream City was also designed to lure back cane workers that the company had lost to high-paying military jobs during wartime. These first tract homes are at the southern edge of town.

Information

The main road, Kaahumanu Ave, is a collection of stores, banks and office buildings and a mile-long strip of shopping centers.

The Kahului post office (☎ 871-2487), 138 S Puunene Ave, is open 8:30am to 5pm weekdays, 9am to noon Saturday. The public library (☎ 873-3097), 90 School St, which has a few Internet terminals, is open 10am to 5pm Monday, Thursday, Friday and Saturday and 10am to 8pm Tuesday and Wednesday.

The 24-hour Kinko's (☎ 871-2000), in the Dairy Center at 395 Dairy Rd, offers Internet access for 20¢ per minute, photocopying, faxing and other business services. From time to time other Internet kiosks pop up around town, sometimes free of charge. At the time of writing, the McDonald's kiosk had a cupholder and tray for your burger. There's an expensive pay-per-use kiosk at the Coffee Store (see Places to Eat, later).

The island's biggest bookstore is Borders Books & Music Café (☎ 877-6160), Maui Marketplace, 270 Dairy Rd. Here you'll find Hawaiiana books, maps, surfing magazines, foreign newspapers and Hawaiian CDs and DVDs. It's open 9am to 10pm Sunday to Thursday, 9am to 11pm Friday and Saturday.

Maui Memorial Hospital (☎ 244-9056), 221 Mahalani St, Wailuku, is the island's main hospital and has 24-hour emergency services. Despite the address, it is actually closer to Kahului.

Kanaha Beach Park

If you're stuck in Kahului, Kanaha Beach Park is OK for swimming, though most locals prefer the cleaner, clearer waters of Kihei. A lifeguard is on duty daily. That hasn't stopped Kanaha from acquiring a reputation for petty crime and violence, however.

It has a long white-sand beach, a roped-off swimming area and a nice view of the West Maui Mountains all the way up the coast to Hakuhee Point. There are restrooms, showers and pay phones, as well as a campground and picnic tables under the shade of hau, ironwood and kiawe trees.

Kanaha is a popular windsurfing and kiteboarding spot, and when the wind is right, both draw a crowd. It's the best place on Maui for beginners, and many of the windsurfing and kiteboarding shops give their lessons here. Everyone gets pretty territorial, so it's best not to go alone without some kind of local introduction.

The beach access sign is down by the car rental lots at the airport. From central Kahului take Amala Pl, the coastal road that starts from the Chevron storage tanks off Kaahumanu Ave.

Kanaha Pond

Kanaha Pond is a kind of respite in the midst of suburbia, beneath the flight path for the airport and beside the highway where trucks go barreling along. Yes, it's noisy.

The pond is a wildlife sanctuary for the endangered black-necked stilt, a wading bird that feeds along the marshy edges of the pond. It's a graceful bird in flight, with long orange legs that trail behind. Even though the stilt population in all Hawaii is estimated at just 1500, the birds can commonly be spotted here.

An observation deck just beyond the parking lot is a good site for spotting stilts, coots, ducks and black-crowned night herons. Bring binoculars. Upon entering the sanctuary, if you close the gate behind you and walk in quietly, you should be able to make some sightings right there along the shoreline.

If you'd like to hike on the service roads in the sanctuary, it's possible to do so September through March (when the birds aren't nesting) by obtaining a permit from the Division of Forestry and Wildlife (☎ 984-8100), State Office Building, 54 High St, room 101, Wailuku. Permits are valid for one weekday only, 8am to 3pm.

Maui Arts & Cultural Center

The island's home for the arts is this $32 million-dollar center *(MACC; 242-2787 ext 228 tour reservations,* W *www.mauiarts.org, 1 Cameron Way).* The center was built on the site of Pa Hula Heiau, and some temple remains can still be seen. The art gallery exhibits change frequently and are open 10am to 5pm Tuesday to Sunday, as well as before and after films at the Castle Theatre (see Entertainment, later). Free tours are given at 11am Wednesday (reservations required).

Places to Stay

With an island as small as Maui, there is absolutely no need to stay near the airport. If you get stuck, however, there are only a few options.

Kanaha Beach Park Campground While it's nice to be at the beach, flights rumble overhead from dawn until 11pm, and without any county campground monitors, safety is a real concern. For permit information, see Accommodations in the Facts for the Visitor chapter. Kahului's two hotels are on the main commercial strip in an area that hardly conjures up images of vacationing in Hawaii.

Maui Beach Hotel *(☎ 888-649-3222, fax 871-5797, 170 Kaahumanu Ave)* Rooms from $90. You'll recognize this modern concrete-block motel by the faux-Polynesian lobby. All rooms have modern amenities, but some really show their age. There's an indoor swimming pool and a buffet-style restaurant that is inexplicably popular with local families. Free shuttle service is provided from the airport.

Maui Seaside Hotel *(☎ 877-3311, 800-560-5552, fax 877-4618,* W *www.mauiseaside hotel.com, 100 Kaahumanu Ave)* Standard/deluxe rooms $130/150, rooms with kitch-

enettes $160. Daily car rental add $29. Don't be misled by this hotel's fanciful name as it's an even older motel, with standard rooms that are way overpriced. For discounts, check the Web site.

Places to Eat

There is no excuse for not eating well (and very affordably) in Kahului, where strip malls hide everything from organic grocery shops to local grinds to upscale world cuisine.

Self-Catering ***Down to Earth Natural Foods*** *(☎ 877-2661, 305 Dairy Rd)* Open 7am-9pm Mon-Sat, 8am-8pm Sun. Opposite Maui Marketplace, this well-stocked natural foods store offers reasonable prices, fresh organic produce, bulk foods, juices and a salad bar. It also has a buffet with a few hot dishes ($5 per pound) and a vegetarian deli with things like tofu-rice loaf.

Mercado Latino *(☎ 871-5067, 325 Huki-like St)* This market, started by two Mexican sisters in search of decent tortillas on Maui, sells hot-plate lunches (around $6), Mexican soda pop and other Latin grocery essentials.

Cheapskates will find ***Orowheat Bakery Thrift Store*** and ***Family Mart & Fast Food*** for fresh fish (raw, dried or fried) and thrifty Asian imports, both hidden on the same industrial loop. ***Safeway*** supermarket is on Kamehameha Ave, and there's a ***Foodland*** at Queen Kaahumanu Center, 275 Kaahumanu Ave. See Shopping, later, for Costco.

Budget ***Ba Le*** *(☎ 877-2400, Maui Marketplace, 270 Dairy Rd)* Most items $3-7. Open 8am-9pm daily. Good, inexpensive French-Vietnamese fare includes twenty kinds of vegetarian and meat sandwiches on French bread. You'll also find flaky croissants, tofu shrimp rolls, salads, plate lunches, Vietnamese pho soups and noodle dishes, with a rainbow of tapioca pudding flavors for dessert.

Aloha Grill *(☎ 893-0263, Maui Marketplace, 270 Dairy Rd)* Most items $6. Open 8am-9pm Mon-Sat, 8am-7pm Sun. This miniaturized '50s-style diner has just six bar stools and a single jukebox. What it lacks in size, it makes up for with lots of food choices. House specials include gourmet burgers and Kahului's largest vegetarian take-out menu. The soda fountain has banana splits and homemade chocolate, cherry and vanilla Cokes.

Maui Coffee Roasters (☎ *877-2877, 444 Hana Hwy*) Items $2-7. Open 7:30am-6pm Mon-Fri, 8am-5pm Sat, 9am-2:30pm Sun. Some say the coffee here is better than anywhere on the island, and java goes for just 50¢ a cup or $1 for a large mug. Locals also linger here for the scones, muffins and sandwiches, plus free newspapers and chess sets.

The Coffee Store (☎ *871-6860, Queen Kaahumanu Center, ground level*) Items $3-7, all-day breakfasts $5. Open from 7:30am daily. This little place also roasts its own coffee and offers tempting salads, sandwiches and quiches. Some come just for the pastries, like baklava or raspberry cheesecake.

The Queen Kaahumanu Center *food court* (*second level*) has a handful of fast-food ethnic eateries. *Maui Tacos* and *Maui's Mixed Plate* both have some appetizing dishes for around $6.

Wow-Wee Maui's Cafe & Oxygen Bar (☎ *871-1414, 333 Dairy Rd*) Most items $5-8. Open 5:30am-6pm daily. This eatery has loads of local hippie color. The bagels aren't cheap ($1.25 and up) and neither are the few deli items, but breathing stations deliver pure oxygen for only $1 per minute to patrons in need of a boost.

If you poke around the back roads of Kahului, there are countless hole-in-the-wall ethnic joints. *Ajiyoshi* (☎ *877-9080, 385 Ho'ohana St*) serves fresh sushi with sake and *Ono Kine* (☎ *873-0100, 180 W Wakea Ave*), whose Hawaiian pidgin name loosely translated means 'number-one stuff,' cooks up Filipino and local food.

Mid-Range *Kahului Ale House Sports Bar & Restaurant* (☎ *877-9001, 355 E Kamehameha Ave*) Pupu $5-10, mains $7-10. Open 11am-2pm daily. Muhammad Ali stares down from posters on the wall as you consume beer-battered shrimp, cheese fries, pork sandwiches or a bowl of Portuguese bean soup.

Brigit & Bernard's Garden Café (☎ *877-6000, 335 Ho'ohana St*) Lunch special $8, entrées $9-15. Open for lunch 10:30am-3pm Mon-Fri, dinner 5pm-9pm Wed-Fri. In a shady spot, this European caterer has a full bar with import beers and an outdoor garden. The menu weighs heavily with dishes like chicken cordon bleu and schnitzel burgers, but there are healthy-minded salads and seafood.

Cary & Eddie's Hideaway Restaurant & Bar (☎ *873-6555, 500 N Puunene Ave*) Lunch/brunch buffet $9-11, dinner buffet $16-21. Open 11am-2pm & 5pm-9:30pm Mon-Sat, 8am-9:30pm Sun. This oceanfront family restaurant and lounge is nothing fancy, but the local food is filling. Look for BBQ ribs, pork or the daily fresh fish, caught perhaps just outside Cary & Eddie's great harborside windows.

Mañana Garage (☎ *873-0220, 33 Lono Ave*) Lunch $7-13, dinner entrées $16-26. Since this Latin-flavored restaurant has been voted everyone's favorite spot, it's hard to get reservations. An impeccable menu lets your taste buds rove from Cuba and the Caribbean to South America, throwing together *picadillo* empanadas with tamarind-glazed salmon or guava chicken. On Amigo Mondays, all seafood dinners are $10 off regular price.

Entertainment

Kahului Ale House Sports Bar & Restaurant (☎ *877-9001, 355 E Kamehameha Ave*) Cover under $5. It's one of the only places to knock back a beer in Kahului, but things can get rowdy. Of course, the big-screen satellite TV, darts, pool tables and arcade games are all perks. Live music and DJs alternate with karaoke nights. Happy hour 2pm to 6pm daily.

Maui Arts & Cultural Center (*MACC;* ☎ *242-7469 box office,* **w** *www.mauiarts.org, 1 Cameron Way*) Off Kahului Beach Rd, MACC is the island's main venue for live theater, traditional Hawaiian music and hula performances, Maui Symphony concerts and big-name touring rock musicians. The Castle Theater shows foreign and independent films pretty much weekly.

The shopping mall cinemas **Consolidated Theatre Kaahumanu** (☎ 873-3137, Queen Kaahumanu Center) and **Wallace Theatres Maui Mall Megaplex** (☎ 249-2222, Maui Mall, 70 E Kaahumanu Ave) both show first-run movies for $7.50/4.25 per adult/child, albeit a bit delayed after mainland releases; bargain matinees (usually before 4pm) are $4.75.

Shopping

Kahului has the island's only major discount stores and everyday shopping malls. Did you just arrive on Maui? Stop long enough to stock up on groceries, anything you forgot to bring from home and new outdoor activity gear for sale or rent (see the Activities chapter).

Costco (☎ 877-5241, 540 Haleakala Hwy) This giant wholesale outlet is one of the best places to purchase food if there are enough of you to warrant the membership fee. It sells just about everything in bulk, from groceries to batteries, or anything else you might need at a steep discount. The quality is excellent. It has one-hour photo processing and sports gear. At the time of writing, it planned to open a gas station where it will sell gas probably 10¢ to 20¢ cheaper than anywhere else on the island (to members only). The annual membership costs $45.

Other discount stores include **Wal-Mart** (☎ 871-7820, 101 Pakaula St), **K-Mart** (☎ 871-8553, 424 Dairy Rd), and **Ross** (☎ 877-5483, 200 E Kamehameha Ave) for cheap aloha wear or cold-weather gear for trips to the Upcountry.

Maui Swap Meet (☎ 242-0240, Puunene Ave) Admission 50¢. Open 7am-noon Sat. For some local flavor and unique souvenirs, this gargantuan fairlike swap meet sets up just south of the post office.

The three major malls are all nearby:

Queen Kaahumanu Center (☎ 877-4325, 275 Kaahumanu Ave) This is Kahului's largest mall, with about 50 shops and department stores. There are free performances by the Old Lahaina Luau at 11:30am Tuesday and Saturday, and a farmers market on Friday. Local ventures include **Camellias Seeds** for traditional dried fruit and candy, **Maui Hands** art gallery and **Sew Special** (☎ 877-6128) for Hawaiian quilting classes and bolts of aloha print material.

Maui Marketplace (☎ 873-0400, 270 Dairy Rd) At Maui's newest mall you'll find **Office Max** for cheap photocopies, **Borders Books & Music Café**, camping and outdoor gear at **The Sports Authority** and **Hawaii Liquor Superstore**.

Maui Mall (☎ 877-7559, 70 E Kaahumanu Ave) Anchored by **Longs Drugs**, this mall is strangely empty. **Tasaka Guri Guri** is famous islandwide for its homemade sweets and exotic sherbets (2 scoops cost just $1). The **Paper Airplane Museum** is really just a shop with over 2500 paper airplane kits, but also a few photo displays on Hawaiian aviation and military history.

Discount Fabric Warehouse (☎ 873-7454, 444 Hana Hwy) and **Fabric Mart** (☎ 871-5770, 55 Kaahumanu Ave) These are two more places to pick up aloha fabric for perking up your vacation rental. The Fabric Mart is inside historic Old Kahului Store, dating from 1916.

HALEKII-PIHANA HEIAU STATE MONUMENT

After the decisive battle of Iao in 1790, Kamehameha I came to these heiau to worship his war god Ku and offered what is thought to have been the last human sacrifice on Maui. Kahekili, the last ruling chief of Maui, lived here prior to his defeat, and the priestess Keopuolani, later the wife of Kamehameha I and the mother of Kamehameha II and III, was born here.

The two adjoining heiau sit atop a knoll and have a commanding view of the entire region, clear across the plains of Central Maui out to sea and up the slopes of Haleakala volcano. The temples were built with stones carried up from Iao Stream.

The first heiau, Halekii (literally 'House of the Images'), has stepped stone walls and a flat grassy top. Watch out for bullhead thorns if you're wearing rubbah slippah. Kii (deity images) used to sit atop these terraces covered by a grass structure. Individual Hawaiian families built their own heiau nearby for making offerings.

Heiau

Visiting the sites of heiau, or temples, of ancient Hawaii can be an odd experience, by turns disappointing, puzzling and overwhelming. First you have to imagine what mostly isn't there anymore. In the early 19th century after the *kapu* system was broken by Queen Kaahumanu, almost all of the heiau in Hawaii were looted, hacked and burned to the ground.

Previously heiau had been erected using lava or limestone rock and came in two basic styles. One was a more substantial structure of high-terraced platforms. A second kind was a simple rectangular enclosure of stone walls, probably introduced later for *luakini,* or temples of human sacrifice. Theoretically, both styles were at times constructed via human chains up to 20 miles long that hauled rocks hand over head up to the chosen site.

Heiau were built in auspicious places, often perched on cliffs above the coast or in other places thought to have *mana,* or 'spiritual power.' A heiau's significance lay not in the structure itself, but in the mana of the site. When a heiau's mana was gone, it was abandoned. Of course, conquering ali'i (chiefs) could sometimes consecrate new heiau upon the ruins of the old in a potent symbolic gesture, thereby restoring the mana of the site.

Atop or inside the heiau boundaries were *hale,* traditional structures made of native ohia wood and thatched with pili grass. Some of these were used as drumming houses or places for *tele* (altars). Around the *anuu* (oracle towers) were placed carved wood *kii* (deity images), a word whose roots are in *tiki,* meaning 'first image' in the early Polynesian language.

Surprisingly the luakini, which were dedicated to the bloody war god Ku, were far less common than those reserved for Lono, the god of fertility and peace. The latter were used for birthing, everyday rituals of prayer, food distribution and the healing arts. Besides heiau, a whole range of religious sites were worshipped, from *ko'a* (fishing shrines) to weathered stones thought to have special healing properties, like the Hauola Stone in Lahaina or the phallic rock above Kalaupapa on Molokai.

Today there is not much left of any of them. Most heiau look like nothing more than a pile of stones, many overgrown with jungle vegetation and fairly precipitous to walk upon (which, by the way, is disrespectful, not to mention intensely hot, because the lava reflects the sun's rays straight upward onto your face). When you visit a heiau, the fine for taking stones or otherwise altering the site is $10,000. Offerings of coins, candles, incense or fruit also damage the integrity of the structure. Recently some heiau have been adopted by community groups for restoration. The best example on Maui – in fact, the largest extant heiau in all of Hawaii – is Piilanihale Heiau near Hana.

The pyramid-like mound of Pihana Heiau is directly ahead. Pihana, which means 'gathering place of supernatural beings,' is fairly overgrown with thorny kiawe, wildflowers and weeds. Few people come this way, and birds fly up from the bushes as you approach. Much larger than Halekii, this *luakini* (temple for human sacrifice) was dedicated to Ku and reserved for worship by royal *ali'i* (chiefs).

Despite the state monument status, the government has been negligent in protecting the heiau. The area is one of the fastest-growing residential areas on Maui, and construction and gravel removal along both sides of the hill have been widespread. Conservationists are ensuring that plants grow wild in order to stabilize the lava rock and prevent the ancient heiau from being undermined.

Even though the temples don't look like much, a sense of *mana* (spiritual power) still emanates from the site. To imagine it all through the eyes of the Hawaiians 200 years ago, ignore the industrial warehouses and tract homes and concentrate instead on the heiau and wild ocean vistas. It must have been an incredible scene.

To get there from Waiehu Beach Rd, turn inland onto Kuhio Pl, three-quarters of a mile south of the intersection of Hwys 340 and 330 near the 3-mile marker, then hang a left onto Hea Place and drive up through the gates. The heiau are less than half a mile from Hwy 340.

WAILUKU

Sitting beneath the eastern flank of the West Maui Mountains, Wailuku has long been a center of religious and political power in ancient Hawaii. Kahekili, Maui's last ruling chief, built his royal palace at the entrance to Iao Valley where today, at the intersection of Main & High Sts, the Kaahumanu Church and government offices are found. One translation of Wailuku is 'waters of slaughter,' after the bloody battles that took place in the Iao Valley, while others translate it as 'destroying waters,' referring to frequent flooding of nearby freshwater rivers.

Wailuku is unabashedly local – there's nothing touristy in the whole town. It is an arresting juxtaposition of old and new; the central area serves as the county seat, while old-fashioned backstreets show a colorful hodgepodge of curio shops and neighborhood restaurants. The charm of Wailuku is that here it's easy to sense the aloha of everyday life that existed all over Hawaii before WWII and the tourist boom of the '60s and '70s changed everything.

The photographic history book *Exploring Historic Wailuku* by George Engebretson brings alive the past by gathering together oral history from residents of old Wailuku. This soft-cover book, which is being developed into an audiotape walking tour, is sold at the Bailey House Museum.

Orientation & Information

Traffic from Kahului crawls along Kaahumanu Ave west into Wailuku town, where the road turns into W Main St. N Market St, just one of downtown's many one-way roads, is crowded with parking spots, but there's also a free municipal parking lot just off the intersection with Vineyard St.

Maui Visitors Bureau (see Tourist Offices in the Facts for the Visitor chapter) is near the main Wailuku post office (☎ 244-1653), 250 Imi Kala St, which is open 8:30am to 5pm weekdays, 9am to noon Saturday.

Travelers avail themselves of free Internet terminals at the hostels. Hale Imua Internet Café (☎ 242-1896) at the Dragon Arts Center charges 20¢ per minute or $8 per hour for high-speed access. Café Marc Aurel (see Places to Eat, later) has one Internet terminal costing $1 per 10 minutes.

Paperback Plus (☎ 242-7135, 1977 Main St) has bargain books for beach reading. The Wailuku public library, 251 High St, is open 10am to 8pm Monday and Thursday, 10am to 5pm Tuesday, Wednesday and Friday.

For outpatient-clinic services, try Maui Medical Group (☎ 249-8080, 2180 Main St) next to Valley Isle Pharmacy. Also, see Kahului, earlier, for information on Maui Memorial Hospital.

Bailey House Museum

Bailey House, a five-minute walk up West Main St from Kaahumanu Church, was home to the family of missionary Edward Bailey, who came to Hawaii from Boston. Nearby stood Wailuku Female Seminary, where Hawaiian girls were schooled by the missionaries in Western ways.

Built on the site of an earlier royal compound belonging to Chief Kahekili, the home is now the headquarters of the Maui Historical Society. The organization curates a worthwhile little museum (☎ 244-3326, W www.mauimuseum.org, 2375A Main St; adult/child $5/1; open 10am-4pm Mon-Sat). A highlight is the lovingly restored surfboard used by Olympian Duke Kahanamoku; it's above the parking lot at the side of the shed. Compare it to today's sleek fiberglass boards – this 6-footer is made of redwood and weighs in at a hefty 150lb!

Edward Bailey himself was a painter and engraver, and many of his works are on display alongside period furniture from the missionary days. There's also a Hawaiian section with stone adzes, *tapa* (bark cloth), bottle gourds, calabashes and artifacts from

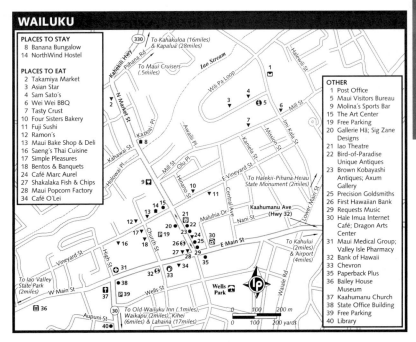

WAILUKU

PLACES TO STAY
8 Banana Bungalow
14 NorthWind Hostel

PLACES TO EAT
2 Takamiya Market
3 Asian Star
4 Sam Sato's
6 Wei Wei BBQ
7 Tasty Crust
10 Four Sisters Bakery
11 Fuji Sushi
12 Ramon's
13 Maui Bake Shop & Deli
16 Saeng's Thai Cuisine
17 Simple Pleasures
18 Bentos & Banquets
24 Café Marc Aurel
27 Shakalaka Fish & Chips
28 Maui Popcorn Factory
34 Café O'Lei

OTHER
1 Post Office
5 Maui Visitors Bureau
9 Molina's Sports Bar
15 The Art Center
19 Free Parking
20 Gallerie Hã; Sig Zane Designs
21 Iao Theatre
22 Bird-of-Paradise Unique Antiques
23 Brown Kobayashi Antiques; Axum Gallery
25 Precision Goldsmiths
26 First Hawaiian Bank
29 Requests Music
30 Hale Imua Internet Café; Dragon Arts Center
31 Maui Medical Group; Valley Isle Pharmacy
32 Bank of Hawaii
33 Chevron
35 Paperback Plus
36 Bailey House Museum
37 Kaahumanu Church
38 State Office Building
39 Free Parking
40 Library

Kahoolawe, as well as the only wooden temple image ever found on Maui. On the 2nd floor of the museum, look carefully for the Western-style top hat crowned with a pheasant feather lei once worn by Sam Kalama, the Maui county superintendent who made possible the construction of the Hana and Haleakala Hwys.

The downstairs **gift shop** has quality crafts and Hawaiiana books for sale. For docent-led tours and special programs, anything from slack-key guitar concerts to Hawaiian herbalism field trips, call ahead to make reservations. These events are usually free.

Kaahumanu Church

Kaahumanu Church, on the corner of W Main and High Sts, was first established in 1832, making it the oldest Congregational church on Maui. The present building, erected in 1876 by missionary Edward Bailey and built over the site of an old

heiau, is on the National Register of Historic Places.

The church was named in honor of Queen Kaahumanu, who cast aside the old gods and burned temple idols, allowing Christianity to flourish. She visited Wailuku in 1832 and in her ever-humble manner requested that the first church bear her name.

The old clock in the steeple was brought around the Horn in the 19th century, and it still keeps accurate time. Hymns are still sung in Hawaiian at Sunday morning services, and there's an old Hawaiian cemetery next door.

Places to Stay

Wailuku has two of the three hostels on Maui, as well as an elegant old-fashioned 1920s inn.

Budget *NorthWind Hostel* (☎/fax 242-1448, ☎ 866-946-7835, w *www.northwind hostel.com, 2080 Vineyard St)* Dorm beds

$16, singles/doubles with shared bath $29/38. In a funky old building with international flags draped from the balcony, the NorthWind Hostel is central. It's certainly not fancy, and be aware that the management changes hands frequently. There is a kitchen, TV and free Internet access. For a fee, guests can use a secure storage area, borrow bicycles and 'Road to Hana' cassette-tape tours. Accommodations on the seventh night are free.

Banana Bungalow (☎ 244-5090, 800-746-7835, ☎/fax 244-3678, W www.mauihostel .com, 310 N Market St) Dorm beds/private rooms with shared bath from $17.50/32. Younger shoestring travelers are happy enough here, considering that Internet access, daily island tours, backyard Jacuzzi and hammocks are all free. Still there's plenty not to love, from cramped dormitories to dank private rooms with sagging mattresses, and lots of creepy critters. Common amenities include a TV room, group kitchen, coin laundry and a shed for storing windsurfing gear, and there is a free airport shuttle once a day. Weekly discounts are available.

If you end up stranded, *Molina's Sports Bar* (see Entertainment, later) has utilitarian rooms out back that are rented by the day, week or month. Wailuku also has more than its fair share of down-and-out boarding houses, albeit with tropical style.

Top End *Old Wailuku Inn* (☎ 244-5897, 800-305-4899, fax 242-9600, W www.mauiinn.com, 2199 Kahookele St) Rooms $120-180. This elegant 1920s home was a wedding gift from a wealthy banker to his new daughter-in-law. Shaded by trees and very private, this regal building has been beautifully restored by two island-born innkeepers and filled with bamboo furniture, artwork and antiques. All of the beds have traditional Hawaiian quilts, while the Bird of Paradise room has eucalyptus floors and the Ilima room its own whirlpool tub.

Places to Eat

Within a few minutes' walk from the intersection of Vineyard and N Market Sts, you can sample Thai, Japanese, Mexican and just plain local Hawaiian food, all at reasonable prices.

Take-Out Food *Takamiya Market* (☎ 244-3404, 359 N Market St) Open 6am-6pm daily. This market stocks hard-to-find specialty soda pops in old-fashioned glass bottles and ethnic picnic foods. If you're in the mood for a snack, *Maui Popcorn Factory* (☎ 242-9888, 21 N Market St) sells snacks and bags of fresh caramel corn for the price of peanuts.

Which family-run bakery is the best? *Maui Bake Shop & Deli* (☎ 242-0064, 2092 Vineyard St) has the advantage of being the most central. It also has the largest selection of baked goods, including elaborate French pastries. Yet you can't beat the prices at *Four Sisters Bakery* (☎ 244-9333, 1968 E Vineyard St), where everything is oh so ooey-gooey. Meanwhile *Sam Sato's* (☎ 244-7124, 1750 Wili Pa Loop) makes such famous *monja* (Japanese custard cakes) that even visitors from Honolulu rave about them. It's open 7am to 2pm from Monday to Saturday.

Budget *Café Marc Aurel* (☎ 244-0852, 28 N Market St) Items under $5. Open 7am-6pm Mon-Fri, 7am-1pm Sat & Sun. Vintage coffee burlap bags cover the seats and black-and-white diamond tiles cover the floor, while up front the display case is stuffed with homemade bon-bons, fruit scones, sandwiches and slices of quiche. Sip a very rich mocha or cappuccino on streetside tables with high-backed stools, where regulars look over the newspapers and watch their neighbors pass by.

There are plenty of weekday lunch deals available, since this is Maui's business and government center. On the other hand this means that on the weekend many restaurants either close or open only for dinner.

Saeng's Thai Cuisine (☎ 244-1567, 2119 Vineyard St) Lunch specials $7, mains $9-12.50. Open lunch 11am-2:30pm Mon-Fri, dinner 5pm-9:30pm daily. Alluring Saeng's offers open-air dining and a wide range of Thai food, including excellent curries, traditional savory salads and at least a dozen vegetarian dishes. Best of all, they don't water down the spices, and the high roof beams look almost like teak, making you think of Chiang Mai. Open-air tables on raised platforms look out upon a small garden with a fountain.

Simple Pleasures (☎ 249-0697, 2103 Vineyard St) Open Tues-Sat 11am-3pm. When things aren't busy, they don't offer the full menu, but whatever the friendly gourmets at this basic vegetarian café do have on hand will be delicious. Savor the Indian curries, Swedish soups and desserts, perhaps coconut haupia pie or lilikoi-lemon tart. Except for some local artwork, however, the atmosphere is bare.

Bentos & Banquets (☎ 244-1124, 85 N Church St) Lunch specials $6-8. Open 10am-2pm Mon-Fri. Local businesspeople and government employees favor this busy catering outlet. The menu of local food changes daily, although a few dishes such as pork adobo or teriyaki beef are standard. If you can't get a seat (yes, they are that popular), try takeout.

Fuji Sushi (☎ 244-2399, 1951 E Vineyard St) Meal combos under $8. Open 11am-1pm & 5pm-8:30pm Mon-Sat. Tucked down a side street, this tiny sushi bar also makes steaming bowls of udon noodles and a healthy number of other dishes that feature unagi (eel).

On Main Street, quick cheap eats include **Shakalaka Fish & Chips** (☎ 986-0855, 2010 Main St), which has fried fish meals under $7 and guava cheesecake, or **Café O'Lei** (☎ 244-6816, 2051 Main St) for gourmet local plate lunches (with some interesting perks, say crab), pasta or salads, each under $8.

Heading east toward the post office and the industrial loop are a few places worth going out of your way for.

Tasty Crust (☎ 244-0845, 1770 Mill St) Open 5:30am-10pm Mon-Fri, 5:30am-11pm Sat & Sun. Bad coffee, good diner. Famous homemade hotcakes have been served here since 1944.

Wei Wei BBQ (☎ 242-7928, Millyard Plaza, 210 Imi Kala St) Most dishes & combos $5-8. Open 7:30am-9pm daily. A be-

wildering number of Chinese, Japanese and multi-ethnic fast food crowds the menu at Wei Wei, but we mean that in a good way, and it's all cheap. Naturally, the BBQ pork is the thing that locals most favor.

Asian Star (☎ 244-1833, 1764 Wili Pa Loop) Dishes $6-12. Open 10am-10pm Mon-Sat, 10am-9pm Sun. Without a doubt, this place wins the prize for superb Vietnamese food on Maui. True, there is about zero ambience here, but good-humored servers and tantalizing dishes more than make up for it. The menu of Vietnamese classics is extensive, anything from vegetarian pho noodle soup to banh hoi, a Vietnamese version of rice-paper fajitas, with a plate of mint leaves, rice noodles, assorted vegetables and shrimp or tofu.

Mid-Range Ramon's (☎ 244-7243, 2101 W Vineyard St) Combination platters $13-20. Open 10am-9pm Mon-Fri, 10am-10pm Sat & Sun. Mexican Ramon's is Wailuku's most expensive restaurant, and yet it still feels like eating at your mother's house. Portions are huge, perhaps to compensate for unexpectedly high prices, and the seafood enchiladas tasty.

Entertainment

Iao Theatre (☎ 242-6969, N Market St) Built in 1928, the landmark Iao Theatre has been restored after years of neglect for use by local theater groups. It's pleasantly casual, and cross breezes keep it cool and comfortable inside. Don't get too excited, though, since most of the productions are recycled musicals – Rocky Horror was playing when we were in town.

Molina's Sports Bar (☎ 244-4100, 197 N Market St) Molina's, midway between the two hostels, often has DJ or live-music nights with $2 drinks. Overall it's the kind of place where you can kick back, watch the game on satellite TV and not feel funny about spilling your beer on the floor.

Shopping

Wailuku is an ideal place for lazily wandering around. Begin walking on N Market St, which has a handful of pawnshops, galleries and antique shops, some of them intriguingly cluttered affairs stocking a mishmash of Hawaiiana items, Asian handicrafts and lots of odds and ends. Don't forget the Bailey House Museum gift shop, either (see Bailey House Museum, earlier).

Bird-of-Paradise Unique Antiques *(☎ 242-7699, 56 N Market St)* Bird of Paradise has it all: old cruise-liner memorabilia, Depression glass, kimonos and vintage California ware.

Brown Kobayashi Antiques *(☎ 242-0804, 60A N Market St)* This elegant antique shop has koa wood furnishings, Japanese tansu chests and painted Chinese cabinets, among other gems.

Dragon Arts Center *(1980 Main St)* A newly restored landmark near N Market St, the Dragon Arts Center houses a few art galleries and import shops. Truly alternative ***Wild Banana Gallery*** *(☎ 242-4943)* represents emerging visual artists and keeps stacks of free local publications on hand.

Other galleries with rotating exhibitions of works by Hawaiian and mainland artists include ***Axum Gallery*** *(☎ 244-1900, 40 N Market St)*, ***Gallerie Hā*** *(☎ 244-3993, 51 N Market St)* and ***The Art Center*** *(☎ 243-0027, 2070 Vineyard St)*, which is managed by a local watercolor painter.

Sig Zane Designs *(☎ 249-8997, 53 N Market St)* Sig Zane's aloha-print clothing from the Big Island is handmade and beautiful to behold (but pricey).

Precision Goldsmiths *(☎ 986-8282, 26 N Market St)* This award-winning custom jewelry store has a myriad of island-born settings and stones.

Requests Music *(☎ 244-9315, 10 N Market St)* Open 10am-6pm Mon-Sat. Maui's best and biggest range of cheap used CDs is sold here.

IAO VALLEY ROAD

In 1790, as part of his plan to conquer and unite all of the Hawaiian Islands, Kamehameha I attacked Kahului village by sea and quickly chased the defending Maui warriors up into precipitous Iao Valley. Those unable to escape over the mountains were slaughtered along the stream. The waters of Iao Stream were so choked with bodies that the area was called Kepaniwai, meaning 'Damming of the Waters.'

Today the area is choked with tourists. Iao Stream is still the largest of the *Na Wai Eha*, or 'four traditional waters,' which flow from the West Maui Mountains down onto the central plains. The quick Iao Valley Road conducts tsunami waves of visitors each day into Iao Valley State Park, which encompasses much of the upper valley along the stream, passing just a few minor sights along the way.

If you're looking for a botany lesson, try **Tropical Gardens of Maui** *(☎ 244-3085; admission $3, children under 12 free; open 9am-4:30pm Mon-Sat)*. It's less than a mile up Iao Valley Rd from Wailuku. Interpretive plaques identify many of the varied flora species displayed here. Even though it's a relatively new garden, the plantings have matured enough in the past few years to make this a worthwhile stop, if you haven't visited any other botanical gardens Upcountry yet.

Another mile up the road is **Kepaniwai Heritage Gardens County Park**, supposedly dedicated to Hawaii's varied ethnic heritage. Iao Stream runs through the park, but the picnic shelters and BBQ pits are rusty. Around the run-down grounds stands a traditional Hawaiian *hale* (house) with a roof made of *pili* grass, and a New England missionary home. The Asian gardens, which harbor stone pagodas, a carp pond and a Chinese pavilion, are nearby. A bronze statue of two Japanese sugarcane workers commemorates the 1985 centennial of Japanese immigration to Hawaii.

At the western edge of the park is **Hawai'i Nature Center** *(☎ 244-6500, 875 Iao Valley Rd; adult/child $6/3.25; open 10am-4pm daily)*. This excellent nonprofit educational facility designed for kids has over two dozen exhibits, some interactive, that identify local birds, explain native stream life and the like. Pick up adult-oriented field guides, natural history books and maps in the gift shop. Short guided walks through the nearby rain forest cost $25; reservations are required.

At a bend in the road about half a mile after Kepaniwai County Park, you'll likely see a few cars pulled over and their occupants staring off into Pali Eleele gorge on the right. One of the rock formations shows a vague **profile** that erosion is continuing to shape. Some locals associate the profile with a powerful *kahuna* (priest) who lived here during the 1500s, while others think it bears an uncanny resemblance to President John F Kennedy's profile. Both stories are a bit suspicious. If parking is difficult here, just continue on to Iao Valley State Park, as it's only a couple of minutes' walk from there back to the profile viewing site.

Iao Valley State Park

Nestled in the mountains, and only three miles out of central Wailuku, lies Iao Valley State Park *(admission free; open 7am-7pm daily)*. The valley itself extends all the way to 5788-foot Puu Kukui, West Maui's highest – and wettest – point.

Legend has it that the valley is named for Iao, the beautiful daughter of Maui. **Iao Needle**, a rock pinnacle that rises 1200 feet from the valley floor, is said to be Iao's clandestine warrior lover, found by Maui and turned to stone. Interestingly, the pinnacle was used by warriors as a lookout during the centuries when heiau and taro patches

The Makahiki

All of the Iao Valley, which is perhaps best known for its bloody war history, was once strewn with heiau.

Each year for four months, all fighting ceased here while Hawaiians remembered the god Lono with a harvest festival, called the *makahiki*. Celebrations began in late autumn with the rising *(hiki)* of the Pleiades constellation *(maka)*, the sun's northward turn signaling the sprouting season for plants and the spawning of fish. Lono, the god of fertility and peace, was thought to reign over the skies until February, when he returned to Tahiti and the war god Ku took over in his manifestation as the gods of farming and abundant seas.

Life didn't get much better than during the makahiki. For the first four days of the festival anything but rest and relaxation was strictly *kapu*, and then all work, apart from that which was still necessary for survival, was forbidden until the end of January. Interisland athletic competitions similar to the Olympics were held, including outrigger canoe races, fishing and surfing tournaments, foot races, wrestling matches and *holua* (sled) racing contests. *Ali'i* (chiefs) debated each other in tests of logic while plentiful food was distributed among the people.

Quite a party, wasn't it? Except for one thing: *hookupu* (taxes). Before any of the games or festivities could begin, taxes were collected. A cross-shaped pole over 12 feet high was tied with billowing clouds of tapa (pounded bark cloth) and royal feathers. This *akua loa,* or representation of the god, was carried in slow procession around the islands while people came out to give 'Father Lono' a share of the first fruits of the harvest and gourds filled with poi or *awa,* and anything else required as tribute-tax by the ali'i. Some were offered to Lono in his pig-god manifestation on altars made of kukui, whose leaves were thought to look decidedly snoutish. Even today Hawaii's unofficial state fish is the *humuhumunukunukuapuaa,* or snout-faced triggerfish.

Some Hawaiians say they can still hear the drumbeats and sight royal processions of ghosts on sites where the makahiki was once celebrated. Starting in the 1980s a few native Hawaiian groups revived the makahiki as a way of bringing about cultural renewal, but most of these ceremonies are closed to outsiders – one event that is open to all is Ka Molokai Makahiki (see Special Events in the Facts for the Visitor chapter). Among the first was the Protect Kahoolawe movement, which still prays each year for Lono to raise the water table of that devastated island and 'green Kahoolawe in our lifetime.'

filled the valley (later plantation owners used the same irrigation ditches and fertile soil to grow sugarcane).

Clouds often rise up the valley, forming a shroud around the top of Iao Needle. Wild ginger and guava trees are all around. A stream meanders beneath the needle, and the steep cliffs of the West Maui Mountains make an impressive backdrop. That's why all the tour buses stop here!

A two-minute walk from the parking lot, you'll reach a bridge where most people stop to photograph Iao Needle. However, just before the bridge, the walkway that loops downhill by the stream leads to the nicest photo angle – one that captures the stream, bridge and Iao Needle together. There are some swimming holes along the streambed.

Over the bridge, a short paved walkway leads up to a sheltered lookout with another fine view of Iao Needle. The whole jaunt will take only about five minutes and will leave most people itching to go farther past the 'No Trespassing' signs.

PUUNENE

Puunene is a working plantation village surrounded by sugarcane fields. Puunene's main attraction is the sugar museum opposite the mill.

Run by the Hawaiian Commercial & Sugar (C&S) Company, the sugar mill is the last of its kind still in operation on Maui. Usually the air hangs heavy with the strange, but sweet smell of sugar. When fields are burned off during harvest, the Puunene area can get clogged with smoke. The power plant next to the mill burns residue sugarcane fibers (called bagasse) to run the mill machinery that extracts and refines the sugar. With a capacity of 37,000 kilowatts, it's one of the world's largest biomass power plants. Excess electricity is sold to Maui Electric.

Information

The Puunene post office (☎ 871-1352), Hansen Rd at Helm St, is open 8am to noon and 1pm to 4:30pm weekdays.

The '10¢ Bookstore' (☎ 871-6563;), operated by the Friends of Maui Library, has stacks of used volumes on all imaginable subjects that cost only a dime each, hardback or softcover. The bookstore can be a little tricky to find, however; head south down S Puunene Ave, take a left onto Camp Rd 5 and follow the 'Books' arrow signs past the school. It is open 8am to 4pm Monday to Saturday.

Alexander & Baldwin Sugar Museum

Housed in the former mill superintendent's house, this worthwhile little museum (☎ 871-8058, Cnr Puunene Ave & Hansen Rd; adult/child 6-17 years $5/2; open 9:30am-4:30pm daily, closed Sun off-season) tells the history of sugar in Hawaii.

The curator, Gaylord Kubota, is an avid photographer and local historian who has worked hard to restore the old machinery outside in the gardens, including a cane hauler, ditch trencher, two tractors and a hand ice-shaver. Inside, museum displays, which explain how sugarcane grows and is harvested, include an elaborate working scale model of a cane-crushing plant mill.

Most interesting, however, are the images of people. The museum traces how Samuel Alexander and Henry P Baldwin gobbled up vast chunks of Hawaiian land, how they fought tooth and nail with an ambitious Claus Speckles to gain access to Upcountry water, and how they dug the extensive irrigation systems that made large-scale sugarcane plantations a possibility on Maui.

The two partners were typical of their generation. As many sons of Hawaii's first missionaries did, they went into business and agriculture instead of the ministry. They bought their first fields near Haiku in 1869 and, after mutual friends curried favor with King David Kalakaua, they quickly received permission to construct a groundbreaking irrigation ditch. When work on the ditch hit solid rock, Henry Baldwin, who had previously lost his right arm in a mill accident, impressed his employees by clambering down a 200-foot cliff without any

Sticky & Sweet

Driving through the corporate sugar fields of Central Maui, it's hard to realize that it was the Polynesians who first planted and harvested sugarcane on Maui. Although they didn't refine it (that had to wait until the 19th century), these ancient Hawaiians did chew its sweet stalks. Visitors today can still buy bags of cut-up cane along the roadside or at neighborhood stores.

In the past century it required about one ton of precious water to produce one pound of sugar, but that ratio is now 1:1 thanks to a new type of drip irrigation. Sugarcane plants take two years to grow to maturity and grow up to 30 feet high, eventually falling over under their own weight at harvest time. The fields are burned to rid them of useless dried grasses and leaves, leaving the cane stalks with their high moisture content unharmed. The water that does evaporate from the stalks condenses their sugar content, speeding up the time needed to refine it later.

The back-breaking labor of harvesting cane by hand and machete has long been replaced with rakes, cranes and rail machinery in Hawaii. The last sugar refining mill on Maui, which is also the only one remaining in the US, does not use the more common method of squeezing the sugarcane with rollers but instead flushes juice out of the shredded sugarcane in a process resembling that of a drip coffeemaker. Each acre of raw sugarcane can produce 12 tons of sugar once refined.

A few weeks after harvesting, the sugar plants send out new shoots (called ratoons) from the rich volcanic soil, and the cycle starts over again – at least for the time being, until sugar becomes an even less profitable crop, and all of the island's beautiful cane fields are sold for golf resorts and condo developments.

help. After that, it was all downhill, so to speak, and the ditch was completed in less than a decade.

Representing the other end of the scale is a turn-of-the-19th-century labor contract from the Japanese Emigration Company stating that the laborer shall be paid $15 a month for working 10 hours a day in the field, 26 days a month (minus $2.50 banked for return passage to Japan). Wives worked the same hours and got only $10. Other illuminating period photos and artifacts of plantation camp life are also on display.

WAIKAPU

The Honoapiilani Hwy (Hwy 30), which runs along the east side of the West Maui Mountains, passes through the town of Waikapu just a couple of miles south of Wailuku. Waikapu remains quite rural, despite the new golf course above its pineapple fields, and an old-fashioned general store stands at the crossroads.

Waikapu's only sight is **Maui Tropical Plantation & Country Store** (☎ 244-7643, *1670 Honoapiilani Hwy; open 9am-5pm daily, tours 10am-4pm)*. Kids might be entertained by the touristy narrated **tram ride** *(adult/child $9.50/3.50)* past fields of sugarcane, pineapple and tropical fruit trees. Past the shop selling fresh fruit, there's a free section that includes a nursery, a few taro plants and a couple of very simple exhibits on agriculture. Two caged monkeys from the defunct Maui Zoo are a sad sight, even for the thick-skinned among us.

KEALIA POND

Kealia Pond National Wildlife Refuge *(☎ 875-1582, Milepost 6, Mokulele Hwy;*

open 8am-4:30pm) is a saltwater marsh and bird sanctuary. From the side of the road, you can usually spot Hawaiian stilts, an endangered species, wading in the water. The pond is also a habitat for the Hawaiian coot, ducks, egrets and black-crowned night herons.

Other migratory birds make their appearance here, including *kolea* (Pacific golden plovers), which fly at least 2500 miles from Alaska to Hawaii every winter; some travel even as far as the South Pacific Islands, such as Samoa. You'll see them mostly between December and February. This is the best time for viewing a mix of native and non-native species.

In summer the pond water levels recede, resulting in brackish salty water (Kealia means 'salt-encrusted place' in Hawaiian), perfect for native species who nest nearby to teach their young to feed on exposed fish and invertebrates in the mud. However, non-native plant species are always threatening to choke the open waters, and food is scarce due to competition from invasive avian species. The cattle egret, originally brought from Florida to control ranch insects, is now the species that is most out of control.

The ancient Hawaiians used this area as a fishpond. The wildlife refuge extends across the highway out to the ocean shore, where it is planned to make an elevated boardwalk with interpretive kiosks.

MAALAEA BAY

Maalaea Bay runs along the south side of the isthmus that connects the West Maui Mountains with Haleakala. Prevailing winds from the north, which funnel between the mountains straight out toward Kahoolawe, create strong midday gusts.

In fact, Maalaea has the strongest winds on the island and in winter, when the wind dies down elsewhere, windsurfers still fly along in Maalaea Bay. The bay also has a couple of hot surfing spots. The **Maalaea Pipeline**, south of the harbor, freight-trains right and is the fastest break in Hawaii. Summer's southerly swells produce huge tubes.

Maalaea Bay is fronted by a continuous 3-mile stretch of sandy beach that runs from Maalaea Harbor south to Kihei Wharf. Unfortunately, theft and car break-ins are a persistent problem, so there are better beaches (and condos) to be found in Kihei (see the South Maui chapter).

For travel by bus to Maalaea Bay, see the Getting Around chapter. See the Hiking special section at the end of the Activities chapter for details of the nearby Lahaina Pali trail into the West Maui Mountains.

Maui Ocean Center

At Maalaea Harbor, this state-of-the-art facility *(☎ 270-7000, W www.mauioceancenter .com, 192 Maalaea Rd; adult/child 3-12 years $18.99/12.99; open 9am-5pm daily)* holds the largest tropical reef aquarium in the US. Some 60 self-paced exhibits of indigenous Hawaiian marine life spread over three acres, proceeding from creatures of the shallowest intertidal waters out into deep ocean life. You could spend hours just listening to all the hand-held audio guide has to say, while trained ocean naturalists wander through periodically and give on-the-spot educational talks.

The extensive 'Living Reef' section focuses on the myriad types of coral and fish you may see while snorkeling or diving in Hawaiian waters. Interpretive displays explain reef formations and identify butterfly fish, wrasses and eels. Don't miss the tank full of eerily glowing jellyfish.

The Open Ocean tank, which holds 750,000 gallons of seawater, has a walk-through acrylic tunnel where schools of fish and meandering sharks swim overhead. It's as close as you can get to being underwater without donning dive gear. Elsewhere there are interactive whale displays, outdoor tanks that harbor sea turtles and stingrays, and a small tidal touch pool.

Places to Eat

Maui Ocean Center has its own restaurant and fast-food cart, but there are equally scenic and more reasonably priced restaurants in the adjacent Ma'alaea Harbor Village shopping center.

Café O'Lei's Maalaea Grill *(☎ 243-2206, 300 Maalaea Rd)* Lunch $6-9, dinner entrées $13-18. Open 10:30am-9pm Tues-Sun. Fresh sea breezes waft through the harborfront windows and everything feels so very tropical, what with the bamboo wood furniture and cream-colored tablecloths. All in all quite a step up for this Wailuku-based caterer, but it's good to see they've brought sensible prices along with them. Fresh seafood and produce dominate the menu.

Capische *(☎ 243-9001, 300 Maalaea Rd)* Entrées $16-25. Open 5pm-10pm daily. Another newcomer is this intimate Italian seafood joint run by some of Maui's top restaurateurs. Recent menu creations have won prizes at the Taste of Lahaina festival, and on Sunday nights there are light opera performances. If you're in the mood for oven-fired pizza, kiawe-grilled Portobello mushrooms in Chianti wine sauce with herbed goat cheese, or calamari and a range of fresh fish and pastas, look no farther.

West Maui

West Maui is built on the smaller of the island's two volcanoes, but today it snares the lion's share of tourists. The region encompasses a large oval of land, from Kahului west to the coast and from Honokohau Bay south to Papawai Point. Behind it all, the dramatic West Maui Mountains dominate the landscape with cliffs casting long shadows over pineapple fields.

To many people, West Maui conjures up images of the heavily urbanized strip running between Lahaina and the coastal beach resorts from Kaanapali to Kapalua. In Lahaina town there is almost no escaping the crowds of honeymooners and cruise-ship passengers, but nevertheless, a few rustic 19th-century buildings and historic sites have survived the onslaught. Lahaina also has over half of the island's nightlife and a variety of restaurants.

Heading north on the Honoapiilani Hwy (Hwy 30) you can leave behind Lahaina's notorious humidity, bypassing a string of beach parks, condos and hotels all the way to the northern tip.

First come the Kaanapali resorts, with their beachfront bars, shopping center and the tiny jewel of a whaling museum. You'll find great snorkeling around Puu Kekaa, where ancient Hawaiians believed souls leapt into the afterlife. At Honokowai, an older area with a mix of residential and condo accommodations, Lower Honoapiilani Rd departs from the highway and twists along the coast. Prices rise as you drive oceanside through Kahana and Napili, Maui's sunniest neighborhood, finally ending up at the exclusive Kapalua golf resort.

Although the curving golden sands of Napili and Kapalua beaches make for pretty swimming spots, for most water enthusiasts the real goal is the far northern shore of West Maui. In summer, Slaughterhouse Beach has excellent snorkeling and kayaking; in winter when the waves rise, Honolua Bay becomes one of the world's premier surfing spots.

Highlights

- Surfing the perfect wave or summer kayaking and snorkeling at Mokuleia & Honolua Bays

- Being awed by the acrobatics of migrating humpback whales and poking around Kaanapali's tiny whaling museum

- Striding the sea cliffs of the Kahekili Hwy out to the natural ocean baths and lava blowholes

- Imagining Hawaiian history at Lahaina's heritage sites and the Olowalu petroglyphs

- Charging up the Waihee Valley and Ridge Trails via swinging rope bridges or rainforest overlooks

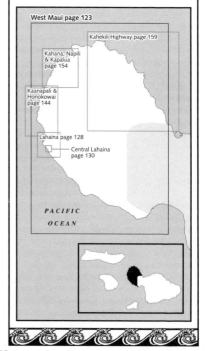

West Maui page 123

Kahekili Highway page 159

Kahana, Napili & Kapalua page 154

Kaanapali & Honokowai page 144

Lahaina page 128

Central Lahaina page 130

PACIFIC OCEAN

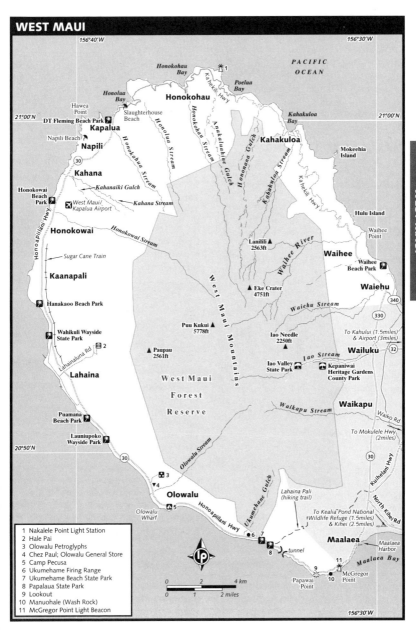

WEST MAUI

156°40'W

156°30'W

PACIFIC OCEAN

Honokohau Bay

1

Poelua Bay

Honolua Bay

Honokohau

Hawea Point

Slaughterhouse Beach

21°00'N

DT Fleming Beach Park

Kahakuloa Bay

Kapalua

Mokeehia Island

Napili Beach

Napili

30

Kahana

Kahanaiki Gulch

Hulu Island

Honokowai Beach Park

West Maui/ Kapalua Airport

Kahana Stream

Waihee Point

Honokowai

Honokowai Stream

Waihee

Lanilili ▲ 2563ft

Wahee River

Waihee Beach Park

Sugar Cane Train

Waiehu

Kaanapali

▲ Eke Crater 4751ft

340

Hanakaoo Beach Park

Waiehu Stream

330

Wahikuli Wayside State Park

Puu Kukui ▲ 5778ft

Iao Needle 2250ft ▲

To Kahului (1.5miles) & Airport (3miles)

2

Wailuku

32

Lahainaluna Rd

▲ Paupau 2561ft

Iao Stream

Lahaina

West Maui

Iao Valley State Park

Kepaniwai Heritage Gardens County Park

Forest

Waikapu

Reserve

Waikapu Stream

Waiko Rd

Puamana Beach Park

To Mokulele Hwy (2miles)

30

Launiupoko Wayside Park

20°50'N

30

Olowalu Stream

Lahaina Pali (hiking trail)

3

4

Olowalu

Honoapiilani Hwy

Ukumehame Gulch

To Kealia Pond National Wildlife Refuge (1.5miles) & Kihei (2.5miles)

Olowalu Wharf

5

To Kahului

North Kihei Rd

6 7

tunnel

Maalaea

8

Maalaea Harbor

11

9

Maalaea Bay

10

McGregor Point

Papawai Point

1 Nakalele Point Light Station
2 Hale Pai
3 Olowalu Petroglyphs
4 Chez Paul; Olowalu General Store
5 Camp Pecusa
6 Ukumehame Firing Range
7 Ukumehame Beach State Park
8 Papalaua State Park
9 Lookout
10 Manuohale (Wash Rock)
11 McGregor Point Light Beacon

0   2   4 km

0   1   2 miles

156°30'W

Just beyond them lies the start (or end) of the Kahekili Hwy, an untrammeled back route to (or from) Kahului. The narrow, twisting road passes sea cliffs, natural ocean baths, lava blowholes and countless jaw-dropping views. Its old-fashioned Hawaiian village of Kahakuloa, with working taro patches and mission churches, is decades removed from the mai tai resorts of the west coast.

MAALAEA TO LAHAINA

The stretch of Hwy 30 between Maalaea Bay and Lahaina certainly has distracting mountain scenery, but during winter most people are craning their necks to look seaward as they drive along. Why?

The popular bumper sticker 'I Brake For Whales' says it all. The ocean between Maalaea and Olowalu is prime humpback cow/calf territory in winter. Although humpback whales are usually spotted farther offshore, they occasionally breach as close as 100 yards from this coast. Forty tons of whale suddenly exploding straight up through the water can be a real showstopper.

Unfortunately, some of the drivers hit their brakes and others don't, making for high rear-ender potential. Other folks are just cruising looking for good surf and snorkeling spots, or maybe a beachfront campground and the Olowalu Petroglyphs trail.

For bus schedules between Maalaea and Lahaina, see the Getting Around chapter.

Papawai Point

Papawai Point is a clearly marked scenic lookout between the 8- and 9-mile marker, with a parking lot and protected turn lanes off the highway. Because the point juts into the waters at the western edge of Maalaea Bay, it's a good whale-watching spot during winter, when volunteer naturalists staff the lookout. Bring your own binoculars, if you have them.

A couple of inconspicuous dirt roadside lookouts also lie just south of the 10-mile marker, but they're both unmarked and difficult to negotiate in heavy traffic since they are on the *makai* (ocean) side of the road.

So is the pull-off for **McGregor Point**, which is farther back before Papawai Point just shy of the 8-mile marker. A dirt path leads down from the impromptu lookout to a light beacon. It's an excellent place for taking in the sunset or Lanai, Molokai and Kahoolawe. Some dive and snorkel boats anchor offshore here or farther west at **Wash Rock**, where even beginners can enjoy the lava mountains, coral, underwater arches and reef fish.

Ukumehame & Papalaua Beaches

Past the 10-mile marker and after the highway tunnel, keep an eye out for the **Lahaina Pali** trailhead on the *mauka* (mountain) side of the road (see the Hiking special section at the end of the Activities chapter). To the makai side are two roadside beaches, easily found by the tents along the shore. Unofficial *camping* here is currently illegal, although the county might make it legit soon (see Accommodations in the Facts for the Visitor chapter).

If traffic is heavy, pull off to the right and either park or wait for a chance to dart across the road to the beaches when traffic clears. If you reach Ukumehame Firing Range, you've driven too far.

At the 11-mile marker **Papalaua State Park** is the beach furthest south, immediately past the tunnel. Papalaua has limited facilities and doesn't seem to have much else to offer (certainly not appealing swimming), except that there is a rich ocean **reef** far offshore. Dive and snorkel boats anchor offshore near the eastern side at Coral Gardens where you can expect to see a variety of tropical fish, sea turtles and the occasional reef shark. This reef also creates the Thousand Peaks toward its west end, with right- and left-hand breaks favored by longboarders and beginning surfers. A few kayakers hit the waters when conditions are calm.

North at the 12-mile marker is **Ukumehame Beach State Park**. Shaded by ironwood trees, this sandy beach is marginally better for sunbathing or taking a quick dip, but because of the rocky conditions most locals stick with picnicking or fishing.

Cetacean Hit Parade

Humpback whales are remarkable not only for their acrobatics but also for their singing. They are the only species of large whales known to do either with such complexity and precision.

Every male member of the humpback herd sings the same set of eerily melodic songs, all in the same order. Each phrase of the melody is composed of repeated single elements, anything from a low moan to a chirp or trill, even roars. The songs cover the full range of frequencies audible to the human ear, and sometimes you can hear them while snorkeling.

Humpback songs last anywhere from six to 30 minutes and evolve as the season goes on, with new phrases being added and old ones dropped, so that the songs the whales sing when they arrive in Hawaii become different songs by the time they leave.

It's thought that humpbacks don't sing in their feeding grounds in Alaska, or that if they do, it's only to locate krill, not for mating. When the whales return to Hawaii six months later, however, they recall the same songs sung last season and again begin exactly where they left off singing on their last tropical honeymoon.

WEST MAUI

Olowalu

Olowalu, which means 'many hills,' has a lovely setting, with cane fields backed by the West Maui Mountains. There's little to mark it other than the general store and a seemingly misplaced expensive French restaurant.

A dirt access road leads through the fields behind the general store to the **Olowalu Petroglyphs**. No special permission is needed to do the hike, even though it is on private land. Park near the signposted gate and walk inland along the hot, dusty road for about 15 minutes, always keeping the cinder cone straight ahead of you. As with most of Maui's extant petroglyphs, these figures are carved into the vertical sides of cliffs rather than on *pahoehoe* lava like on the other Hawaiian Islands. Most of the Olowalu figures have been damaged or otherwise covered up by graffiti, but you can still make out some triangular-shaped human figures, animals and claw-shaped Hawaiian sails. There is a rickety old viewing platform but no interpretive signs.

When waters are calm, there may be OK snorkeling at **Olowalu Beach** south of the general store, stretching between mile markers 13 and 14. Since there is no parking lot, pull off safely anywhere along the highway and trek on down. There's a narrow sandy beach to lie on, although be

careful of kiawe thorns. The coral reef is large and shallow, but when the wind and waves pick up conditions are silty and visibility is poor. There are better snorkeling spots north of Lahaina.

Olowalu Beach was the site of an infamous massacre. In 1790 some Hawaiians stole a skiff from the US ship *Eleanora*, which was anchored at Honuaula Bay a few miles north of Olowalu. A sailor was killed and the skiff burned for its iron nails and fittings. Ever since the first foreign ships to visit Hawaii gifted the *ali'i* (chiefs) with Western weapons, the theft of guns, ammunition and any kind of scrap metal had become commonplace. This time Captain Simon Metcalfe retaliated by burning the village at Honuaula with its grass huts and *heiau* (temples) to the ground. He then sailed a few miles south to Olowalu, where he tricked the Hawaiians into sailing out in their canoes to trade. He and his crew mercilessly gunned them all down with cannons, killing an estimated 100 people.

This incident set in motion a chain of karmic events that led to the death of the captain's son Thomas, who was bludgeoned to death on the Big Island by Hawaiians wielding canoe paddles.

Places to Stay *Camp Pecusa* (☎ 661-4303, W *www.maui.net/~norm/pecusa.html,*

Cryptoglyphs

The ancient Hawaiians had no written history, although they did cut petroglyphs. The problem is that no one alive today can decipher their meaning with accuracy. Some petroglyphs may have been intentionally cryptic, while others were perhaps artistic expressions or carved holes in which to hide the umbilical cords of newborns to ensure longevity. Others think that petroglyphs were a memory aid, similar to *mele* (chants) that documented significant events.

Most petroglyphs are found along ancient footpaths or burial sites and may have been clustered at sites thought to have mana, or spiritual power. Petroglyphs were often carved by pecking into *pahoehoe* (smooth, ropy lava), sandstone beach shelves or, as on Maui, into sheer cliff faces. But unlike hieroglyphics, Hawaiian petroglyphs do not tell a story. There is probably no Rosetta stone waiting to be found that will ever unlock the mystery.

Many of these carved petroglyphs are stylized stick figures depicting warriors with rainbows, birds, canoes and other easily recognizable images. The large, triangular bodies are thought to represent the ali'i, while other important figures are of sea turtles (whales are conspicuously absent). Other petroglyphs are just linear marks, which may have been made to record important events and journeys or represent calendars or genealogical lines.

Most Hawaiian petroglyphs are probably no more than a few hundred years old, with an apparent surge in carving activity just prior to Western contact. These later petroglyphs even depicted guns, churches and other Western imports, with Roman script dated as late as the 1860s.

Today many petroglyph sites are being ruined by graffiti and erosion. The Olowalu site is in poor condition, but those over on Lanai, especially in the Palawai basin, are better preserved. Some misguided tourists walk on top of them to get a better view, or use chalk or burning sticks to re-engrave faded petroglyphs, all of which actually damages them. The best thing you can do is quietly look and then leave them alone.

800 Olowalu Village Rd) Tent sites $5 per person; no reservations. Check-in before 5pm only. A caretaker lives on the grounds, making this church-sponsored campground the most secure place on Maui to camp. Sites are available to individuals on a first-come, first-served basis (don't worry, you have a 95% chance of finding available space). No alcohol is allowed, and there's a maximum stay of seven nights a month.

The sites are extremely basic, but lie in the shade alongside a rocky beach. It's not suitable for swimming, but there's good snorkeling farther out on the reef (watch out for reef sharks). There is a solar-heated shower, a couple of outhouses, fire pits, drinking water and picnic tables. The kitchen, washing machines and other amenities near the private cabins are strictly off-limits to campers.

Look for a small blue Camp Pecusa sign at the side of a cane field, about half a mile south of the Olowalu General Store.

Places to Eat *Olowalu General Store* (☎ 661-3774, 820 Olowalu Village Rd) This landmark store is the only budget option for miles. A few cheap snacks, hot takeout items, drinks or ice cream each cost a few bucks.

Chez Paul (☎ 661-3843, Olowalu Village Rd) Entrées $22-45. Open for dinner daily; reservations required. Out in the middle of nowhere, this French seafood restaurant has been building its stellar reputation since 1968. The interior feels very European, with old-fashioned artwork, white linens and just a dozen tables. The classic French menu is spiced up with Hawaiian touches, perhaps Kona lobsters or a tropical fruit salsa. Look for the flags and strings of lights out front.

Launiupoko Wayside Park

Launiupoko Wayside Park, south of Lahaina at the 18-mile marker, is popular for picnicking and watching the sun set behind Lanai. It has showers, toilets, BBQ grills, picnic tables and changing rooms.

Although the small grey-sand beach is unappealing for swimming, offshore is a favorite place for beginning surfers, many of whom seem to be content to just sit floating on their boards out in the water. Back on the beach there is a small *keiki* wading pool that fills up at high tide.

Farther north toward Lahaina is **Puamana Beach Park**, another grassy picnic area. Although it's not much to look at nowadays, decades ago it inspired the 1930s Hawaiian classic tune 'Puamana,' written by Irmgard Farden Aluli, the most prolific female composer since Queen Liliuokalani.

LAHAINA

Lahaina was once the breadbasket, or, more accurately, the breadfruit basket, of West Maui and the royal court of Maui chiefs. According to legend, it was one of these ali'i who gifted the town with its name, meaning 'cruel or unmerciful sun.' And yes, the sweltering heat and humidity are still more oppressive in Lahaina than anywhere else on the island. The coastal setting and mountain backdrop *is* pretty, however, and it's easy to see why people have been drawn here over the centuries. Soft breezes blow off the ocean and there are fine sunset views of Lanai from the seawall.

By the mid-19th century, two-thirds of all the whalers coming into Hawaii were landing in boisterous old Lahaina town, which had replaced Honolulu as the favored port. Today the narrow streets are jammed with tourists and the historic wooden shops along Front St that once housed whalers' saloons and provision stores are crammed with souvenir shops. If you're expecting something quaint and romantic, you may be disappointed. The chief attractions are restored 19th-century buildings, including the homes of missionaries, prisons for sailors, and graveyards for both.

History

After Kamehameha the Great conquered and unified the Hawaiian Islands, he half-heartedly took up residence in Lahaina, and the royal capital remained here until Kamehameha III moved it to Honolulu to 1845. He may have done it just to get away from his dueling neighbors, both whalers and missionaries whose venom for each other was obvious.

Shortly after his arrival in 1823, William Richards, Lahaina's first Protestant missionary, converted Maui's native governor, Hoapili, to Christianity. Under Richards' influence, the new convert began passing laws against drunkenness and debauchery. But after months at sea, whalers weren't looking for a prayer service when they pulled into port. To most sailors there was 'no God west of the Horn.'

In 1826, when English captain William Buckle of the whaler *Daniel* pulled in to port, he was outraged to discover Lahaina had a new missionary taboo against womanizing. Buckle's crew came to shore seeking revenge against Richards, but a group of Hawaiian Christians came to Richards' aid and chased the whalers back to their boat.

When Captain Buckle decided to purchase a Hawaiian woman instead, Richards wrote a letter home about it, which ended up being printed in a prominent New York newspaper and made the captain out to be a slave trader and pirate. A libel suit soon followed and the missionary was summoned to Honolulu to be tried by Hawaiian chiefs, but he was acquitted.

The next year the good governor arrested the captain of the *John Palmer* for allowing women to board his ship, and the angry crew shot a round of cannonballs at Richards' house. The captain was arrested and then released, but laws restricting liaisons between seamen and native women stayed. Hawaii's first stone church, first missionary school and first printing press were all in place by the early 1830s.

After Governor Hoapili's death, sailors once again began to heed Maui's siren call. The whaling years reached their peak in

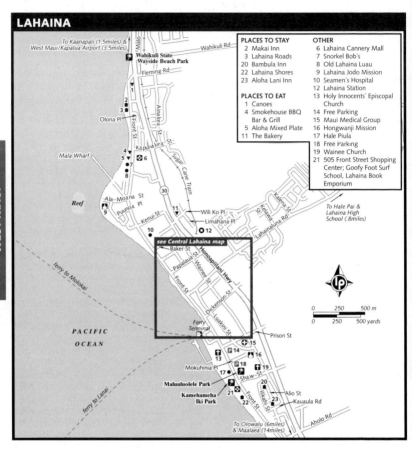

LAHAINA

To Kaanapali (1.5miles) &
West Maui/Kapalua Airport (3.5miles)

Wahikuli Rd

Wahikuli State
Wayside Beach Park

Fleming Rd

Olona Pl

Mala Wharf

Reef

Ala-Moana St

Puunoa Pl

Kenui St

Kapulakea St

Sugar Cane Train

Wili Ko Pl

Limahana Pl

see Central Lahaina map

Baker St

Honoapiilani Hwy

Papalaua St

Wainee St

Front St

Dickenson St

Luakini St

Ferry
Terminal

Prison St

PACIFIC
OCEAN

ferry to Molokai

ferry to Lanai

Mokuhinia Pl

Shaw St

Maluuluolele Park

Kamehameha
Iki Park

Alio St

Front St

Iliikahi St

Kauaula Rd

Aholo Rd

To Olowalu (6miles)
& Maalaea (14miles)

Kelawea St

Kenui Rd

Lahainaluna Rd

Kahena St

To Hale Pai &
Lahaina High
School (.8miles)

PLACES TO STAY	OTHER
2 Makai Inn	6 Lahaina Cannery Mall
3 Lahaina Roads	7 Snorkel Bob's
20 Bambula Inn	8 Old Lahaina Luau
22 Lahaina Shores	9 Lahaina Jodo Mission
23 Aloha Lani Inn	10 Seamen's Hospital
	12 Lahaina Station
PLACES TO EAT	13 Holy Innocents' Episcopal
1 Canoes	Church
4 Smokehouse BBQ	14 Free Parking
Bar & Grill	15 Maui Medical Group
5 Aloha Mixed Plate	16 Hongwanji Mission
11 The Bakery	17 Hale Piula
	18 Free Parking
	19 Wainee Church
	21 505 Front Street Shopping
	Center; Goofy Foot Surf
	School, Lahaina Book
	Emporium

0   250   500 m
0   250   500 yards

WEST MAUI

Lahaina in the 1840s, with hundreds of ships pulling into port each year. The town took on the whalers' boisterous nature, opening dance halls, bars and brothels. Hundreds of sick or derelict sailors, who had either been abandoned or jumped ship, roamed the streets. Among the multitudes that landed in Lahaina was Herman Melville, who later penned *Moby Dick*.

By the 1860s, the depletion of the last hunting grounds in the Arctic and the emergence of the petroleum industry spelled the end of the US whaling era. As whaling had been the base of the island's economy,

Lahaina became all but a ghost town until the Pioneer Mill Co was founded in 1862. For the next century, Lahaina remained a sleepy plantation settlement until major resort development farther up the coast at Kaanapali in the 1960s revived it. The international jet-set crowd favored down-and-out Lahaina, but this time instead of wine, women and whaling songs, it was 1970s sex, drugs and rock & roll that did the trick. Since then, the town has mellowed except for every year on Halloween, when it hosts the 'Mardi Gras of the Pacific' (see Special Events in the Facts for the Visitor chapter).

A lava cave entices a diver.

Hawaii's original mode of transport, the outrigger canoe

Maui is named after the demigod who pulled the Hawaiian Islands out of the sea with a fish hook.

The beginnings of a Mai Tai – Maui pineapple fields

And the beginnings of a hibiscus lei

Tourists wonder at the beautiful Iao Needle, Central Maui

Uncle Sol Kawaihoa with his ukulele, Wailuku

Blending in with Moorish idols, Central Maui

Orientation

Lahaina's focal point is its busy, small boat harbor, which is backed by the oldest banyan tree in the USA. Half of Lahaina's historic sights are clustered in this area, while the other half are scattered around town.

Finding parking can be a nightmare, especially on weekends or after dark. Front St has street parking, but there's always a line of cruising cars. The town is fairly compact, so don't worry about parking too close to your final destination – just grab the first spot you see.

There are also free public parking lots at the southern end of Front St, while those closer to the center around Dickenson St average $5 per day. If you're only in Lahaina for a few hours, you could park at one of the shopping centers and then make a small purchase (suntan oil, a bottle of water etc) to get your parking stub validated free of charge.

For information on limited bus services from Lahaina south to Maalaea Bay and north to Kapalua, see the Getting Around chapter.

Information

There's a small information desk (see Tourist Offices in the Facts for the Visitor chapter) inside the old courthouse, 648 Wharf St, in Banyan Tree Square.

ATMs are found everywhere. At the Lahaina Shopping Center, Bank of Hawaii (☎ 661-8781) is open from 8:30am to 4pm Monday to Thursday and 8:30am to 6pm Friday. First Hawaiian Bank (☎ 661-3655), 215 Papalaua St, keeps about the same hours but stays open until 5pm Monday to Thursday.

The downtown post office station, 132 Papalaua St, in the Lahaina Shopping Center, is open 8:15am to 4:15pm Monday to Friday. There's often a long queue inside. If you just want to buy stamps or ship a package via FedEx or UPS, try Lahaina Mail Depot (☎ 667-2000), 658 Front St, in the Wharf Cinema Center. They also mail coconuts. You can pick up general delivery mail at the main Lahaina post office (☎ 661-0904), 1760 Honoapiilani Hwy, next to the civic center a few miles north of town. It's open 8:30am to 5pm Monday to Friday, 9am to 1pm Saturday.

The Lahaina public library (☎ 662-3950), 680 Wharf St, is open noon to 8pm Monday and Tuesday, 9am to 5pm Wednesday and Thursday, and 12:30pm to 4:30pm Friday. Otherwise Internet access is expensive (up to $12 per hour) and found only at a few cafés, including the Swiss Cafe (☎ 661-6776), 640 Front St, as well as at Karma Cafe and Westside Natural Foods & Deli (see Places to Eat, later).

For nonemergencies, Maui Medical Group (☎ 249-8080) has an office at 130 Prison St. There is a Longs Drugs at the Lahaina Cannery Mall.

Beaches

Lahaina is not known for its beaches, which are largely shallow and rocky. The section near Lahaina Shores is swimmable. It was once a royal surfing ground and here young local kids still paddle out to wait for waves, meanwhile dodging the ferries and cruise ships. Your best bet for snorkeling or swimming is to go farther north to Kaanapali.

Baldwin House

Lahaina's oldest building and also its most distinguished-looking landmark is the Baldwin House (☎ 661-3262, 696 Front St; adult/family $3/5; open 10am-4:30pm daily). Originally built in 1834, it was the home of Reverend Dwight Baldwin, a Protestant missionary doctor, until the late 1860s. A grand lanai looks out onto Front St, and its coral and rock walls beneath the exterior plaster are a full 24-inches thick, which keeps the house, now a museum, cool year-round.

It took the Baldwins 161 days to get to Hawaii from their native Connecticut. These early missionaries traveled neither fast nor light, and pieces from the weighty collection of china and furniture they brought with them around Cape Horn are on display. Others are reproductions or period antiques, including some fine Hawaiian-style quilts. The entrance fee includes a brief tour

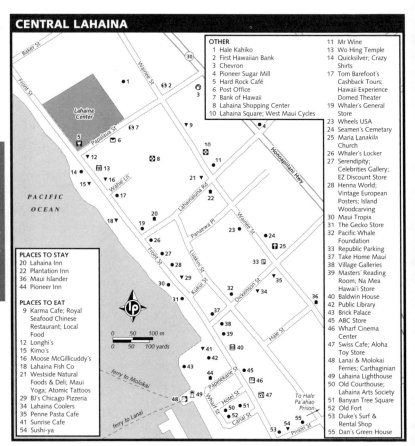

CENTRAL LAHAINA

OTHER
1 Hale Kahiko
2 First Hawaiian Bank
3 Chevron
4 Pioneer Sugar Mill
5 Hard Rock Café
6 Post Office
7 Bank of Hawaii
8 Lahaina Shopping Center
10 Lahaina Square; West Maui Cycles
11 Mr Wine
13 Wo Hing Temple
14 Quicksilver; Crazy Shirts
17 Tom Barefoot's Cashback Tours; Hawaii Experience Domed Theater
19 Whaler's General Store
23 Wheels USA
24 Seamen's Cemetary
25 Maria Lanakila Church
26 Whaler's Locker
27 Serendipity; Celebrities Gallery; EZ Discount Store
28 Henna World; Vintage European Posters; Island Woodcarving
30 Maui Tropix
31 The Gecko Store
32 Pacific Whale Foundation
33 Republic Parking
37 Take Home Maui
38 Village Galleries
39 Masters' Reading Room; Na Mea Hawai'i Store
40 Baldwin House
42 Public Library
43 Brick Palace
45 ABC Store
46 Wharf Cinema Center
47 Swiss Cafe; Aloha Toy Store
48 Lanai & Molokai Ferries; Carthaginian
49 Lahaina Lighthouse
50 Old Courthouse; Lahaina Arts Society
51 Banyan Tree Square
52 Old Fort
53 Duke's Surf & Rental Shop
55 Dan's Green House

PLACES TO STAY
20 Lahaina Inn
22 Plantation Inn
36 Maui Islander
44 Pioneer Inn

PLACES TO EAT
9 Karma Cafe; Royal Seafood Chinese Restaurant; Local Food
12 Longhi's
15 Kimo's
16 Moose McGillicuddy's
18 Lahaina Fish Co
21 Westside Natural Foods & Deli; Maui Yoga; Atomic Tattoos
29 BJ's Chicago Pizzeria
34 Lahaina Coolers
35 Penne Pasta Cafe
41 Sunrise Cafe
54 Sushi-ya

PACIFIC OCEAN

WEST MAUI

---

led by a Hawaiian docent; the last tour begins at 4:15pm. You can pick up a free Lahaina walking tour brochure here.

Next door the old missionary storehouse was turned into an officers club called the **Masters' Reading Room** during Lahaina's whaling heyday. From here, sea captains could keep an eye on the harborfront rabble-rousers across the road while they read the newspapers. It now houses the offices of Lahaina Restoration Foundation (☎ 661-3262, **w** www.lahainarestoration .org), the organization that has been most instrumental in preserving the historic sites around town. Downstairs is Nā Mea Hawai'i Store (see Shopping, later).

Banyan Tree Square

In 1873, reputedly the largest banyan tree in the USA was planted here to commemorate the 50th anniversary of the first missionary arrival in Lahaina. With its shaded benches and walkways, the square makes a nice spot to take a break from the crowds on Front St. The tree has 16 major trunks and scores of branches reaching across the better part of an acre. It's so sprawling that it appears to be on the verge of pushing the old courthouse, which shares the square, clear off the block. Local kids like to use the aerial roots to swing Tarzan-style from branch to branch, and craftspeople and artists set up booths here every other weekend. In late April the town throws a birthday bash in honor of this living landmark.

On the harbor side of the banyan tree stands the old **courthouse**, dating from 1859 but restored in 1925. It once served as a government center, housing a post office, governor's office and customs house, which was also a hotbed of illegal smuggling. The courthouse was originally built with stones from Lahaina's unfinished royal palace nearby, and in 1898 the US annexation of Hawaii was formally concluded here. The last trial took place in 1987.

The **old jail** *(courthouse basement; open 9am-5pm daily)* belongs to the Lahaina Arts Society (☎ 661-0111), and the cells that once held drunken sailors now display artwork. As the society is a nonprofit collective, it charges roughly half of the commission charged by private galleries for paintings, jewelry, pottery, woodcarvings and basketwork by contemporary island artists. The basement entrance is on the north side of the building. Around the back on the ground floor is another art gallery and a visitor information desk. Upstairs are the beginnings of a modest history museum (free).

Canal St, bordering Banyan Tree Square, used to be part of an extensive canal system that ran through Lahaina. Most of it was filled in around 1913 due to problems with mosquitoes, which didn't exist in Hawaii until whalers brought them from North America in their water barrels. An enterprising US consul officer built this section of the canal in the 1840s to allow whalers easier access to freshwater supplies – for a fee, of course.

At the corner look for a reconstructed section of coral wall from an **old fort** built in 1832. At the height of its use, the fort had 47 cannons, mostly for show and salvaged from foreign ships that sank in Hawaiian waters. The nearby public market was nicknamed 'Rotten Row' for all of its drunks, gamblers and licentious Hawaiian women. Each day at dusk, a Hawaiian sentinel beat a drum to alert sailors to return to their ships. Those who didn't make it back in time ended up imprisoned in the fort. The fort was dismantled in 1854 and its coral blocks used to build the new prison on Wainee St.

Lahaina Harbor Area

The four remaining cannons on the waterfront opposite the old courthouse were raised from the wreck of a Russian ship that went down in Honolulu Harbor in 1816. Amusingly they now point directly at the tourists crowding Lahaina's harbor. Booths lining the edge of the harbor sell tickets for most of the sunset sails, sport-fishing expeditions, snorkeling and whale-watching cruises. Interisland ferries to Molokai and Lanai dock at the public pier.

Quietly floating in the waters is the *Carthaginian* *(☎ 661-8527; adult/senior/ family $3/2/5; open 10am-4pm daily)*. The original wooden-hulled *Carthaginian* belonged to a class of swift brigantines that made freight runs in the 19th century between New England, China and the Sandwich Islands, as Hawaii was then called by Westerners. She was one of the last square-riggers left in Hawaii, and after being brought to Lahaina and restored, she appeared in the film version of James Michener's *Hawaii*. On Easter Sunday 1972, when the ship set sail for additional repairs in Honolulu, the 960-ton vessel hit a reef outside Lahaina Harbor, splintered and sank.

The present *Carthaginian* is actually a steel-hulled vessel built in Kiel, Germany, in 1920 that has been painstakingly converted into a replica of the original. The 97-foot brig had to be completely restored and all the masts and yards handcrafted – a process that took a full seven years. Below deck you'll find an Alaskan whaling boat, photographs donated by National Geographic and a tiny theater where a one-hour film on whales is shown continuously (to watch the whole thing show up by at least 3pm). You can squash yourself into the snug old captain's chairs and listen to recordings of whale songs.

The Fragrance of Famine

Hawaii's forests of sandalwood were once so vast that the Chinese name for Hawaii was Tahn Hueng Sahn, or the 'Sandalwood Mountains.' Then why has the fragrant iliahi nearly disappeared from the modern landscape?

By the mid-1780s, Hawaii was becoming a popular port of call for Yankee traders plying the seas between North America and China. Sea captains quickly discovered that Hawaii had great stores of sandalwood, worth a premium in China. When the captains showed interest in it, Hawaiian chiefs readily began bargaining the wood away in exchange for foreign weapons.

A lucrative triangle of trade emerged. From Hawaii, the ships sailed to Canton and traded loads of sandalwood for Chinese silks and porcelain, which were then carried back to New England ports and sold at a high profit. In New England, the ships were reloaded with goods to be traded with the Hawaiians. Kamehameha the Great eventually put a *kapu* (taboo) on all sandalwood forests, giving himself total control over the trade. Even under his relatively shrewd management of resources, the bulk of the profits ended up in the sea captains' fat pockets because payment for the sandalwood was made in overpriced goods.

Kamehameha's successor, Liholiho, partially lifted the royal kapu, allowing island chiefs to get in on the action. The chiefs began purchasing foreign luxuries by signing promissory notes to be paid in future shipments of sandalwood. To pay off the rising 'debts,' Hawaiian *makaainana* (commoners) were forced into virtual servitude. Used like packhorses, with sandalwood logs strapped to their backs under bands of ti leaves, these men who hauled the wood were called *kua leho,* literally 'calloused backs.' It was not uncommon for them to carry heavy loads 20 miles from the interior to ships waiting on the coast. Soon all makaainana were forced to pay their taxes in sandalwood. Crops were neglected and famine soon followed.

In a few short years after Kamehameha's death, Hawaii's sandalwood forests were nearly exhausted. Today the tree is not extinct in Hawaii, but it is rare. In the past few years a grassroots reforestation program on Maui has re-established the fragrant trees first outside Kahakuloa and then in Kula Forest Reserve. Hikers will spy a native species of dryland sandalwood along the Lahaina Pali Trail (see the Hiking special section at the end of the Activities chapter).

In the same area stands the **Lahaina Lighthouse**, probably the oldest lighthouse in the Pacific. It was commissioned in 1840 to aid whaling ships pulling into Lahaina and was fueled by sperm whale oil. The current structure, which dates from 1905, flashes red with a photoelectrical cell courtesy of the Coast Guard. About 100 feet north, the **Hauola Stone** is a water-worn lava stone on the shoreline. To spot it, look to the right as you face the ocean – it's the middle stone. The ancient Hawaiians believed this stone emitted healing powers to those who sat upon it.

The entire area surrounding the Lahaina public library was once the site of a royal taro field as well as the first Western-style building in Hawaii, the **Brick Palace**, erected by Kamehameha I so he could keep watch on arriving ships. Despite the grand name, this 'palace' was a modest two-story structure built around 1800 by two ex-convicts from Botany Bay, Australia. All that remains today is the excavated foundation and cornerstones, which can be found on the makai side of the library.

The most prominent landmark in the harbor area is the old green-and-white **Pioneer Inn**, now a Best Western hotel. It's got a faux whaling-era atmosphere, with swinging doors, ship figureheads and signs warning against womanizing in the rooms. It was actually built in 1901 long after the whaling boom had passed, but nobody seems to care. Rumors fly about the hotel's original owner, a Canadian named George Freeland, a one-time member of the British Columbia provincial police who allegedly tracked a criminal all the way to Hawaii only to lose the man (and himself, it seems) in tropical Lahaina. Until the 1950s, the hotel provided Lahaina's only visitor accommodations. The famous guests who slept here included Jack London (Queen Liliuokalani only stopped by).

Front Street

If you walk north down Front St past the Pioneer Inn and Baldwin House, you'll come to a row of **historical buildings**, which date from the turn of the 19th century. They are best appreciated from the seawall sidewalk or from the upstairs balcony of any of the Front St restaurants, especially during happy hour.

Wo Hing Temple One of the most unique buildings is the Wo Hing Temple (☎ 661-3262, 858 Front St; admission by donation; open 10am-4:15pm daily). It opened in 1912 as a meeting hall for the fraternal order of Chee Kung Tong, a Chinese benevolent society. After WWII when its members started leaving for new economic opportunities on Oahu, it was used as a home for elderly Chinese men.

As Lahaina's ethnic Chinese population declined, so too did the building. The Lahaina Restoration Foundation took it over and turned it into a museum in 1984. Inside you'll find cultural artifacts and period photos, a ceremonial dancing lion, two Fu dogs made of British Columbia jade and carved in Hong Kong, plus a collection of opium bottles found during the cleanup of the grounds. Upstairs is the only public Taoist shrine on Maui.

Even if you linger, it won't take long to tour the house, which is okay because nothing deserves your attention more than the tin-roof cookhouse out back. Here an impromptu theater has been set up to show films shot by Thomas Edison during his 1898 and 1906 visits to Hawaii, soon after he invented the motion picture camera. Set to slack-key guitar music, these black-and-white movies capture old Hawaii in a way nothing else in Lahaina does. Settle back on the benches and watch royalty parade to traditional luau, *paniolo* (Hawaiian cowboys) swimming their horses onto market-bound steamships, rigorous plantation labors and everyday street scenes from the Honolulu of yesteryear.

Wainee Street

Hale Pa'ahao ('stuck-in-irons house'), Lahaina's old **prison** *(admission free)*, was built in 1852 by convicts, who dismantled the old harborside fort and carried the stone blocks here to construct these eight-foot-high prison walls. Hawaiians could collect bounties by turning in sailors who jumped ship or fooled around with local women. Outside is a 1923 Model T Ford that once belonged to a Japanese wholesaler from Hana.

Even though the prison was restored in 1988, it's not well taken care of. Inside one of the whitewashed cells an 'old seadog' mannequin repeats a recorded story about 'life in this here calaboose.' In another cell, you'll find a list of offenses and arrests for the year 1855. The top three offenses were drunkenness (330 arrests), adultery and fornication (111) and 'furious riding' (89). Other no-nos included profanity, lascivious conduct, aiding deserting sailors and drinking *awa* (kava moonshine). There's also a copy of a 16-year-old seaman's diary, vividly describing his time spent in this prison – not surprisingly, he thought the meals were excellent compared to ship's rations.

A few blocks north of the old prison is the **Seamen's Cemetery**, which lies beside Maria Lanakila Church, Maui's first Catholic church. It's basically a local cemetery, with only one seaman's tombstone that can be identified. However, historical records indicate that numerous sailors from the whaling era were buried here, including one of Herman Melville's cousins and a shipmate from the *Acushnet*, who apparently died of a 'disreputable disease.'

Heading south from the prison, **Hongwanji Mission** (☎ 661-0640, 551 Wainee St) dates from 1927. It's usually locked, but the front doors are glass so you can glance in at the beautiful gilt altar and painted screens. Unlike Buddhist temples in Japan, this one has rows of wooden pews and the exterior resembles a mission church, except with silver pagoda spires in place of steeple bells. In 1904 the first Buddhist priest to establish a mission here commuted on horseback from Wailuku – over 25 miles of steep mountain trails. The venture came of age when Japanese plantation workers moved out of the camps and established homes and businesses in Lahaina.

Dating from 1832, **Wainee Church** *(535 Wainee St)* was the first stone church in Hawaii and was cursed with bad luck. The steeple and bell collapsed in a whirlwind in 1858. Then the church was torched by royalists in 1894 because its minister supported the annexation of Hawaii. A second church, built to replace the original, also burned to the ground in 1947, and the third was blown away during a storm a few years later. One could get the impression that the old Hawaiian gods didn't take kindly to the house of this foreign deity! The fourth church, optimistically named Waiola ('Waters of Life') Congregational Church (☎ 661-4349), has been standing since 1953.

In the **cemetery** next door lie several notables: Governor Hoapili, who ordered the original church built; Queen Keopuolani, once the highest-ranking woman in Hawaii and wife of Kamehameha I; and the Reverend William Richards, Lahaina's first missionary. Many of the old tombstones are for children who died young, while others have cameo photos and intriguing inscriptions.

Around Maluuluolele Park

The name of this public park means 'the breadfruit shade of Lele' ('Lele' was the ancient name for Lahaina). Today, it has basketball courts, tennis courts, a baseball field and shows not a hint of its fascinating past.

On this site was once a royal pond called Mokuhimia, the legendary home of water spirits. For centuries the *Moku'ula*, which means 'sacred island,' was the abode of

Maui chiefs. The islet held an ornate royal burial chamber that was likely covered in featherwork, mirrors and exquisite draperies. In the 16th century when the young daughter of Piilani died, she was ceremonially deified here as Kihawahine, the *mo'o akua* (water lizard god) who visits all the islands of Hawaii to unify the royal blood lines.

In later years the site became the abode of the first three Kamehameha kings. The Princess Nahienaena, who was in love with her brother King Kamehameha III, also died here in 1836. Polynesian tradition dictated that royal siblings should marry to keep the bloodline pure, but the missionaries preached against incest and constantly tried to pry the pair apart. After a child fathered by her brother was stillborn, the princess quickly died of a broken heart at the tender age of 21. The king reacted by drowning himself in liquor and often came here on the anniversary of her death to drink and lose himself in reverie.

The pond was filled in before the 1920s and the sacred island was thought to have been leveled. However, an archaeological study in 1993 confirmed that the island still lies beneath Maluuluolele Park. The Moku'ula site is currently marked with a plaque affixed beneath a stand of tall palm trees at the southern edge of the park. The Friends of Moku'ula (☎ 661-3659, **w** www .mokuula.com, 505 Front St, suite 234), is working with Mayor James Apana to rezone the land as a public historic site with an interactive interpretive center for Hawaiian culture, instead of allowing yet another shopping mall to be built. You can contribute by going on the organization's historic walking tour of Lahaina (see Organized Tours in the Getting Around chapter).

Across the street from the park, a couple of steps and a grassy building foundation is all that remains of Kamehameha the Great's attempt at a royal palace, **Hale Piula** (literally 'iron-roof house'). Construction on the palace was started in the late 1830s but was never completed, as Queen Kaahumanu and later kings preferred to sleep in traditional thatched houses, and the capital was moved to Honolulu halfway through the project. The building was used for a short time as a government office, but was damaged in a storm, and most of the stones were carted away to build the old courthouse in Banyan Tree Square.

The interior of **Holy Innocents' Episcopal Church** (☎ 661-4202, 561 Front St) is decorated with a Hawaiiana motif. Paintings on the front of the koa altar depict a fisher in an outrigger canoe and Hawaiian farmers harvesting taro and breadfruit. Above the altar is a Hawaiian Madonna and Child, for which a Lahaina mother and infant were the models.

Hale Kahiko

At the rear of the Lahaina Center (☎ 667-9216) is Hale Kahiko *(admission free; open 9am-6pm daily)*. The three *pili* (bunchgrass) houses, or *hale,* that are found here are replicas of an old Hawaiian village. Despite the irony of standing off to the side of a shopping center parking lot, they have been faithfully reconstructed using ohia lehua wood posts from the Big Island and 20 tons of pili thatch with *senit* (coconut twine) fiber lashings. Each hale is designed for a different function; one as the family sleeping quarters, another as a men's eating house (traditional *kapu,* or taboos, forced men and women to eat separately), and the third as a workshop where women made tapa. Inside are a few simple everyday implements, such as gourd containers, woven baskets and weapons.

The tiny grounds have been landscaped with a fascinating cross-section of native plants traditionally used by Hawaiians for food or herbal medicine. You could easily spend a half-hour bumping elbows with other tourists and identifying plants using the guide brochure, including the all-purpose kukui (candlenut), which was used for lamp oil, relish, tapa dye, seed lei and as a natural laxative, as well as the unusual shampoo ginger.

Seamen's Hospital

In 1844, this building *(1024 Front St)* was leased by the US government and turned into a hospital for sick and abandoned seamen. Officials at the hospital became notorious for embezzlement. Sailors who weren't sick and others long since dead were commonly signed onto the hospital books. A US warship with a board of inquiry was sent by the American government to investigate the corruption in 1859, but the ship and her findings mysteriously disappeared at sea on the return home!

The seamen's hospital has been completely restored and is now used as a private office. A huge anchor on the lawn marks the site. Next door the residence maintained by the Lahaina Restoration Foundation resembles early sugar plantation camp housing.

Lahaina Jodo Mission

A large bronze statue of Buddha overlooks Lahaina Jodo Mission, located off the north end of Front St just before crossing the bridge. With its back to the mountains, the Buddha looks out over the Pacific Ocean toward Japan. It was completed in 1968 in celebration of the centennial of Japanese immigration to Hawaii. There is a 90-foot pagoda and an enormous temple bell cast in Kyoto that weighs 3½ tons. Inside are priceless Buddhist paintings by Haijin Iwasaki.

Across the road is the long **Mala Wharf**, constructed in the 1920s to allow interisland ferries to land passengers directly ashore. It never made the grade. Rough seas prevented the ferries from pulling up alongside the pier, forcing them to continue shuttling passengers across the shallows of Lahaina Harbor in small boats. The wharf is now crumbling and closed, although Mala does have a new launch ramp for small boats nearby.

Lahainaluna Road

Lahainaluna Seminary, established by Christian missionaries in 1831, was the first US educational institution west of the Rockies and is now Lahaina's public high school. It is the alma mater of David Malo, the first Hawaiian to be ordained in the Christian ministry. Amazingly, Malo was also one of the strongest spokespeople for native Hawaiian rights during the early years of foreign invasion. He is buried on the hillside above the high school, which is considered to be one of the finest in the state. The school celebrates David Malo every year in late April.

The school is at the end of Lahainaluna Rd, just over a mile east of the old **Pioneer Sugar Mill**. Only recently did the mill company sell off its sugarcane fields, which once stretched along the coast from Lahaina past Kaanapali. The smokestacks are a West Maui landmark, but the company wants to tear them down to make way for some more profitable use of the land. It seems inevitable that they will be lost.

Hale Pai North of the main school parking lot, the fully restored Hale Pai *(admission by donation; open 10am-3pm Mon-Fri)* was the site of the first printing press in Hawaii. A limited corps of volunteers staff the building, so the hours are a bit flexible.

Although the main purpose of the press was to make the Bible available to Hawaiians, it also was used to produce other works, including the first Hawaiian botany book and, in 1834, Hawaii's first newspaper. Renegade students even used it once to counterfeit currency! *Mo'olelo Hawaii,* a collection of oral history written by David Malo and his students that was later translated into English as *Hawaiian Antiquities,* is widely regarded as the preeminent published account of ancient Hawaiian history and culture.

Examples of early books are on display and a replica of the original ramage press (shipped here from Honolulu) can be used to print a page copied from the first Hawaiian primer. Don't overlook the allegorical Temperance Map drawn by an early missionary to illustrate the perils of drunkenness – Beer Inlet leads to Stupidity Island, remember. Reproductions cost only $5 including a hilarious explanatory pamphlet.

Places to Stay

Lahaina has a few atmospheric inns that are worth a romantic splurge, as well as a handful of modern B&Bs and condos. Most are right along Front St. The nearest campground is at Olowalu, about five miles south of town. There are no hostels.

B&Bs The minimum stay is usually three days and advance reservations are often necessary.

Bambula Inn (☎ 667-6753, 800-544-5524, fax 667-0979, ⓦ www.maui.net/~bambula) Rooms $80, cottages $100-110. Both cottages and the garden room are white, tropical delights, with private bath and free snorkel gear. The studio cottages also have full kitchens. As a bonus there are free sunset cruises on the family sailboat, with whale sightings practically guaranteed during winter. French and German are spoken here.

Aloha Lani Inn (☎ 661-8040, 800-572-5642, fax 661-8045, ⓔ melinda@maui.net, ⓦ www.maui-vacations.com/aloha, 13 Kauaula Rd) Singles/doubles $69/79. This modest contemporary home is a quick walk south of Lahaina Shores (see Condos, later). All rooms have a shared bathroom and breakfast is not included, although guests are free to use the kitchen and fill the coffee pot. The accommodating owner, Melinda, has added tropical colors, piled the living room with Hawaiiana books and made it all quite cozy.

Old Lahaina House (☎ 667-4663, 800-847-0761, fax 667-5615, ⓦ www.oldlahaina.com, PO Box 10355, Lahaina, HI 96761) Standard/deluxe rooms from $70/115, suite $150-205. Also just a few minutes south of Lahaina Shores, this plantation-style house is romantic enough for honeymooners. The garden hides a small swimming pool, and all rooms have TV, phone and air-con. Except Sunday, a breakfast of pastries and fruit is included in the rates.

Hotels *Best Western Pioneer Inn (☎ 661-3636, 800-457-5457, fax 667-5708, ⓦ www.pioneerinn-maui.com, 658 Wharf St)* Rooms $100-165. Parking $5. This two-story hotel has some character left, even if the historic harborfront rooms for which it was best known for are no longer available. Rooms face either Front St, Banyan Tree Square or the inn's garden courtyard. Considering the room size, simple motel furnishings and the less-than-soundproof walls, the rates are pricey. It's better just to come for a drink at the downstairs **restaurant** and **bar**.

Maui Islander (☎ 667-9766, 800-367-5226, fax 661-3733, **w** www.ohanahotels.com, 660 Wainee St) Rooms $139, studios with kitchen $159, 1-bedroom suites $199. Parking $5. Set a few blocks off Front St, this sprawling low-rise hotel set among palm trees nevertheless has some retro appeal. Even if rooms are nothing special, they do have air-con and discount promotions can knock 30% or more off the price. On the grounds are a pool, tennis court and barbecue area; discount passes for nearby Gold's Gym are available.

Inns If you can afford it, these exquisite places are where you should be staying.

Lahaina Inn (☎ 661-0577, 800-669-3444, fax 667-9480, **w** www.lahainainn.com, 127 Lahainaluna Rd) Rooms $109-129, suites $159-169. Parking $5. Lahaina Inn is a project of Crazy Shirts originator Rick Ralston, who spent over $3 million restoring the early 20th-century building as a jewel of a hostelry. The twelve rooms are small but delightful, each with hardwood floors, antique furnishings, floral wallpaper, private bathroom and lanai. Modern conveniences include air-conditioning, telephone and piped-in classical music, but purposefully no television.

Plantation Inn (☎ 667-9225, 800-433-6815, fax 667-9293, **w** www.theplantation inn.com, 174 Lahainaluna Rd) Rooms $145-185, suites $225. Complimentary parking. This elegant two-story Victorian-style inn is arguably the classiest place to stay in Lahaina. Each of the 19 sound-proof rooms and suites boasts antiques, hardwood floors, air-con, TV/VCRs and tiled baths. Rates include use of the swimming pool and a continental breakfast at **Gerard's**, which is the French restaurant situated downstairs at the inn.

Condos If you're looking for a beachfront condo, Lahaina is really not the place to do

it. Try farther up the coast between Honokowai and Napili instead.

Lahaina Shores (☎ 661-3339, 800-642-6284, fax 667-1145, **w** www.lahaina shores.com, 475 Front St) Mountain-view studios low/high season $160/170, 1-bedroom ocean-view units $225/270. This 155-room condo complex is run like a casual seaside resort hotel. It is located right on the beach, next to the 505 Front St shopping plaza, and has a small swimming pool. Each unit is generously sized and has a full kitchen and large lanai. The fifth night is usually free, but if you have to pay rack rates, don't bother.

Makai Inn (☎ 662-3200, fax 661-9027, **w** www.makaiinn.net, 1415 Front St) Rooms $70-105. The friendly Makai Inn is north of the town center, near the Lahaina Cannery Mall, which is on the shopping shuttle route. All of the 400-sq-foot units have full kitchens and some have panoramic ocean views. Although it is a smaller, older complex, there is free parking and no minimum stay. Ask about discounts for longer visits.

Klahani Resorts (☎ 667-2712, 800-669-0795, fax 661-5875, **w** www.klahani.com, PO Box 11120, Lahaina, HI 96761) Personable Klahani handles condo rentals at the oceanfront **Lahaina Roads** (1403 Front St) complex and the clubhouse condos next to Puamana Beach Park, just south of town.

Places to Eat

Like any beachfront resort town, Lahaina has too many just-average pizza kitchens, burger joints and seafood restaurants that survive only because of their waterfront setting. There are a few landmark places if you're willing to splash out (and make advance reservations), or assorted cafés, delis and local food counters if you're not.

Lahaina Square, off Wainee St, has a **Foodland** supermarket. The Lahaina Cannery Mall has a 24-hour **Safeway** (☎ 667-4392) supermarket with takeout salads and deli sandwiches.

Mr Wine (☎ 661-5551, 808 Wainee St) Open 11am-7pm Mon-Sat. Mr Wine has vast cellars and sells Hawaiian microbrews.

Westside Natural Foods & Deli (☎ 667-2855, 193 Lahainaluna Rd) Open 7:30am-9pm Mon-Sat, 8:30am-8pm Sun. Westside Natural Foods sells organic produce, yogurt, fresh juice and a variety of bulk trail mixes and granolas. The deli has a salad bar and hot vegetarian dishes, plus a few café tables where you can sit and eat.

Budget Most of Lahaina's budget eats are found in strip malls and shopping centers, but that doesn't make them bad – honest. The barn-size ***Paniolo Coffee Co*** in the open-air Lahaina Center serves strong java.

The Bakery (☎ 667-9062, 991 Limahana Place) Items under $6. Open 5:30am-3pm Mon-Fri, 5:30am-2pm Sat, 5:30am-noon Sun. On the north side of town this is Lahaina's best bakery. You can get freshly baked artisan breads, croissants, tempting sticky buns and huge muffins, plus sandwiches made to order.

Sunrise Cafe (☎ 661-8558, 693-A Front St) Most dishes $5-8. Open 6am-6pm daily; full menu until 3pm only. Sunrise Cafe, just steps away from Lahaina Harbor, is an arty little hole-in-the-wall selling cinnamon rolls, bagels, pancakes, salads and sandwiches at reasonable prices. Sidewalk tables look out over the ocean.

Gaby's Pizzeria & Deli (☎ 661-8112, 505 Front Street) Mains $5-10, pizzas from $13 or $2 per slice. Locals keep Gaby's, a combo sports bar and family-style pizzeria, pretty busy. Take your pick of toppings from the sea (garlic clam), Upcountry farms (feta, sun-dried tomatoes and spinach), or pasta salads and hot Italian sandwiches.

Sushi-ya (☎ 661-5679, 117 Prison St) Meals $5-7.50. Open 6am-4pm Mon-Fri. Opposite a parking lot, this little hut is bursting with a big reputation where Japanese meets local Hawaiian grinds. The two-scoop plate lunches with macaroni salad are enormous, and there's saimin and Spam tempura, too.

Karma Cafe (☎ 662-1250, 888 Wainee St) Most items $3-7.50. Open 7am-7pm Mon-Fri, 9am-7pm Sat & Sun. Bohemian staff whip up specialty smoothies and frappés, and the atmosphere breathes in meditative

calm with a tiny waterfall and silky floor cushions. The short menu of 'quick grinds' includes wraps, burgers and vegetarian food, but perhaps you'd like the Path to Enlightenment (chocolate, milk, mint and espresso)?

Almost next door to Karma Cafe, ***Royal Seafood Chinese Restaurant*** has a daily hot lunch buffet for $7.25. Around the back in the parking lot is a takeout hut aptly named ***Local Food*** serving inexpensive mixed-plate lunches, *kalua* (traditional method of baking) pig and other Hawaiian faves (under $6).

If it's the middle of the night, Lahaina Square mall down the street has a 24-hour ***Denny's*** restaurant, as well as a branch of ***Maui Tacos***.

Farther north at Lahaina Cannery Mall, ***Ba Le*** has good Vietnamese takeout (see Kahului in the Central Maui chapter). The upscale Mexican chain ***Compadres*** is well known for its Taco Tuesday, when all margaritas cost $2 and tacos only a buck.

Smokehouse BBQ Bar & Grill (☎ 667-7005, 1307 Front St) Platters $13-20, lunch/dinner sandwiches $7/12. Open noon-9pm Mon-Sat, 3pm-9pm Sun. Opposite the Lahaina Cannery Mall, and far enough north to get away from most of the tourists, this local waterfront bar serves *kiawe* (mesquite) smoked barbecue with baked beans, cornbread with macadamia-nut butter and your choice of sides. Outside, lanai tables are right on the beach.

Aloha Mixed Plate (☎ 661-3322, 1285 Front St) Mini/regular/jumbo mixed plates from $3/5/7, other dishes $3-7. Open 10.30am-10pm daily. It looks like a fast-food joint, but the local food is real enough and the oceanfront setting great. If you come to eat around sunset, you'll be able to overhear the music from the Old Lahaina Luau free.

Mid-Range ***Penne Pasta Cafe*** (☎ 661-6633, 180 Dickenson St) Mains $6-12. Open 11am-9:30pm Mon-Fri, 5pm-9pm Sat & Sun. Chef Mark Ellman of Maui Tacos fame has opened this modest Italian *cucina* that garners big praise. There are plenty of daily pasta specials to match the home-baked cheese flatbreads and generous caesar salads. The pastas can be bland, but the pizza and desserts are nearly perfect.

Lahaina Coolers (☎ 661-7082, 180 Dickenson St) Breakfast/lunch dishes $5-11, dinner entrées $11-18. Open 8am-midnight daily. Casual Lahaina Coolers has open-air tables, a beach atmosphere (even though it's not on the water) and by all accounts serves decent food. Dive masters from nearby scuba shops like to hang out here. Apart from the usual menu of burgers, salads and pasta, there's papaya salad, vegan eggs Benedict and a surfers special burrito made with Portuguese sausage.

Most people start looking for a place to eat along Front St, where tables either face the ocean or overlook the street scene.

BJ's Chicago Pizzeria (☎ 661-0700, 730 Front St) Most mains are $6-15. Open 11am-11pm Sun-Thur, 11am-midnight Fri & Sat. This Southern California chain takes a stab at Chicago-style pizza (basically just thick-crust pizza, not quite the real thing) that is pretty tasty. Hot Italian sandwiches, pasta and salads round out the menu, and the upstairs tables overlook Front St. If you come before 4pm, the lunch special includes a minipizza and salad for $6.50.

Moose McGillicuddy's (☎ 667-7758, 844 Front St) Breakfast/lunch dishes $6-11, dinner entrées $11-23; early-bird breakfast $2 (7.30am-8.30am) and dinner $10 (4pm-7pm). Open 7:30am-10pm daily. All day and into the night, Moose's buzzes with merry vacationers. And you know what? The food ain't half bad. Old license plates, movie posters and other Americana kitsch fill the walls, and the super-long menus stick to the same theme. Seafood dinners get a bit fancier than lunch (mostly burgers, salads and fajitas), but breakfast is your best bet. How about a Señor Chicken omelette or yummy Meadow Muffin, basically a butter-milk biscuit crowned in cinnamon? Don't forget that wakey-wakey cocktail either, since 'It's always noon somewhere in the world.'

Kimo's (☎ 661-4811, 845 Front St) Lunch mains $7-11, dinner entrées $15-25. Open 11am-11pm daily. Reservations advised. Rustic Kimo's is an extremely popular oceanfront restaurant boasting sunset views and live music on weeknights. It's all pretty straightforward but elegant, with a good reputation dating back to 1977. Skip lunch, which is mostly unexciting salads and sandwiches, and go straight for dinner, including steak or market-fresh fish done in a dozen different styles, each accompanied by fresh-baked carrot muffins, sourdough rolls, herb rice and a caesar salad.

Maui Brews (☎ 667-7794, Lahaina Center, 900 Front St) Breakfast $4-8, appetizers $6-9, mains $8-18. Restaurant open 11am-10pm daily, bar menu until 11:30pm. Maui Brews, in the Lahaina Center, is the island's perennially popular sports bar/music club/restaurant, serving exactly the kind of food you'd expect: burgers, pizza, ribs and steak.

Lahaina Fish Co (☎ 661-3472, 831 Front St) Mains $10-24. Open 11am-midnight daily. This salty-dog–style wooden eatery concentrates on the essentials, offering a rainbow variety of fresh fish and a raw bar for sashimi, oysters and clams. The lunch and late-night grill menus are far simpler, with fish & chips, chowder and lava rock crab Louie salad.

Top End Seafood is what everyone is here for – and also a table with a view, naturally. Reservations are advised.

Canoes (☎ 661-0937, 1450 Front St) Entrées $21-40, early-bird dinner $16 (5pm-6pm). Open 4pm-10pm daily; food available 5pm-9:30pm. Anyone could fall in love at Canoes at the very quiet end of Front St. The architecture resembles a traditional Hawaiian canoe house, or *hale waa,* and waves can be heard crashing across the road while the torchlight flickers. All of the upper-storey tables are open to the ocean breezes and the food emphasizes classic steak and Hawaiian seafood with lilikoi cheesecake afterward.

Longhi's (☎ 667-2288, 888 Front St) Breakfast $3-11, lunch $9-16, dinner entrées $17.50-30. Open 7:30am-10pm daily. So popular that it even has its own cookbook,

Longhi's used to have a solid-gold reputation with tourists and locals alike. The open-air lanai affects a wealthy plantation ambience, but the menu is mostly limited to 'signature' dishes such as Shrimp Longhi, Scallops Longhi et al. There's an extensive wine list and the homemade breakfast quiche and frittata look promising.

Pacific'O (☎ 667-4341, fax 661-8399, 505 Front Street Shopping Center) Lunch mains $10-15, dinner entrées $19-28. Open 11am-3pm & 5:30pm-10:30pm daily. Pacific'O is perhaps Lahaina's most reputable spot for contemporary Pacific cuisine. The seaside setting and attentive service are impeccable and the food imaginative. Start with the signature seafood chowder or a hot calamari salad. Main courses get adventurous with seafood tempura in white miso-lime-basil sauce or fresh fish with banana curry sauce and sun-dried fruit chutney. The lunch menu sticks with tamer fare, like a goat-cheese salad, shrimp satay or fish & chips.

David Paul's Lahaina Grill (☎ 667-5117, 800-360-2606, fax 661-5478, W www.lahaina grill.com, 127 Lahainaluna Rd) Entrées $26-33. Open from 6pm nightly. In the historic Lahaina Inn, this popular chef-driven restaurant has excellent food and an intimate setting. Splashes of art make it feel almost like a gallery space. Chef's David Paul Johnson's self-described 'New American' cuisine takes local Hawaiian Island produce and mixes it with tastes from around the Americas and Pacific Rim. The Sonoma Duck is a ménage à trois of shredded duck confit, macadamia-nut smoked chicken and foie gras with plum sauce. House specialties include spicy tequila shrimp with firecracker rice and a vintage Hawaiian chocolate soufflé.

I'o (☎ 661-8422, 505 Front Street) Entrées $18-28. Open 5:30pm-10pm daily. Across from Pacific'O, this is Chef David Paul Johnson's other venture, this time into modern Hawaiian cuisine. The dining space exhibits a postmodern aquarium chic and, probably because the restaurant is right on the beach, the idea works. The martini and wine lists go on forever, while you can count on a short, but surprising specials menu

along the lines of fresh oysters topped with bacon and star anise–coconut cream or Lobster Tahitian stir-fry with bamboo shoots and dark cane rum. If you dine early enough, you'll overhear the Feast at Lele luau.

Gerard's (☎ 661-8939, 877-661-8939, fax 667-5392, W www.gerardsmaui.com, 174 Lahainaluna Rd) Entrées $29-40. Open 6pm-9:30pm daily. At the Plantation Inn, stylish Gerard's serves 'contemporary French island cooking,' with all the romance of candlelight, wine and an open-air lanai. Gascony-born chef Gerard Reversade apprenticed under four-star Michelin restaurant chefs, and when he opened his own place in Lahaina in 1982, he supported Maui farmers and fishers from the very start. The menu changes regularly, with such seasonal specials as quail stuffed with corn or ahi tartare and taro chips, but rack of lamb and duck confit are house standards. Service is stellar and the traditional French desserts show tropical flair ($8.50), not surprising when the chef makes his own sorbet.

Entertainment

A lot of what's happening on Maui happens in Lahaina, and has done ever since the whaling days of yore. But things aren't quite that wild anymore, and most of the nightlife seems aimed at vacationers desperate to revive their younger days. Magic shows and spectacular Las Vegas–style extravaganzas are predictably popular with the cruise-ship crowd.

If you keep your ear cocked toward the grapevine (or just check the entertainment listings in Thursday's *Maui News* or *Maui Time*) you will find something you like, whether that's a live band, first-run movies, happy hour at a historic hotel or a traditional hula show. Or take a walk down Front St and check it out for yourself. If everything looks a bit too plasticky, try instead the Maui Arts & Cultural Center in Kahului (see the Central Maui chapter).

Alternative types can soothe their souls at *Maui Yoga (☎ 661-7272, W www.mauiyoga .com, 181 Lahainaluna Rd, suite D)*, which has a few drop-in classes every day.

Bars, Clubs & Live Music Happy hour in Lahaina is pretty much 3pm to 6pm nightly. For those who believe in drinking cheaply well after the sun sets, *Lahaina Coolers* (see Places to Eat, earlier) has another happy hour from 10pm until 2am, which is when most bars and clubs close. Restaurants that have entertainment usually stay open until midnight. Cover charges during the week are usually free or only a few bucks, rising to $5 to $10 on weekends.

Maui Brews (☎ 669-7794, *Lahaina Center, 900 Front St)* Entertainment until 2am nightly. Good ol' Maui Brews has a sports bar with big-screen TVs and a nightclub, both pouring Lahaina's largest selection of draft beers, including Hawaiian microbrews. Starting around 9pm, the club presents live reggae early in the week, with salsa, jazz, island bands, hip-hop or retro DJs seeing you through the weekend.

Moose McGillicuddy's (see Places to Eat, earlier) Honeymooners, frat boys and just about anyone else you can think of rub shoulders (and other body parts) while dancing here, with DJs or live music nightly from 9:30pm.

Hard Rock Café (☎ 667-7400, *Lahaina Center, 900 Front St)* Yes, we know: it's just another Hard Rock. But sometimes you can catch big-name acts or Club 808 radio DJs here on weekends. There is usually no cover charge, either, so who's complaining?

Hop Tomato Italian Bistro & Brewery (☎ 661-8580, *Lahaina Center, 900 Front St)* Open until 11pm daily. Revolutionizing the concept of happy hour, Hop Tomato offers a pitcher of beer with pizza for just $12. Copper beer vats may make you thirsty for the microbrew sampler ($5.25), or some homemade root beer at least. Recently, DJs for global house, trance and drum 'n bass have been settling into this indoor/outdoor space on Friday nights.

Pioneer Inn (☎ 661-3636, *658 Wharf St)* This century-old landmark has a harborside verandah made for people-watching and live musicians stroll among the tables almost nightly starting around sunset.

Many other Front St restaurants (see Places to Eat, earlier) use live music or dancing to lure customers, but there may be a cover charge if you're not eating or drinking. *Longhi's* has an interesting koa-wood dance floor and live rock bands starting around 9:30pm Friday. *BJ's Chicago Pizzeria*, which happens to be housed in the legendary Blue Max club of the 1970s, has live music nightly 6pm to 8pm. *Pacific'O*, overlooking the beach, features live jazz 9pm to midnight weekends. Nearby *Ali'i Mocha House* (☎ 661-7800, *505 Front St)* has jazz or blues singers on certain weeknights.

Hula & Luau You can enjoy free keiki hula shows at 2.30pm Wednesday and 6pm Friday at *Hale Kahiko* (see Hale Kahiko, earlier) outside Lahaina Center, as well as at the *Lahaina Cannery Mall* at 1pm Saturday and Sunday. The Cannery also has Polynesian dance performances at 7pm Tuesday and Thursday.

Old Lahaina Luau (☎ 661-8455, **w** *www .oldlahainaluau.com, 1251 Front St)* Adult/child $70/40. Luau 5:30pm-8:30pm daily. Old Lahaina Luau, on the beach behind the Lahaina Cannery Mall, has a buffet dinner with open bar, Hawaiian music and a show. Often voted the most authentic for its traditional luau and feast, if you go to one luau on the island for the cultural aspect this should be it.

The Feast at Lele (☎ 667-5353, *800-248-5828, **w** www.feastatlele.com, 500 Front St)* Adult/child $90/60. Luau 6pm-9pm Tues, Thur & Sat. On the waterfront behind the 505 Front Street shopping center, this Polynesian dance show has four courses and four acts brought to you by the Old Lahaina Luau and the I'o (see Places to Eat, earlier) chefs.

Cinemas The *Lahaina Wharf Cinemas* (☎ 244-8934 ext 2004, *Wharf Cinema Center)* and *Front Street Theatres* (☎ 244-8934 ext 2004, *Lahaina Center)* Adult/child $7.50/4.25, matinees $4.75. Both multiscreen theaters show first-run movies, albeit a little later than on the US mainland.

Hawaii Experience Domed Theater (☎ 661-8314, *824 Front St)* Adult/child 4-12 years $7/4. Hourly screenings noon-9pm daily. This Omnivision theater has been showing the same 40-minute, 70mm film 'Hawaii: Island of the Gods' for ages. The aerial photography may be worth the price of admission, especially shown on this enormous 180-degree screen.

Shopping

It is hard to separate the pearls from the pigs in Lahaina. There are so many tourist rip-off shops that sell fake Hawaiiana or low-quality gear, that you may be tempted to give up.

Lahaina touts itself as an art gallery mecca. 'Art Night,' held from 6pm to around 9pm on Friday, is when galleries schedule their openings, occasionally with entertainment, artist appearances and hors d'oeuvre. However, most of these galleries carry nothing but schlock. **Celebrities Gallery** (☎ 667-0727, 764 Front St) is at least amusing for its reproductions of works by famous folks like David Bowie or Miles Davis. **Vintage European Posters** (742 Front St) sells the real deal, with giant early 20th-century posters.

If you're looking for fine art by island painters, sculptors, woodcarvers and printmakers, there are a few worthy places. One is the **Lahaina Arts Society** in the old courthouse (see Banyan Tree Square, earlier).

Village Gallery (☎ 661-4402, 800-246-0585, 120 Dickenson St) and **Village Gallery Contemporary** (☎ 661-5559, 800-483-8599, 180 Dickenson Square) Carved wooden lei, paintings, blown glass, modern woodblock prints and jewelry made from recycled antiques are just a few of the unique pieces found at both these places.

Island Woodcarving (740 Front St) This master woodcarver can also often be found sitting under the banyan tree on Wednesday.

Whaler's Locker (☎ 661-3775, 780 Front St) There are many, many scrimshaw and netsuke shops on Front St. This place has the best quality and prices, plus amber and shark's teeth for sale.

Island Sandals (☎ 661-5110, W www .islandsandals.com, Wharf Cinema Center, 658 Front St) Tucked around the side of the shopping center, handmade leather sandals are put together while you wait. Quality costs: one pair $125-155.

Nā Mea Hawai'i Store (☎ 661-3262, 698 Front St) Next to the Baldwin House, this shop carries aloha shirts, feathered lei hats, native flora and fauna prints and Hawaiiana books that you could buy to take with you and stretch out on the rocks by the harbor to read.

Dan's Green House (☎ 661-8412, W www .dansgreenhouse.com, 133 Prison St) Dan's sells *fuku-bonsai*, a quasi-bonsai effect created when the roots of the common houseplant schefflera (octopus tree) grow around a lava rock. It also sells blooming orchids, protea, plumeria, coconut tree sprouts and Hawaiian ti leaf plants.

For island-style clothing, try **Serendipity** (☎ 667-7070, 752 Front St) and **Maui Tropix** (☎ 661-9296, 715 Front St) or **Quicksilver** (☎ 667-7978, 851 Front St) for that instant surfer look. Every other store on Front St seems to be a T-shirt warehouse; homegrown **Crazy Shirts** (☎ 661-4775, 865 Front St) uses unique dyes (hemp, beer, even Blue Curaçao) and **The Gecko Store** (☎ 661-1078, 703 Front St) has a funky sand floor.

Discount tourist shops like **ABC Store**, **Whalers General Store** and the even cheaper **EZ Discount Store** are everywhere. Major shopping malls are **Lahaina Center** (☎ 667-9216, 900 Front St), which has international chains and a cinema, and **Lahaina Cannery Mall** (☎ 661-5304, W www .lahainacannerymall.com, 1221 Honoapiilani Hwy), which is good for special events or the Hawaiian CDs and ukuleles at **Groove 2 Music**.

The grooviest little place to shop is peaceful **505 Front Street** (☎ 667-2514, 505 Front St) shopping center, beside the beach on the quiet side of town:

Old Lahaina Book Emporium (☎ 661-1399) Open 10am-9pm Mon-Sat, 10am-6pm Sun. Lose yourself inside Maui's largest independent bookstore, stacked with all types of new and used volumes and vintage Hawaiian collectibles.

Right around the corner from Maui Yoga (see Entertainment, earlier) is **Atomic Tattoos** (☎ 667-2156, 193 Lahainaluna Rd).

Those looking for less permanent thrills can duck into **Henna World** (☎ 662-8789, 744 *Front St*).

LAHAINA TO KAANAPALI

On the stretch from Lahaina to Kaanapali, the driving can be aggressive, and traffic can jam up quickly, particularly during rush hours. Most people are either commuters or in a big hurry to get to the better beaches farther north.

For details about coastal bus services, see the Getting Around chapter.

Sugar Cane Train

The old steam-powered train that once carried sugarcane from the fields along the coast to the Pioneer Sugar Mill has been restored by the Lahaina, Kaanapali & Pacific Railroad (☎ 667-6851, 800-499-2307, w *www .sugarcanetrain.com; Roundtrip adult/child 3-12 years $15.75/8.75*). Unfortunately, the train tracks run close by the highway and sugarcane isn't raised here anymore so unless you really feel the need for a joyride with singing conductors or a cowboy cookout, you can safely skip it.

Wahikuli Wayside State Park

About two miles north of Lahaina, this wayside park occupies a narrow strip of beach squeezed next to the highway opposite the main post office and the civic center. With a gift for prophecy, the Hawaiians named this coastal stretch Wahikuli, or 'noisy place.'

The beach is mostly backed by a black-rock retaining wall, although there's a small amount of sand. If you don't mind the traffic noise, the swimming conditions are usually only a bit murky. But why bother? When the water's calm, you can snorkel near the lava outcroppings at the park's south end. There are showers, restrooms, pavilions, picnic tables and free parking.

Hanakaoo Beach Park

Hanakaoo Beach Park is a mile-long sandy beach just south of Kaanapali Beach Resort. The park has full facilities and a lifeguard on duty daily. The beach is also known as Canoe Beach, since local canoe clubs store their outriggers here. You can watch them paddling along the coast either early in the morning or during late afternoon.

The beach has a sandy bottom and water conditions are usually quite safe for swimming. You can snorkel down by the south side of the beach park, although it doesn't even compare with Puu Kekaa (Black Rock) farther north.

Bodyboarders and surfers like the gentle shorebreaks here. However, southerly swells in summer can create powerful waves and shorebreaks, and the occasional kona storm can kick up rough water conditions in winter.

KAANAPALI

In the late 1950s, Amfac corporation, owner of the Pioneer Sugar Mill, earmarked 600 acres of relatively barren sugarcane land for development of the first Hawaiian resort outside Waikiki. While modern Kaanapali is not a 'getaway' in the sense of avoiding crowds, it does boast three miles of sandy beach with views across the channel to Lanai and Molokai.

Today the resort area is crowded with two 18-hole golf courses, 30 tennis courts, Whalers Village shopping center, six high-rise oceanfront hotels and six condo complexes. It is all rather nouveau riche and looks as much like Southern California as Hawaii.

Kaanapali Beach

Kaanapali is really two beaches divided by Puu Kekaa (Black Rock) at the Sheraton. Officially the stretch north from Black Rock to Honokowai is Kaanapali Beach, and everything south is just an extension of Hanakaoo Beach Park, also nicknamed 'Dig Me Beach.' Since the resort was built, however, the whole thing has generally been called Kaanapali Beach.

Public beach parking is ridiculously limited to a few slots along the beach hotels and Whalers Village. The Hyatt has free 'self parking' for hotel visitors at its south side. Whalers Village also has public parking

KAANAPALI & HONOKOWAI

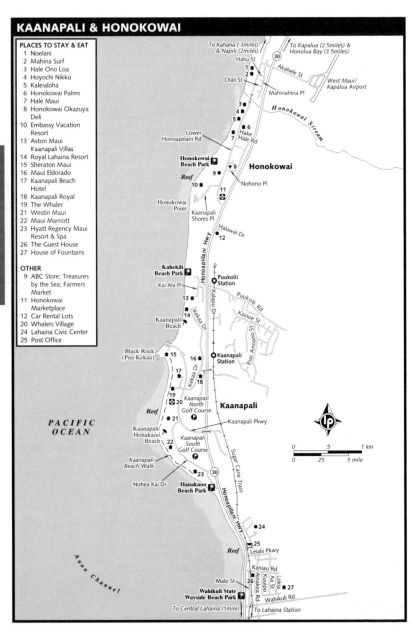

PLACES TO STAY & EAT
1 Noelani
2 Mahina Surf
3 Hale Ono Loa
4 Hoyochi Nikko
5 Kaleialoha
6 Honokowai Palms
7 Hale Maui
8 Honokowai Okazuya Deli
10 Embassy Vacation Resort
13 Aston Maui Kaanapali Villas
14 Royal Lahaina Resort
15 Sheraton Maui
16 Maui Eldorado
17 Kaanapali Beach Hotel
18 Kaanapali Royal
19 The Whaler
21 Westin Maui
22 Maui Marriott
23 Hyatt Regency Maui Resort & Spa
26 The Guest House
27 House of Fountains

OTHER
9 ABC Store; Treasures by the Sea; Farmers Market
11 Honokowai Marketplace
12 Car Rental Lots
20 Whalers Village
24 Lahaina Civic Center
25 Post Office

WEST MAUI

To Kahana (.3miles) & Napili (2miles)
To Kapalua (2.5miles) & Honolua Bay (3.5miles)
Haliu St
30
Akahele St
West Maui/ Kapalua Airport
Olali St
Mahinahina Pl
Honokowai Stream
Lower Honoapiilani Rd
Hake
Hale Rd
Honokowai Beach Park
Reef
Honokowai
Nohono Pl
Honokowai Point
Kaanapali Shores Pl
Halawai Dr
Honoapiilani Hwy
Kahekili Beach Park
Kai Ala Pl
Puukolii Station
Puukolii Rd
Kalapu Dr
Kainoe St
Kaanapali Beach
Kekaa Dr
Puu Anoano St
Black Rock (Puu Kekaa)
Kaanapali Station
Kaanapali North Golf Course
Kaanapali
Kaanapali Pkwy
PACIFIC OCEAN
Reef
Kaanapali/ Honakaoo Beach
Kaanapali South Golf Course
Kaanapali Beach Walk
30
Nohea Kai Dr
Hanakaoo Beach Park
Sugar Cane Train
Honoapiilani Hwy
Auau Channel
Reef
Leialii Pkwy
Kaniau Rd
Malo St
Alaikea Rd
Kuuipo
Aa St
Uokla
Wahikuli State Wayside Beach Park
Wahikuli Rd
To Central Lahaina (1mile)
To Lahaina Station

0   .5   1 km
0   .25   .5 mile

with free validation if you spend more than $10 at any of the shops or restaurants. You can also park at Kahekili Beach Park and stroll down along the beach.

Kaanapali Hanakaoo Beach Much of the stretch between the Sheraton and the Hyatt can be dangerous, particularly on the point in front of the Marriott, where strong currents sometimes develop. As a general rule, waters are rougher in winter, although the worst conditions can actually occur in early summer if there's a southerly swell.

Be careful in rough surf, as the waves can pick you up and bounce you onto the coral reef that runs from the southern end of the Westin down to the Hyatt. It is possible to snorkel near the Hyatt, but check with the hotel beach huts for the day's water conditions before jumping in.

Puu Kekaa (Black Rock) Black Rock, the nickname for Puu Kekaa ('Kekaa Point'), is the rocky lava promontory that protects the beach in front of the Sheraton. This is Kaanapali's safest and best spot for swimming and snorkeling.

You can snorkel along the southern side of Black Rock, where you'll find some nice coral and schools of fish that are used to being fed. The real prize, however, is the horseshoe cove cut into the tip of the rock, where there's more pristine coral, abundant fish and the occasional turtle. It's also a popular shore dive spot. However, there's often a current to contend with off the point, which can make getting to the cove a little risky, but when it's calm you can swim right around into the horseshoe. Check with the Sheraton beach hut about current water conditions.

If you just want to see what the cove looks like, you can peer down into it after taking the short footpath along the top of Black Rock from in front of the Sheraton.

Kaanapali Beach Walk A paved beachfront walk connects the Hyatt and the Sheraton, passing other resort hotels along the way. If you breeze by around sunset, you may catch some free entertainment, notably musicians outside Whalers Village and the Marriott luau. In addition to the coastal scenery, both the Hyatt and Westin have some striking landscaped gardens and artwork collections valued at $2 million each.

The Hyatt's lobby and grounds shelter Ming vases, Balinese paintings, Hawaiian quilts, ceremonial drums, and New Guinean

WEST MAUI

Black Rock

According to legend Puu Kekaa (Black Rock) was created by the demigod Maui, who apparently had a wicked appetite for turning anyone he didn't like into stone. In this case the victim was a shape-shifter who unwisely taunted Maui about his lack of strength. After the demigod climbed Haleakala and lassoed the sun, Maui walked back to Kaanapali and chased the shape-shifter out to sea, freezing his body into stone upon the shore.

Black Rock was also believed to be the island's *uhana lele,* the place where the souls of those who had recently died leapt into the afterlife. Only someone with great *mana* (spiritual power) could jump from the rock and return to the land of the living unscathed. In the 18th-century Chief Kahekili performed this feat, perhaps to rid his people of their superstitions or to increase his own prestige. He must've also done it for his own pleasure, as he was a legendary athlete of *lele kawa,* the ancient Hawaiian sport of cliff-jumping.

By the end of the 1800s, this sacred site was being used by trains from the Lahaina sugar mill to unload sweet cargo onto waiting ships. Today Black Rock is in the clutches of the Sheraton hotel, which employs a torchbearer to leap into the sea every night around sunset for tourists. The spirit of Kahekili, who was quite the showman back in his own day, must feel flattered.

artifacts, storyboards and war shields. Among the other noteworthy pieces: a bronze sculpture from Thailand of King Rama battling with the King of Demons; a large wooden Buddha, lacquered and gilded, from Mandalay; and a spirit figure from the Misingi village in Papua New Guinea.

It's hard not be impressed by the Hyatt's lobby atrium with its jungle foliage, waterfalls, pools and gardens with strutting flamingoes and talking macaw. The more austere Westin Maui is landscaped with five free-form pools and a network of artificial streams and ponds with swans and crowned cranes. The Westin's collection of Asian and European garden statuary can look a bit odd, however, especially the bronze dogs in somewhat menacing poses at the edge of the walkways.

Kahekili Beach Park This beach park at the north side of Kaanapali Beach is dedicated to Kahekili Nui Ahumanu, the last king of Maui. It is also called Airport Beach, after the old Kapalua airport that once stood nearby.

The beach has golden sands, shady palm trees and gentle slopes. The water is open ocean, but most of the time inshore it's placid and crystal clear, perfect for swimming.

If you walk north for about 20 minutes, you'll come to a reef around Honokowai Point, where there is good snorkeling when conditions are calm. Keep your eyes on the shore, though, as currents can be strong.

Kahekili Beach Park has showers, changing rooms, toilets, a picnic pavilion, barbecue grills and free parking. To get there from Honoapiilani Hwy, turn west onto Kai Ala Pl (opposite Puukolii Rd) just past the 25-mile marker and then bear right.

Whalers Village Museum

A highlight of any trip to Kaanapali is this tiny **whaling museum** (☎ 661-4567, 3rd level, Whalers Village, 2435 Kaanapali Pkwy; admission free; open 9:30am-10pm daily).

In the 19th century, whales were considered a 'floating gold mine' of oil, spermaceti and blubber. Whale baleen, prior to the in-

vention of durable plastic, was used for things like corsets and umbrella stays. Ambergris was a perfume fixative, but so rare that in four decades the entire US whaling fleet only harvested 1 ton!

Period photos and interpretive exhibits sound the depths of all aspects of whaling history, from hunting methods to everyday shipboard life. There are harpoons, whale jawbones and displays of scrimshaw, perhaps the only folk art unique to the USA. For a small donation, riveting audio guides are available in four languages.

A lot of the character of the whalers comes through, and you'll get a feel for how rough and dirty the work was. Wages were so low that sailors sometimes owed the ship money by the time they got home and had to sign up for another four-year stint just to pay off the debt.

A short film on whales plays continuously in the small theater next to the **Whalers Village Museum Shoppe** that sells excellent scrimshaw carvings and recordings of traditional whaling songs from New England. There's a full-size **sperm whale skeleton** at the front entrance to the shopping center, which is a short walk from the museum.

Activities

Kaanapali Golf (☎ 661-3691, w www .kaanapali-golf.com, 2290 Kaanapali Pkwy; Green fees & shared cart for guests/nonguests $130/150, twilight rate (after 2:30pm) $75). The Tournament North course here is slightly less windy than golfing at scenic Kapalua, but the fairways are right near the highway and the condo complexes.

Royal Lahaina Tennis Ranch (☎ 667-5200, Royal Lahaina Resort; Daily pass $10, child under 18 free with playing adult). It's the largest tennis complex in West Maui with a 3500-seat stadium and six courts lit for night play. During the day there are clinics and 'Stroke of the Day' sessions taught by pros. Once you pay the daily fee, you can also play at the tennis courts found at the **Maui Marriott Beach & Tennis Club** (100 Nohea Kai Dr) and the **Sheraton Maui** (2605 Kaanapali Pkwy).

Places to Stay

Kaanapali has high-priced resort hotels right on the beach, equally expensive condos up on the golf-course links and a couple of modern B&Bs in an average residential neighborhood back toward Lahaina and far from the beach. If the truth be told, none of these options is terribly exciting, although if you can snag a special discount it might be worth it.

B&Bs *House of Fountains* (☎ 667-2121, 800-789-6865, fax 667-2120, **W** *www.aloha house.com, 1579 Lokia St)* Rooms/studios/suites $95/115/145. All accommodations, varying from simple rooms to spacious suites, come with air-con, private bath and a German-style breakfast. Amenities at this contemporary 7000-sq-foot home include a guest kitchen, ocean-view sundeck, swimming pool and Jacuzzi. German is spoken.

The GuestHouse B&B (☎ 661-8085, 800-621-8942, fax 661-1896, **W** *www.mauiguest house.com, 1620 Ainakea Rd)* Suites per person/two people $115/130. This is another morden home but this time with more tropical Hawaiian touches. Each of the four large suites has air-con, telephone, private lanai and its own hot tub or Jacuzzi. Privacy is easy to come by, and it's got a circular swimming pool, too. Rates include breakfast and free email, laundry facilities, full kitchen access and use of beach gear, including boogie boards and snorkel sets.

Condos What you're paying for is location mostly. There are more affordable condos farther north at Honokowai.

Aston Maui Kaanapali Villas (☎ 667-7791, 800-922-7866, fax 667-0366, 45 Kai Ala Dr)* Hotel rooms low/high season $160/210, studios with kitchen $215/275. Overall, it's of a less meticulous standard than other Kaanapali properties, and if you can't get any discounts, it's not a great deal. However, its location near the south end of Kahekili Beach Park makes it worth recommending.

Both of the following low-rise condo complexes are in a hillside location near the golf course, a few minutes' walk from the beach.

Kaanapali Royal (☎ 667-7200, 800-676-4112, fax 661-5611, **W** *www.kaanapaliroyal .com, 2560 Kekaa Dr)* 2-bedroom units low/high season from around $225/275. These large two-bedroom, two-bath condos with a full kitchen and washer/dryer can sleep up to six people, which makes this place a bargain for families. There is a heated swimming pool and tennis courts onsite.

Maui Eldorado (☎ 661-0021, 800-688-7444, fax 667-7039, **W** *www.outrigger.com, 2661 Kekaa Dr)* Studios/1-bedroom units from $195/255. Outrigger's Maui Eldorado is a more posh condo resort. The studios are big, with kitchens completely set apart from the bedrooms. The rack rates are a joke, but the Outrigger chain offers numerous discount schemes (see the Web site **W** www .outrigger.com for details). If you ask for the 'Free Ride' special, rates include a free rental car.

Hotels All Kaanapali resort hotels are either on the beach or within walking distance of it. They've all got the expected modern amenities, impressive swimming pools and activity programs for adults and keiki. However, rooms tend to be boxy, and these days some of the hotels are showing their age. Other places nickel-and-dime you to death with 'daily resort use fees' (around $10 per guest) for things that really should be free, such as local telephone calls and extra towels.

The cheapest rates listed here are generally during low season for rooms that have garden views and are set farther back from the ocean. Promotions can often cut even these rates by a substantial amount. For general information on current promotions, visit the Kaanapali resort Web site at **W** www.maui.net/~kbra.

Kaanapali Beach Hotel (☎ 661-0011, 800-262-8450, fax 667-5987, **W** *www.kbhmaui .com, 2525 Kaanapali Pkwy)* Rooms/suites from $165/250. Parking $5. This hotel has an enviable beachside location between Whalers Village shopping center and Black Rock. Although it's an older complex, it's pleasantly low-key and gets top marks for overall value and Hawaiian-style hospitality.

Free introductory scuba lessons are given daily in the whale-shaped swimming pool.

The Whaler (☎ 661-3484, 800-676-4112, fax 661-8338, ⓦ www.vacation-maui.com/whaler, 2481 Kaanapali Pkwy) Studios $175-205, 1-bedroom units $225-340, 2-bedroom units $400-580. Check-in fee $35, daily parking $7. Right next to Whalers Village, this flower-laden, high-rise condo complex may not look like much from outside, but each unit has a fully equipped kitchen, marble bathroom and private lanai overlooking a boisterous (that is, noisy) section of beach. Make sure you get a discount from Whalers Realty, or search the Web for ads by private condo owners. If you want to be in the thick of things, this is the place.

Royal Lahaina Resort (☎ 497-7934, 800-222-5642, fax 494-3960, ⓦ www.2maui.com, 2780 Kekaa Dr) Off-peak specials: standard garden/ocean-view rooms $110/145, 1-/2-bedroom suites $275/375. Admittedly, this place is past its prime. But it sits on a broad, less busy stretch of beach on the northern side of Black Rock. The cheapest rooms can feel cramped and totally lack views, but there are a few cottages closer to the beach, as well as tennis courts and three swimming pools. Internet promotions can knock 50% off the regular rates.

Hyatt Regency Maui Resort & Spa (☎ 661-1234, 800-233-1234, fax 667-4498, ⓦ www.maui.hyatt.com, 200 Nohea Kai Dr) Terrace/partial ocean-view rooms from $275/395, suites from $600. Newly renovated rooms have standard Hyatt décor, but some of the hotel perks include priceless artwork, an oceanfront spa, guided stargazing programs and an outdoor swimming pool that meanders through waterfall grottoes with a 150-foot water slide.

Sheraton Maui (☎ 661-0031, 800-782-9488, fax 661-0458, ⓦ www.sheraton hawaii.com, 2605 Kaanapali Pkwy) Garden/ocean-view rooms from $350/500, suites from $750. There is no more prime beachfront location than directly in front of Black Rock. Although the hotel was completely rebuilt in 1997 to the tune of $150 million, rooms are not quite all you'd except for the

rates they're charging. Still, there is a 142-yard swimming lagoon and just think: location, location, location.

Places to Eat

You have only two choices in Kaanapali: eating at resort hotels or the Whalers Village shopping center (2435 Kaanapali Pkwy), and only a few places are relatively good value for the money.

Whalers Village *Coffee, Etc* (☎ 667-8672, 2nd level) Items $2-6. Kaanapali's best-kept secret is this down-to-earth café, hidden inside Waldenbooks megachain bookstore opposite the whaling museum. Healthy and creative wraps, fresh salads, giant muffins and cookies are easy on both your wallet and your taste buds. Wash it all down with Hawaiian-grown coffee or an Italian soda while you revel in luxurious air-conditioning.

The basement ***food court*** has a few fast-food options with plate meals under $7, including Village Korean BBQ and Takase Soba Shop.

Hula Grill & Barefoot Bar (☎ 667-6636) Appetizers $7-15, entrées $10-25. Hula Grill open for dinner 5pm-9:30pm daily; Barefoot Bar open 11am-10:30pm daily. Among the beachfront restaurants, this one distinguishes itself with the culinary arts of chef Peter Merriman, known throughout the islands for his Hawaii Regional cuisine. Laidback ambience (yes, the sandy beachfront bar really does allow bare feet) belies an inventive menu of *pupu*. For example: crab and macadamia-nut wontons, or more substantial kiawe-grilled pizza or Tahitian-style fish in fresh lime and coconut juices. Inside, the more formal and expensive Hula Grill brings on the heavy-hitters: fish, lobster and steak.

Hotels You could easily while away the better part of a morning at one of the hotel buffets before hitting the beach.

Kaanapali Mixed Plate Restaurant (Kaanapali Beach Hotel) Buffet adult/child $9.50/6.50. Open for breakfast 6am-10:45am, lunch 11am-2pm. While not a notable for its culinary delights, you can certainly eat your fill here of fresh pineapple, eggs, sausage, cereals and coffee.

If you can afford to spend twice as much, you can stuff yourself in style at the more lavish resorts, where the breakfast buffet usually includes an omelette station, fresh fruit and pastries. The **Swan Court** *(Hyatt Regency Maui Resort & Spa)* has a superb movie-star setting that overlooks a large swan pond with artificial waterfalls and a Japanese garden.

You'd better eat well early in the day, because lunch options are not promising. You can pick up affordable picnic fixings at **Beachfront Market & Pantry** outside the Maui Marriott, on the Kaanapali Beach Walk.

Tropica *(☎ 667-2525, Westin Maui, 2365 Kaanapali Pkwy))* Bar menu $7-15, dinner entrées $17-34, 3-course tasting menu $25. Open 3pm-midnight; dinner 5:30pm-10:30pm, bar 3pm-midnight daily. This poolside bar and grill has a 'fire and ice' concept menu, shooting from lobster with chili-pepper butter to Hawaiian oyster shooters with cool tropical salsa. The desserts are equally dramatic, with the chocolate lava of Pele's Inferno ($9) being big enough to share.

The Maui Marriott **Nalu Sunset & Sushi Bar** has a harmonious mix of Pacific Rim styles and perfect ocean views, but true sushi lovers should make the trek to **Sansei Seafood Restaurant & Sushi Bar** at Kapalua (see Kapalua, later).

Teppanyaki Dan *(Sheraton Maui)* Complete dinners $20-42. Open 6pm-9:30pm Thur-Mon. Chefs prepare *teppanyaki* (Japanese grilling) at your table, and with fresh Hawaiian ingredients and whispers of the ocean, how could they go wrong? You just have to choose your main grill dish, perhaps steak or Maui lobster with lemongrass essence finished off with a light citrus or nut dessert (under $5).

The Coral Reef *(Sheraton Maui)* Entrées $25-45. Open 5:30pm-9pm daily. Rattan furniture and ceiling fans are reminiscent of old colonial outposts, but the concept is tropically aquatic. The austere menu focuses

on market-fresh fish prepared in over a dozen styles, the most elaborate à la Oscar, stuffed with king crab, asparagus and covered with Béarnaise sauce.

Entertainment

Whalers Village *(☎ 661-4567, Ⓦ www.whalersvillage.com, 2435 Kaanapali Pkwy)* This open-air shopping complex has a full schedule of lei-making, sand sculpture and other art classes in the afternoon, with live music, hula and Polynesian dance performances starting at 7pm on the lower-level stage.

There's often contemporary or Hawaiian music outdoors in the evening at one of the Whalers Village restaurants:

Hula Grill & Barefoot Bar *(☎ 667-6636)* Happy hour, 3pm to 5pm, at the Barefoot Bar is followed by sunset Hawaiian music until 8pm daily.

Rusty Harpoon *(☎ 661-3123)* Many people come here for the longer happy hours (2pm to 6pm and 10pm to closing), elevated views over the beach and sports on the three big-screen satellite TVs.

Many of the major Kaanapali hotels such as the following (see Places to Stay, earlier) have a variety of entertainment after dark, including live bands, jazz pianists, and traditional and contemporary Hawaiian music.

Sheraton Maui The Sheraton has a torch-lighting and cliff-diving ceremony at sunset nightly, with hula dancing from 6pm to 8pm nightly at its Lagoon Bar.

Hyatt Regency Maui Resort & Spa The Hyatt has a torch-lighting ceremony nightly at around 6:15pm, followed by mellow Hawaiian music until 9:30pm in the Weeping Banyan Lounge.

Kaanapali Beach Hotel Every night in the hotel courtyard, there's a free hula show starting at 6:30pm followed by Hawaiian music until 9:30pm at the Tiki Terrace.

Westin Maui *(☎ 667-2525, 2365 Kaanapali Pkwy)* There is live Hawaiian entertainment at the poolside bar & grill 5pm to 7pm Monday to Friday and live bands or DJs at its Tropica bar (see Places to Eat, earlier) almost nightly starting at 7pm.

WEST MAUI

You can sneak-preview the flashy Polynesian dance revues with dinner buffets (which they like to call 'luaus') by walking along the beach around sunset.

***Drums of the Pacific** (Hyatt Regency Maui Resort & Spa)* Nonguests adult/teen/child $78/49/34. Luau 5:30pm-8pm nightly. Probably the most thrilling of the Kaanapali offerings, the Hyatt holds its 'Drums of the Pacific' luau most nights (reservations required). Just don't expect anything authentically Hawaiian.

Shopping

Whalers Village** (☎ 661-4567, 2435 Kaanapali Pkwy)* Open 9:30am-10pm daily. Kaanapali's only shopping mall has three levels and over 50 shops. There's a ***Waldenbooks (2nd level), ***Wolf Camera*** (lower level), ***Crazy Shirts*** (main level), ***DFS*** (lower level) duty-free store with free coffee samples and ***ABC Store*** (main level) for cheap beach essentials and more. There is also a branch of ***Noa Noa*** for unique Polynesian batik clothing (see also Wailea in the South Maui chapter).

***Lahaina Printsellers** (☎ 667-7617, 800-669-7843, ⓦ www.printsellers.com, ground level, Whalers Village)* This antiquarian print shop is fascinating. Here you can peruse old explorers' maps of the Sandwich Islands (as Hawaii was once known abroad), reprints of whale etchings or watercolors of Hawaiian flora and fauna, each costing from $20 to thousands of dollars.

***Hawaiian Quilt Collection** (☎ 667-7660, Hyatt Regency Maui Resort & Spa)* This islandwide chain of Hawaiian quilting shops sells handmade pillows, bedcovers and kits with traditional designs. Call to sign up for three-hour quilting workshops ($50).

Getting Around

A free shuttle (☎ 800-262-8450) runs between the Kaanapali hotels, Whalers Village shopping center, the golf course and the Kaanapali Sugar Cane Train station about every half-hour from 9am to 8pm.

For information on limited bus services from Kaanapali to Lahaina and Kapalua, see the Getting Around chapter.

HONOKOWAI

North of Kaanapali, the road forks. If you want to zip up to the better beaches, bypassing the condos and resorts, stick to the Honoapiilani Hwy (Hwy 30). Cyclists may want to come this way, as the highway has a wide shoulder lane marked as a bike route.

Meanwhile the parallel shoreline road, Lower Honoapiilani Rd, leads into Honokowai. Kaanapali is a planned community; Honokowai is an unplanned one, consisting of an assorted stretch of condos squeezed between the shoreline and the Lower Honoapiilani Rd. Rates are more affordable, but that's because the beach isn't good for much except fine views of Molokai and Lanai. See map page 144.

Honokowai Beach Park

The waters off Honokowai Beach are largely lined with shelves of submerged rock shelf and offer poor swimming conditions. Young keiki might enjoy splashing around in the shallows, but most visitors staying here head straight for the Kaanapali beaches to the south.

Places to Stay

Condos These condo complexes are relatively inexpensive and decent, although a bit older when compared to other West Maui resorts. Usually the minimum stay is three days, with cleaning surcharges for stays of less than a week.

***Hale Maui** (☎ 669-6312, fax 669-1302, ⓦ www.maui.net/~halemaui, Lower Honoapiilani Rd)* 1-bedroom units $75-95, 3rd guest add $15. There are no views and no telephones, but it is right on the beach and each unit has a full kitchen. Just look for the mustard-yellow apartment building next to the park. German is spoken.

***Honokowai Palms** (☎ 667-2712, 800-669-0795, fax 661-5875, 3666 Lower Honoapiilani Rd)* 1-/2-bedroom units $75. It's a simple, two-story cinder-block building across the road from the beach. Rates and décor are cheap, but at least it has a swimming pool and kitchens.

***Kaleialoha** (☎ 669-8197, 800-222-8688, fax 669-2502, ⓦ www.mauicondosoceanfront*

.com, 3785 Lower Honoapiilani Rd) Studios $95, 1-bedroom units $115-125. All of these beachfront condos have full kitchens and washer/dryers. Studios face the road (fancifully called 'mountain view'), while one-bedroom units have ocean views and lanai. There is a swimming pool and barbecue area, but it's nothing special. Ask about off-season and other promotional discounts, however.

Hale Ono Loa (☎ 662-0807, 800-487-6002, fax 662-1277, W www.mauilodging.com/lodging/haleonoloa.htm, 3823 Lower Honoapiilani Rd) 1-bedroom units low/high season $85/100, 2-bedoom units $135/165. The few rental units in this high-rise complex are rented by Maui Lodging. All of them having sliding *shoji* (rice-paper screen) bedroom walls that pull back to reveal full ocean views. Some units also have koa-wood or rattan furniture, even though the décor is otherwise average. Larger suites have a Jacuzzi or waterfront lanai.

Hoyochi Nikko (☎ 662-0807, 800-487-6002, fax 662-1277, W www.mauilodging.com/lodging/hoyochi.htm, 3901 Lower Honoapiilani Rd) 1-/2-bedroom units $95-160. Another Maui Lodging property, this looks like a traditional Japanese inn, but with disappointingly modern interiors. It is almost hidden from the road, however, and every unit faces the ocean (and swimming pool) and is fully equipped with a kitchen and washer/dryer. Unit Nos 203 and 204 have second-bedroom lofts.

Mahina Surf (☎ 669-6068, 800-367-6086, fax 669-4534, W www.mahinasurf.com, 4057 Lower Honoapiilani Rd) Low/high season rates; 1-bedroom units from $110/125, 2-bedroom units from $135/145. Bordering Kahana, this low-rise condo complex is centered on a grassy lawn with a heated pool. All of the units are spacious and have kitchens, VCRs, phones and lanai with ocean views. Weekly and monthly rates and discounts for automobile club members and seniors are available.

Noelani (☎ 669-8374, 800-367-6030, fax 669-7904, W www.noelani-condo-resort.com, 4095 Lower Honoapiilani Rd) Studios/1-/2- bedroom units from $110/150/210. Noelani offers friendly aloha atmosphere, palm trees, two freshwater pools and a bewildering array of discounts. Over 50 tastefully furnished beachfront units have ocean-facing lanai, telephones, full kitchens, TV/VCRs and sofa beds; all but the studios have washer/dryers, too.

Hotels *Embassy Vacation Resort* (☎ 661-2000, 800-362-2779, fax 667-5821, W www.embassyvacationresorts.com, 104 Kaanapali Shores Place) 1-bedroom garden-view/oceanfront suites from $340/390. This aging flamingo-pink resort sits on Honokowai Point just north of Kaanapali. Each of the 820-sq-foot suites has everything you could imagine, right down to a kitchenette and big-screen TV/VCR. Amenities include a gigantic pool with a 60-foot water slide and indoor gym. Promotional rates can drop as low as $200 for up to four adults, including full breakfast and evening cocktails.

Places to Eat

Farmers market (Lower Honoapiilani Rd) Open 7am-11:30am Mon, Wed & Fri. For fresh fruits and vegetables, visit this market that sets up in the *ABC Store* shopping plaza parking lot near the beach. Local farmers sell fresh fruit and vegetables, homemade chips and salsa, assorted cheeses, fresh juices and macadamia nuts. There's also a small *Treasures by the Sea* that really sells seashells by the seashore, as the tongue-twister goes.

Out on the highway, the sprawling *Honokowai Marketplace* (3350 Lower Honoapiilani Rd) has a *Star Market* for groceries, a surprising range of budget-minded eateries, from $1 tacos to cheapskate sushi, and award-winning desserts at *Hula Scoops*.

Java Jazz & Soup Nutz (☎ 667-0787, Honokowai Marketplace) Items $2-5. At last, there's a real coffee shop in Honokowai, one that's arty and jazzy, with strong java to boot. The small adjoining kitchen serves an abbreviated menu of gourmet soups, sandwiches and pastas (under $10).

Honokowai Okazuya & Deli (☎ 665-0512, 3600 Lower Honoapiilani Rd) Dishes

$6-10. Open 10am-2:30pm, 4:30pm-9pm Mon-Sat. This long-running local fave makes a good chicken caesar salad and delicious mahimahi with lemon, capers and rice.

KAHANA

Kahana is the newer high-rise stretch immediately north of Honokowai. It's more upscale, with condo and room rates swinging well above $100.

The white, sandy beach here has reasonable swimming conditions, although sometimes things get a little murky with seaweed. For snorkeling, a good area is along the rocky outcropping at the north side of the Kahana Sunset condominium complex. However, there is technically no public beach access anywhere nearby.

There's an ATM, Internet café, coin laundry (last wash 8pm) and gas station at the Kahana Gateway shopping center (☎ 669-9669), 4405 Honoapiilani Hwy. Close to the beach, the Kahana Manor condo complex, 4310 Lower Honoapiilani Rd, has a convenience store, pub and one-hour photo lab.

Places to Stay

As with most Maui condo complexes, there is usually a three-day minimum stay.

Aston Kahana Beach Resort (☎/fax 669-8611, 800-922-7866, W www.astonhotels.com, 4221 Lower Honoapiilani Rd) Studios low/high season $185/225, 1-bedroom units $225/260. Newly renovated as an Aston property, this tall condo complex stands at the southern edge of Kahana Beach. All of the bright, white tropical units have kitchenettes and oceanfront lanai. Rack rates are seriously overpriced, but check the Web site for promotional deals.

Royal Kahana (☎ 669-5911, 800-688-7444, fax 669-5950, 4365 Lower Honoapiilani Rd) Low season value rates: garden-/ocean-view studios $139/154, 1-bedroom units $180. Although the Royal Kahana is an enormous white high-rise complex, the location is excellent, on the beach and just a few minutes' walk from the Kahana Gateway shopping center. Most of the comfortable, modern units have full kitchens,

washer/dryers and private lanai. Perks include a heated swimming pool, tennis courts, fitness room and sauna, plus a weekly mai tai party. This is an Outrigger property, so check its Web site (W www.outrigger.com) for special promotions and discounts.

Kahana Village (☎ 669-5111, 800-824-3065, fax 669-0974, W www.maui.net/~village/kahana.html, 4531 Lower Honoapiilani Rd) 2-bedroom loft units low/high season $185/220, 3-bedroom ground-floor units $295/355. Although the buildings are quite close together, large units can accommodate quite a few people. Some are right on the ocean and there's a small swimming pool, too.

Places to Eat

At the *Kahana Gateway (4405 Honoapiilani Hwy)* is a *Whalers General Store* for groceries and *Ashley's Internet Café (☎ 669-0949)*, serving prize-winning ice cream sundaes, deli sandwiches and local mixed-plate lunches (under $8).

Roy's Kahana Bar & Grill (☎ 669-6999, Kahana Gateway) and *Roy's Nicolina Restaurant (☎ 669-5000, Kahana Gateway)* Appetizers $6.50-12, dinner entrées $16.50-27. Open 5:30pm-9:30pm daily. Everyone knows Roy's, and so they should. These two sister restaurants are the original Maui outposts of the eating empire owned by chef Roy Yamaguchi, a local boy who has created a signature version of what most of us think of as Pacific Rim cuisine, but he calls it a Euro-Asian blend of French techniques with Japanese and Hawaiian traditions.

Roy's Kahana Bar & Grill has 40-foot-high ceilings, koa-wood tables and artwork dominated by a copper exhibition kitchen, while the quieter Nicolina is just next door. Half of each menu is devoted to Roy's classic dishes, such as Szechuan ribs and farm-fresh salads from the Upcountry or more substantial 'Mama Yama' meatloaf and inventive seafood. A fresh sheet of daily specials is created by each restaurant's head chef. It's an unforgettable experience, especially the deep chocolate soufflé.

Fish & Game Brewing House & Rotisserie (☎ 669-3474, Kahana Gateway) Bar menu $5-13, lunch mains $8-18, dinner entrées $24-35. Open 11am-1am daily; lunch until 3pm, dinner from 5:30pm. It takes chutzpah to open a restaurant anywhere near Roy's, but they've done it. Plantation Pale Ale or Wild Hog Stout microbrews go down well with rotisserie chicken, sandwiches or shellfish flown in from the Pacific Northwest. Whether you eat in the clubby restaurant or sports bar, it's a winning pitch either way.

NAPILI

Some visitors fall in love with Napili, which happens to be Maui's sunniest neighborhood, and return year after year. Napili Kai Beach Club, built in 1962, was the first hotel north of Kaanapali. To protect the bay, as well as its investment, Napili Kai organized area landowners and petitioned the county to create a zoning bylaw restricting all Napili Bay buildings to the height of a coconut tree.

It worked, and today Napili remains one of the most relaxed niches on the west coast. Napili Bay has a beautiful, curved golden-sand **beach**, with excellent swimming and snorkeling when it's calm. Big waves occasionally make it into the bay in the winter, attracting bodysurfers but also creating strong rip currents.

Places to Stay

Most of Napili's condos are on the beach, and for the most part, away from the road and traffic noise. Expect a minimum stay of three to five days.

Hale Napili (☎ 669-6184, 800-245-2266, fax 665-0066, **W** www.maui.net/~halenapi, 65 Hui Dr) Garden-view/oceanfront studios from $100/140, 1-bedroom units from $160. The aloha of the Hawaiian management ensure lots of repeat guests. This well-maintained little condo complex couldn't be better placed either, since it's right on Napili Bay (obviously, there's no need for a pool). All units have full kitchens, queen and sofa beds, TVs, telephones, ceiling fans and lanai. Off-season and promotional rates are a bit less.

Napili Surf (☎ 669-8002, 888-627-5457, fax 669-8004, **W** www.napilisurf.com, 50 Napili Place) Garden-/ocean-view studio $125/170, 1-bedroom units $200-270. Napili Surf is a motel-style place made of painted cinder blocks at the south end of Napili Bay. It's far from luxury, but the grounds are decently kept, there's a pool and weekly discounts are possible.

Napili Shores (☎ 669-8061, 888-462-7454, fax 669-5407, 5315 Lower Honoapiilani Rd) Garden-view/oceanfront studio $177/233; garden-view/ocean-view 1-bedroom unit $211/239. This is another Outrigger property, so remember to check the Web site (**W** www.outrigger.com) for discounts and promotions. Staff are extremely helpful, and it's quiet enough that you can really appreciate the setting. Low-lying condo buildings stretch all the way down to the beach along a grassy expanse, passing the swimming pool and *Gazebo Restaurant*. Also on site is a small grocery store and pan-Asian café.

Napili Kai Beach Club (☎ 669-6271, 800-367-5030, fax 669-0086, **W** www.napilikai.com, 5900 Lower Honoapiilani Rd) Hotel rooms $190-245, studios with kitchenette $220-325, suites with full kitchen $360-760. At the northern end of Napili Bay, the staff at this sprawling place are almost pampering. Polynesian-style buildings enclose beautiful units, each with Japanese shoji dividers and private lanai. There is an oceanfront swimming pool. The catch here is the price, which varies depending on the season, view and proximity to the beach, but is still never cheap. Then again, the maximum number of people allowed per unit is gratifyingly high, and there are special deals on car and tennis-court rentals.

Places to Eat

Napili Plaza (☎ 665-0546, cnr Napilihau St & Hwy 30) This shopping center has a grocery store and lots of cheap budget eats, including *The Coffee Store* and *Maui Tacos*. For something a notch better than fast food, try *Mama's Ribs 'n Rotisserie* for local mixed-plate lunches ($7-10) with great sides like tricolor pasta salad or baked beans. It's open 11am to 7pm daily.

Sea House Restaurant (☎ 669-1500, Napili Kai Beach Club) Breakfast or lunch $4-12,

WEST MAUI

KAHANA, NAPILI & KAPALUA

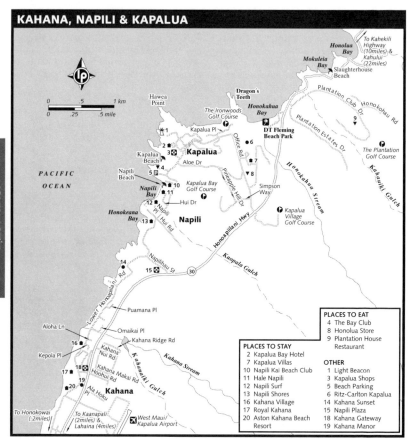

To Kahekili
Highway
(10miles) &
Kahului
(22miles)

Honolua Bay

Mokuleia Bay

Slaughterhouse Beach

Plantation Club Dr

Honokohau Rd

Dragon's Teeth

Honokahua Bay

Hawea Point

The Ironwoods Golf Course

Kapalua Pl

DT Fleming Beach Park

Plantation Estates Dr

9

The Plantation Golf Course

*1

2

Kapalua Beach

3

Kapalua

Aloe Dr

6

7

Office Rd

Honokahua Stream

Kahaaiki Gulch

Napili Beach

4

5

10

8

Kapalua Bay Golf Course

Pineapple Hill Dr

Simpson Way

Kapalua Village Golf Course

PACIFIC OCEAN

Napili Bay

11

12

Hui Dr

Napili Pl

Honokeana Bay

13

Napili Hui Rd

Napili

Honoapiilani Hwy

Kaopala Gulch

14

15

Napilihau St

30

Puamana Pl

Lower Honoapiilani Rd

Aloha Ln

Omaikai Pl

Kahana Ridge Rd

16

Kahana Nui Rd

Kepola Pl

17

18

19

20

Kahana Makai Rd

Hoohui Rd

Ala Hoku Pl

Kahana Stream

Kahanaiki Gulch

Kahana

To Honokowai (.2miles)

To Kaanapali (2miles) & Lahaina (4miles)

West Maui/ Kapalua Airport

WEST MAUI

0   .5   1 km
0   .25   .5 mile

PLACES TO EAT
4 The Bay Club
8 Honolua Store
9 Plantation House Restaurant

PLACES TO STAY
2 Kapalua Bay Hotel
7 Kapalua Villas
10 Napili Kai Beach Club
11 Hale Napili
12 Napili Surf
13 Napili Shores
16 Kahana Village
17 Royal Kahana
20 Aston Kahana Beach Resort

OTHER
1 Light Beacon
3 Kapalua Shops
5 Beach Parking
6 Ritz-Carlton Kapalua
14 Kahana Sunset
15 Napili Plaza
18 Kahana Gateway
19 Kahana Manor

dinner mains $18-27. Open for breakfast 8am-10:30am, lunch 11:30am-2pm, dinner 6pm-9pm. For a more appealing setting than the shopping center, this restaurant features open-air dining with a sunset view and Hawaiian music early in the week. The problem is the food, which is mostly standard American fare that is not done particularly well. A Friday night dinner buffet features hula dancing performed by local children; all proceeds benefit the Napili Kai nonprofit cultural foundation. The dinner show is at 6pm Friday; adult/child costs $35/20.

KAPALUA

The Kapalua resort development has the Kapalua Bay and Ritz-Carlton hotels, some luxury condos, a few restaurants and three golf courses. It's a small, uncrowded development – the most exclusive in northwest Maui.

The beaches here are beautiful, but many visitors bypass Kapalua for more dramatic beaches and bays farther north. It is, however, the last place to stop for supplies before the Kahekili Hwy. It also happens to have the finest sushi anywhere on Maui and this alone makes it worth the drive.

Kapalua Beach

Kapalua Beach, at Kapalua Bay, is a pretty white-sand crescent beach with clear views of Molokai across the channel. The long rocky outcroppings at both ends of the bay make it the safest year-round swimming spot on this coast.

There's good snorkeling on the right side of the beach, where you'll find lots of large tangs, butterfly fish, wrasses and orange slate-pencil sea urchins. For unique kayak-dive or snorkel tours led by Kapalua Dive Company, see the Activities chapter.

To get to Kapalua Beach, take the paved drive immediately north of Napili Kai Beach Club. A blue shoreline access sign points to a parking area with about 25 public spaces, restrooms and showers. A tunnel from the parking lot leads under the Bay Club restaurant to the beach.

Oneloa Beach

This forgotten beach is near the Ritz-Carlton resort, off the lower links of the Ironwoods golf course. There are a few casual parking spaces reached by turning right (north) at the end of Office Rd. Most of the beachfront itself is rocky, except at the very western end, and rip currents and swells usually make for bad swimming or snorkeling, especially during high winds (which are common).

If you walk around the monument (see 'Bone Rattling') and out to Makaluapuna Point, you'll reach the spiky lava formations of the almost human-size **Dragon's Teeth**, that have been carved by erosion and sea salt. You can also get here without trampling on any burial sites (an advisable precaution) from the west end of DT Fleming Beach Park (see Northern Beaches, later), but this requires picking your way carefully across fields of light-colored lava.

Activities

All three **golf** courses are run by Kapalua Golf (☎ 669-8044, 877-527-2582, Ⓦ www.kapaluamaui.com, 2000 Village Rd; Greens fees & cart for resort guests $115-135, for nonguests $160-220). The Plantation Course is home to the PGA Mercedes Champi-

onships held each January. The Bay and Village courses were designed by Arnold Palmer, and the former is also the nation's first certified Audubon Cooperative Sanctuary. Handouts on tropical birds (not birdies) are available.

A match of **tennis** (Tennis Garden ☎ 669-5677; Village Tennis Center ☎ 665-0112) costs resort guests/nonguests $10/12. Near the Ritz-Carlton beach, the Village Tennis Center is the newer of Kapalua's two tennis court complexes. Racquet rental costs $6, shoes come free.

Check the **Kapalua Shops** (☎ 800-527-2582) calendar link at Ⓦ www.kapalua maui.com for information on free slack-key guitar and hula kahiko performances, as well as beginners hula and lei-making classes. You can also make reservations with the **Hawaiian Quilt Collection** (☎ 665-1111) shop for friendly, three-hour Hawaiian quilting workshops ($50, includes materials).

Maui Pineapple Plantation Tour

Lovers of all things pineapple can go on this plantation tour (☎ 669-8088) 2½-hour tour $26. Tours 9:30am & 1pm Mon-Fri. The Maui Pineapple Company, which is the only pineapple canning company operating in the US, opens its fields to educational tours led by the Kapalua Nature Society. Reservations are required, and you must wear covered shoes (no sandals). Check in 30 minutes in advance at the Kapalua Villas reception center opposite Honolua Store on Office Rd.

Places to Stay

Kapalua Villas (☎ 669-8088, 800-545-0018, 0031-113094 in Japan, fax 669-5234, Ⓦ www.kapaluavillas.com, 500 Office Rd) 1-bedroom 2-bath condos $199-279, 2-bedroom 3-bath units $299-469. These luxury condo units in the Kapalua Bay Hotel resort development can sleep from four to six people, making them quite a bargain. Perks include complimentary tennis and full amenities, including a kitchen and washer/dryer in each condo. The Bay Villas are closest to the beach, but the Ridge Villas up on the golf course also

Bone Rattling

When the Honokahua sand dunes at Oneloa Beach were excavated in 1988 during the construction of the Ritz-Carlton hotel, a lot more than simple bones was unearthed. The controversy that started here permanently changed Hawaii's cultural landscape.

Keeping the bones of ancestors safely undisturbed was of great importance to ancient Hawaiians, so much so that they went to great lengths to hide the bones inside burial chambers, lava tubes and underwater grottoes. Some believed that by 'planting' the bones in the ground, their ancestors would nourish them, both spiritually and physically, with food grown in that spot.

The Honokahua burial ground at Kapalua was thought to contain the remains of over 2000 Hawaiians who had returned to their *one hanau* (birth sands) between AD 850 and the 18th century. After 100 skeletal remains of ancestral Hawaiians had been exhumed and examined, protests by native Hawaiians took on momentum, and a candlelight vigil took place at the state capital. Construction at the Ritz-Carlton was eventually halted, the skeletons were reinterred and the hotel site was relocated mauka of the seaside graves.

Soon after, Hui Malama I Na Kupuna o Hawai'i Nei, literally 'a group caring for the ancestors of Hawaii,' helped enact the Native American Grave Repatriation Act of 1990, which extends rights to native Hawaiians as well. Islandwide burial councils now oversee the return of ancestral remains to Hawaii from wherever they have been scattered around the world. So far the Bishop and Smithsonian museums have fully cooperated in returning all of their holdings, as have the Royal Ontario Museum and the South Australian Museum in Adelaide.

As for the Ritz-Carlton, the luxury hotel now prides itself on leading 'culturally sensitive' tours of the burial site. Ironically, its literature even makes it sound as if protecting the legacy of Honokahua was its idea in the first place.

have ocean views. Ask about special promotional packages.

Kapalua Bay Hotel (☎ 669-5656, 800-367-8000, fax 669-4649, **w** www.kapaluabay hotel.com, 1 Bay Dr) Garden-/ocean-view hotel rooms from $350/510, 1-/2-bedroom condos $500/800. This is a stylish complex right on the beach. Open-air walkways breathe with sea breezes, and tropical cane and koa furniture fills the lobby. Everything looks so tropical, white and appealing, but considering the prices you're probably better off at the Kapalua Villas. Demonstrations of Hawaiian arts and crafts take place in the day in the lobby, and there's a Hawaiian guitarist at night in the ***Lehua Lounge***.

Places to Eat

Honolua Store (☎ 669-6128, Office Rd) Plate lunch $4-6. Open 6am-8pm daily. This general store is a historic landmark serving strictly local food, cafeteria- or deli-style. Plate-lunch specials, available until 3pm only, include scoops of stew, fried chicken or kalua pig, all of which have been sitting under heat lamps. The store sells drinks, produce, sandwiches and snacks for a picnic.

Sansei Seafood Restaurant & Sushi Bar (☎ 669-6286, Kapalua Shops) Sushi rolls, sashimi and appetizers $4-19, entrées $16-24. Open 5:30pm-10pm daily; early-bird special (25% off entire menu) 5:30pm-6pm only; laser karaoke & late-night menu 10pm-2am Thur & Fri. No matter where on the island you have to drive from, you won't regret making the pilgrimage to Sansei. With antique sake bottles and Japanese paper kites all around, you can feast on prize-winning, creative hot appetizers and classic chilled sushi and sashimi. Among the most memorable are the Asian rock shrimp cakes with ginger-lime-chili butter and mango crab salad roll with crunchy peanuts and Kula greens.

Plantation House Restaurant (☎ 669-6299, 2000 Plantation Club Dr) Breakfast dishes $3-11, lunch mains $7.50-14, dinner mains $22-30. Open for breakfast & lunch 8am-3pm, dinner 5:30pm-10pm. Although the setting is exclusive and the attitude snobby, this is the best place for a reasonably priced sit-down meal. The restaurant has a fine view across the fairway clear down to the ocean. The morning menu includes such dishes as field-picked pineapple in cinnamon–sour-cream sauce or Cajun-spiced sashimi eggs Benedict. Above-average salads and sandwiches appear at lunch, including a daily fish special. Dinner is a pricier affair with seafood, duck, lamb and steak entrées, but you could just come for sunset cocktails at the bar.

The Bay Club (☎ 669-5656) Dinner entrées $33-55, 4-course tasting menu $75. Open 6pm-9:30pm daily; reservations advised. This establishment, perched atop a promontory at the southern end of Kapalua Bay, has beautiful waterfront views and an open-air setting. Inside it feels just like a gentleman's club, with exorbitant prices to match and reservations are required. Sumptuous main courses include seafood truffle risotto or pan-roasted Kona lobster with caramelized fennel.

NORTHERN BEACHES

Kapalua marks the end of development on the West Maui coast. From there on, it's all rural Hawaii, with golf carts giving way to pickup trucks and old cars with surfboards tied on top. The coast gets more lush and scenically rugged as you go along.

DT Fleming Beach Park

DT Fleming Beach Park, at the north side of Kapalua on Honokahua Bay, is a county beach park with restrooms, picnic facilities and showers. It was named after the Scotsman who first helped to develop West Maui's pineapple industry.

The park is a long, sandy beach backed by trees. There's good bodysurfing and surfing, with winter providing the biggest waves. The shorebreaks can be tough, and this beach is second only to Hookipa for injuries.

Take notice, too, of the signs warning of dangerous currents – the beach has seen a number of drownings over the years. Rip tides are common, especially in winter when you'll see red flags posted along the beach.

The reef out near the southern rocks is good for snorkeling, but only when it's very calm. Kayakers also launch here, mostly in summer (see the Activities chapter). There's a lifeguard on duty daily.

The beach is close to the Ritz-Carlton hotel, but public access is via a paved road that cuts down to the shore about a mile north of Office Rd. Look for the blue shoreline access sign after the 31-mile marker on the makai side of the highway. If you reach the Plantation golf course driveway, you've gone too far.

Slaughterhouse Beach & Honolua Bay

Slaughterhouse Beach (Mokuleia Bay), named for the ranch slaughterhouse sheds that once sat on the cliffs above, is a hot bodysurfing spot during the summer when the rocks aren't exposed. Unlike rocky Honolua, this bay has a white-sand beach.

In winter, Honolua Bay has such perfect waves that it's made the cover of numerous surfing magazines. The bay faces northwest, and when it catches the winter swells, it has some of the best surfing to be found anywhere in the world. Dolphins can be seen spinning offshore sometimes.

In summer, snorkeling is excellent in both bays, which are separated by narrow Kalaepiha Point and together form a marine-life conservation district. Fishing is prohibited, as is collecting shells, coral, rock or sand. Both sides of Honolua Bay have good reefs with lots of different coral formations, while the midsection of the bay has a sandy bottom. Since Honolua Stream empties into the bay, visibility is often poor after heavy rains, especially around the boat ramp area. When it's calm, you can snorkel around its small caves and archways from one bay to the other.

For Honolua Bay, beachgoers have traditionally parked their cars at a few pull-offs along the road, then scrambled along rough paths down to the beach. Slaughterhouse Beach is farther back at the 32-mile marker, about a mile north of DT Fleming Beach Park, and is marked with a blue shoreline access sign. There are limited parking spaces on the makai side of the highway and a concrete stairway leads down to the beach.

Honokohau Bay

As you continue north beyond Honolua Bay, the road climbs with expansive coastal views. The beaches along this section are all open ocean with rough water conditions. Some experts do surf, snorkel and dive at Honokohau Bay. However, this is only when waters are extremely calm and it's strictly at your own risk. When surf is up, beware of rip currents.

KAHEKILI HIGHWAY

Pretty soon comes the beginning of the Kahekili Hwy (Hwy 30), the serpentine coastal road that curves around the undeveloped northeastern side of the West Maui Mountains toward Wailuku. It's ruggedly scenic, with deep ravines, eroded red hills, rock-strewn sea cliffs and pastures. You're likely to spot paniolo and egrets lazily hitchhiking upon cows. Skies are usually clear, if windy. All around the colors are intense, from aquamarine waves to the white brilliance of the sun above, and the air is clean and pure.

Like its counterpart to the south, the Piilani Hwy around the south flank of Haleakala (see Beyond Hana in the East Maui chapter), the Kahekili Hwy is shown either as a black hole or an unpaved road on many tourist maps. In fact the approximately 20-mile road is paved its entire length – although much of the drive is very winding and narrow, with blind curves and the occasional sign warning of falling rocks. During heavy rain, the road may be closed due to landslides.

The two-lane road between Honokohau and Kahakuloa is easy going, while the southern section between Kahakuloa and Waihee is mostly one lane with a few hair-raising cliff sections without shoulders. While the posted speed limit on most of the road is 15mph, in some sections it's a mere

5mph. But taking it slowly is the whole point anyway.

Traffic flows in both directions, but it's best to start from the Kahului-Wailuku area early in the morning. That way you can hike, go horseback riding or even whack a few golf balls around before lunch, then stop for banana bread or a picnic in Kahakuloa village and spend the afternoon at the natural ocean baths or the Northern Beaches (see Northern Beaches, earlier). Driving time is at least 1¼ hours without stops; be sure to fuel up first and bring lots of water.

Waiehu & Waihee

Waiehu Beach Rd turns into the Kahekili Hwy at the northern end of Wailuku, past the turnoff for the Halekii-Pihana Heiau State Monument (see Central Maui chapter).

The highway then heads through the little towns of Waiehu and Waihee. Down near the shore is **Waiehu Municipal Golf Course** (☎ 243-7400, 200 Halewaiu Rd; green fees $30-35, club rental $15). This popular, old-fashioned set of links is the cheapest course on Maui and it's easily walkable, so you don't need a cart. It's so no-frills that you may find some holes unmarked! If a stray ball lands in the nearby ocean surf, kiss it goodbye. Farther on at the 5-mile marker is Waihee Valley Rd, the turnoff for the **Waihee Valley Trail** (see the Hiking section at the end of the Activities chapter).

As the highway climbs into Waihee, subdivisions give way to scenery. Just before the 7-mile marker is **Mendes Ranch** (☎ 244-7320, 871-5222 24-hr answering service, ⓦ www.maui.net/~mendes, 3530 Kahekili Hwy; trail rides $130 Mon-Sat). Established in 1941, this working cattle ranch offers trail rides to rain forest and sea cliff overlooks before finishing off with a barbecue lunch.

Opposite the Mendes Ranch is the side road up to the Boy Scouts' Camp Maluhia. A pretty, winding drive through open pasture leads to the start of the **Waihee Ridge Trail** (see the Hiking special section at the end of the Activities chapter), a varied scenic route offering rare views of West Maui's interior valleys. The trailhead is a mile up from the highway, on the left just

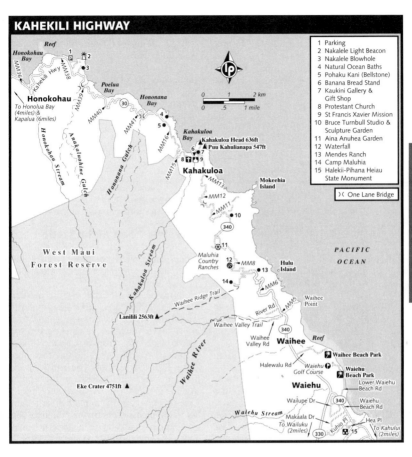

KAHEKILI HIGHWAY

1 Parking
2 Nakalele Light Beacon
3 Nakalele Blowhole
4 Natural Ocean Baths
5 Pohaku Kani (Bellstone)
6 Banana Bread Stand
7 Kaukini Gallery & Gift Shop
8 Protestant Church
9 St Francis Xavier Mission
10 Bruce Turnbull Studio & Sculpture Garden
11 Aina Anuhea Garden
12 Waterfall
13 Mendes Ranch
14 Camp Maluhia
15 Halekii-Pihana Heiau State Monument

)(One Lane Bridge

WEST MAUI

before Camp Maluhia. It's marked with a Na Ala Hele sign and a squeeze-through turnstile fence.

Waterfalls, Gardens & Galleries

Back on the highway, you'll pass a gentle **waterfall** on the left, rain permitting. For another waterfall view, stop at the pull-off a tenth of a mile north of the 8-mile marker and look down into the ravine below; you'll see a picture-perfect waterfall framed by double pools.

Shortly before the 9-mile marker, a sign marks the driveway up to **Aina Anuhea** (ad-

mission $4) gardens, basically just a few tropical plantings and a tiny banana patch on a private estate. You'll probably end up feeling suckered by the price of admission, even if it does include a cup of free pineapple juice at the run-down gift shop.

Continuing around the hairpin turns, the highway gradually levels out atop the sea cliffs. Before the 10-mile marker is **Bruce Turnbull Studio & Sculpture Garden** (☎ 667-2787, 800-781-2787), built on the site of an ancient Hawaiian garden. If you haven't made an appointment to see the artist's studio, you can still catch a glimpse of his bronze and wood creations set facing the ocean by peering through the gates.

Just before Kahakuloa and the 14-mile marker, on the mauka side of the road, is the wonderful, lemon-colored **Kaukini Gallery & Gift Shop** (☎ 244-3371). Owned by an artist, on display here are finely selected works by dozens of island artists, from watercolorists to koa woodcarvers and Japanese-influenced potters. A few drinks and snacks are sold, too.

Kahakuloa Village

The village of Kahakuloa lies at the base of a small green valley with working taro patches and cliffs standing like centurions on each side of the bay. Although tiny – you blink, you miss it – Kahakuloa is arguably the most Hawaiian place in West Maui; certainly the mana here feels right.

Before the road plunges down into the valley, there is a dirt pulloff fronting two peaks. On the left is **Kahakuloa Head** (636 feet), yet another of the daredevil Chief Kahekili's favorite cliff-diving spots, while to your right is **Puu Kahulianapa** (547 feet), which can be scaled if you're up for playing 'King of the Mountain.'

Although it contains only a few dozen simple homes, Kahakuloa ('Tall Lord') village has two churches. As the highway skitters down into the valley, opposite a *banana bread stand*, the first you'll come to is the little tin-roofed **St Francis Xavier Mission**. Off to the north, the green-wood and red-tiled **Protestant church** hunkers down on the valley floor.

As you come out of the valley, a number of viewpoints and pulloffs look down over cliff-top plateaus with rugged coast and crashing surf. Lush stretches of turf invite you to take a walk from the road down to the cliffs and out along the coastline.

Bellstone & Ocean Baths

Just past the 16-mile marker is **Pohaku Kani**, a large bellstone. If you hit it with a rock on the Kahakuloa side where the deepest indentations are, you might be able to get a resonant, if hollow sound, but it takes some imagination to hear it ring like a bell.

Just opposite, a couple of vague 4WD tracks lead off toward the coast. If you park just off the highway, you can pretty much walk down any of them and eventually head right (south) to reach an overlook. From there you can plan how to navigate your way down the lava cliffs into the **natural ocean baths** at the ocean's edge. These baths, bordered by lava rock and encrusted with semi-precious olivine minerals, are an incredible sight: clear, calm pools in the midst of roaring surf. Some have natural steps, while others are quite deep or warmed by the sun. Take care not to sit near any blowholes, and skip the whole idea if the waves look too high or the area is covered in silt from recent storm run-offs.

Nakalele Point Light Station

As the road begins to improve, you'll see stone cairns piled everywhere. They look like religious offerings, but most are just the creations of sightseers.

Between the 39- and 38-mile markers there is another large, dirt area of pull-offs and 4WD trails. As elsewhere on Maui, don't leave valuables in your parked car. The smashed glass from broken windshields is indicative of the break-ins that take place here. In a few minutes you can walk out toward the **light beacon** at the end of Nakalele Point. The coastline here has interesting pools, arches and other formations worn out of the rocks by the pounding surf.

Continue walking right along the coast (there is no real trail) for another 15 or 20 minutes to the impressive **Nakalele Blowhole**; if you see only a little sputtering, that's most likely because you haven't reached *the* blowhole yet, so keep going.

When the water is really surging, the Nakalele Blowhole is even visible from back along the highway toward the 40-mile marker. During the winter season, you can sometimes spot humpback whales breaching offshore in this area as well.

As you continue north along the highway toward Kapalua, Molokai comes into view, and the scenery is very lush all the way to Honokohau Bay, the furthest point north on Maui.

As humming as it gets, Front St, Lahaina

Nap time at Lahaina Harbor

Steam train on a sugar rush, West Maui

Today a golden-sand beach, tomorrow a black-sand beach...western Maui

Lounging at the Hyatt Regency, Kaanapali

Strolling on the beach in Kapalua

South Maui

South Maui offers a mixed plate of aquatic adventures, spread out from Kihei to La Perouse Bay along the island's southwest coast, on the drier side of Haleakala volcano. Here you have clear views of Lanai and Kahoolawe as well as West Maui, which because of the deep cut of Maalaea Bay looks like a separate island. As diverse as the sunny, sandy beaches are, they are nothing compared to the varied development strategies (or the lack of them), which have resulted in congested condovilles or exclusive golf resorts, even state parks and national marine sanctuaries.

On the northern side is Kihei. Although it has become synonymous with out-of-control eyesore development, Kihei has premier beaches along its entire length and near-constant sunshine. It has long attracted sunbathers, boogie boarders, windsurfers and local families on weekend picnics. Travelers can find decent deals, and the nightlife is booming.

Farther south are the meticulously planned Wailea and Makena resorts, with four championship golf courses and a tennis club nicknamed 'Wimbledon West.' Landscaped oceanfront hotels preside over fabulous beaches that are all open to the public. If you'd like to dine in a teahouse made of rocks from Mt Fuji or indulge in the island's grandest spa, bring your platinum credit card.

The high-rise hotels finally give way to a state park that now protects the old hippie camp of unsurpassed Big Beach. At at the end of the coastal road, aquamarine waters throw themselves against the rough, black lava fingers of Maui's youngest volcano flow at the untamed nature reserve at Cape Kinau and La Perouse Bay.

KIHEI

Thirty years ago, Kihei was a long stretch of undeveloped beach with kiawe trees, a scattering of homes and a church or two. Even earlier, Hawaiian fisherman lived here and

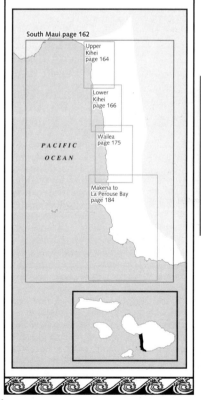

Highlights

- Snorkeling and diving with octopus and butterfly fish inside Molokini crater
- Grooving on the nightlife along Kihei strip
- Repenting the morning after and singing hymns in Hawaiian at historic churches
- Lazing on the glorious beaches that stretch all the way to Makena
- Hiking atop ancient coals of a'a (jagged lava) beside aquamarine La Perouse Bay
- Spotting sea turtles, spinner dolphins and, in winter, humpback whales just offshore

South Maui page 162

Upper Kihei page 164

Lower Kihei page 166

Wailea page 175

PACIFIC OCEAN

Makena to La Perouse Bay page 184

SOUTH MAUI

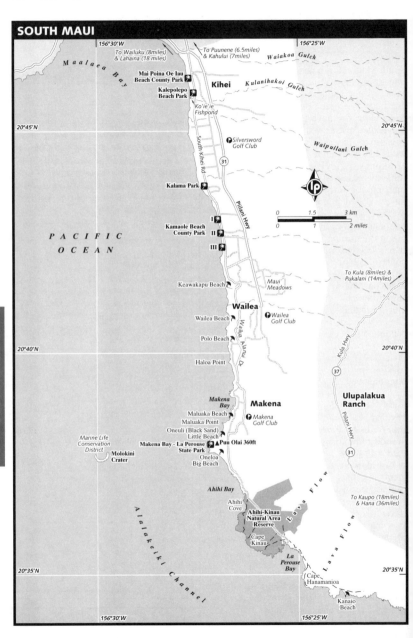

SOUTH MAUI

manned the royal fishpond, quite close to where Captain Vancouver landed his ship in 1792.

Since the 1970s developers have pounced on Kihei with such intensity that it has gained the dubious distinction of being Maui's fastest-growing community. Much of the development was haphazard, and it's painfully obvious. S Kihei Rd, which runs the full length of Kihei, is lined with condos, gas stations, shopping centers and fast-food places in such congestion that it is the example most often cited by the anti-development forces on the Neighbor Islands. To them, Kihei is what no town wants to become.

While Kihei's 'condoville' character doesn't win any prizes for aesthetics, it has one advantage for visitors – the sheer abundance of condos means that Kihei's accommodations rates are among the cheapest on Maui. In addition, the infrastructure has begun to catch up with the rampant commercial growth; bike lanes are being added to S Kihei Rd, a library and other public facilities have evolved, and steps have been taken to ameliorate some of the traffic problems. With some of the island's best beaches, Kihei justifiably remains a favorite destination for all types of traveler.

Orientation & Information

The Piilani Hwy (Hwy 31) bypasses the start-and-stop traffic of parallel Kihei Rd. Several residential streets connect the two. Although Kihei traffic isn't as bad as locals say (and visitors may be accustomed to much worse), it is still slow. If you can manage it, try to plan your stops in geographical order to avoid the headache of trying to make a left turn. Of course, renting a bicycle or scooter may be a solution, but you still have to contend with Kihei Rd in the midday heat.

There are 24-hour ATMs in the various shopping plazas and grocery stores. City-Bank (☎ 891-8586), 1819 S Kihei Rd, in the Kukui Mall, charges just about the lowest ATM fees. American Savings Bank (☎ 879-1977), 1215 S Kihei Rd, in Longs Center, is open from 9am to 6pm Monday to Friday and 9am to 1pm Saturday.

The Kihei post office (☎ 879-1987), 1254 S Kihei Rd, near Azeka Place, is open 9am to 4:30pm Monday to Friday, 9am to noon Saturday.

For private shipping, photocopying and faxing, try Mail Boxes Etc (☎ 874-5556), 1215 S Kihei Rd, in Longs Center, or the Postal Plus (☎ 891-8585, fax 891-0084), 2463 S Kihei Rd, below Denny's in the Kamaole Shopping Center.

Cybercafés in South Maui are generally expensive. At Cyber Surf Lounge (☎ 879-1090), in Azeka Place II, high-speed Internet access costs 10¢ per minute with a $2 minimum. Bubba's Burgers (☎ 891-2600), 1945 S Kihei Rd, offers free email access while you wait. Other Internet kiosks in coffee shops tend to be unreliable and more expensive.

The modern Kihei public library (☎ 875-6833), 35 Waimahaihai St, is directly behind the fire station. It's open noon to 8pm Tuesday, 10am to 6pm Wednesday and Friday, and 10am to 5pm Thursday and Saturday.

Longs Drugs (☎ 879-2669), 1215 S Kihei Rd in the Longs Center, offers one-hour photo processing. Pro Photo Lab (☎ 879-1508), 2395 S Kihei Rd at Dolphin Plaza, handles B&W photo processing, slides and transparencies and sells professional film and underwater cameras.

There are coin laundries at most condominium complexes. Otherwise the Lipoa Laundry Center (☎ 875-9266), 40 E Lipoa St in the Lipoa Center, is open 8am to 8pm daily. As a bonus, it's right next to Hapa's Brew Haus.

For serious medical emergencies, the nearest hospital is in Wailuku (see Kahului in the Central Maui chapter). Urgent Care Kihei Physicians (☎ 879-7781), 1325 S Kihei Rd at Lipoa St, can handle minor matters and is open 6am to midnight daily. Urgent Care Kihei Physicians accepts walk-ins and

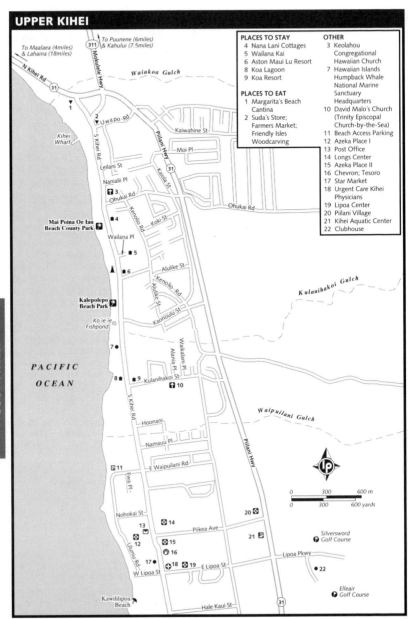

UPPER KIHEI

PLACES TO STAY
4 Nana Lani Cottages
5 Wailana Kai
6 Aston Maui Lu Resort
8 Koa Lagoon
9 Koa Resort

PLACES TO EAT
1 Margarita's Beach Cantina
2 Suda's Store; Farmers Market; Friendly Isles Woodcarving

OTHER
3 Keolahou Congregational Hawaiian Church
7 Hawaiian Islands Humpback Whale National Marine Sanctuary Headquarters
10 David Malo's Church (Trinity Episcopal Church-by-the-Sea)
11 Beach Access Parking
12 Azeka Place I
13 Post Office
14 Longs Center
15 Azeka Place II
16 Chevron; Tesoro
17 Star Market
18 Urgent Care Kihei Physicians
19 Lipoa Center
20 Piilani Village
21 Kihei Aquatic Center
22 Clubhouse

most kinds of medical insurance, including travel insurance.

Kihei Wharf

In 1899, Henry Baldwin built a wharf at the north end of Kihei for landing supplies for his sugar plantation. Later a plantation workers camp grew up around the wharf. Things stayed pretty lively until sand accretion eventually made the wharf – which once jutted some 200 feet into the bay – obsolete.

The remains of the wharf, which now only extends about 30 feet, are mostly used by local fishers and their *keiki* (children). It's convenient for catching the sunset if you happen to be in the area.

Keolahou Congregational Hawaiian Church

Doused with ocean spray, this little green-and-white church (☎ 879-4963, 177 S Kihei Rd) dates from 1920. Many of the Tongans living on Maui belong to the congregation. Sunday service is held at 9:30am.

Captain Vancouver Monument

Captain Cook never set foot on Maui, but one of his enterprising crew members, George Vancouver, did. After returning to the islands in command of his own ship, he came ashore at the small village of Kihei in 1792. When he returned the next year, he dropped off the first cattle and horses ever to set foot (or hoof, rather) in Hawaii.

By all accounts he was a fairly enlightened explorer. At first Vancouver tried to make peace between the warring *ali'i* (chiefs) on Maui and refused to trade with them in arms or ammunition. Eventually he became an impromptu advisor to Kamehameha the Great, who was so impressed by Vancouver's talk of the British Empire that he adopted the Union Jack into his royal flag (which still symbolizes the Hawaiian sovereignty movement today).

A small **totem pole** commemorates Captain Vancouver's landing on the beach. In between trips to Hawaii, he went on to 'discover' British Columbia, a journey now done in the reverse by thousands of Canadian tourists who flock to Maui each year.

Coincidentally, the monument sits directly opposite Auntie Aloha's Hawaiian Hut, now part of the Aston Maui Lu Resort, which is said to have been built by a rich Canadian logger.

Humpback Whale National Marine Sanctuary

The Hawaiian Islands Humpback Whale National Marine Sanctuary (whew, say that three times fast) headquarters (☎ 879-2818, W www.hihwnms.nos.noaa.gov, 726 S Kihei Rd; open 10am-4pm Mon-Fri) maintains a work-in-progress visitor center, with simple exhibits, videos and free literature on whales, sea turtles and other endangered marine life that the sanctuary protects, as well as traditional Hawaiian aquaculture.

During Maui's whale-watching season, roughly from December to April, the center comes alive. Maui's warm offshore waters are the favored breeding and nursing grounds for two-thirds of the North Pacific humpback whale population. The center's oceanfront verandah makes a great spot for sighting the whales that frequent the bay. Trained volunteers act as guides and a scope is set up for public viewing. Just to the north, natural sand dune restoration efforts are ongoing.

Free lectures on marine conservation are given about once a month year-round. The National Oceanic and Atmospheric Administration (NOAA), which manages the sanctuary, estimates that the migrant whale population is increasing at an annual rate of 7%. Each year it trains hundreds of volunteers to participate in the Great Whale Count; call the visitor center to ask about these and other educational opportunities.

David Malo's Church

The church on this historic site was built in 1852 by David Malo, a notable scholar and the first Hawaiian ordained to the Christian ministry. Malo, who was born on the Big Island, had the foresight to worry about the effects of early Western contact on traditional Hawaiian culture. He became a trusted advisor of Kamehameha III, whom he helped to compose Hawaii's first declaration

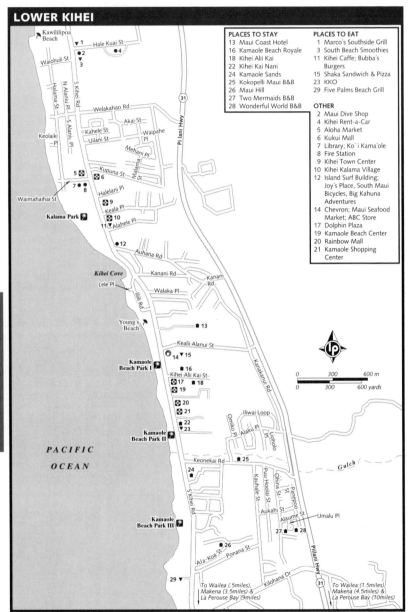

LOWER KIHEI

PLACES TO STAY
13 Maui Coast Hotel
16 Kamaole Beach Royale
18 Kihei Alii Kai
22 Kihei Kai Nani
24 Kamaole Sands
25 Kokopelli Maui B&B
26 Maui Hill
27 Two Mermaids B&B
28 Wonderful World B&B

PLACES TO EAT
1 Marco's Southside Grill
3 South Beach Smoothies
11 Kihei Caffe; Bubba's Burgers
15 Shaka Sandwich & Pizza
23 KKO
29 Five Palms Beach Grill

OTHER
2 Maui Dive Shop
4 Kihei Rent-a-Car
5 Aloha Market
6 Kukui Mall
7 Library; Ko'i Kama'ole
8 Fire Station
9 Kihei Town Center
10 Kihei Kalama Village
12 Island Surf Building; Joy's Place, South Maui Bicycles, Big Kahuna Adventures
14 Chevron; Maui Seafood Market; ABC Store
17 Dolphin Plaza
19 Kamaole Beach Center
20 Rainbow Mall
21 Kamaole Shopping Center

Kawililipoa Beach
Hale Kuai St
Waiohuli St
Halama St
N Alanui Pl
S Kihei Rd
N Alanui Pl
S Alanui Pl
Welakahao Rd
Akai St
Kahele St
Waipahe Pl
Keolaiki Pl
Uilani St
Mehani Pl
Malama St
Kupuna St
Halelani Pl
Waimahaihai St
Keala Pl
Kalama Park
Alahele Pl
Auhana Rd

Pi Iani Hwy
31

Kihei Cove
Lele Pl
Kanani Rd
Kanani Rd
Iliili Rd
Walaka Pl
Young's Beach
13
Kealii Alanui St
Kamaole Beach Park I
14   15
Kihei Alii Kai St
16
17   18
19
20
21
22
23
Iliwai Loop
Aleku Pl
Omiko Pl
Lioholo Pl
Kamaole Beach Park II
Keonekai Rd
25
24
Puu Hoolai St
Kauhale St
Ohina St
Parepoo St
Aukahi St
Gulch
Kanakanui Rd

PACIFIC OCEAN

Kamaole Beach Park III
26
Ala-Koa St
Ponana St
Alaume St
Umalu Pl
27   28
29
Kilohana Dr
To Wailea (.5miles),
Makena (3.5miles) &
La Perouse Bay (9miles)
To Wailea (1.5miles),
Makena (4.5miles) &
La Perouse Bay (10miles)
31
Piilani Hwy

0   300   600 m
0   300   600 yards

SOUTH MAUI

of rights in 1839, as well as the first constitution the following year.

Malo died here one year after his church was completed. He was buried in Lahaina at his alma mater, Lahainaluna Seminary (see Lahaina in the West Maui chapter). Most the original church was dismantled long ago, but a three-foot-high section of the stone walls still stands next to a grove of palm trees and a small cemetery. Eighteen pews are lined up inside the walls, and an open-air service is held here courtesy of **Trinity Episcopal Church-by-the-Sea** (☎ *879-0161, 100 Kulanihakoi St*), at 9am Sunday.

Ko'a i Kama'ole

When ground was broken for construction of the new Kihei library, an ancient *ko'a* (fishing shrine) was unearthed. Before setting out to sea, Hawaiian fisherman would leave offerings here, perhaps a piece of coral, a sea urchin or some fish hooks. When they returned, a slice of the first catch of the day would be left to thank the gods for their favors. Today the site is just a pile of rocks, but it is marked with an interpretive plaque.

Beaches

Kihei's southern beaches are postcard perfect. Most popular are Kamaole Beach County Parks I, II and III, while farther south Keawakapu Beach is an uncrowded gem. The northern beaches up around Kihei Wharf, where swimming is definitely not advised, are the domain of windsurfers and a few kayakers. Kayakers also launch from Kihei Cove opposite Kanani Rd. Snorkelers and divers head straight for Wailea and Makena beaches instead.

Mai Poina Oe Iau Beach County Park This park at the northern end of Kihei has a long, sandy beach and full facilities. The park, whose name means 'forget me not,' is dedicated to Maui's war veterans.

Sunbathing is best in the morning before the wind picks up, but water conditions are murky and swimming isn't recommended. Windsurfing is generally good in the afternoon; many people take windsurfing lessons

Molokini

The largely submerged volcanic crater of Molokini lies midway between the islands of Maui and Kahoolawe. Half of the crater rim has eroded away, leaving a crescent moon that rises 160 feet above the ocean surface with a land surface area of about 18 acres. So tiny is Molokini that King David Kalakaua once wagered it all in a game of poker at the Ulupalakua Ranch; when he lost, he claimed that he had only bet *omole kini,* a bottle of gin.

According to ancient legend, Molokini was a beautiful woman who was turned to stone by jealous Pele, goddess of fire and volcanoes. Other stories say that one of Pele's lovers angered her by secretly marrying a *mo'o,* or shape-shifting water lizard. Pele then chopped the sacred lizard in half, leaving Molokini as its tail and Puu Olai in Makena as its head. Still other tales allege that Molokini, which means 'many ties' in Hawaiian, is the umbilical cord leftover from the birth of Kahoolawe.

Today, Molokini draws scores of snorkelers and divers, who come here for its clear waters with abundant fish and coral. Most of the black coral that was once prolific in Molokini's deeper waters made its way into Lahaina jewelry stores before the island was declared a marine conservation district in 1977. During WWII the US Navy shelled Molokini for target practice, and live bombs are still occasionally found on the crater floor. A decade ago, demolition experts removed three bombs that were in just 20 feet of water. Bullets are still seen protruding from the naked cliffs, which are recovering from being stripped of native foliage by shrapnel and feral rabbits.

here, and outrigger canoes and kayaks also launch from the beach.

Kalepolepo Beach Park The waters off this beach park aren't good for much, but this is one of the few places on Maui where you can see the remains of a fishpond.

Ko'ie'ie Fishpond (W *www.formaui.org*) was built in the 16th century by King Umi and was used to raise mullet for the ali'i. Rising tides poured sea life into the pond through the sluice gate, which could then be closed to trap the mature fish inside. Over 1 ton of fish is thought to have been harvested annually after the fishpond was rebuilt in the 1800s by Kamehameha I. The fishpond is now on the National Register of Historic Places, thanks to volunteer restorers who reset each lava stone by hand during low tide. For more on fishponds in Hawaiian history, see 'Fishponds' in the Excursions chapter.

Kalama Park Opposite Kihei Town Center, Kalama Park has an inline skating hockey rink, baseball field, soccer pitch, tennis and volleyball courts, playground, picnic pavilions, restrooms and outdoor showers. The park is broad and grassy, but its beach is shallow and unappealing for swimming.

Kamaole Beach County Parks The Kamaole parks are essentially one long beach divided into three sections (Kam I, II and III) by rocky points. All have full facilities, lifeguards on duty and stretches of beautiful golden sand, although powerful *kona* storms can temporarily wipe them out.

Water conditions vary greatly with the weather, but there's usually good swimming. For the most part, these shores have sandy bottoms with a fairly steep drop, which tends to create good conditions for bodysurfing, especially in winter. For snorkeling, the north and south ends of Kam III have some nearshore rocks harboring a bit of coral and a few tropical fish, but the Wailea beaches are far better.

All three beach sections are along S Kihei Rd, opposite the condos and shopping centers. Kam I and Kam III have parking lots, while most people heading for Kam II either walk or park their cars just on the west side of the road.

Keawakapu Beach Park More scenic and less crowded than the roadside Kihei beaches, sandy Keawakapu Beach straddles the border between the southernmost Kihei hotels and Mokapu Beach in Wailea. Snorkeling is fairly good in the mornings at the rocky outcrop at the southern end, but be careful not to disturb the sea turtles.

As there's no reef off Keawakapu, the state has been working to develop an artificial reef here for the past 30 years. The original drop consisted of piles of abandoned car bodies collected from around the island, but in recent years the state has switched to using 'fish shelters' made of old tires embedded in concrete dropped some 500 yards offshore.

There's a fine view from the beach, and during the winter whales cavort in the surrounding waters and sometimes come quite close to shore.

To get to Keawakapu, go south on S Kihei Rd almost until it ends. You'll see the blue shoreline access sign pointing down past the outdoor showers to the beach. There is a parking lot with about 40 spaces on the *mauka* (inland) side of the road.

Places to Stay

The bulk of Kihei accommodations are in condo complexes, as well as a few cottages, hotels and subdivision B&Bs. There are no hostels, but budget travelers could double, triple or even quadruple up together in a cheap condo or cottage.

Rates peak during high season, usually mid-December to mid-April, while substantial discounts and packages are offered at other times of year.

Cottages A beachfront cottage in Hawaii may sound like a dream, but the reality doesn't quite measure up in Kihei. Most cottages are squeezed onto relatively small parcels of land next to noisy Kihei Rd and are far north of the best swimming beaches.

Nona Lani Cottages (☎ 879-2497, 800-733-2688, W *www.nonalanicottages.com, 455 S Kihei Rd*) Rooms low/high season $65/75, cottages from $85/100. One-week minimum stay is usually required. Nona Lani cottages are managed by a friendly island family who sell lei made from flowers grown in their roadside gardens. Rooms in the main house have air-con, private bath and TV. A range of small cottages, from simple accommodations to secluded honeymoon suites, have kitchens, lanai and hammocks. Guests may be able to negotiate discounts for longer stays.

B&Bs The typical minimum stay is three days, with discounts possible for visits of a week or longer. Advance reservations are necessary.

Two Mermaids on the Sunny Side of Maui B&B (☎ 874-8687, 800-598-9550, fax 875-1833, **W** www.twomermaids.com, 2840 Umalu Pl) Poolside studio $95, 1-/2-bedroom apartment $125/175. Happy guests rave about the hospitality of these two mermaids, who bring a basket of fresh-cut fruit to your door every morning. The cheery rooms all have private baths, minikitchen facilities and acoustic guitars. Outside the small pool has a naturalistic border of rocks and leafy gardens. Look for a tall, modern white house tucked at the end of a residential cul-de-sac, not too far from the beach.

Kokopelli Maui B&B (☎/fax 891-0631, 169 Keonekai Rd) Rooms with shared bath low/high season $70/80, suites $85/95. Convenient to the highway, this no-frills B&B offers a couple of upstairs rooms with ceiling fans in a modern home. Continental breakfast and shared kitchen access is included. It is often full with long-term guests. Ask about weekly and monthly discounts.

Wonderful World B&B (☎ 879-9103, 800-943-5804, **W** www.wonderfulbnb.com, 2828 Umalu Pl) Suites $75-100. This is another contemporary home, right near Two Mermaids. It is about half a mile inland from Kamaole Beach Park III. Rates include breakfast served on the lanai with ocean views. Each ample suite has its own private bath, telephone, cable TV/VCR and varying kitchen facilities, but not a hint of Hawaiiana.

Condos In a nutshell, Kihei is 'condoville.' Condos in South Kihei are close to the best beaches and usually have staffed front desks. Many of the complexes on noisy Kihei Rd can make sleep a bit elusive, so ask for a unit farther back when making reservations

if you don't mind sacrificing the ocean view. The minimum stay is usually three days, and cleaning surcharges may apply for short stays of less than a week. For rental policies and procedures, see Accommodations in the Facts for the Visitor chapter.

Wailana Kai (☎ 891-1626, 866-891-1626, fax 891-8855, **W** www.wailanakai.com, 34 Wailana Pl) 1-bedroom units low/high season $75/90, 2-bedroom units $90/110. At the 1-mile marker, this well-maintained minicomplex resides on a cul-de-sac set one block back from the beach. Each of the small apartment units has a full kitchen, cable TV, lanai and floral-print furniture, everything you'd expect in a more expensive condo (except for the space, perhaps). A pint-size pool, laundry facilities and onsite manager are the perks. Credit cards are not accepted.

If the Wailana Kai is full or you haven't made reservations, there are a handful of other budget complexes on the same street.

Kihei Kai Nani (☎ 879-9088, 800-473-1493, fax 879-8965, **W** www.kiheikainani.com, 2495 S Kihei Rd) 1-bedroom units low/high season $70/95; mid-Apr-mid-Dec $1200 per month. Not only is this the friendliest place on the whole strip, but it's directly opposite Kamaole Beach Park II. All of the low-rise buildings have one-bedroom units with full modern kitchens, ceiling fans, spacious balconies and telephones with free local calls. Some units may come with cable TV/VCR and free beach equipment. The Kihei Kai Nani has a good-size pool and several barbecue grills, and there are restaurants and shops within easy walking distance.

Kamaole Beach Royale (☎ 879-3131, 800-421-3661, fax 879-9163, **W** www.mauikbr .com, 2385 S Kihei Rd) 1-bedroom units low/high season $80/105, 2-bedroom units $95/120, 3-bedroom units $100/125. Kamaole Beach Royale is a well-managed, seven-story condo set back from the road on a hillside opposite Kamaole Beach Park I. It's quiet, with open range behind and ocean views from the top floors, but the pool is small. Units are spacious and well furnished with private lanai, modern kitchens, air-con, cable TV/VCR, phones with free local calls and washer/dryers. Credit cards are not accepted.

Kihei Alii Kai (☎ 879-6770, 800-888-6284, fax 879-6221, 2387 S Kihei Rd) 1-bedroom units low/high season $75/100, 2-bedroom units $95/120. Set back from the main road and a two-minute walk from Kamaole Beach Park I, this 127-unit complex has a pool, sauna and tennis courts. The low-rise buildings are crowded together like apartment blocks, but most units are comfortable enough for the money; all have cable TV and washer/dryers.

Koa Resort (☎ 879-3328, 800-541-3060, 811 S Kihei Rd) 1-bedroom units low/high season $100/130, 2-bedroom units $130/160. This condo complex can look a little deserted, especially since it doesn't really have a front desk. Most rentals are handled by Bello Realty, whose address follows below. All units are equipped with full kitchens, private lanai and cable TV. You'll also find two tennis courts, a putting green, a swimming pool and a spa spread out across 5½ landscaped acres with flowering trees.

Koa Lagoon (☎ 879-3002, 800-367-8030, fax 874-0209, W www.koalagoon.com, 800 S Kihei Rd) 1-bedroom units low/high season $100/130, 2-bedroom units $130/160. This white concrete high-rise enjoys unbeatable views and the units are fairly soundproof, but the beach out front is often filled with seaweed that makes it unsuitable for swimming. Perks include BBQ grills and a heated pool, plus air-con, full kitchen, TV/VCR and washer/dryer in each apartment. Most of the units are rented by Bello Realty, whose address follows below.

Kamaole Sands (☎ 874-8700, 800-367-5004, Neighbor Islands 800-272-5257, fax 477-2329, W www.castleresorts.com, 2695 S Kihei Rd) 1-bedroom units low/high season from $155/175, 2-bedroom units $230/255. Kamaole Sands is its own condo city with 270 rental units in almost a dozen four-story buildings, most set well back from the road opposite Kamaole Beach Park III. All of the large units are fully-equipped with modern amenities. Barbecue grills and small waterfall pools are scattered around the green, landscaped grounds. Tennis courts, a

Jacuzzi, a swimming pool and a weekly welcome party with live Hawaiian music are also provided. Still, the complex can seem a bit impersonal, but steep Internet discounts may balance that.

Maui Hill (☎ 879-6321, 800-922-7866, fax 879-8945, 2881 S Kihei Rd) 1-bedroom 2-bath units low/high season $150/199, 2-bedroom 2-bath units $195/248. Regally set on a hillside above Keawakapu Beach Park, these Mediterranean-style villas prove that condo living can be luxurious. Nothing has been spared to outfit these 21st-century condos. Weekly *mai tai* parties are a fixture. Look for the retro 1970s whale sign pointing to the resort from the Kihei Rd turnoff.

Scores more Kihei condos can be booked through rental agents.

Bello Realty (☎ 879-3328, 800-541-3060, fax 875-1483, W www.bellomaui.com, PO Box 1776, Kihei, HI 96753) Condo properties from under $100 per night, mostly right in Kihei.

Condominium Rentals Hawaii (☎ 879-2778, in the USA 800-367-5242, in Canada 800-663-2101, fax 879-7825, W www.crhmaui.com, 362 Huku Lii Pl, No 204, Kihei, HI 96753) Car/condo packages and Internet deals for mid-range Kihei properties.

Kihei Maui Vacations (☎ 879-7581, 888-568-6284, fax 879-2000, W www.kmvmaui.com, PO Box 1055, Kihei, HI 96753) Condos from $60 to $600 per night, as well as a few luxury homes for rent.

Kumulani Rentals (☎ 879-9272, 800-367-2954, fax 874-0094, W www.maui.net/~putt3/kumulani, PO Box 1190, Island Surf Bldg, 1993 S Kihei Rd, Kihei, HI 96753) Condos from $450 per week, including upscale Kihei and Wailea Properties.

Hotels *Aston Maui Lu Resort* (☎ 879-5991, 800-922-7866, fax 879-4627, W www.astonhotels.com, 575 S Kihei Rd) Standard rooms low/high season from $110/130. Unlike many chain resorts, this low-rise complex achieves a rustic Polynesian feel with all the standard modern amenities. Some units front the beach, while others are across the road and set back from the highway. There is also an island-shaped swimming pool and what they say is the oldest coconut grove on Maui. Check the Web site for steep discounts and package deals.

Maui Coast Hotel (☎ 874-6284, 800-895-6284, fax 875-4731, **W** www.westcoasthotels.com/mauicoast, 2259 S Kihei Rd) Standard rooms/suites from $165/195. A favorite with older package tourists and business travelers, this is an expansive, modern, seven-story hotel affiliated with the Canadian Coast Hotels chain. It is set back from the road, so it's quieter than many of the Kihei condos. All rooms have minifridges and lanai; suites have whirlpool tubs. Guests can use the complimentary washer/dryers, two Jacuzzis, a heated pool and tennis courts, plus there's live Hawaiian music at the poolside bar nightly. Ask about the off-season and senior discounts.

Places to Eat

With a few happy exceptions, Kihei restaurants just aren't good value, and tasty food with an ocean view is hard to find. You may find yourself doing a little self-catering from your condo kitchen instead. There's a ***Star Market*** with a bakery and deli south of Azeka Place and a 24-hour ***Foodland*** at Kihei Town Center. Farther east on the highway, there's a ***Safeway*** grocery store and pharmacy at Piilani Village. Behind the ABC Store and Chevron Gas Station, there's a small ***Maui Seafood Market*** (☎ 874-1221, 2349 S Kihei Rd) shop that serves hot local plate lunches (under $6).

Kihei Farmers Market (Next to Suda's Store parking lot) Open 1:30pm-5:30pm Mon, Wed & Fri. Farmers give free samples of their fruits and vegetables, fresh juices, salsas and cheeses to entice you to buy more.

Hawaiian Moons Natural Foods (☎ 875-4356, Kamaole Beach Center, 2411 S Kihei Rd) Open 8am-8pm Mon-Sat, 8am-6pm Sun. This shop has an organic produce section, yogurts, juices, trail mix, bulk grains, pineapple-coconut muffins, granolas and a few organic wines. The salad bar ($5 per pound) and fresh juice and espresso bar both close a bit earlier than the store itself.

Budget Fast-food chains are everywhere, so if you're on a tight budget you won't have to spend more than a few bucks to get your fill of greasy hamburgers or cheap Chinese food. But tastier options exist, too, if you poke around the strip malls long enough.

Home Maid Bakery & Deli (☎ 874-6035, Azeka Place I, 1280 S Kihei Rd) Local plate lunches $6. Open 6am-9pm daily. This humble bakery is a local mecca for hot *malasadas* (Portuguese doughnuts).

Taj Mahalo (☎ 874-1911, Lipoa Center, 41 E Lipoa St) Dishes $5-10.50. Open 10.30am-9pm Mon-Sat, 4pm-9pm Sun. This Indian takeout cafeteria fries up a rainbow of fiery curries to go along with its cool *lassi* shakes.

South Beach Smoothies (☎ 875-0594, 1455 S Kihei Rd) Items under $5. Open 8am-4pm Mon-Fri, 9am-2pm Sat (closed Sun). Luscious smoothies are chock-full of fresh fruit and only cost about $3.50, including an extra 'side car' free. This friendly local place also sells cheap hot dogs, granola and health-food bars.

Shaka Sandwich & Pizza (☎ 874-0331, 1295 S Kihei Rd) Pizza slices $2, whole pizzas from $13, sandwiches $4.50-11. Open 10:30am-9pm daily. In the strip mall behind Jack in the Box, this place is a favorite of surfers. The pizza is actually pretty greasy, but try the Philly cheesesteaks or Italian-style sandwiches, calzone and *stromboli*.

Maui Tacos (☎ 879-5005, Kamaole Beach Center, 2411 S Kihei Rd) Items around $6. Open 9am-9pm daily. This Hawaii-wide chain is the brainchild of a respected Maui chef, who grew tired of never finding good Mexican food on the islands. It's actually more California-style, but who cares when the whopping beef, chicken or veggie burritos are made with five kinds of lard-free beans and fresh local salsa. Chimichangas, quesadillas and nachos are à la carte.

Tobi's Ice Cream & Shave Ice (☎ 891-2440, Kihei Kalama Village, 1913 S Kihei Rd) Icy delights $3-5.25. Open 10am-9:30pm daily. Finally, an ice-cream shop for *kamaaina* (island folks). Thick, tall milk shakes, 'Wild Wahine' shave ice and tropical smoothies are always mo' bettah here.

Alexander's (☎ 874-0788, Kihei Kalama Village, 1913 S Kihei Rd) Meals $7-10. Open

11am-9pm daily. Alexander's is a great spot for fish & chips, made with your choice of fresh mahimahi, ono or ahi. They also make combo meals and hush puppies (fried cornmeal dough balls), fried zucchini, corn bread and cole slaw. There are a few tables outdoors where you can scarf it all down.

Kihei Caffe *(☎ 879-2230, 1945 S Kihei Rd)* Dishes $5-7. Open 5am-3pm daily. This casual café, opposite Kalama Park, is an excellent little breakfast spot, perfect for jet-lagged travelers who wake up early. It serves cappuccino, Kona coffee, homemade pastries and good karma. Tempting banana–macadamia nut pancakes, superfresh salads and sandwiches are just a few of the offerings, while the in-your-face local attitude seems to be free. If you're lucky, one of the crowded outdoor tables will already have the morning paper on it.

Bubba's Burgers *(☎ 891-2600, 1945 S Kihei Rd,* w *www.bubbaburger.com)* Items $2.75-7.50. Open 10:30am-9pm daily. Thank God for Bubba's, because it's the only self-respecting burger joint in town. Hailing from Coors Tavern in Pueblo, Colorado, Bubba's swears, 'We cheat tourists, drunks and attorneys.' All the burgers are guaranteed to contain 88% fat-free beef direct from Upcountry ranches on the slopes of Haleakala. It charges an outrageous 75¢ for lettuce and tomato because, well, it doesn't believe real people should eat them on their burgers. Other notables are the famous Budweiser beer chili and free email access.

Joy's Place *(☎ 879-9258, Island Surf Bldg, 1993 S Kihei Rd)* Items $4-7. Open 10am-5pm Mon-Sat, 10am-3pm Sun. Joy's Place, a small restaurant with a dozen café tables, has mostly vegetarian home-style food. You can get organic salads, soups and tortilla-wrapped sandwiches, which are all delicious. Vegans will savor the curried hummus and cheeseless pesto.

Kamaole Shopping Center *(2653 S Kihei Rd)* This busy shopping center has a 24-hour **Denny's** and **Cinnamon Roll Fair** for instant sugar highs ($3 each). The upstairs billiards bar **Dick's Place** *(☎ 874-8869)* often advertises all-you-can-eat fajita or seafood nights (around $15).

Mid-Range *Margarita's Beach Cantina (☎ 879-5275, Kealia Beach Plaza, 101 N Kihei Rd, 2nd level)* Mains $11-22. Open 11:30am-10pm daily. Margarita's has acceptable Mexican food and a great sunset-facing deck overlooking the water. The menu shows the usual burgers, fajitas and Mexican combo plates with rice and beans (under $15). Best of all are all-you-can-eat prime rib or lobster nights for about the same price.

Marco's Southside Grill *(☎ 874-4041, 1445 S Kihei Rd)* Breakfast $6-10, lunch & dinner mains $10-26. Open 7:30am-10pm daily. A glittering outpost of Kahului's Italian restaurant Marco's, this place has sparkling white marble columns, Spanish leather chairs, a baby grand piano and 24-karat beer tap pulls. The wood oven–fired pizzas, oversize hot Italian sandwiches and signature pastas, such as vodka rigatoni, are a steal. The dessert menu is almost as long as the wine list. Breakfast is all over the place, wandering from *huevos rancheros* to eggs Benedict, and the chocolate-cinnamon French toast comes highly recommended.

Pita Paradise *(☎ 875-7679, Kihei Kalama Village, 1913 S Kihei Rd)* Lunch dishes or combos $6-16, dinner mains $8-19. Open for lunch 11am-3pm Mon-Sat, dinner 5pm-9:30pm daily. It's a perennial favorite for fresh pita with gourmet stuffings, such as sirloin steak with Kula onions or grilled vegetables. Get your *ziziki* bread or fish kababs and sit at an open-air table.

La Creperie *(☎ 891-0822, Kihei Kalama Village, 1913 S Kihei Rd)* Savory crepes $11-18, entrées $15-25. Open 5pm-10pm daily. This tiny spot on the side of a lively outdoor shopping center has a long list of savory and sweet crepes and a surprisingly good wine list. It has live jazz some nights.

Maui Pizza Café *(☎ 891-2200, Rainbow Mall, 2439 S Kihei Rd)* Pizza & pasta $8-16. Open 11:30am-1am daily. The ambience at this bar-restaurant couldn't be more welcoming, and pizza is deservedly its signature dish. Homemade thin-crust rounds are piled high with local produce and seafood, perhaps with a little *kalua* pig with Maui onions or scampi in citrus-garlic sauce. Traditionalists can stick with Italian sausage and mozzarella, or go for a fresh salad with pesto or wild mushroom pasta.

Top End *Roy's Kihei Bar & Grill (☎ 891-1120, fax 891-1104, Piilani Village, 303 Piikea Ave)* Appetizers $8-12, entrées $21-29. Open 5:30pm-10pm daily. Famous local chef Roy Kahana has opened yet another winning restaurant, this time on the outskirts of Kihei. As always, the emphasis is on Hawaiian seafood, excellent wine and relaxed sophistication. Half of the menu is reserved for Roy's classic recipes, while the other half features nightly specials found only at this location, perhaps scallops in dragon sauce or the chef's dim-sum canoe for two. If you can't make it to the more established Roy's in Napili (see the West Maui chapter), this might do nicely.

Kaui Ku Ono (KKO) (☎ 875-1007, 2511 S Kihei Rd) Pupu $8-13, dinner mains $10-15. Open 8am-midnight daily. KKO's torchlights blaze nightly and the sun often sets to the tune of live Hawaiian music. An expansive lanai looks out over the road toward the ocean. If its inventive pupu doesn't satisfy your hunger, there is a serious steakhouse upstairs.

Five Palms Beach Grill (☎ 879-2607, fax 875-4803, 2960 S Kihei Rd) Breakfast & lunch $10-15, dinner entrées $20-30, 5-course chef's tasting menu $65 (2-person minimum). Open 8am-9:30pm daily; pupu only 2:45pm-5pm. Around the back of the Mana Kai resort, this established restaurant looks charming at night when palm trees are waving in the moonlight. The stiffly formal dining room has chandeliers, but you can choose to sit outside on the edge of the waterfront gardens. The cooking emphasizes local produce, such as Molokai sweet potatoes, Maui onions and fresh seafood. Dinner brings on the heavy-hitters: lobster, steak, lamb and Hawaiian market fish. Everyone raves about the Sunday champagne brunch ($20, 8am to 2pm), although regular breakfast and lunch can be skipped.

Entertainment

After Lahaina, Kihei has the liveliest entertainment scene on Maui. Don't expect Oahu-style nightlife, however. There are only a handful of bars and clubs for DJs and live music, but they stay hoppin' all through the week. Check the Thursday *Maui News* or the free *Maui Time* for events calendars.

Happy hour is usually from 3pm to 6pm, and most bars and clubs stay open until 2am. The former usually has no cover charge, while the latter are free only on certain weeknights; expect to pay $5 to $10 on weekends.

Hapa's Brew Haus (☎ 879-9001, Lipoa Center, 41 E Lipoa St) There's something happening nightly at Hapa's Brew Haus, a combination bar and nightclub that bizarrely, also serves sushi. Local legend Willie K owns Monday night, while queer-friendly Ultra Fabulous Night is on Tuesday. On other nights you might get live music or DJs. With a heavy-hitting sound system and sweaty singles scene, you can be sure this place will stick around.

The key triumvirate of bars and clubs gather at Kihei Kalama Village, across from Kam II beach park.

Bada Bing's(☎ 875-0188, Kihei Kalama Village, 1945 S Kihei Rd) South Maui's newest and biggest dance floor is found inside this self-proclaimed 'New Jersey-style Italian bistro' (OK, whatever boys). DJs from Oahu and the mainland keep things spinning, and $2 drink specials certainly don't hurt either.

Life's a Beach (☎ 891-8010, Kihei Kalama Village, 1913 S Kihei Rd) This is the kind of grass shack, Bob Marley–lovin' bar you're gonna find on every tropical island in the world. Surfboards hog the walls, and the tables out front are crowded with all the usual suspects, from young beach mamas to laid-back local boys. Live music or DJs play almost nightly.

Kahale Beach Club (☎ 875-7711, Kihei Kalama Village) This is a local watering hole, stripped to the essentials and hidden at the back of the parking lot. Hard-drinkin' patrons demand live, loud homegrown music every day.

The Sports Page Grill & Bar (☎ 879-0602, Kamaole Beach Center, 2411 S Kihei Rd) Another local establishment, but this

SOUTH MAUI

one has big-screen TVs, satellite sports and a bar menu named after sports heroes. If you have to nosh, try the Yogi Berra corned beef or Sunday NFL breakfast specials.

Dick's Place (☎ 874-8869, *Kamaole Shopping Center, 2463 S Kihei Rd*) Swing upstairs to this huge billiards bar and shoot some stick.

A few of South Maui's restaurants (see Places to Eat, earlier) also have bars and entertainment. ***Maui Pizza Café*** has live music and DJs a few times a week, including reggae and a queer-friendly Friday. It has cheap drink specials and usually no cover charge. Happy hour starts early at 2:30pm at ***Margarita's Beach Cantina*** and lasts almost until the sun sets on its oceanfront sundeck.

Consolidated Theatres Kukui Mall (☎ 878-3456, *Kukui Mall*) Adult/child $7.50/4.25, bargain matinee (usually before 4pm) $4.75. This four-screen cinema complex shows new Hollywood releases, but parking can be a problem.

Shopping
Kihei overflows with souvenir shops of all sorts, with most aimed squarely at the el cheapo tourist market.

Aloha Market (*Cnr S Kihei Rd & Waimahaihai St*) Near the public library, this outdoor market has a collection of stalls selling cheap T-shirts, swimwear, jewelry as well as souvenirs.

Kihei Kalama Village (*1913 S Kihei Rd*) Whatever you cannot find at the aforementioned Aloha Market, you can probably purchase at the outdoor stalls here.

ABC Discount Store (☎ 879-6305, *2349 S Kihei Rd*) Opposite Kamaole Beach Park I, the ubiquitous ABC sells cheap beach mats, suntan lotion, sunglasses, liquor and other discount beach essentials.

Friendly Isles Woodcarving (*Outside Suda's Store*) An exception to the rule, here you can watch a real local woodcarver at work on beautiful authentic pieces. He sets up shop on the *makai* (seaward) side of the farmers market (see Places to Eat, earlier).

Locals usually shop the Hawaiian and international chain stores at ***Piilani Village***

(☎ 874-8900, *225 Piikea Ave*), which has a branch of ***Waldenbooks***, homegrown ***Crazy Shirts*** and ***Tropical Disc*** (☎ 874-3000), the well-established music shop. Tropical Disc has an excellent selection of Hawaiian tunes and headphone setups for previewing popular releases. The hip, young staff can help you choose a ukulele, too.

Maui Dive Shop (☎ 879-3388, *1455 S Kihei Rd*) The main outlet for this dive-shop chain sells discount reef walkers, boogie boards, snorkels, fins and wet suits.

WAILEA
At the end of the S Kihei Rd lies the fastidious resort of Wailea, a world away from the cluttered commercialism of Kihei. Why the difference? Wailea was developed solely by the Alexander & Baldwin sugar company in the 1970s, at the same time construction in Kihei was running amok.

As soon as you enter Wailea, you'll be struck by the contrast with its northern neighbor. Here everything is green, manicured and precise – which is only natural (or artificial, rather) given that the resorts were built alongside championship golf courses. Farther south, Makena has followed Wailea's lead, with a luxury hotel and golf course of its own catering to Japanese tourists. And to think there was nothing but ranch land here before.

All this greenery comes with a price tag. It is mostly paid by Upcountry farmers, whose water is drained through irrigation ditches to provide the millions of gallons required by resort guests daily. But as one local activist slogan points out, 'No one can eat golf balls.' Plans for further development are fiercely opposed by a wide coalition of local and international environmental groups.

Still, swimmers, snorkelers and sunbathers will love Wailea for its lava-rock coastline broken by golden-sand beaches. They offer panoramic views of Lanai, Kahoolawe and Molokini, and during winter there's superb shoreline whale watching. Incidentally, the name Wailea means 'waters of Lea,' the Hawaiian goddess of canoe-making, and the kayaking farther south past Makena is superb.

WAILEA

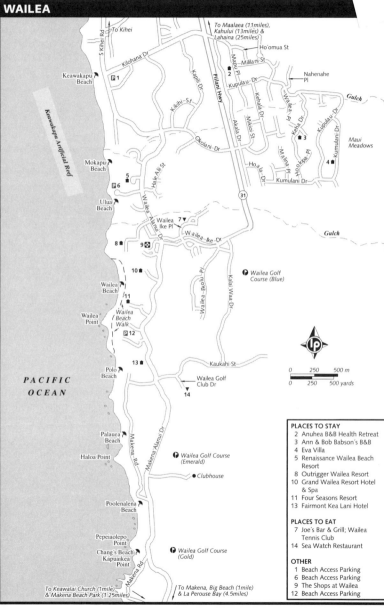

To Kihei
S Kihei Rd
Kilohana Dr

Keawakapu
Beach

P 1

To Maalaea (11miles),
Kahului (13miles) &
Lahaina (25miles)

Ho'omua St
Mililani St
Mapu Pl
2
Kupulau Dr
Nahenahe Pl
Gulch

Kapili Dr
Kihihi St
Pi'ilani Hwy
Okolani Dr
Akala Dr
Kehala Dr
Mikioi St
Wailea Pl
Kehi Pl
Kupulau Dr
Maui
Meadows

Mokapu
Beach

5
P 6

Ulua
Beach

Hale Alii St
Wailea Alanui Dr

31

Kapili Dr
Malina Pl
Ho'ali Dr
Ho'olai Pl
Kipa Pl
Kumulani Dr

3
4
Kumulani Dr

Wailea
Ike Pl
7
Wailea-Ike Dr

Gulch

8
9

10

Wailea
Beach
11
Wailea
Beach
Walk

Wailea
Point

P 12

13

Polo
Beach

14

Wailea Golf
Course (Blue)

Wailea-Ekolu Pl
Kilai Waa Dr

Kaukahi St

Wailea Golf
Club Dr

PACIFIC
OCEAN

Palauea
Beach

Haloa Point

Makena Rd
Makena Alanui Dr

Wailea Golf Course
(Emerald)

Clubhouse

0   250   500 m
0   250   500 yards

Poolenalena
Beach

Pepeiaolepo
Point

Chang's Beach
Kapuaikea
Point

Wailea Golf Course
(Gold)

Makena Rd

To Keawalai Church (1mile)
& Makena Beach Park (1.25miles)

To Makena, Big Beach (1mile)
& La Perouse Bay (4.5miles)

Keawakapu Artificial Reef

SOUTH MAUI

PLACES TO STAY
2 Anuhea B&B Health Retreat
3 Ann & Bob Babson's B&B
4 Eva Villa
5 Renaissance Wailea Beach
   Resort
8 Outrigger Wailea Resort
10 Grand Wailea Resort Hotel
   & Spa
11 Four Seasons Resort
13 Fairmont Kea Lani Hotel

PLACES TO EAT
7 Joe's Bar & Grill; Wailea
   Tennis Club
14 Sea Watch Restaurant

OTHER
1 Beach Access Parking
6 Beach Access Parking
9 The Shops at Wailea
12 Beach Access Parking

Orientation & Information

If you're heading to Wailea from up north, take the Piilani Hwy (Hwy 31). Otherwise the Kihei Rd strip can be a tedious 30 minutes through congested traffic. Wailea's main road is Wailea Alanui Dr, which turns into Makena Alanui Dr after Polo Beach, and continues south to Makena.

In addition to a few high-priced hotels on the beach, Wailea has a number of low-rise condo villas, a shopping center, a trio of pro golf courses and a famous tennis club.

If you're looking for a post office, library, medical clinic or cheap cybercafé, head north to Kihei. Resort guests can avail themselves of expensive business centers, on-call doctors and activity concierge desks at their own hotels.

A complimentary shuttle bus runs around the Wailea resorts every 30 minutes from 6:30am to 8pm, connecting the hotels, condos, shopping center and golf courses. Pickup from The Shops at Wailea is from the parking lot in front of the east-wing entrance.

Beaches

While Wailea's beaches generally have good swimming conditions, occasional high surf and kona storms can create dangerous shorebreaks and rip currents. Obey the posted warning signs.

These beaches start at the southern end of Keawakapu Beach (see Kihei, earlier) and continue south toward Makena. All are lovely strands of sand with free public access, limited parking, outdoor showers and restrooms. Those beaches fronting the resorts get the most crowded, while the quieter county beach parks sometimes have picnic tables and barbeque grills.

If you can't find a public parking spot (follow the blue shoreline access signs), you'll have to risk parking in hotel guest lots, which usually isn't too much of a problem.

Ulua & Mokapu Beaches Ulua Beach is a little gem between the Outrigger Wailea Resort and the Renaissance Wailea Beach Resort. The first road south of the Renaissance leads to the beach parking lot.

There's colorful coral at the rocky outcrop on the right side of the beach, where it borders its rougher twin Mokapu Beach. Beginners can usually spot long needlefish, schools of goatfish, unicorn tangs and other tropical fish. Snorkeling is best in the morning before the winds pick up. When the surf's up, forget snorkeling – go bodysurfing instead.

During WWII, US Marines trained for the invasion of Tarawa off this beach, and consequently it was referred to locally as Tarawa Beach – but the developers of the Wailea resort area didn't think that conjured up holiday images, so they renamed it Ulua.

Wailea Beach Wailea Beach is, naturally, the longest and widest beach in the area. The sands slope gradually, making the inshore waters excellent for swimming. When the water is calm, there's good snorkeling around the rocky point on the south side of the beach. Divers entering the water at Wailea Beach can follow a reef that runs down to Polo Beach. At times, there's a gentle shorebreak that is suitable for bodysurfing.

Beach access is from the road running between the Four Seasons Resort and the Grand Wailea Resort Hotel & Spa, both of which front Wailea Beach.

Polo Beach Small, golden Polo Beach is fronted by a condo development and the Fairmont Kea Lani Hotel, but its southern end is seldom crowded.

When there's wave action, boogie boarders and bodysurfers usually find a good shorebreak here. When the waters are calm, the rocks at the north end of the beach provide snorkeling along a rocky reef where you'll see the occasional turtle. At low tide, the lava outcropping at the south end of the beach has some interesting little tide pools that harbor spiny sea urchins and a few small fish.

To get to Polo Beach heading south, turn down Kaukahi St after the Kea Lani Hotel. There's a large beach parking lot on the right, near the end of the road.

Wailea Beach Walk

For an educational stroll that's easy on the eyes, take the shoreline path that runs for 1¼ miles from the Renaissance to the Fairmont Kea Lani, connecting all the Wailea beaches and the resort hotels that front them.

In winter, this is one of the best walks in all of Hawaii for spotting humpback whales – on a good day, you may be able to observe more than a dozen of them frolicking in the waters offshore. Drop a coin in the telescope just north of the Outrigger if you forgot to bring binoculars. Near the Outrigger *luau* (Hawaiian feast) grounds, there's a sacred stone where local fishers occasionally leave offerings.

Some of the luxury hotels you pass are worth strolling through, most notably the Grand Wailea Resort Hotel & Spa, which has $30 million of artwork and some strikingly elaborate waterways and landscaping. On its section of beach, look for the rusted military machinery dating from WWII, when US armed forces used this area to prepare for an invasion by Japan.

At its southern end, the path winds above the jagged lava points that separate the beaches. An interesting landscape of native Hawaiian flora appears, with over 60 varieties identified by plaques. Most are found near the Wailea Point Condminiums, where on a grassy area you'll see a remnant of an ancient Hawaiian home. There's a quaint bench for watching the sunset, too.

Palauea Beach Palauea Beach is along Makena Rd, a quarter of a mile south of Polo Beach. A fair number of people use the beach for surfing and bodysurfing. It's more secluded and less frequented than Polo Beach, but otherwise it's much the same, *sans* the development.

You can walk to Palauea Beach from Polo Beach in less than 10 minutes. The kiawe brushland between the beach and the road is marked private property, although there are gigantic breaks in the fence where beachgoers cross.

Chang's Beach Sandwiched between the end of the Wailea resort strip and Makena Rd, Chang's Beach is a sandy half-mile-long crescent with too many names. You may see or hear it referred to as Paipu Beach, Makena Surf Beach (after the closest condominium complex to the south) or even Love Beach.

That last name may be best, because it's hard not to love this place. Not only is the beach usually uncrowded, but the shallow, sandy bottom and calm waters make for excellent swimming. There is good snorkeling off both the southern and northern lava points, but be careful not to damage the live

coral or disturb the sea turtles. Haloa Point, a bit farther north, is a popular scuba-diving spot.

There is one main access point with parking spaces and limited facilities; look for a hand-drawn sign pointing off Wailea Alanui Dr, before the Makena Rd turnoff.

Activities

The **Wailea Golf Club** (*☎ 875-5111, 100 Golf Club Dr; Green fees & cart $140-160, resort guests less $25*) has championship courses. The Emerald is a tropical garden that consistently ranks top and the Gold is an interesting rugged course that takes advantage of volcanic landscapes.

If you want to play tennis at 'Wimbledon West,' try **Wailea Tennis Club** (*☎ 879-1958, 800-332-1614, 131 Wailea Ike Pl; Hourly court rental $35, resort guests $28*). Lessons and equipment rentals are available. Expect a dress code.

Places to Stay

Staying in Wailea requires shelling out a fair amount of cash, except if you stay at one of the B&Bs in the exclusive Maui Meadows subdivision, which sits about a mile above the beach on the slopes of Haleakala.

SOUTH MAUI

B&Bs **Ann & Bob Babson's B&B** (☎ 874-1166, 800-824-6409, fax 879-7906, W *www .mauibnb.com, 3371 Keha Dr*) Suites $100-130, 2-bedroom 2-bath cottage $135. From the living room of this modern hillside home, guests can see Kahoolawe, Molokini and Lanai, not to mention the Babson family's blooming landscaped gardens. All rooms have private bath. Rates include breakfast except Sunday and for cottage guests (who have their own kitchen). The master bedroom suite has its own private sundeck, Jacuzzi and wraparound windows. There's a five-day minimum stay (cottage one week).

Eva Villa (☎ 874-6407, 800-884-1885, in Germany 0800-182-1980, W *www.maui.net/~pounder, 85 Kumulani Dr*) Rates $115-140. This luxury B&B is inside a private hilltop villa that looks dazzlingly white in the sun. Guests share a swimming pool, Jacuzzi and rooftop sundeck. The gardens also hide a koi pond. The poolside studio and two-bedroom suite each has a private bath, while the stand-alone cottage has a full kitchen, washer/dryer and wrap-around lanai with a barbecue grill.

Anuhea B&B Health Retreat (☎ 874-1490, 800-206-4441, fax 874-8587, W *www .anuheamaui.com, 3164 Mapu Pl*) Rooms with shared bath low/high season from $115/105. This B&B, whose name means 'cool, sweet breeze,' is run by natural-health practitioners. Rooms are simple and modern, but most guests will want to spend more time outdoors anyway in the Jacuzzi, gazebo or gardens. Massage services and off-season discounts are available. En suite and ocean-view rooms cost a bit more.

Condos **Destination Resorts** (☎ 891-6200, 800-367-5246, fax 874-3554, W *www.drhmaui .com, The Shops at Wailea, ground level unit B51*) Studios/1-bedroom garden-view units from $155/205, 2-bedroom ocean-view from $310, 3-bedroom oceanfront from $600. Destination Resorts books about 300 units in half a dozen complexes around Wailea and Makena. While they aren't cheap, most of the condos tend to be better value than Wailea's luxury hotels, if you won't miss an elaborate swimming pool or beachfront

locale. There's a nasty $50 check-in fee, although package discounts for car rental and golf or tennis may somewhat ease the pain. A few Kihei condo agents (see earlier) also rent properties in Wailea.

AA Oceanfront Condominium Rentals (☎ 879-7288, 800-488-6004, fax 879-7500, W *www.makena.com, 2439 S Kihei Rd, No 102A, Kihei, HI 96753*) AA Oceanfront has high-end rentals in Wailea and Makena.

Hotels All of these resorts offer a full range of guest amenities, whether this translates as spas, fitness centers, jungle-like swimming pools, free hula classes or discounts on golf and tennis. The only differences between these hotels is in style (Polynesian or Western), attitude (how much of it can you take) and what kind of luxury you can afford.

Outrigger Wailea Resort (☎ 879-1922, 800-367-2960, fax 874-8331, W *www.out riggerwailea.com, 3700 Wailea Alanui Dr*) Garden-/mountain-/ocean-view rooms $325/375/425. Of all the Wailea resorts, the Outrigger is the one most in harmony with its Polynesian surrounds. For Wailea, it's an unpretentious, low-key operation that was recently renovated to the tune of $25 million dollars. An open-air tropical lobby leads straight back to the beach. Favored by families and conventioneers, the Outrigger chain that manages the hotel often offers substantial discounts and promotional packages. They also operate a condo property, **The Palms at Wailea**, where you can get a one-bedroom suite on the golf course for less than a hotel room here.

Fairmont Kea Lani Hotel (☎ 875-4100, 800-659-4100, fax 875-1200, W *www.kealani .com, 4100 Wailea Alanui Dr*) 1-bedroom suites $325-700, oceanfront villas $1100-1700. This fanciful resort hotel resembles something out of *The Arabian Nights,* and is an amusing credit to its Mexican architect. Somehow the Kea Lani manages to be exceedingly luxurious and not take itself too seriously. Each of the suites has a lanai, marble bathroom and separate living room with a sofa bed. The most expensive one-bedroom suites sleep up to four adults, and oceanfront villas come with private pools.

Renaissance Wailea Beach Resort (☎ 879-4900, 800-992-4532, fax 879-6128, W *www.renaissancehotels.com, 3550 Wailea Alanui Dr)* Terrace-/garden-/ocean-view rooms from $259/279/309. This is a tasteful resort hotel – upscale, but not as lavish as its neighbors to the south – done in an out-of-the-box tropical style. It's nothing special, but the grounds are lush, the rooms are furnished with rattan and wicker, and it's on a quieter beach. Special discounts packages can throw in a car and breakfast for about $100 less than the regular room rate.

Grand Wailea Resort Hotel & Spa (☎ 875-1234, 866-702-9177, fax 874-2442, W www.grandwailea.com, 3850 Wailea Alanui Dr) Low-/high-season rooms from $410/435, seasonal specials $310. Without a doubt, the Grand Wailea is the most extravagant resort on Maui. The lobbies are filled with priceless sculptures and artwork, while the grounds are given over to elaborate gardens, fountains, a multimillion-dollar, mosaic-tile pool (modeled after the one at California's Hearst Castle) and a 2000-foot-long system of water slides and waterfall grottoes. Officially, the guided tours of the artwork (10am Tuesday and Friday) and landscaped grounds (10am Thursday) that meet in the front lobby are only for guests. Be forewarned that security can be a bit paranoid. The peach exterior of the resort makes it look like Monaco or Macau, and all of the rooms are unabashedly opulent. The Grand Suite in the hotel's exclusive Napua Tower is the islands' most expensive night's sleep, setting you back (well, not *you* probably, but setting someone back) a cool $10,000. One would hope the bed is comfortable.

Places to Eat

Hotel restaurants or golf course clubhouses, these are your main choices. That said, if you're looking to splurge, there are worthy options.

Mid-Range When a coffee and muffin can easily cost $6 and a burger with fries more than $10, there is no such thing as budget food, except perhaps for the fresh-baked goodies and exceptional Java roasted by

Honolulu Coffee Co (The Shops at Wailea, 3750 Wailea Alanui Dr, 2nd level).

Caffe Ciao (Fairmont Kea Lani Hotel) Items $3-10. Deli open 6:30am-10pm daily. Caffe Ciao has both a deli shop and an expensive outdoor café. Inside the shop you'll find shelves stocked with such gourmet food stuffs as herbal Hawaiian teas, Dean & Deluca miscellany and Ghirardelli chocolate. Most takeout items are made with beach picnics in mind, including thick sandwiches on artisan bread, cold tortellini or caponata. Healthy drinks fill the fridge.

There's a similar, if even more overpriced deli at the Grand Wailea Resort called *Café Kula Hawaiian Marketplace*, right next door to *Bistro Molokini*, which has reputable kiawe-wood–fired pizzas ($12-20) served between 11am and 9pm daily.

Maui Onion (Renaissance Wailea Beach Resort). Lunch mains $10-15. Open 11am-6pm daily. This poolside bar and restaurant has sealed its reputation with specialty Maui onion rings (but try the traditional French onion soup instead) as well as gourmet burgers that almost seem worth the expense.

Tommy Bahama's Tropical Café & Emporium (☎ 875-9983, The Shops at Wailea, 3750 Wailea Alanui Dr, 2nd level) Lunch mains $10-14. Open 11am-10pm daily. You may snicker at this faux tropical 'emporium,' but the lunch menu is divine, especially the grouper fish, the Cayman citrus crab salad and Havana Cabana, a pork sandwich with blackberry brandy–barbecue sauce.

Top End *Joe's Bar & Grill (☎ 875-7767, fax 875-1827, 131 Wailea Ike Pl)* Entrées $18-38. Open 5:30pm-9:30pm daily. This deceptively casual bar and grill overlooking the courts at the Wailea Tennis Club is run by the same folks as the famed Haliimaile General Store (see the Upcountry chapter). Some classic menu items are the same, but the emphasis here is on hearty American standards of prime rib, meatloaf and a very popular New York steak. Waiting for your table is a pleasure at the copper-top bar.

SeaWatch (☎ 875-8080, fax 875-7462, 100 Wailea Golf Club Dr) Breakfast dishes

$3-10, lunch mains $7.50-12, dinner entrées from $24. Open 8am-3pm & 5:30pm-10pm daily. On a hillside with a grand ocean view, this restaurant is a favorite with wedding parties and honeymooners. Dining is either indoors or outside on the plantation-style verandah. Although breakfast can be over-priced, one of the renowned favorites is the crabcake Benedict with roasted pepper hollandaise. Lunch dishes up salads, sandwiches and fish with only a bit of Hawaiian flair. At dinner, expect something special such as citrus-*ponzu* pork chops with asparagus or fresh fish with mango chutney and yams in coconut milk.

The Shops at Wailea (*3750 Wailea Alanui Dr*) mall has a few branches of well-to-do chains, including a svelte **Ruth's Chris Steak House** (*☎ 874-8880, 2nd level*), open 5pm to 9:30pm daily, and a breezy **Longhi's** (*☎ 891-8883, ground level*), open 8am to 10pm daily, with tropical plants, white stucco and an oceanfront sundeck.

At the major resorts, the Fairmont Kea Lani Hotel and Outrigger Wailea each has an outstanding restaurant, while the most visually astonishing places are found at the Grand Wailea.

Nick's Fishmarket (*Fairmont Kea Lani Hotel*) Mains $26-45. Open from 5:30pm daily. Sunset ocean views, torch lighting and an ocean-facing Mediterranean-style dining room only enhance this restaurant's first-class reputation for talent and creativity with market fresh fish. The most expensive item on the menu? A surf-and-turf combo of Tristan lobster and Angus steak.

Hula Moons (*Outrigger Wailea Resort*) Dinner entrées $28-35. Open 6am-10:30am, 11am-3pm & 5:30pm-10pm daily. The brainchild of a successful San Francisco restaurateur, Hula Moons is named after a book by Don Blanding, the Oklahoma-born wanderer and unofficial poet laureate of Hawaii from the 1920s steamship era. Whispers of nostalgic aloha waft over curvy romantic booths that overlook the ocean. The cuisine plays lightly with Hawaiian fusion ideas, such as shrimp and lobster martini or *lilikoi*-glazed rack of lamb. It's all charming, right down to the PanAm clipper swizzle sticks.

The Friday seafood buffet costs $39/15 adult/child, the Sunday champagne brunch (10am-2pm) $37/15.

Humuhumunukunukuapua'a (*Grand Wailea Resort*) Entrées $22-32. Open 5:30pm-10pm daily. Here's your chance to practice saying the name of Hawaii's unofficial state fish, or just say 'Humuhumu' and be done with it. Any way you pronounce it, this place inhabits a Polynesian-style longhouse floating on a 70,000-gallon saltwater lagoon. The food is seafood and steaks, but you can gaze inside the giant tropical aquarium just by visiting the cocktail lounge, where pupu costs under $12.

Kincha (*Grand Wailea Resort*) Appetizers $8-18, entrées $26-53. Open 5:30pm-9:30pm Thurs-Mon. As beautiful as a teahouse in Kyoto, this restaurant is made from over 800 tons of rocks from Mt Fuji, all hand-chosen and specially shipped to Hawaii. Tatami rooms overlook a contemplative pond. Expect Japanese haute cuisine with strokes of Pacific Rim.

Entertainment

Most of the Wailea resort hotels have live Hawaiian music or jazz in their restaurants and cocktail lounges nightly.

The Shops at Wailea (*see Shopping later*) has live jazz on Sunday and Thursday nights, Hawaiian music on Saturday and varying performers on Wednesday's art night. Also in the shopping center, **Longhi's** (*see Places to Eat, earlier*) has a live band on Saturday night until 1:30am.

Both the **Outrigger Wailea Resort** and **Renaissance Wailea Beach Resort** (*see Places to Eat, earlier*) have touristy luau that start shortly before sunset a few evenings per week. Expect to pay around $60/30 per adult/child for an all-you-can-eat buffet and Polynesian dance show, but there are better ones in West Maui. You might catch part of the revue free of charge or overhear some drumming by walking along the beach.

Shopping

The Shops at Wailea (*☎ 891-6770, 3750 Wailea Alanui Dr*) Open 9:30am-9:30pm daily, Wed art night with live music 6:30pm-

9:30pm. Exclusivity is the norm at this shopping mall, with the likes of Prada, Guess and Louis Vuitton among others. Some of the more unique shops are the Hawaiian fine jeweler *Na Hoku* (2nd level), which has been making Tahitian black-pearl pieces since 1924, and *Noa Noa* (ground level) for one-of-a-kind, hand-batiked, Polynesian-print island wear, most of it designed by the owner herself, including amazing Japanese-style *yukata*. Some Hawaiian chains include *Crazy Shirts* (2nd level), *Honolua Surf Co* (ground level) and the discount *ABC Store* (ground level) for inexpensive beach wear, pineapple potholders, Kona coffee and the like. Many of the much-touted art galleries sell nothing but schlock. *Dolphin Galleries* at least represents some real Hawaiian artists and traipsing through *Celebrities* can be fun if you've never seen art by John Lennon or David Bowie before.

All of the resort hotels have their own upscale shops and island chain outlets. The branch of *Lahaina Printsellers* in the Grand Wailea Resort Hotel & Spa (see Places to Stay, earlier) sells reprints of beautiful antique maps and sketches of Hawaiian flora & fauna.

MAKENA

Even during the 1970s resort boom, Makena was a sleepy and largely overlooked area at the end of the road. That is, until the Seibu Corporation gobbled up 1800 acres above the old Makena landing and developed it into a Japanese-style resort, complete with a high-rise hotel, golf course and tennis center, plus a new paved road to access it all.

During the 19th century, Makena was the busiest settlement on this side of Maui. Cattle from Ulupalakua Ranch and the other pastures in the Upcountry were corralled down the mountain to Makena Landing and shipped to the market in Honolulu. By the 1920s interisland boat traffic had shifted to other ports on the island, however, and Makena withered.

Thankfully, much of Makena remains wild and free for public use. Puu Olai, a 360-foot cinder hill a mile south of the landing,

dominates the shoreline and backs two knockout beaches at Makena Bay-La Perouse State Park. Makena Bay has great snorkeling and diving near the old landing, including lots of sea turtles.

Makena Bay

To explore the older side of Makena, heading south on Makena Rd make a quick right after the Makena Surf condos and head toward the bay.

Makena Beach Park is a local recreational area with boat-launching facilities, showers and toilets. When seas are calm, there's good snorkeling along the rocks at the south side of the landing. Many dive trips start from here and head for the **5 Graves**, also known as the 5 Caves or Turtle Town, just to the north, so it can get crowded in the waters here.

South of the landing is the **Keawalai Congregational Church** (☎ 879-5557), which dates from 1832 and is one of Maui's early missionary churches. The present building was constructed in 1855 and features 3-foot-thick walls made of burnt coral rock. The bayside graveyard has interesting old tombstones with cameo photographs. A small congregation meets for an atmospheric Sunday service at 9:30am, which is held in a combination of Hawaiian and English.

Makena Rd ends shortly after the church at a cul-de-sac on the ocean side of Maui Prince Hotel. There is beach parking and restrooms on the mauka side of the road.

Maluaka Beach

At the southern end of Makena Bay is Maluaka Beach, a short beige-sand beach fronting the Maui Prince Hotel. It is often called simply Makena Beach, which is confusing because there is a Makena Beach Park just to the north.

The beach, which slopes down from a low sand dune, has a sandy bottom in its center, but strong currents occasionally make swimming iffy. Rocky formations at the southern end provide decent snorkeling and overall, it's lovely.

You can either park opposite Keawalai Congregational Church and walk through the resort, or drive on Makena Alanui Rd past the Maui Prince Hotel, take the first road on your right and backtrack around to the official beach parking lot (with a laughable 15 parking spaces), where you'll find restrooms and a paved sidewalk leading through the resort to the beach.

Oneuli (Little Black Sand) Beach

Going south, past the Maui Prince Hotel, S Makena Rd winds past private villas. The next posted beach access sign is for Oneuli (Little Black Sand) Beach. (If you see the sign for the first Makena Bay-La Perouse State Park parking lot, you've gone too far.) A rutted access road bounces you along to a tiny black-sand beach.

Strong offshore currents make it dangerous for swimming, but it's atmospheric for ocean gazing with Puu Olai to the south and the Neighbor Islands clearly in view. Salt-and-pepper sand and windy conditions make for brisk beach walks, during which you can sometimes spot turtles poking their heads out of the water.

Makena Bay-La Perouse State Park (Big Beach & Little Beach)

In the late 1960s, Big Beach was the site of an alternative-lifestyle camp that took on the nickname 'Hippie Beach.' The tent city lasted until 1972, when police finally evicted everyone on health code violations. Rumors of legendary rock stars jamming on the sand still fly around the island, and more than a few of Maui's now-graying residents can trace their island roots to infamous Hippie Beach.

It's now the sort of scene that people conjure up when they dream of a Hawaiian beach – beautiful and expansive, with virtually no development on the horizon. Big Beach is a huge sweep of glistening sand and a prime sunset spot with straight-on views of Molokini and Kahoolawe. Little Beach is a secluded cove and Maui's most popular nude beach.

The Hawaiian name for Big Beach is Oneloa, literally 'Long Sand.' This golden-sand beach is well over half a mile long and as broad as they come, with clear turquoise

waters. But the open ocean beyond Big Beach can have powerful rip currents and dangerous shorebreaks during periods of heavy surf. These killer breaks are for experienced bodysurfers only.

Little Beach, also known as Puu Olai Beach, is a popular nude beach, despite a rusty old sign and many arrests to the contrary. Sunning yourself in the buff is illegal and citations cost a pretty penny. All the uproar is probably less due to any supposed Hawaiian cultural issues with naked sunbathers and more to do with the beach being one of the few gay meeting places on Maui.

Little Beach is hidden by a rocky outcrop that juts out from Puu Olai, the cinder cone that marks the north end of Big Beach. A trail leads up over the rocks and links the two, taking just a few minutes to walk. From the top of the trail, there's a splendid view of both beaches. Little Beach fronts a small sandy cove that usually has a gentle shorebreak ideal for bodysurfing and boogie boarding. Snorkeling along the rocky lava outcrops at both ends is good when the water is calm.

Makena Beach (a collective name for Little Beach and Big Beach) has recently become a state park, which may eventually lead to the addition of full beach facilities, but for now it remains in a natural state except for a couple of pit toilets and picnic tables. The turnoff to the main parking area for both beaches is exactly a mile past the Maui Prince Hotel. A second parking area sits a quarter mile to the south. You can also park alongside the road and walk in. Car break-ins and thefts are commonplace in the parking lots, so many locals prefer the latter option. The safest place is probably farthest from the beach, right before the road narrows heading toward La Perouse Bay, just opposite the roadside *Makena Grill*. Watch for kiawe thorns in the woods behind the beach.

Activities

Although not as prestigious as the Wailea courses, **Makena North Golf Course** (☎ 879-3344, 5415 Makena Alanui Dr; Greens fees

& *cart $140)* offers a challenging round and is still of championship caliber.

Smaller than Wailea, **Makena Tennis Club** (☎ *879-8777, 5414 Makena Alanui Dr; Guests/nonguests $18/22 per hour, daily clinics $20)* is just as professional. Advance reservations are necessary; bring proper tennis attire.

Places to Stay
Destination Resorts *(see Wailea, earlier)* also handles condo rentals in Makena.

Maui Prince Hotel (☎ *874-1111, 800-321-6284, fax 879-8763,* w *www.mauiprince hotel.com, 5400 Makena Alanui Dr)* Rooms $310-460, suites from $600. From the outside it looks like a fortress, but the interior incorporates a finer sense of Japanese aesthetics. The five-story hotel turns inward around a courtyard with waterfalls, running streams, carp ponds and raked rock gardens. All of the 310 rooms have at least partial ocean views and the resort can be quiet, even deserted. Special promotions often undercut the rack rates, combining rooms with car rental, free activities or discounts on golf.

Places to Eat & Drink
A short distance past the parking lots for Big Beach, you'll find a **lunch cart** run by a longtime island resident who hails from LA. Daily specials cost only $6, but portions aren't very big; still, it's cheaper than anything offered at the Maui Prince Hotel.

Hakone *(Maui Prince Hotel)* Complete dinners $26-45. Open 6pm-9:30pm Tues-Sat. This refined Japanese restaurant serves scores of *sunomono* dishes and a *rakusen kaiseki* multicourse chef's tasting menu. Entrées show some elegant Kyoto haute cuisine influences, along with Hawaiian ingredients and tropical flourishes. Sushi includes the funny 'I No Like Fish' roll for vegetarians, and there's tempura-taro ice cream or green-tea brulée for dessert ($6). The Monday dinner buffet (6pm to 9pm) costs $40/25 per adult/child.

Prince Court *(Maui Prince Hotel)* Brunch $40, dinner mains $24-32. Open 6pm-9:30pm daily. Overwhelmingly formal,

the resort's premier dining room offers an indulgent Sunday champagne brunch (seatings 9am, 9:30am, 11:30am & noon) with a splendid array of seafood dishes. At night, it specializes in tantalizing Hawaiian fusion, such as half-stuffed Kona lobster with caramelized Maui onion sauce or kalua duck with sugarcane-speared prawns. The five-onion herb bisque is a signature dish.

Molokini Lounge *(Maui Prince Hotel)* This quiet cocktail lounge often has live Hawaiian music and great sunset views.

MAKENA TO LA PEROUSE BAY
The tourist traffic thins out somewhat beyond Makena. Advanced snorkelers and divers revel in the motorboat-free waters, abundant sea life and coral reefs around Cape Kinau. Meanwhile expert kayakers and surfers challenge the offshore swells at La Perouse Bay, where hikers and horseback riders trek across jet-black lava on ancient Hawaiian trails.

After Big Beach, S Makena Rd continues as a narrow, bumpy paved laneway for 2½ miles. The road goes through the Ahihi-Kinau Natural Area Reserve before deadending at La Perouse Bay. Because of the road's narrow width and two-way traffic, it can be a slow drive, so take it easy. Many people mistake this road for the one that rings around the island to Kaupo Gap and Hana. Nope, for that road you've got to backtrack all the way to Kahului Airport and take the Haleakala Hwy (Hwy 37) up through Pukalani and Kula until it joins the upper Piilani Hwy.

Ahihi-Kinau Natural Area Reserve
This 2045-acre protected nature reserve includes sections of Ahihi Bay and Cape Kinau, which was created when Haleakala last spouted out lava toward the coast. The remains of a coastal Hawaiian village – its old sites marked by walled and terraced platforms – sit between lava flows around Ahihi Bay.

No one knows for sure when this last lava flow happened, though 1790 is the date most people will tell you. But that is only an approximation. Maps drawn by the French

MAKENA TO LA PEROUSE BAY

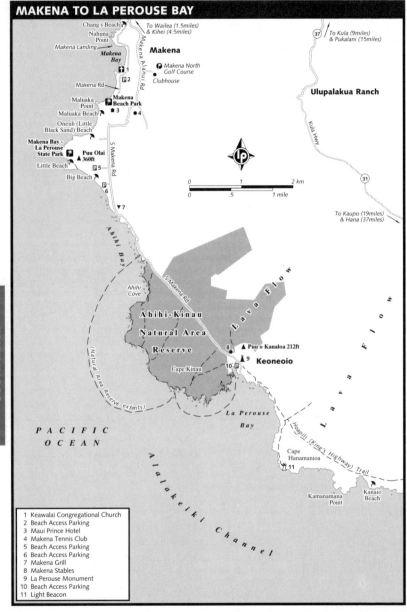

Chang's Beach
Nahuna Point
Makena Landing
Makena Bay
Makena Rd
Maluaka Point
Maluaka Beach
Oneuli (Little Black Sand) Beach
Makena Bay – La Perouse State Park
Little Beach
Big Beach
Puu Olai ▲ 360ft

To Wailea (1.5miles) & Kihei (4.5miles)

Makena Alanui Rd

Makena

Makena North Golf Course
Clubhouse

37   To Kula (9miles) & Pukalani (15miles)

Ulupalakua Ranch

Kula Hwy

S Makena Rd

31

To Kaupo (19miles) & Hana (37miles)

0   1   2 km
0   .5   1 mile

Ahihi Bay

Ahihi Cove

(Natural Area Reserve extents)

Ahihi-Kinau Natural Area Reserve

Cape Kinau

La Perouse Bay

Lava Flow

Lava Flow

S Makena Rd

▲ Puu o Kanaloa 212ft
Keoneoio

Hoapili (King's Highway) Trail

PACIFIC OCEAN

Alalakeiki Channel

Cape Hanamanioa

Kamanamana Point

Kanaio Beach

1 Keawalai Congregational Church
2 Beach Access Parking
3 Maui Prince Hotel
4 Makena Tennis Club
5 Beach Access Parking
6 Beach Access Parking
7 Makena Grill
8 Makena Stables
9 La Perouse Monument
10 Beach Access Parking
11 Light Beacon

SOUTH MAUI

The Enlightened Explorer

In May 1786, the renowned French admiral and explorer Jean-François de Galaup, Comte de La Perouse, became the first Westerner to land on Maui. As he sailed into the bay that now bears his name, scores of Hawaiian canoes came out to greet him and trade. Since Captain Cook had given the ali'i (chiefs) weapons a few years back, all the Hawaiians wanted in exchange for food and fresh water was more iron. After all, metals had been totally absent from the islands before Western contact in 1778.

La Perouse was a student of the French enlightenment. His two ships, the *Boussole* (meaning 'compass') and the *Astrolabe*, carried soldiers and sailors, but also botanists, astronomers, geographers, zoologists, naturalists and clergy. When he came ashore on Maui, the admiral visited four villages around Keoneoio, noting especially that the island had 'a burning climate.' One of his officers received the gift of a royal feathered cape.

He stayed on Maui just two days. After leaving Hawaii, La Perouse sailed across the Pacific, visiting countless countries and islands, including Yezo (modern-day Hokkaido, now part of Japan), where he spent quite some time with the aboriginal Ainu. Eventually he arrived in Australia, just days after the First Fleet landed at Botany Bay. The British soldiers were quick to inform him that they had already claimed the continent for the King, but La Perouse didn't mind. Reflecting upon his sojourn in Hawaii, he wrote that, 'Although the French were the first in these latest times on Maui, I did not think it was my right to take possession of it in the name of the King. The customs of Europeans in this respect are completely ridiculous.'

Unfortunately this enlightened explorer was never heard from again. After leaving Australia, he mysteriously disappeared into the South Pacific. Some historians speculate that he and his crew were eaten by cannibals when their ships were wrecked in the New Hebrides – which only goes to prove that nice guys like La Perouse really do finish last.

explorer La Perouse showed no cape here in 1786, while those penned by Captain Vancouver just a few years later did. Then again La Perouse may have been smoking some *pakalolo*, because geologists date the volcanic flow back as early as the 1400s. To complicate matters further, native Hawaiians told missionaries in the 1840s that their own grandparents had witnessed the event.

Whatever the true date may be, it doesn't change the fact that this is Maui's youngest and wildest spot. The nature reserve legally protects its unique marine life and geological features, including anchialine pools, lava tubes, *kipuka* ('islands' of land surrounded by lava flows) and all the a'a you would ever want to see. Fishing and the removal of any flora, fauna or lava pieces are prohibited.

As motorized boats are also not allowed, the entire area is a snorkeler's dream. A little roadside cove just one-tenth of a mile south of the first reserve sign (which is

about 2½ miles south of Big Beach) offers good snorkeling. It's quite rocky and can be a bit challenging getting in, but the cove has lots of coral and fish whenever silt doesn't limit the visibility. There are several pull-offs along the road, some just presenting views and others with rough tracks leading across the lava field to untouched snorkeling spots on the coast. If you are up for an adventure, this is the place. Those trails just before La Perouse Bay are closest to the shoreline, but generally speaking the good snorkeling is farther north. A good compromise is to take the trail at the very southern tip of the reserve on the makai side of the road, two-tenths of a mile before Makena Stables (to the north of the stables). The trail is clearly marked with a signboard. Follow it to the coast and then walk north and snorkel wherever takes your fancy. Always bring a buddy along and test the waters before jumping in.

La Perouse Bay

This astoundingly beautiful natural area is steeped in history. In earlier times, it was the site of the Hawaiian village of Keoneoio. The broken archaeological remains of *hale* (thatched house) platforms and *heiau* (temples) by the sea are still found among the lava patches. Nowadays, the area is part public beach and part private ranch land, which means that many of its unique features have ended up getting trampled or vandalized over the years.

Environmental groups, Maui County officials and the state legislature have all urged the federal government to conduct a feasibility study on declaring La Perouse Bay a national park. Although this is unlikely to happen soon, volunteers are already patrolling the area to help visitors learn to treat the *aina* (land) with respect and discourage car break-ins.

Spinner dolphins come into the bay during the day and can be seen resting offshore (they never actually sleep). Even for expert kayakers, surfers and divers, La Perouse Bay presents a real challenge, but the sea life is amazing. Don't even think about going out into the water if the waves are high, as they are often due to strong off-shore winds. Swimming and snorkeling are pretty much out of the question.

The paved road ends after about three miles past Big Beach, and just short of La Perouse Bay. Although it may be possible to drive all the way in on the 4WD road, you're okay parking just past where the asphalt ends at **La Perouse Monument**. From there you walk down to the coast in only a few minutes. From La Perouse Monument, it's also possible to hike along the **King's Hwy Coastal Trail** (see the Hiking special section at the end of the Activities chapter). From the monument, walk to the bay's edge and head south along the coastline.

Activities

Just before reaching the monument on the mauka side of the road sits **Makena Stables** (☎ 879-0244, fax 879-0744, ⓦ *www.makena stables.com; rides $110-175*). The proprietor guides a variety of trail rides for all skill levels up on the volcanic slopes of the Ulupalakua Ranch. The ranch *ohana* (family) is very down-to-earth and friendly, providing homemade snacks and lots of aloha. The sunset rides are especially popular. Advance reservations are required.

East Maui

The famed Hana Hwy runs from Central Maui to the village of Hana and beyond to the pools of Oheo Gulch. While all of the Hawaiian Islands have incredible scenery, the Hana Hwy ranks as *the* most spectacular coastal drive in Hawaii. Waterfalls and rain forest play hide and seek along its serpentine length, with ocean vistas and little-used dirt roads leading who knows where.

Timeless Hana town sits beneath the rainy slopes of Haleakala volcano, surrounded by green pastures and a jagged black coastline. In ancient times, it was the heart of one of Maui's largest population centers, and the village itself was thought to have been reserved for the *ali'i* (chiefs). Today that same royal pride is displayed by the few thousand residents of this heavenly backwater, where the very absence of development is the lure – almost too much of a lure. Tourists follow on each other's heels at every stop, both rushing by the northern end of the road at Paia and then turning around before the rewarding Piilani Hwy at the southern end. That's lucky for you, since both deserve a healthy chunk of your time.

Paia is an old sugar town with a fresh coat of paint. Many people treat it like a breakfast stop on the way to Hana (Paia has the best-value eats on Maui), but it's so much more. A mix of surfers and hippies keep the local culture juicy, and outside town, cliffs pillowed by green drop to dramatic stretches of beach for as far as the road seems to wind. The most famous, Hookipa Beach, is a mecca for windsurfers, especially in summer.

At the opposite end of the Hana Hwy, the road morphs into the Piilani Hwy (Hwy 31) and continues right around the island past Oheo Gulch, Kipahulu and Kaupo back into the Upcountry. After Hana, the waterfalls may be fewer but are every bit as divine. If you're tempted to linger, there is free camping atop the sea cliffs near Kipahulu. Or press on to more off-beat sights, including Charles Lindbergh's grave. As the highway gives way to gravel and

Highlights

- Windsurfing with the experts at Hookipa Beach

- Stopping at fruit stands and for sea views along the serpentine Hana Hwy

- Walking the black-sand beach and ancient Hawaiian ruins of Waianapanapa

- Splashing in waterfall pools and camping atop the sea cliffs of Oheo Gulch

- Slowing down your biorhythms in 'Heavenly Hana'

- Adventuring on the lonely, wild highway around Kaupo Gap

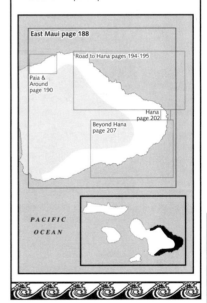

splendid isolation, you can beat your own path to unnamed beaches or ancient *heiau* (temples) and catch sunset views up Kaupo Gap before rolling around Maui's southwestern tip and back to civilization.

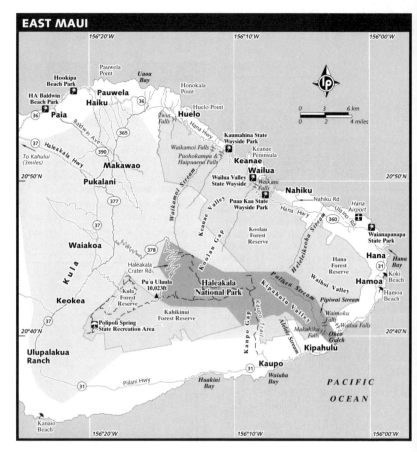

EAST MAUI

PAIA & AROUND

As part of the original Alexander & Baldwin sugar plantation, Paia in the early 20th century had a population more than triple its present size. In those days most of the town's almost 10,000 residents lived in plantation camps on the cool slopes above the sugar mill. That is, until WWII changed the island's industrial landscape forever, when many residents moved to Kahului or Oahu seeking new economic opportunity.

Shops closed and Paia began to collect cobwebs. As the Age of Aquarius dawned, hippies seeking paradise were the first to revive it, followed by windsurfers who began to discover nearby Hookipa Beach in the 1980s. Today, Paia has just as many surfers as it once had sugarcane workers, and they hail from as many parts of the world, which gives Paia more international flavor than any other small town in Hawaii. Many of the old wooden storefronts in town are painted in bright tones of rosy pink, sunshine yellow and sky blue, adding to the town's unique character. They house natural food stores, local arts & crafts galleries and surf supply stores, plus some of the island's tastiest eateries.

Orientation & Information

The Hana Hwy (Hwy 36) runs straight through the center of Paia. This is the last real town before Hana and the last place to gas up your car. Paia is also a link to the Upcountry; Baldwin Ave (Hwy 390) leads from the center of town past the old sugar mill to Makawao. Although the mill was long past its heyday by the time it closed in late 2000, its smokestacks up on the hillside above town still look oddly silent.

Absolutely everything is on one of these two roads, and the whole town is walkable. The Bank of Hawaii (☎ 575-9511), 35 Baldwin Ave, is open 8:30am to 4pm Monday to Thursday, 8:30am to 6pm Friday. The post office (☎ 579-8866), 120 Baldwin Ave, is open 8am to 4:30pm Monday to Friday, 10:30am to 12:30pm Saturday.

The Minit Stop gas station (☎ 579-9227), 123 Hana Hwy, stays open until 11pm daily and has an ATM. There's a coin laundry nearby on Baldwin Ave, just south of the Vegan Restaurant. Mana Foods has a community bulletin board, with notices tacked up for everything from rooms for rent to classes in windsurfing and Ashtanga yoga.

If it's equipment rentals and professional lessons you're after, most sports shops are found back up the road in Kahului (see the Activities chapter).

Spreckelsville Beach

Spreckelsville Beach, by the golf course between Kahului Airport and Paia, is a long stretch of sand punctuated by lava outcrops. It's one of the windiest places on the north shore, particularly in summer, making it a prime windsurfing spot mostly for beginners. Of course, its attraction may change if the Spreckelsville resort development goes ahead despite protests by environmentalists and the local community. As much of the beach is rocky, only a few spots offer reasonable swimming. Snorkelers will want to head elsewhere.

To get to the beach, turn at the 5-mile marker onto Nonohe Pl, which runs along the west side of the Maui Country Club. Turn right when the road ends and keep an eye out for the blue beach access sign.

HA Baldwin Beach Park

HA Baldwin Beach Park, a big county park about a mile west of Paia, has a long sandy beach offering good bodysurfing. Swimmers and snorkelers might find favorable conditions only in the morning, since the wind really kicks up after noon. Windsurfing is possible but not popular here.

The park has showers, restrooms, picnic tables with barbecue grills and a well-used baseball and soccer field. Look for the sign and turnoff to the dirt and grass parking areas at the 6-mile marker.

A word of caution: this park tends to be a rather congested scene, and things can quickly turn nasty if large groups have been hanging out drinking. Theft and violent assaults are not unheard of, unfortunately.

A bit farther east closer to town at Paia Bay, **Jaws** has become famous for its giant waves, second only possibly to Oahu, where surfers are towed in by Waverunners.

Mantokuji Buddhist Mission

On the Hana side of town, Mantokuji is a 1921 Buddhist temple with ocean views and a massive temple gong. During the summer, the Obon holidays are observed here with religious services and Japanese folk dances. The temple is fronted by a graveyard with kanji-engraved headstones and tropical flowers.

Hookipa Beach Park

Hookipa, which has long been one of Maui's prime surfing spots, has established itself as Hawaii's premier windsurfing beach too.

The beach has good year-round action – winter has the biggest waves for board surfers, and summer has the most consistent winds for windsurfers. The unspoken agreement is surfers go out in the morning, while windsurfers take the afternoons, but it all depends on the weather.

Between the strong currents, dangerous shorebreak and razor-sharp coral, this is unquestionably an area for experts. As a spectator venue, it's great – if you come at the right time, you'll see some of the best action to be found anywhere. The world's top windsurfers show up for the Da Kine Classic

PAIA & AROUND

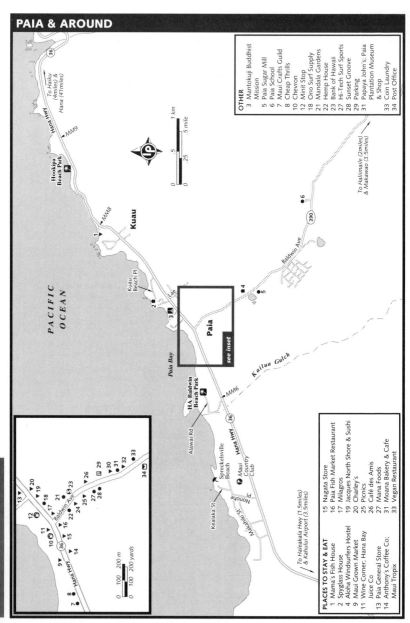

To Haiku
(4miles) &
Hana (41miles)

Hana Hwy

MM9

Hookipa
Beach Park

MM8

Kuau

Kuau
Beach Pl

Lae

PACIFIC
OCEAN

Paia Bay

Paia

see inset

Kailua Gulch

H.A. Baldwin
Beach Park

MM6

Hana Hwy

Alawai Rd

Spreckelsville
Beach

Maui
Country
Club

Nonohe
Pl

Kealaka St

Mahihi St

To Haleakala Hwy (1.5miles)
& Kahului Airport (3.5miles)

Baldwin Ave

To Haliimaile (2miles)
& Makawao (3.5miles)

1 km
.5 mile

0   .5
0   .25

EAST MAUI

13

12
6

11

10   36

9

7   8

Hana Hwy

14

20
19

18
17

16   23
22   21

15

24

25
27
28

26

30
31   32

29

33

34

0   100   200 m
0   100   200 yards

in May and the Aloha Classic in late October or early November.

The park has restrooms, showers and picnic pavilions. Look for the line of cars on the lookout above the beach, the turnoff for which appears just before the 9-mile marker.

A few territorial windsurfers also use Kuau Cove fronting Mama's Fish House at the 8-mile marker, but don't go without an introduction and beware of sharp, shallow coral. Offshore is the **Kuau Pipeline**, a hard-breaking left tube that is tackled by serious surfers only.

Places to Stay

Although many people stay in rural Haiku (see the Upcountry chapter), Paia has quite a few private places to stay along the coast. If you're planning to stay any length of time, check bulletin boards around town or look in the 'Vacation Rentals' column of the *Maui News* classifieds for rooms in shared houses starting at $300 a month.

Aloha Windsurfers Hostel (☎ 579-6480, 866-242-8999, e *alohawindsurf@yahoo.com*, w *www.accommodations-maui.com*, 181 Baldwin Ave) Beds in 4-bed dorms $18/105 per night/week, private singles/doubles $180/225 per week. This house-hostel primarily caters to windsurfers and international travelers. It sits right in the center of Paia town, and shared amenities include kitchen, laundry, storage area, satellite TV and free Internet access. Call ahead for airport pickups.

Many of Paia's beach cottages, B&Bs and vacation houses are booked through rental agents, who can almost always find you a good deal. Whether you take advantage of their handy services or make reservations directly with the owners, count on a minimum stay of at least three days to avoid any 'cleaning fee,' usually around $30.

Hookipa Haven (☎ 579-8282, 800-398-6284, fax 579-9953, w *www.hookipa.com*, 62 Baldwin Ave No 2A, PO Box 791658, Paia, HI 96779) Rooms or studios from $50. This well-established vacation rental service makes bookings around Paia and the Upcountry, as well as elsewhere on Maui. German is spoken.

Chameleon Vacation Rentals Maui (☎ 575-9933, 866-575-9933, fax 340-8537, w *www.donnachameleon.com*, PO Box 350, Haiku, HI 96708) Rooms or cottages from $65. This friendly, ecominded booking agent handles everything from oceanfront windsurfer properties to rustic, romantic cabins in Paia and Haiku, and down toward Hana.

The Spyglass House (☎/fax 579-8608, 800-475-6695, w *www.spyglassmaui.com*, 267 Hana Hwy) Rooms $90-150. This wonderfully eccentric retreat has porthole windows, bits of stained glass and plenty of hidden nooks and crannies. Located well off the highway beside the ocean, those rooms in the original Spyglass House are better furnished than those in the garden Dolphin House. Guests have access to hammocks, a Jacuzzi, a barbecue grill and even yoga classes.

The Inn at Mama's Fish House (☎ 579-9764, 800-860-4852, fax 579-8594, w *www.mamasfishhouse.com*, 799 Poho Pl) 1-bedroom garden-view duplex $140-160, 2-bedroom beachfront cottages $350. At Kuau Cove and adjacent to Mama's Fish House restaurant, this hospitable inn offers a few units near the beach that boast nothing so much as prime location. Although each unit comes with full kitchen, cable TV/VCR, stereo and phone, guests could spend far less for more elsewhere.

Places to Eat

Any excuse for stopping in Paia around mealtime will do. The food is, in short, wonderful. Nothing better awaits you in Hana, so stock up here on picnic supplies and takeout meals.

The *Wine Corner* (☎ 579-8904, 111 Hana Hwy) sells microbrews from Hawaii and California and import beers. Next door, the *Hana Bay Juice Co* shakes up fresh smoothies.

Self-Catering *Mana Foods* (☎ 579-8078, 49 Baldwin Ave) Open 8am-8pm daily. Mana Foods is a large, down-to-earth health-food store with a good variety of juices, yogurts, bulk nuts, granolas, cheeses and organic produce. It also offers freshly baked artisan breads, a salad bar and a few inexpensive, hot takeout items.

Out on the Hana Hwy, *Nagata Store* sells the basics, as does the *Paia General Store,* which also has a takeout window for cheap local fare.

Maui Grown Market (☎ 579-9345, 93 Hana Hwy) Simple picnic lunches (around $8.50) can be picked up here. It offers some unbelievable perks: a cooler and a Hana Hwy guide cassette or CD to borrow, free pineapple or coffee and – you're never going to believe this – one of its loveable, well-trained dogs to accompany you on your road trip (24-hour advance notice required). This is a branch of its main store (see Road to Hana, later).

Budget & Mid-Range *Café des Amis (☎ 579-6323, 42 Baldwin Ave)* Breakfast or lunch $4-8, dinner $8-12. Open 8:30am-8:30pm daily. This tiny French café is a sunny morning spot, especially for savory or sweet crepes and rich coffee.

Anthony's Coffee Co (☎ 579-8340, 90 Hana Hwy) Dishes $5-10. Open 5:30am-6pm daily. Surfers fuel up here with big breakfast plates and deli lunches, or just drink big ol' cups of regular joe out on the busy sidewalk.

Picnics (☎ 579-8021, 30 Baldwin Ave) Dishes $5-8, picnic lunches $8.50-13 per person. Open 7am-5pm daily. This famous deli has a few eat-in tables and publishes a free menu with an entire driving guide to the Hana Hwy on the reverse. If you don't get a boxed picnic lunch, consider the plantation breakfasts or local plate lunches, fruit or vegetable salads and vegetarian spinach-nut burgers with cheddar cheese.

Vegan Restaurant (☎ 579-9144, 115 Baldwin Ave) Dishes $9-11. Open 11am-9pm daily. As there are only a dozen small café tables, it's best to arrive early. No one can forget the yummy mashed potatoes with gravy or vegan burgers, large salads and dishes with a touch of Thai cooking. Look for daily specials and a variety of teas, along with chocolate cake.

Paia Fish Market Restaurant (☎ 579-8030, 2A Baldwin Ave) Dishes $5-15. Open 11am-9:30pm daily. Obviously this restaurant specializes in fresh fish, which you'll find on display in a refrigerated case at the counter. At any time of day, you'll find locals hunkering down with fish & chips ($8-10) at the wooden tables inside. Another good choice is the grilled fish sandwich on a whole-wheat bun, with either ono or ma-himahi ($6).

Moana Bakery & Cafe (☎ 579-9999, 71 Baldwin Ave) Breakfast or lunch $6-10, dinner $8-23. Open 8am-9pm daily. A soothing spot down the way, this place is jointly run by a chef and a French pastry master. Some of the dishes feature herbs, vegetables and fruits from the café's own garden. The emphasis here is on familiar dishes prepared gourmet-style, perhaps chilled seared ahi with Molokai sweet potatoes or Hana Bay crab cakes at dinner. At breakfast you can get gourmet omelettes, Italian frittata and malted Belgian waffles.

Milagros (☎ 579-8755, 3 Baldwin Ave) Lunch $6-10, dinner mains from $12. Open 8am-9:30pm daily. Milagros is a justifiably popular Tex-Mex café with both indoor and sidewalk dining on Paia's liveliest corner. The freshness of ingredients shine through in near-perfect salsas and fish tacos, but there's also a range of enchiladas, salads, fajitas, gourmet sandwiches and burgers on the menu.

Jacques North Shore & Sushi (☎ 579-8844, 120 Hana Hwy) Breakfast or lunch $5-8, dinner entrées $10-25. Open 8am-midnight daily; bar menu only after 10pm. Jacques, who did a stint as the personal chef of the king of Sweden, specializes in Pacific regional dishes with a French accent. You might try the spicy oni salad or banana vegan curry. The grilled fresh fish of the day, which is offered nightly, costs from $22.

Charley's (☎ 579-9453, 142 Hana Hwy) Breakfast or lunch $8-10, dinner mains $10-17. Open 7am-2:30pm & 5pm-10pm. Charley's, a self-styled Western saloon, hooks the late breakfast crowd. At dinner, the menu leans toward your basic pizza, pasta and calzone, with a few more gourmet ideas thrown in – nothing unforgettable. It serves a late-night menu until midnight.

Scuba diving in La Perouse Bay

If it lands in the Pacific, leave it there.

Molokini volcanic crater offers a diving heaven.

Sailing canoes, Wailea

Hui Aloha Church, Kaupo, with Kaupo Gap and Haleakala peak in the distance

Keanae Peninsula, Hana Hwy, East Maui

All the time in the world, Hana Hwy, East Maui

Wailua Falls near Oheo Gulch, East Maui

Top End *Mama's Fish House* (☎ 579-8488, 799 Poho Pl) Appetizers $8-20, dinner entrées $28-35. Open 11am-2:30pm & 5pm-9:30pm daily. Set in its own coconut grove in Kuau Cove, no one does fresh fish like Mama's. All of the fish is locally caught (your menu will introduce you to all of the fishers by name) and excellently cooked. Luau-style dinners, *kalua* pig sandwiches and Maui onion or Kona lobster soup are a few of the other menu highlights. Lunch is only slightly cheaper than dinner. Oh and yes, there's a beautiful ocean view. To get here, take the Hana Hwy east of Paia center to the 8-mile marker; look for Mama's boat up on a small rise to your left.

Entertainment
A few of Paia's restaurants also have bars, live music and other happenings. If you want more action, head for *Casanova* in Makawao (see the Upcountry chapter).

Jacques has a tropical garden that makes it feel as if you're on the beach instead of the highway, especially with the island's longest monkeypod bar.

A bit farther down the road, *Charley's* saloon has live music every other Sunday night and late night jams on Wednesday and Saturday. Cover varies from nothing to $5.

Back on Baldwin Ave, *Moana Bakery & Cafe* has jazz and flamenco on weekends, but that might change to Hawaiian music or even belly-dancing by the time you get here.

Shopping
Art and funky clothing are the things to buy in Paia.

Maui Crafts Guild (☎ 579-9697, W www .mauicraftsguild.com, 43 Hana Hwy) Open 9am-6pm daily. Even if you're not looking to buy, this gallery operated by a collective of Maui artists and craftspeople is worth a stop. It's a virtual museum of dyed cloth, woodcarving, pottery, natural fiber baskets, beadwork and more. There's a nice view of the surrounding sugarcane fields from the top floor.

On the way into town, *Cheap Thrills* vintage clothing shop also sells handmade jewelry. *Mandala Gardens* (☎ 579-9555,

29 Baldwin Ave) sells Indian-inspired wear, while *Hemp House* (☎ 579-880, 16 Baldwin Ave) specializes in hemp-fiber clothing and tie-dyed skivvies. Other notable local shops include *Sunset Groove* (☎ 579-9090, 62 Baldwin Ave).

Paia Plantation Museum & Shop (☎ 579-9174, 113 Baldwin Ave) Assorted photos and artifacts from the now defunct mill are hidden behind a few assorted souvenirs.

Papaya John's (☎ 579-9608, 105 Baldwin Ave) Get your papaya natural health products and energy bars for hiking here, all excellent for digestion.

PAIA TO HIGHWAY 360
Beyond Hookipa Beach Park, fields of sugarcane give way to long rows of pineapples. Immediately after the 10-mile marker, a short gravel road leads down to Maliko Bay, where there's a small boat ramp frequently used by scuba divers in summer. Uphill lies the hamlet of Haiku, which has a few cafés and heaps of wonderful B&Bs (see the Upcountry chapter).

Hwy 365, which leads up the long way to Makawao and other Upcountry towns, comes in just after the 16-mile marker. At this point, the Hana Hwy changes numbers from Hwy 36 to Hwy 360 and the mile markers begin again at zero. The road then changes dramatically, slicing through cliffs and becoming more of a mountain road than a highway. Hana is 35 scenic miles away.

ROAD TO HANA
The Hana Hwy is a cliff-hugger as it winds its way deep into valleys that drip with vegetation and back out above a rugged coastline, snaking around more than 600 twists and turns along the way. African tulip trees add bright splashes of orange to the dense rain forests, bamboo groves and fern-covered hillsides.

All of the 54 bridges to Hana have poetic Hawaiian names taken from the streams, gulches and waterfalls they cross – names that mean such things as Heavenly Mist, Burning Star and Reawakening. This road, which was completed in 1927 using convict labor, is very narrow; in many places, it is

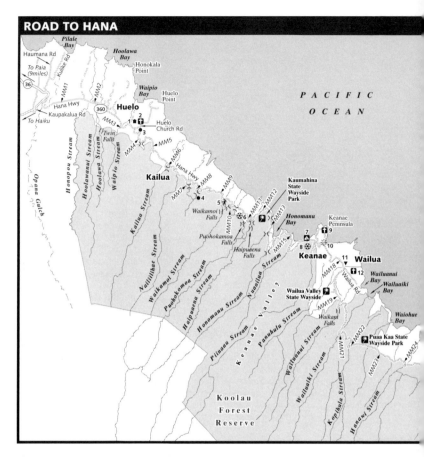

ROAD TO HANA

Pilale Bay
Haumana Rd
Hoolawa Bay
To Paia (9miles)
Honokala Point
Kulike Rd
36
MM1
MM2
Hana Hwy
Waipio Bay
Huelo Point
PACIFIC OCEAN
360
Huelo
Kaupakalua Rd
MM3
Huelo Church Rd
To Haiku
2
Twin Falls
3
MM4
MM5

Honopou Stream
Hoolawanui Stream
Hoolawa Stream
Waipio Stream
MM6
Hana Hwy
Kailua
MM7
Kailua Stream
Kaumahina State Wayside Park
MM8
MM9
4
5
Waikamoi Falls
6
MM10
MM11
MM12
MM13
Honomanu Bay
Keanae Peninsula
Opana Gulch
Naililihae Stream
Waikamoi Stream
Puohokamoa Falls
7
Haipuaena Falls
MM14
MM15
8
10
Keanae
9
11
Wailua
12
Wailuanui Bay
Wailuaiki Bay
Puohokamoa Stream
Haipuaena Stream
Honomanu Stream
Nuaailua Stream
MM16
MM17
MM18
Wailua Rd
MM19
Wailua Valley State Wayside
Waikani Falls
Waiohue Bay
Piinaau Stream
Keanae Valley
Panuhulu Stream
Wailuanui Stream
MM20
Puaa Kaa State Wayside Park
Wailuaiki Stream
MM21
Kopiliula Stream
MM22
MM23
MM24
Hanawi Stream

Koolau Forest Reserve

essentially 1½ lanes wide, with two-lane traffic! Recently honored as 'Hawaii's Millennium Legacy Trail,' the road has its roots in the royal trail system constructed by Chief Piilani and completed in the 15th century. You can still hike along the old King's Hwy at Waianapanapa State Park just north of Hana (see the Hiking special section at the end of the Activities chapter).

One more caveat: the Hana Hwy is not quite the *ono* attraction everyone believes it to be. Those who have been on other pretty, twisting coastal drives elsewhere in the world won't find much that's new here. The point is to get off the highway and go out of your way to visit quiet waterfall pools, tropical gardens, lava tubes or even Maui's best-restored heiau (see Ulaino Rd, later).

You won't need to save too much time for sleepy Hana, since there's not much there at the end of the road (that's precisely what makes it so alluring for overnight retreats). Once you drive beyond the town, crowds thin and anything is possible – as long as you get an early start from Paia and allow yourself a full day.

Everywhere on Maui you'll see Hana driving guide cassettes and CDs for rent or

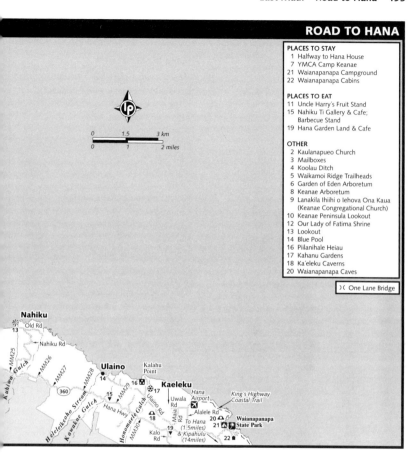

ROAD TO HANA

PLACES TO STAY
1 Halfway to Hana House
7 YMCA Camp Keanae
21 Waianapanapa Campground
22 Waianapanapa Cabins

PLACES TO EAT
11 Uncle Harry's Fruit Stand
15 Nahiku Ti Gallery & Cafe;
   Barbecue Stand
19 Hana Garden Land & Cafe

OTHER
2 Kaulanapueo Church
3 Mailboxes
4 Koolau Ditch
5 Waikamoi Ridge Trailheads
6 Garden of Eden Arboretum
8 Keanae Arboretum
9 Lanakila Ihiihi o Iehova Ona Kaua
   (Keanae Congregational Church)
10 Keanae Peninsula Lookout
12 Our Lady of Fatima Shrine
13 Lookout
14 Blue Pool
16 Piilanihale Heiau
17 Kahanu Gardens
18 Ka'eleku Caverns
20 Waianapanapa Caves

)(One Lane Bridge

sale. If you feel you need the extra help, they are available free of charge for guests of the Northshore Hostel in Wailuku and from a few B&Bs. *Maui Grown Market* (☎ 572-1693, *Ulumalu Rd*) lends you one if you purchase one of its picnic lunches (see Places to Eat under Paia, earlier). Look for its corrugated-iron plantation shack on the *mauka* side of the highway, just past the 14-mile marker.

It would take about two hours to drive the Hana Hwy straight through from Kahului to Hana. It is fully paved, but this is not a drive to rush. Please remember, pull over if local drivers are behind you, as they have places to get to and move at a different pace.

Some people hitchhike the Hana Hwy, but that's illegal and a bit crazy because there are very few stretches of road wide enough for drivers to safely stop, even if they wanted to, which most tourists don't. You're better off renting your own wheels (see the Getting Around chapter).

Twin Falls

You'll see a dirt pullout on your right and maybe a fruit stand right after the 2-mile

EAST MAUI

Ultimate Hana Highway Guide

The Best of the Hana Hwy...

Least Crowded Waterfall: Blue Pool

Most Suggestive Bridge Name: No 38 *Honoma'ele* (Land of Deep Love)

Best Surprise Attraction: Ka'eleku Caverns or Piilanihale Heiau

Most Perks with a Picnic Lunch: Maui Grown Market

Best Buddhist Stupa: The Tea House B&B

Best Garden: Kahanu Gardens

Most Poi Eaten per Capita: Keanae village

Most Authentic Jungle Digs: Tree Houses of Hana

Most Shades of Green in a Single Mile: Nahiku Rd

Best Fruit Stand: Uncle Harry's

Best Place to Load Up on Kitsch: Hasegawa General Store

Best Reason to Keep Going: The Piilani Hwy

...and the Worst of It

Most Crowded Waterfall: Twin Falls

Least Understandable Bridge Name: No 41 *Kahawai'okapia* (Frugal Valley)

Attraction That Least Fulfills Your Expectations: Hana town

Place That Least Satisfies Your Stomach: Hana town

Biggest Water Drain: East Maui Irrigation (EMI)

Worst Garden: Keanae Arboretum

Ground Zero for Dengue Fever: Nahiku Rd

Most Disappointingly Privatized Land: Huelo Point

Most Treacherous Trail: Red Sand Beach, Hana

Worst Rip-Off: Locals selling fruit that is already falling off the trees all around you

Best Reason to Turn Around Before It's Too Late: The Piilani Hwy after rain

marker. This is the start of the gentle walk to Twin Falls. If you can't find a place to park, don't worry. There are better waterfalls farther down the road.

If you just can't wait to get your feet wet, join the mobs of day trippers and hop over the fence and walk for about 15 minutes down the dirt road. Hand-painted signs point the way first to the lower falls and then, farther along, the upper falls. Both trails can be slippery after rain and are lined by fragrant guava trees.

Places to Stay Most of these hidden B&Bs have a three-night minimum stay, but weekly discounts are usually available.

Halfway to Hana House (☎ 572-1176, fax 572-3609, 100 W Waipio Rd, Ⓦ *www .maui.net/~gailp)* Studio $85, including continental breakfast. This beachside home is not really halfway to Hana but only about 5 miles from Haiku. The sole studio unit has a private entrance and bath and is set among herb gardens, bamboo groves, a banana patch and lily pond. It also enjoys an unobstructed view across the treetops to the sea. Inside are tropical flower arrangements and chocolate macadamia nuts by the pillows.

The Tea House (☎ 572-5610, Ⓦ *www .maui teahouse.com, reservations: Ann DeWeese, PO Box 335, Haiku, HI 96708)* 1-bedroom cottage one/two people $95/110. Secreted down near the ocean, this Asian-style retreat was built with recycled walls from a Zen temple in San Francisco. All courtesy of solar power, guests have a small kitchen with fresh herbs, TV/VCR and an open-air bath in a redwood gazebo. There's also a barbecue grill, plentiful good books, wild ginger and bananas and a Tibetan-style stupa on the grounds.

Maluhia Hale (☎ 572-2959, Ⓦ *www .maui.net/~djg/index.html, PO Box 687, Haiku, HI 96708)* Suite/cottage $105/115.

Meaning 'Peaceful Home,' this airy plantation-style house not far from Twin Falls was built by its owners. Both the suite and cottage come with a kitchenette and private bath, as well as a continental breakfast. The cottage, however, is most striking, its all-white décor splashed with bright blue from the Hawaiian quilt and Chinese porcelain pieces. The attached sitting room and verandah can be left open to the elements if the weather is kind.

Huelo

Dirt-packed Huelo Rd, about half a mile past the 3-mile marker (look for the stand of public mailboxes), leads downhill past Door of Faith church to historic **Kaulanapueo Church** (1853), an austere coral-and-stone building. The church is likely to be locked, however. There are distant views of the ocean if you park by the roadside and walk over the short access road, which is beleaguered by potholes.

It's tempting to follow the road past the church down to the coast, but it's all marked private property, and you'll dead-end at gated vacation homes and a flower farm. There is no public beach access.

Koolau Forest Reserve

Beyond Huelo, the vegetation becomes increasingly lush as the highway snakes along the edge of the Koolau Forest Reserve.

Koolau, which means 'windward,' is the windward side of Haleakala and catches the rain clouds. The coast in this area gets 60 to 80 inches of rain a year, while a few miles up on the slopes the annual rainfall is an impressive 200 to 300 inches.

The reserve is heavily forested and cut with numerous gulches and streams. From here, there seems to be a one-lane bridge and a waterfall around every other bend. Many of the dirt roads leading inland from the highway are the maintenance roads for the **Koolau Ditch**, which runs inland paralleling the highway. The system brings water from the rain forests to the cane fields of dry Central Maui. If you want to take a closer look, stop at the small pullout just before the bridge that comes up immediately after the 8-mile marker. Just 100 feet above the road you can see a section of the ditch – built of hand-hewn stone block – that meanders down the hillside and then tunnels into the rock face.

The village of **Kailua** is home to many of the people who work for the East Maui Irrigation (EMI) Company, which maintains the 75 miles of ditches and tunnels. The century-old system is capable of carrying 450 million gallons of water a day.

As you leave the village, you'll notice Norfolk pines up on the hillside, followed by a grove of painted eucalyptus trees with rainbow-colored bark that were introduced from Australia. Next, there's a long stretch of bamboo and more painted eucalyptus.

Farther on, about half a mile after the 9-mile marker, there's a wide turnoff with space for a few cars below the **Waikamoi Ridge Trail** (see the Hiking special section at the end of the Activities chapter). Stop only if you're itching to get your tootsies off the tarmac; serious hikers should continue to Waianapanapa or Oheo Gulch.

Waterfalls & Gardens

OK, so there are waterfalls and tropical foliage everywhere along the Hana Hwy, but the most popular lie between the 10- and 12-mile markers.

Waikamoi Falls is at the bridge just before the 10-mile marker. One waterfall and a pool are near the road. It's possible to walk a short way up to a higher waterfall, but the rocks can be slippery and the bottom one is prettier anyway. Past Waikamoi, bamboo grows almost horizontally out from the cliffs, creating a canopy effect over the road.

Another half mile along comes the **Garden of Eden Arboretum** (☎ 572-9899, *10600 Hana Hwy; admission $5; open 8:30am-2:30pm daily*), designed by a certified arborist. Before you know it, you've driven in and are being kindly asked for your admission fee. Even if it's a bit of a tourist trap, many people say the price of admission is worth it for all the nature paths, abundant tropical flowers and waterfall overlook.

At the 11-mile marker, **Puohokamoa Falls** is just a few minutes' walk from the road near Puohokamoa Bridge. Because it has more parking space and a couple of picnic tables, this waterfall soaks the majority of visitors.

Half a mile after the 11-mile marker, **Haipuaena Falls** is a gentle, short waterfall with a wonderful pool deep enough for swimming. Most people don't know this one's here, as you can't see the pool from the road. If you're inclined to take a dip but don't have a proper bathing suit, take your chances here. There's space for just one or two cars, on the Hana side of the bridge. To reach the falls, walk upstream for a couple of minutes. Wild ginger grows along the path, and ferns hang from the rock wall behind the waterfall, making for a quite idyllic setting.

If there's no room to park by the bridge, head for **Kaumahina State Wayside Park** shortly after the 12-mile marker. The park has picnic tables and lots of parking spaces, but is of little interest other than as a place to stretch and use the toilets. A two-minute walk up the hill under the park's tall eucalyptus trees opens up a broad view of Keanae Peninsula to the southeast.

Honomanu Bay

For the next several miles, the scenery is particularly magnificent, opening up a new vista as you round each bend. If you're on this road after heavy rains, you can expect to see waterfalls galore crashing down the mountains.

Just after crossing the bridge at the 14-mile marker, an inconspicuous and very rough gravel road heads down to Honomanu Bay. The rocky black-sand beach is used mostly by surfers and fishers. The water's usually too turbulent and the currents too strong for swimming, but on very calm days it's possible to kayak here.

Keanae

Keanae is about halfway to Hana. Keanae Valley, which extends down from the Koolau Gap in Haleakala Crater, averages 150 inches of rain a year.

The YMCA (see below) is midway between the 16- and 17-mile markers. Within the next half mile, the Keanae Arboretum, the road to Keanae Peninsula and the Keanae Peninsula Lookout come up in quick succession.

YMCA Camp Keanae (*☎ 248-8355,* *e ymcacampkeanae@aol.com, 13375 Hana Hwy)* Tent sites or coed dorm beds $15. On a knoll overlooking the coast, this YMCA has guest cabins that can sometimes fill with groups on weekends. Otherwise, they're usually available to individual travelers as hostel-style dorms. The cabins have bunk beds, but you have to bring your own sleeping bag, food and cookware. Kitchen facilities are not available, but the cabins have simple outdoor grills. If you prefer to set up a tent, you can do that instead. Advance reservations are required, and there's a three-night limit. Nicer accommodations are available upon request.

Keanae Arboretum This arboretum has numerous ornamental and food plants along with six acres of trees. Introduced tropical plants seen here include painted eucalyptus trees and golden-stemmed bamboo, whose green stripes look like the strokes of a Japanese *shodo* artist. A short trail leads up past heliconia, ti, banana, guava, breadfruit, ginger and other fragrant plants. The higher ground has dozens of varieties of Hawaiian taro in irrigated patches.

All sounds great, doesn't it? Except that it's unkempt and often dry, with many of the plants looking nearly dead and swarms of mosquitoes buzzing around. A paved path cuts through it all, making it accessible but even less natural. Look for cars parked alongside the road three-quarters of a mile past the 16-mile marker.

Keanae Peninsula The road that leads down to Keanae Peninsula is just beyond the arboretum. Keanae is a quiet little Hawaiian village with colts and goats roaming freely and some vestiges of traditional life. At the end of the road spotted with taro patches is a scenic coastline of jagged rock and pounding waves.

Next door to the ballpark is **Lanakila Ihiihi o Iehova Ona Kaua** (Keanae Congregational Church), an attractive stone church dating from 1860. This is one Hawaiian church made of lava rocks and coral mortar whose exterior hasn't been covered over with layers of whitewash. And rather than locked doors, you'll find a guest book and a 'Visitors Welcome' sign. A small cemetery is sprinkled with tropical flowers and coconut palms.

Keanae Peninsula Lookout There's a good view of Keanae village, with its squares of planted taro fed by Keanae Stream, at an unmarked pullout just past the 17-mile marker. Look for the mailbox under the tsunami speaker.

Keanae Peninsula was formed by an eruption of Haleakala volcano. Outlined by its black lava shores, the peninsula still wears its birthmark around the edges. It's very flat, like a leaf floating on the water.

Just before the pullout is deep **Ching's Pond** where a well-worn, steep trail leads down from the roadside bridge.

Wailua

Shortly after the Keanae Peninsula Lookout, you'll pass a couple of **fruit stands** along the road selling drinks and snacks. Bypass the overpriced Halfway to Hana stand, which does have bathrooms and an authentic thatched *hale* in its favor. Instead, keep going to **Uncle Harry's**, run by the family of the late Harry Kunihi Mitchell, a *kupuna* herbalist and native Hawaiian-rights advocate who penned the popular 'Mele o Kahoolawe' (Song of Kahoolawe). Here giant smoothies ($5) are freshly made or you can just buy a few bananas, papayas or coconuts.

Wailua Peninsula Immediately after Uncle Harry's, Wailua Rd breaks off seaward toward **Our Lady of Fatima Shrine**. This little white-and-blue chapel, built in 1860, is also known as the Coral Miracle Church. The coral used in the construction came from a freak storm that deposited coral rocks onto a nearby beach. Before

this, men in the congregation had been diving quite deep but were only able to bring up a few pieces of coral at a time. After the church was completed, another rogue storm hit the beach and swept all the leftover piles of coral back into the sea. Or so the story goes. The chapel has just half a dozen little pews. The current congregation now uses St Gabriel's Mission, the larger and newer church out front.

From Wailua Rd, you can also get a peek of the long cascade of **Waikani Falls**, which is just to the left of the Wailua Valley State Wayside up on the Hana Hwy.

Wailua Rd dead-ends half a mile down, though you might not want to go that far, as driveways blocked off with logs and milk crates prevent cars from turning around.

Waysides On the Hana Hwy, just before the 19-mile marker, **Wailua Valley State Wayside Lookout** comes up on the right. It has a broad view into Keanae Valley, which appears to be a hundred shades of green. You can see a couple of waterfalls, and if it's clear, you can look up at Koolau Gap, a break in the rim of Haleakala Crater.

If you climb up the steps to the right, you can get a good view of Wailua Peninsula, but there's a better view of it at a large paved turnoff a quarter mile down the road.

Halfway between the 22- and 23-mile markers is **Puaa Kaa State Wayside Park**, where a tranquil waterfall empties into a pool before flowing down into a ravine. The park has restrooms, a pay phone, shaded streamside picnic tables and a pool large enough for swimming. The only disadvantage is a pack of stray cats that might pester picnickers.

Nahiku

Just after the 25-mile marker comes Makapipi Falls and the turnoff to overgrown Nahiku. During 2001 this road was closed to tourists because it was ground zero of Maui's dengue fever outbreak (see Health in the Facts for the Visitor chapter).

Nahiku Rd leads down into a cluttered little village that gets more rain every year than any other town in East Maui, over 300 inches. Rubber trees from a defunct plantation line the road, which is sprouting with rain-forest greenery. A few local fruit and flower stands work on the honor system.

The road ends at a beach with rough sea. When the waters are very calm, snorkeling and diving are possible along the left-hand side, where there's an extensive reef with lava arches and sea turtles. Sometimes dolphins swim into the bay on summer afternoons.

Back on the highway before the 29-mile marker is the *Nahiku Ti Gallery & Café*. Although the café serves decent coffee and sandwiches, it's the barbecue stand next door that makes people stop for kalua pig sandwiches and fresh fried fish. It's probably better food than anything you'll get in Hana.

Ulaino Road

By this point, Hana is foremost on your mind. But nothing really awaits you there (at least, nothing that can't wait a little bit longer). So don't bypass Ulaino Rd at the 31-mile marker. Here you can go spelunking in caves, visit an ethnobotanical garden and ancient heiau and finish up swimming under the epitome of waterfalls at the Blue Pool.

Even when it's very dry, you probably won't be able to go the whole way (about 3 miles) without a 4WD, but you can usually get as far as the gardens (see later). After that, you could always park along the roadside and walk the remaining distance.

Opposite the turnoff on the mauka side of the road is *Hana Garden Land & Cafe* (☎ 248-7340, W www.hanagardenland.com, Kalo Rd), closed at the time of research for renovations. When it reopens you'll find a garden setting and a menu that emphasizes locally grown produce (the banana bread is unforgettable). The grounds were first planted in 1974 and boast over 125 varieties of palm, tropical fruit trees, a koi pond and walking paths across 5 acres.

Ka'eleku Caverns If you want to walk inside lava tubes formed by ancient flows, visit these caverns (☎ 248-7308, W www.mauicave.com; 1- & 2-hr tours $29/69).

Until 1999, these caves were filled with trash (and 17,000lb of cow bones!) when local Chuck Thorne bought the property and cleaned them out, an effort that won an environmental preservation award. Rain or shine, tours are led through the fragile ecosystem of stalactites and stalagmites; guides will teach guests how to 'cave softly.' All gear is provided, including flashlights (torches) and hard hats. Reservations are strongly advised.

Kahanu Gardens & Piilanihale Heiau

These gardens (☎ 248-8912; usually open 10am-2pm Mon, Wed & Fri), comprising a 122-acre botanical garden on Kalahu Point, are under the jurisdiction of the nonprofit National Tropical Botanical Garden group, which manages other gardens in Hawaii and in Florida. Here the group works to propagate and conserve rare and medicinal plants and trees of Polynesia, Melanesia and Micronesia. All in one place you'll see kukui, hala, hau and the largest known collection of ulu (breadfruit) cultivars anywhere in the world.

On the grounds is also the site of Piilanihale Heiau, the most astoundingly huge temple in Hawaii, which has a stone platform the size of two football fields. It was built by Piilani, the 14th-century Mauian chief who is also credited with construction of many of the coastal fishponds and taro terraces in the Hana area.

The heiau's restoration has been the life's work of Yoshihiko Sinoto, a Japanese archaeologist who has been instrumental in preserving and rebuilding other Hawaiian heiau and *marae* across the South Pacific.

The gardens are located approximately 1½ miles along Ulaino Rd on the *makai* side. Admission policies vary; sometimes self-guided

The hala plant

tours are offered ($5), while at other times you must take a guided tour ($10). Call beforehand to avoid being turned away.

Blue Pool Past the gardens, Ulaino Rd quickly becomes rough. Major dips in the road pass over two streambeds that clearly call for 4WD vehicles, especially if it has been raining hard recently. Don't despair, since rainfall only makes your end goal that much more worth trekking out to see.

The best advice is to park well off to the side of the road before the first streambed and walk the final mile to the coast. When you get there, strike out across the beach boulders to your left (northwest) for about five or 10 minutes until you see paradise on earth: the Blue Pool. A waterfall this beautiful is not just a pipe dream and is surely what you've been looking forward to in Hawaii all along. (Unless, of course, things are very dry, in which case you might not see much more than a trickle.)

Waianapanapa State Park

The road into beautiful Waianapanapa State Park comes immediately after the 32-mile marker, half a mile south of the Hana Airport turnoff.

The road veers left and ends at a parking lot above Pailoa Bay, which is surrounded by a scenic coastline of low, rocky cliffs. There are picnic pavilions, potable water, restrooms, outdoor showers and a campground. If you turn right instead at the earlier T-intersection, you'll reach the state park cabins.

There's a natural lava arch on the right side of the bay. A short path from the parking lot leads down to the small black-sand beach, which is unprotected and usually has strong rip currents. When it's very calm, the area around the arch is said to be good for snorkeling. Check it out carefully, though, as people have drowned here. Regardless of the weather, the crescent beach practically calls out for you to plant footprints upon its simple sands. There are also hiking trails along the coast, some well traveled and some monkish, including the King's Highway Coastal Trail (see the

Hiking special section at the end of the Activities chapter); the marked trail starts from near the Waianapanapa parking lot and campground.

The park has a *campground* and a dozen *housekeeping cabins*. See Camping under Accommodations in the Facts for the Visitor chapter for details on rates, campsite permits (required) and cabin reservations.

The secluded cabins here book up months in advance, especially the few with ocean views. Tent sites sit right beside the main parking lot, but this isn't a problem after the day trippers go home and campers get the whole moonlit beach to themselves. Expect wet conditions at any time of year.

Caves Two lava-tube caves are just a five-minute walk from the parking lot along a loop path. On the outside, the caves are covered with ferns and flowering impatiens. Inside, they're dripping wet and cool. Waianapanapa means 'glistening waters,' and should you be tempted to take a dip in the small cave pools, the clear mineral waters will leave you feeling squeaky clean.

On certain nights of the year, the waters in the caves turn red. Legend says it's the blood of an innocent princess, who was killed in a fit of rage by her jealous husband. Less romantic types attribute the phenomenon to swarms of tiny, bright red shrimp called *opaeula,* which occasionally emerge in spring from subterranean cracks in the lava.

HANA

Hana is not a grand finale to the Hana Hwy, and people expecting great things are often disappointed. Separated from Kahului by 54 bridges and almost as many miles, this isolated rural town has thus far successfully avoided development. And even though a line of traffic passes through each day, not many visitors stay on.

While the setting is pretty, the town itself is simple and sedate. What makes Hana special is more apparent to those who linger overnight. There's an almost timeless rural character, and though 'Old Hawaii' is an oft-used cliché elsewhere, it's hard not to think of Hana in such terms.

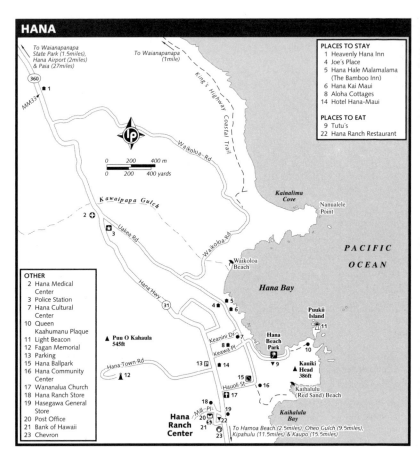

HANA

PLACES TO STAY
1 Heavenly Hana Inn
4 Joe's Place
5 Hana Hale Malamalama (The Bamboo Inn)
6 Hana Kai Maui
8 Aloha Cottages
14 Hotel Hana-Maui

PLACES TO EAT
9 Tutu's
22 Hana Ranch Restaurant

OTHER
2 Hana Medical Center
3 Police Station
7 Hana Cultural Center
10 Queen Kaahumanu Plaque
11 Light Beacon
12 Fagan Memorial
13 Parking
15 Hana Ballpark
16 Hana Community Center
17 Wananalua Church
18 Hana Ranch Store
19 Hasegawa General Store
20 Post Office
21 Bank of Hawaii
23 Chevron

To Waianapanapa State Park (1.5miles), Hana Airport (2miles) & Paia (27miles)

To Waianapanapa (1mile)

King's Highway Coastal Trail

Waikoloa Rd

Kawaipapa Gulch

Uakea Rd

Waikoloa Rd

Kainalimu Cove

Nanualele Point

PACIFIC OCEAN

Waikoloa Beach

Hana Bay

Puukii Island

Hana Hwy

Puu O Kahaula 545ft

Keanini Dr

Keawa Pl

Hana Beach Park

Queen Kaahumanu

Kauiki Head 386ft

Hana Town Rd

Hauoli St

Kaihalulu (Red Sand) Beach

Mill Pl

Kaihalulu Bay

Hana Ranch Center

To Hamoa Beach.(2.5miles), Oheo Gulch (9.5miles), Kipahulu (11.5miles) & Kaupo (15.5miles)

People in Hana cling to their traditional ways and have largely been successful in warding off the changes that have altered much of the rest of Maui. In the latest round, they beat down a plan by outside developers to build a golf course and luxury homes on the pasturelands. Nevertheless, a small community of celebrities, including Carol Burnett and Kris Kristofferson, have long had homes in the Hana area.

Hana is also one of the most Hawaiian communities in the state. Many of its 1900 residents have Hawaiian blood and a strong sense of *ohana*, or extended family. If you spend time around here, you'll hear the words 'auntie' and 'uncle' a lot.

History

For ancient Hawaiians, Hana was the seat of power for East Maui. From this geographically isolated place, the 14th-century chief Piilani set out to conquer the central plains of Wailuku, then marched to Lele (now Lahaina) and united Maui under his rule.

In the tradition of victorious ali'i, Piilani built himself a fine new temple, Piilanihale Heiau (see Ulaino Rd, earlier) to show off his *mana* (spiritual power). It is still the largest heiau extant on Maui, but his public-works projects are more often remembered today. Piilani began construction of the far-reaching King's Hwy footpath that circled the island, and today almost half of Maui's highways still (confusingly) bear his name.

In 1849, along came a whaler by the name of George Wilfong, who bought 60 acres of land for planting sugar and changed Hana's landscape for the next century. According to legend, he used spare blubber pots and a team of oxen to squeeze the juice out of the cane. But he couldn't find enough native Hawaiians willing to work on his fledgling plantation. It wasn't until the Masters and Servants Act of 1850 allowed for the importation of cheap labor from overseas that two Danes were able to make a go of it nearby.

Chinese, Japanese and Portuguese laborers were brought in to work newly planted sugarcane fields, and Hana became a booming plantation town in the late 19th century. A narrow-gauge railroad connected the fields to the Hana Mill. Many planters and foremen were haole, sons of New England missionaries with influence both in Hawaiian politics and sticky fingers that reached all the way back home to the mainland. Following the California Gold Rush and the Civil War, which increased demand for sugar on the US mainland, the Reciprocity Treaty of 1875 exempted sugar from US import duties in exchange for US naval rights at Pearl Harbor.

In the 1940s, Hana could no longer compete with larger sugar operations in Central Maui, so the mill shut down. Enter San Francisco businessman Paul Fagan, owner of the Puu o Hoku Ranch on Molokai, who purchased 14,000 acres in Hana. Starting with 300 Herefords, Fagan converted the cane fields to ranch land. A few years later, he opened a six-room hotel called the Kauiki Inn. Geographically and economically, Hana Ranch and the hotel became the hub of town.

In February 1946, Fagan brought over his minor league baseball team, the San Francisco Seals, for prespring training, and allegedly, that's when journalists first gave the town its moniker 'Heavenly Hana.' On April 1, 1946, a powerful tsunami caused by an earthquake on the US West Coast ripped up the Hana Coast. A dozen people died, businesses were lost and many people went to work on the ranch.

Today, Hana Ranch still has a few thousand head of cattle worked by paniolo (Hawaiian cowboys). When the cattle are ready for Oahu stockyards, they're trucked all the way up the Hana Hwy to Kahului Harbor. The Kauiki Inn survives as the exclusive Hotel Hana-Maui.

Information

Hana Ranch Center is the commercial center of town. It has a tiny Bank of Hawaii (☎ 248-8015), open 3pm to 4:30pm Monday to Thursday and 3pm to 6pm Friday, and a post office, open 8am to 4:30pm weekdays.

The Hana Ranch Store (☎ 248-8261), which sells groceries, liquor and general supplies, is open 7am to 7pm daily. Across the road, Hasegawa General Store (see below) has an ATM. There are community bulletin boards outside the post office and the two grocery stores.

The ballpark has public tennis courts. All other activities can be arranged through the Hotel Hana-Maui (see Places to Stay, later). Its Hana Ranch guides lead 1-hour trail rides ($35) along the Hana coast at 8:30am, or up into the hills at 10am, every day except Sunday. For information on kayaking in Hana Bay, see the Activities chapter.

Hana closes up early. If you're going to be heading back late, fuel up right away. The Chevron station (☎ 248-7256), 5200 Hana Hwy, closes most days around 6pm (5:30pm Sunday).

Hasegawa General Store

This business has been in the Hasegawa family since 1910. The old Hasegawa General Store, Hana's best-known sight, burned to the ground in 1990. After a brief hiatus, it moved to its new location (☎ 248-8231, 5165 Hana Hwy) under the rusty tin roof of the old theater building in the town center. The store is open 8am to 5:30pm Monday to Saturday, 9am to 4:30pm Sunday.

While some of its character was inevitably lost along with its eclectic inventory, the store is still packed with just about everything from bags of poi and aloha dolls to fishing gear and machetes. It also has groceries, hardware, newspapers and the record that immortalized the store in song.

Hana Cultural Center

If you're looking for a good place to get a sense of Hana's roots, drop by the friendly, community-run Hana Cultural Center (☎ 248-8622, ⓦ www.hookele.com/hccm, Uakea Rd; admission $2; open 10am-4pm daily). On the grounds are a couple of authentically thatched hale of the type once found in traditional Hawaiian villages, the newest of which is a *hale wa'a* (canoe house).

Inside the *hale wai o hana* (House of Treasures) is a small museum displaying quilts, early Hawaiian artifacts such as *poi* boards, an *ulu maika* set, woodcarvings, *lomi lomi* sticks for self-massage (unfortunately none for sale!) and historical exhibits with period photographs.

Also on the grounds is the old Hana district police station and three-bench courthouse (1871), now on the National Register of Historic Places. Although it looks like a museum piece, the court is still used a couple of times a month when a judge shows up to hear minor cases such as traffic violations, sparing Hana residents the hassle of driving all the way to Wailuku.

Fagan Memorial

After Paul Fagan died, his family erected a memorial in 1960 on Lyon's Hill, which was Fagan's favorite spot for watching the sunset. The huge hilltop cross is now Hana's most dominant landmark. A trail starts opposite the Hotel Hana-Maui. It is often used by cyclists and joggers. Walkers can reach the memorial in about 15 minutes.

Wananalua Church

Looking like an ancient Norman church, the current structure with thick walls of lava rock and coral mortar was built by missionaries in 1838 to replace the congregation's original grass church. There's a little cemetery at the side with graves randomly laid out, rather than lined up in rows. Even at rest, Hana folks like things casual.

Hana Bay

At the southern end of Hana Bay, **Hana Beach Park** has a black-sand beach, small boat ramp, snack bar, showers, restrooms and picnic tables. Hana folks occasionally come down here with ukulele, guitars and a few beers for impromptu evening parties. When water conditions are very calm, snorkeling and diving are good out in the direction of the light beacon. Currents can be very strong, and snorkelers shouldn't go beyond the beacon. Surfers head to Waikoloa Beach at the northern end of the bay.

Kauiki Head, the 386-foot cinder hill on the south side of Hana Bay, was according to legend the home of the demigod Maui, or alternatively, yet another of his daughter's lovers that he turned to stone. It was the site of an ancient fort. In 1780, Chief Kahekili successfully fought off a challenge by Big Island chiefs here. The islet at the tip of the point, which now holds a light beacon, is **Puukii** or 'Image Hill.' The name can be traced to a huge *kii* (statue) that the great king Umi erected here in the 16th century to ward off invaders.

Queen Kaahumanu (see History in the Facts about Maui chapter), the favorite wife of Kamehameha the Great and one of the most powerful women in Hawaiian history, was born in a cave here in 1768. A trail to a plaque noting the queen's birth starts along the hill at the side of the wharf at Hana Beach Park. It leads through ironwood trees toward the light beacon, passing by a tiny red-sand beach. The walk to the rock where the plaque is mounted is only mildly interesting but takes just five minutes. Watch your step, as most of the trail is a bit crumbly.

Kaihalulu (Red Sand) Beach

Hana's more famous red-sand beach, Kaihalulu Beach, farther down on the south side of Kauiki Head, is favored by nude sunbathers. It's a gorgeous little cove with sand eroded from the red cinder hill and beautiful turquoise waters.

Although the cove is partly protected by a lava outcrop, the currents can be dangerous if the surf is up. There are some tide pools, too. Water drains through a break on the left side, which should be avoided. Your best chance of finding reasonably calm waters is early in the morning.

The path to the beach is at the end of Uakea Rd beyond the ballpark. It starts across the lawn at the lower side of the Hana Community Center, where a steep, treacherous trail continues down to the beach, less than 10 minutes away. Technically you are trespassing. The trail passes around an interesting overgrown Japanese cemetery – a remnant of the sugarcane days – just two minutes' walk east from the community center.

Places to Stay

Hana has a wealth of accommodation gems. If you're looking for a romantic splurge, this is the place. Affordable options are harder to come by. Be aware that most places have at least a two-night minimum stay.

There's tent camping and cabins at Waianapanapa State Park, just north of town on the Hana Hwy (see Road to Hana, earlier). There are also campsites at Oheo Gulch, about 10 miles south of Hana (see Beyond Hana, later). If you plan to camp at Oheo Gulch, you'll need to stock up on food and water in Hana.

Rental Agencies A couple of vacation rental agencies handle cottages and houses in the Hana area. As the properties can vary greatly in quality and maintenance, you'd better get specific details before sending any deposit.

Hana Alii Holidays (☎ 248-7742, 800-548-0478, fax 248-8595, Ⓦ http://hanaalii .com, PO Box 536, Hana, HI 96713) This company manages more than a dozen private homes, apartments and cottages, ranging from $60 for a two-bedroom place outside town to $295 for a deluxe beachfront cottage near Hamoa Beach.

Hana Plantation Houses (☎ 923-0772, 800-228-4262, fax 922-6068, Ⓦ www.hana maui.com, PO Box 249, Hana, HI 96713)

Houses from $72 for two people, $10 each additional person. Hana Plantation Houses rents about a dozen private houses on the lush Hana coast. At the lower end, there's a little Japanese-style studio with an efficiency kitchen or a two-bedroom cottage in a garden setting for a bit more. All have cooking facilities and are about 10 minutes outside town. Ask about discounts for longer stays.

Budget & Mid-Range *Joe's Place* (☎ 248-7033, Ⓦ www.joesrentals.com, 4870 Uakea Rd) Rooms with shared/private bath $45/55. In town, Joe's Place has only small, basic rooms, but they're clean and comfortable enough. Most rooms have two single beds, though a few have double beds. Amenities include a community kitchen, barbecue grills (and *imu!*) and a TV room.

Aloha Cottages (☎ 248-8420, Keawa Pl) Studio/2-bedroom cottages from $65/85. Aloha Cottages is near the Hotel Hana-Maui. Run by the Nakamura family, all the units are straightforward and none has a phone, but messages are taken. The studio has twin beds and a hot plate, toaster and fridge; each of the two-bedroom cottages has its own full kitchen, a queen bed and two twin beds.

Tree Houses of Hana, Maui (☎ 248-7241, Ⓔ hanalani@maui.net) Treehouses $95. These are the real deal: rustic treehouses built deep in the jungle with no electricity or running water. Instead, guests get tiki torches, bamboo outhouses with hot showers, camp-style kitchens and hammocks. Quite an adventure! It also has B&B guesthouse rooms with ocean views for the less wild at heart.

Tradewinds Cottages (☎ 248-8980, 800-327-8097, Ⓦ www.maui.net/~twt/cottage.html) 1- & 2-bedroom cottage $110/135, $10 each extra person. Tradewinds is a 5-acre tropical flower farm a couple of miles north of town, near the airport. Here you can stay in either of two pleasant cottages that let you pretend you are living in your own private garden. Both have full kitchens, cable TV, ceiling fans and covered sundecks with private hot tubs and fine views. Guests are

EAST MAUI

usually free to pick papayas, bananas and avocados gratis.

Hana Hale Malamalama *(☎ 248-7718,* w *www.hanahale.com, Uakea Rd)* Cottage $160, bamboo studio/villa with kitchen $140/185. Centered on a fishpond, this naturalistic village, also called 'The Bamboo Inn,' is fully outfitted in bamboo, right down to the furnishings and outdoor showers. But not all accommodations are created equal. Make sure you reserve one of the suites in the main house (the Bamboo Inn) or the treehouse cottage. All of these come with private Jacuzzi, ocean views and timeless serenity.

Hana Kai Maui *(☎ 248-8426, 800-346-2772, fax 248-7482,* w *www.hanakaimaui .com, 1533 Uakea Rd)* Garden- & ocean-view studios $125/135, 1-bedroom units $145/165. Near Hana Hale Malamalama, this is a modern, though not fancy, 17-unit condo complex. Condo units have full kitchens and lanai, most with fine ocean views of Hana Bay and within earshot of the breaking surf. If you aren't getting any discounts, it's probably not worth it.

Top End *Heavenly Hana Inn (☎ 248-8442,* w *www.heavenlyhanainn.com, Uakea Rd)* 1- & 2-bedroom suites $185-200/$250, breakfast $15. You can't help but notice this landmark *ryokan* (traditional Japanese inn) on the way into town, set back from the 33-mile marker. Every attention has been paid to authentic detail, from gardens and skylights down to *shoji* (rice-paper screens) and rooms for tea and meditation. Each of the apartment suites is exquisitely tasteful. Deluxe breakfasts of Hawaiian or Asian fare must be preselected a week in advance. If no one is around and you've made reservations, just ring the temple bell.

Hotel Hana-Maui *(☎ 248-8211, 800-321-4262, fax 248-7202,* w *www.hotelhanamaui .com, Hana Hwy)* Rooms/cottages $235-275/250-655. In the center of town, the Hana-Maui is low profile, more like a plantation estate than a luxury hotel. Indeed, its history reaches back to the original Kauiki Inn built by Paul Fagan in the 1940s. Everything here is quite airy and open, with Hawaiian accents such as traditional quilts and artwork. Most rooms are in single-story row cottages that have bleached hardwood floors, tiled bathrooms, a view over a private garden and French doors opening to trellised patios. Pampering has its price – ask about multiple-night packages that throw in a bottle of champagne and candlelit dinner, plus a one-hour massage for two, all for less than the regular rates. Even if you can't afford to stay, at least stop by the Hotel Hana-Maui to wander through its fine ***Hana Coast Gallery***.

Places to Eat & Drink

In a word, the pickings are thin. Bring groceries from Kahului or Paia if you plan to stay a while, as the Hana grocery stores have only a limited selection. You should skip the ***Hana Ranch Restaurant*** *(☎ 248-8255, Hana Ranch Center)*. For the desperate there is a takeout counter on the side that offers standard breakfast fare, plate lunches and saimin, burgers and sandwiches (all under $7).

Tutu's *(☎ 248-8224, Hana Beach Park)* Dishes under $5. Open 8am-4pm at least Mon-Thur. This fast-food grill at Hana Beach Park serves hamburgers or mahimahi burgers and veggie sandwiches, as well as local mixed-plate lunches ($6). It's not stellar, but it's probably the best budget eats in Hana. You can eat on picnic tables by the bay.

Hotel Hana-Maui *(see Places to Stay, earlier)* Breakfast $5-16.50, lunch $9-15, dinner from $25. Open 7:30am-10:30am, 11am-2:30pm, 6:15pm-9pm daily. The ranch-style dining room opens onto a sunny lanai that overlooks Hana Bay. Small portions detract from what is finely flavored Hawaii Regional cuisine, but the aloha atmosphere is rewarding. There is live music in the Paniolo Bar from 6:30pm to 9:30pm, Thursday to Sunday. The restaurant hosts a live hula show by local families starting at 7:30pm Thursday and Saturday.

BEYOND HANA

As it continues south from Hana, the road undergoes a transmigration of souls and the name changes to the Piilani Hwy (Hwy 31).

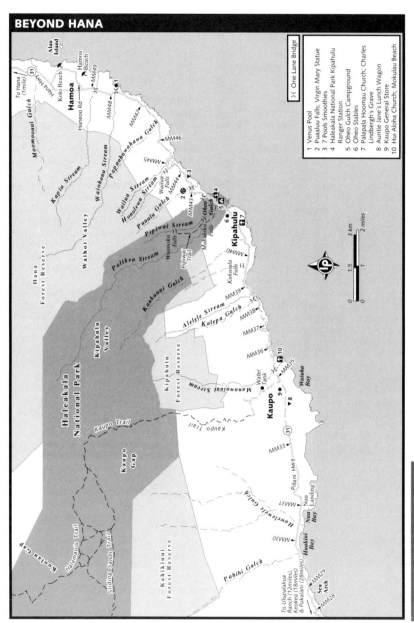

BEYOND HANA

>|< One Lane Bridge

1 Venus Pool
2 Puaaluu Falls; Virgin Mary Statue
3 7 Pools Smoothies
4 Haleakala National Park Kipahulu
   Ranger Station
5 Oheo Gulch Campground
6 Oheo Stables
7 Palapala Hoomau Church; Charles
   Lindbergh's Grave
8 Auntie Jane's Lunch Wagon
9 Kaupo General Store
10 Hui Aloha Church; Mokulau Beach

To Hana
(1mile)
Hana Hwy
31

Alau
Island

Koki Beach

Hamoa
Beach

Hamoa

Haneoo Rd

MM49

MM48

MM47

Moomoonui Gulch

Kapia Stream

Waiohonu Stream

MM46

MM45

Papaahawahawa Gulch

Wailua Stream

Honolewa Stream

Wailua
Falls

MM44

Puaalu Gulch

MM43

Waihoi Valley

Hana

Forest Reserve

Pipiwai Stream

Waimoku
Falls

Makahiku
Falls

Oheo Gulch

Kipahulu

6

7

Palikea Stream

Pipiwai
Trail

Kaukauai Gulch

Kipahulu Valley

Makahiku
Falls

MM40

Kukuiula
Falls

Alelele Stream

Kalepa Gulch

MM39

MM38

Haleakala

National Park

Kipahulu

Forest Reserve

MM37

MM36

10

Manawainui Stream

Water
Tank

MM35

Wainha
Bay

Kaupo

9   8

31

Kaupo Trail

Kaupo Trail

MM33

Pilani HWY

Kaupo Gap

Hawelewele Gulch

Nuu
Landing

LEWW

Nuu
Bay

MM41

Kahikinui

Forest Reserve

MM30

Haukini
Bay

Halemauu Trail

Koolau Gap

Sliding Sands Trail

Pahihi Gulch

To Ulupalakua
Ranch (12miles),
Keokea (18miles)
& Pukalani (28miles)

MM29

Sea
Arch

MM28

0   1.5   3 km
0   1   2 miles

EAST MAUI

Gone are most of the crowds of day trippers as the road slowly winds around past Oheo Gulch and Kipahulu. After that it takes on a rugged, solitary character, and at the right time of day you'll feel like the last person on earth. The road continues right around the southern flank of Haleakala, past Kaupo Gap and ranch lands, back into the Upcountry (see the Upcountry chapter).

Someday, in a *Bladerunner*esque asphalt future, this may well be a real highway with cars zipping along in both directions. For now, it's an unspoiled adventure. Signs such as 'Motorists Assume Risk of Damage Due to Presence of Cattle' and 'Narrow Winding Road, Safe Speed 10mph' give clues that this is not your standard highway. Many tourist maps mark it as impassable, and car rental agencies say that just being on it is a violation of their contracts.

However, the highway is almost entirely paved! The stretch between the Kaupo area and Ulupalakua Ranch has even been upgraded in recent years and is in fairly good condition, even if it does rattle your bones. The trickiest section of the drive is around Kaupo, but even there the road only turns to dirt for five miles. Depending on when this section of road was last graded, you might face a couple of tortuous climbs over rocky riverbeds. These are usually dry and pose little problem, even for standard compact cars. But after hard rains, streams flow over the road, making passage difficult. A 4WD vehicle, or at least a high-riding car with a manual transmission, will minimize your chances of bottoming out.

Flash floods sometimes wash away portions of the road, making it impossible to get through until it's repaired. For the latest road conditions, ask other drivers. You can also call the Oheo Gulch ranger station (☎ 248-7375) between 9am and 5pm daily or the county Public Works Department (☎ 248-8254) between 6:30am and 3pm weekdays.

But really, it's nothing to fear. Start off early and take something to munch on and plenty to drink. Check your oil and spare tire – it's a long haul to Hana or Kula if you break down, and the tow charge is said to be

around $400. Keokea is the last place on the Kula side to get gas and something to eat. In the Oheo Gulch area, you might find a fruit stand, but drinking water, gas stations and other services are nonexistent after Hana. Ain't that grand?

Hana to Oheo Gulch

Between the hairpin turns, one-lane bridges and drivers trying to take in all the sights, it's a slow-moving 10 miles between Hana and Oheo Gulch, the southern portion of Haleakala National Park. Allow yourself at least 45 minutes.

This incredibly lush stretch of highway is perhaps the most beautiful part of the entire drive down from Paia. You'll get extra coastal views by detouring along the quick **Haneoo Rd loop**, near Hamoa, which runs past a couple of beaches and ancient shoreline fishponds. The turnoff is just before the 50-mile marker, about 1½ miles south of Hana.

Koki Beach is at the base of a red cinder hill less than half a mile from the start of the loop. Most of the sand washes away in winter, leaving a rocky shoreline. At other times it's ideal for beachcombing. Local surfers who know the coastline sometimes ride out on the waves here, but rocks and strong currents make it hazardous for newcomers. That offshore rock topped by a few coconut trees is **Alau Island**, a seabird sanctuary. The trees were planted years ago by a couple of Hana residents, allegedly so that they'd have coconuts to drink while fishing off the island. You'll see the remains of Haneoo Fish Pond on the shoreline.

A little farther along is **Hamoa Beach**, a lovely gray-sand beach that's used by the Hotel Hana-Maui but is accessible to everyone. James Michener said it was the only beach in the North Pacific that looked as if it actually belonged in the South Pacific. When the waves are up, there's good surfing and bodysurfing, though be aware that rip currents are sometimes present. When the waters are calm, swimming in the cove is good. Public access is down the steps below the hotel's bus stop sign. There are outdoor showers and restrooms.

Back on the highway, next up is the **Venus Pool** once used by Hawaiian royalty. Park near the bridge just after the 48-mile marker, then squeeze by the gate and follow the worn trail along the stream toward the ocean. In five minutes it reaches a small, serene pool protected from rough surf by lava outcroppings. Take a dip in the cool waters or just sunbathe on the rocks.

As you continue driving south, you'll see waterfalls cascading down the cliffs, orchids growing out of the rocks and lots of bread-fruit and coconut trees. **Wailua Falls**, 3 miles before Oheo Gulch at the 45-mile marker, is particularly attractive, with its almost 100-foot drop visible from the road. At the pullout, you might find a couple of vendors selling hand-painted T-shirts and the like. Halfway between the 43- and 44-mile markers, the *7 Pools Smoothies* stand is run by true hippies who like nothing more than to hang out playing the bongos. After another mile and past the one-lane bridge, start looking for **Puaaluu Falls**. There's even a statue of the Virgin Mary tucked into a rock face on the makai side of the road here.

Oheo Gulch

Oheo Stream dramatically cuts its way through rain forests of the Oheo Gulch (Haleakala National Park – Kipahulu Section) in a lovely series of waterfalls and wide pools, each one tumbling into the next. Not so long ago, Oheo Gulch was dubbed the 'Seven Sacred Pools' in a tourism promotion scheme. There are actually 24 pools from the ocean all the way up to Waimoku Falls, and they were never sacred. When the sun shines they are ideal for swimming, especially before the afternoon day trippers start to swarm.

A large Hawaiian settlement of several thousand people once spread throughout the Oheo area, and archaeologists have identified the stone remains of more than 700 structures here, including fishing shrines and canoe ramps. Prior to Western contact, the villagers also cultivated taro and sweet potatoes in terraced gardens.

One of the expressed intentions of Haleakala National Park is to manage the Oheo area 'to perpetuate traditional Hawaiian farming and *hoonanea*' – a Hawaiian word meaning to pass the time in ease, peace and pleasure. Entrance to this southern section of the park is free and open 24 hours. Entrance to the upper Kipahulu Valley, which stands between Oheo Gulch and the Haleakala volcano crater, is *kapu*. It is a scientific reserve and a sanctuary for native rain-forest flora and fauna.

Programs at the Kipahulu ranger station (☎ 248-7375), open 9am to 5pm daily, include exhibits on Hawaiian culture and short ranger-led walks and talks throughout the day. The 1-mile guided hike up to the Bamboo Forest leaves daily at 9am. A three-hour guided hike to Waimoku Falls is usually offered on Saturday at 9:30am, as long as the weather is accommodating and at least four people want to go.

Restrooms and picnic tables are available – they're near the visitors' parking lot and park campground – but drinking water, food and gas are not.

Kuloa Point Trail A 20-minute loop trail runs from the Oheo Gulch parking lot down to the lower pools and back, passing interpretive signs and archaeological sites along the way. The start of the trail is near the ranger station.

At the junction with the Pipiwai Trail, go right. A few minutes down, you'll come to a broad grassy knoll with a beautiful view of the Hana coast. On a clear day, you can see the Big Island, 30 miles away across Alenuihaha Channel. This would be a fine place to break out a picnic basket – as long as you anchor it from blowing away.

The large freshwater pools along the trail are terraced one atop the other and are connected by gentle cascades. They're usually calm and great for swimming, though the water's brisk. The second big pool below the bridge is a favorite. If it's been raining heavily and the water is flowing too high and fast, the pools are closed and signs are posted.

Still, heavy rains falling on the upper slopes can bring a sudden white-water torrent here at any time. If the water starts to rise, get out immediately. People have been swept out to sea from these pools by flash floods. The ocean below is not at all inviting – the water is quite rough, with gray sharks known to frequent the area.

Actually, most of the injuries that occur here come from falls on slippery rocks. Also hazardous are submerged rocks and ledges in some of the pools, which makes jumping from the bridge or over one waterfall into the next pool a dicey proposition. Please check carefully before diving in.

Pipiwai Trail The Pipiwai Trail starts on the seaward side of the ranger station. Or take a shortcut and cross the road from the parking lot, then veer slightly right along the highway to the pedestrian crossing until you pick up the trail on the other side.

From here it's a half mile to Makahiku Falls and another 1½ miles to Waimoku Falls, for a total of 4 miles roundtrip. It takes about an hour to hike the 1½ miles to Waimoku Falls from the Makahiku Falls viewpoint. The upper part of the trail is muddy, but boardwalks cover some of the worst sections. Ancient farm sites with abandoned taro patches can be spotted along the way, although it takes a keen eye to recognize them.

Initially, you'll pass large mango trees and lots of guava trees before coming to an overlook with a safety railing after about 10 minutes. **Makahiku Falls**, a long bridal-veil waterfall that drops into a deep gorge, is just off to the right. Thick green ferns cover the sides of 200-foot basalt cliffs where the falls cascade. The scene is pretty darned rewarding for such a short walk.

To the left of the overlook, a worn path continues up to the top of the falls, where there's a popular skinny-dipping pool. Around midday the pool is quite enjoyable, but by late afternoon the sun stops hitting it and the mosquitoes move in. Rocks above the falls will keep you from going over the edge as long as the water level isn't high; a cut on one side lets the water plunge over the cliff. But if the water starts to rise, get out immediately – a sheer drop from this height could obviously be fatal.

Back on the main trail, you'll walk under guava and banyan trees before crossing Palikea Stream. Mosquitoes thrive along the stream and the humidity starts to get wearing here; slap on some insect repellant and just keep going. Steps ahead lies the wonderland of the **Bamboo Forest**, where three thick groves of bamboo stalks crash musically together in the wind. When you come out of the first grove, you'll be able to glimpse distant **Waimoku Falls**, a thin, lacy 400-foot waterfall dropping down a sheer rock face. By the time you emerge from the third thicket, you're there.

The pool under Waimoku Falls was partially filled in by a landslide during a 1976 earthquake, so it's not terribly deep. At any rate, swimming is not recommended due to the real danger of falling rocks.

If you want to take a dip, you'll find better places to swim along the way. About 100 yards before Waimoku Falls, you'll cross a little stream. If you go left and walk upstream for 10 minutes (there's not really a trail; just walk alongside the stream), you'll come to an attractive waterfall and a little pool about neck deep. There's also a nice pool in the stream about halfway between Makahiku and Waimoku Falls.

Horseback Riding A mile southwest of Oheo Gulch, *Oheo Stables* (☎ 667-2222, ℗ *www.maui.net/~ray; 3-hr ride (max 6 people) $119; departures 10:30am & 11:30am daily)* offers casually paced trail rides to waterfalls within the Kipahulu section of Haleakala National Park. All rides include a 30-minute stop at a waterfall overlook and start off at the stables with a buffet of hot banana muffins, croissants, tree-ripened fruit and coffee. Bring long pants, closed-toe shoes and sunscreen.

Places to Stay The national park maintains primitive *Oheo Gulch Campground* about half a mile southeast of the main Oheo Gulch visitor's area. The campground is Hawaiian-style: free and undeveloped – just a huge open pasture. There are some incredible places to pitch a tent on grassy cliffs right above the coast and the pounding surf. Not only that, the whole camping area is set amid the ruins of an old Hawaiian village, making this quite a powerful place to be, especially under a full moon.

In winter, there are usually only a handful of tents here. It gets quite a few campers in summer, but even then it's generally large enough to handle everyone who shows up (maximum 100 people). Facilities include pit toilets and a few picnic tables and grills but *no* water. Permits aren't required, though camping is officially limited to three nights each month.

Getting There & Away A lot of people leave the Oheo Gulch area in midafternoon to head east back up the Hana Hwy. Some of them, suddenly realizing what a long trek they have ahead, become very impatient drivers. You might want to consider leaving a little later, which would give you more time to sightsee and allow you to avoid the rush. Getting caught in the dark on the Hana Hwy does have certain advantages. You can see the headlights of oncoming cars around bends that would otherwise be blind, and the traffic is almost nonexistent.

Otherwise, the Piilani Hwy (don't be misled by the term 'highway' – there's no pavement in many places) heads west through Kaupo up to Keokea in Kula. It's usually passable but not always. It shouldn't be done in the dark, even though *kaupo* means 'night landing' in Hawaiian.

The Oheo Gulch ranger station can give you the latest information on road conditions. Another option is to drive to the southern end of Kipahulu and talk to

Lindbergh's Last Flight

When Charles Lindbergh and his wife, the aviatrix and poet Anne Morrow Lindbergh, first began visiting Maui in the 1960s, they were captivated by its beauty. Sam Pryor, a friend who lived at Oheo Gulch, sold them a little plot of Kipahulu rain forest and they built the cliffside home they christened Argonauta in 1971. The Historic Hawai'i Foundation is currently trying to restore and move Argonauta and Anne's writer's cottage within the boundaries of the national park.

It seems that all his life Charles Lindbergh had been seeking the privacy that only Hana could provide. After making the first ever nonstop solo flight across the Atlantic in 1927, this shy man was catapulted into the limelight. During a goodwill tour to Mexico he met Anne Morrow and married her in 1929. A few years later, the famous couple's 20-month-old son was kidnapped and later found dead, during which time they were constantly hounded by the press. Charles's controversial political actions before WWII, which included accepting a Nazi medal of honor and speaking out against US voluntary involvement in the war before Pearl Harbor, earned them further notoriety.

Toward the end of his life Charles frequently retreated to his Hana home, re-emerging into public life only as a spokesperson for the conservation movement, particularly of endangered humpback and blue whales. When he learned that he was dying of cancer in 1974, Lindbergh said, 'I'd rather spend two days on Maui than two months in this hospital in New York City.' He immediately flew back to the island and died a few days later, on August 26, 1974.

Charles Lindbergh is buried in the graveyard of Palapala Hoomau Congregational Church. His simple grave is surrounded by lava rocks, just as he designed it, and sits under a plum tree. He lies buried in a eucalyptus coffin dressed in his favorite work clothes, a plaid shirt and khakis, plus a Hudson's Bay blanket. The gravestone inscription, 'If I take the wings of the morning/And dwell in the uttermost parts of the sea,' is incomplete. The next verse of Psalm 139 is 'Even there shall thy hand lead me/And thy right hand shall hold me.' Anne Morrow Lindbergh died on February 7, 2001, at her home in rural Vermont.

EAST MAUI

people coming from the Kaupo direction. Most likely they've either just driven down from Kula or else have started up the road from Kipahulu, found road conditions bad and turned around.

Kipahulu

The village of Kipahulu is less than a mile south of Oheo Gulch. At the turn of the 19th century, Kipahulu was one of several sugar plantation villages in the Hana area. It had a working mill from 1890 to 1922. Following the closure of the mill, unsuccessful attempts were made to grow pineapples until ranching took hold in the late 1920s.

Today, Kipahulu has both exclusive estates and modest Hawaiian homes. Fruit stands are set up here and there along the roadside; some are attended by elderly women who string lei and sell bananas, papayas and woven *lauhala* (pandanus-leaf) hats. This is the end of the line for most day visitors who have pushed beyond Hana.

Palapala Hoomau Church, with its 26-inch-thick walls and simple wooden pews, dates from 1864. The church is known for its window painting of a Polynesian Christ dressed in the red-and-yellow feather capes worn only by Hawaii's highest chiefs. The churchyard is a peaceful place, with sleepy cats lounging around, waiting for a nice warm car hood to sprawl out on. The church is a quarter mile beyond St Paul's Church, which sits on the highway three-quarters of a mile south of Oheo Gulch. The dirt road down to the church is immediately past the 41-mile marker on the makai side. Turn in at the gate just past the wooden cistern at the end of the field.

Most people make the pilgrimage here just to visit **Charles Lindbergh's grave** (see 'Lindbergh's Last Flight'). Don't get the location mixed up with St Paul's Church.

Kaupo

As the road winds around from Kipahulu, it skirts the edge of rocky cliffs and the vegetation picks up. First the road is shaded with big mango trees, banyans, bougainvillea and wiliwili trees with red tiger-claw blossoms. Then you'll see increasing numbers of hala

and guava trees as the road sporadically bottoms out into gravel after the 39-mile marker, and you bounce along for just under 5 hilly miles to Kaupo. If you've made it this far in under an hour, congratulations.

The village of Kaupo comes after the 35-mile marker. However, don't expect a developed village in any sense of the word, as Kaupo is spread out and there's really not much to see. This is home for the scattered community of paniolo – many of them third-generation ranch hands – who work the Kaupo Ranch.

Kaupo was once heavily settled. It has three historic heiau and two churches from the 19th century. As the road curves in and then out, it's well worth stopping for the picturesque view of the church across the bay. There used to be a landing for shipping Kaupo Ranch cattle, and you can still see steps leading down into the water on a rock jutting out into the ocean. This area is cool and forested, and there are sisal plants on the hillsides.

Loaloa Heiau, the largest of the ancient temples, is a registered national historical monument. All three heiau sites are mauka of **Hui Aloha Church**, which is itself 0.7 miles east of Kaupo General Store. This attractive whitewashed church, built in 1859 and restored in 1978, is surrounded by a stone wall and a few windswept trees beside rocky, black-sand Mokulau Beach. Mokulau, which means 'many small islands,' is named for the rocks just offshore. The area was an ancient surfing site, and occasionally you may see whales breaching offshore or Hawaiian monk seals.

Kaupo General Store (☎ 248-8054) Theoretically open 9:30am-5pm Mon-Sat. On the east side of the gap, Kaupo General Store is 'the only store for 20 miles' and sells snacks, beer and wine. Opening hours can be a bit flexible to say the least, so it's best not to count on it being open.

Auntie Jane's Lunch Wagon This local woman shares her aloha at an afternoon lunch wagon makai of the highway by selling organic beef burgers, simple sandwiches and shave ice. If you're lucky, she'll be open.

Kaupo to Ulupalakua Ranch

Without question this lonely stretch of highway owns Maui's most beautiful and wild landscape. The views up **Kaupo Gap**, a deep and rugged valley eroded into the side of Haleakala volcano, are imbued with mana at sunset.

Makai of the 31-mile marker is **Nuu Bay**. A very rough 4WD road passes through a gate and runs down to the ocean in under 10 minutes. You could also park along the highway and walk it. Families use the black-sand beach at Nuu Bay for swimming when the waters are calm. Spinner dolphins sometimes play offshore. There is good coral and sea life for snorkeling and diving, too, but be sure to stay within the protected section of the bay. Out on the open ocean, strong currents and rip tides are endemic and will catch swimmers unaware.

Another mile farther along there is a wide turnoff on the mauka side of the road for a quick walk out to dramatic **Huakini Bay**. There is not much to do here, except sit on the wonderfully smooth boulders and watch the violent surf. As the road continues, it runs in and out of numerous gulches and crosses a few bridges, gradually getting closer to the coast. You'll notice striations of lava on the mauka side, left over from centuries of repeated volcanic upheaval.

After the 29-mile marker, a natural **lava sea arch** will appear makai of the highway. If you keep driving along just until the arch disappears from sight, look for a turnout on the makai side of the road. Park and take a worn footpath through pastoral green fields down to the cliff's edge. Peering to your left, you'll see the surf crashing through the arch and other blowholes spouting along the harsh lava coast. The road gradually rises but only improves after the 23-mile marker. A few miles south of Ulupalakua Ranch, it crosses an expansive **lava flow** dating from the time of Haleakala's last eruption (see Ahihi-Kinau Natural Reserve in the South Maui chapter). This flow is the same one that covers the La Perouse Bay area of the coast south of Makena. It's still black and barren all the way down to the sea. Just offshore is the crescent island of Molokini with Kahoolawe beyond. The large grassy hills between here and the sea are volcanic cinder cones. There's such a wide-angle view that the ocean horizon is noticeably curved. Time your arrival for just before sunset.

South of Tedeschi Vineyards (see the Up-country chapter), groves of fragrant eucalyptus trees quickly replace drier and scrubbier terrain. It's open range here; cattle graze right beside the road and occasionally mosey in front of you.

Upcountry

Upcountry, the cool highland area on the western slopes of Haleakala, has some of Maui's finest countryside. It is the heart of *paniolo* (Hawaiian cowboy) country, where rodeos, steaks and gargantuan pickup trucks rumbling along the highway are commonplace. Rolling hills, green pastures and grazing cows make it all look more like the American West than tropical Hawaii.

From Olinda Rd or the heights of Kula, there are sweeping views down over sugarcane plains to raucous sea cliffs set against the vast backdrop of the Pacific. The population thins the farther you get from the coast, with only a few scattered towns and settlements higher up. A fair chunk of the land is occupied by only two ranches.

Yet this salt-of-the-earth region is worth visiting on its own merits, if for no other reason than to escape the lowland heat. Daytime temperatures up here are only mildly warm, and after dark, peaceful, starry nights get brisk.

On the main street of Makawao, an old paniolo town that still hosts an annual Fourth of July rodeo parade, you'll see the general store and steakhouse, but also evidence of a growing alternative culture drifting up from Paia on the coast. From Makawao, country roads lead off every which way, perfect for sunset views and drivers without destinations.

Kula, in the navel of the Upcountry, boasts rich farmland where most of Maui's vegetables and flowers are grown. Landscaped botanical gardens and protea shops are open to the public, right up onto the approach road to Haleakala. Above Kula are the delightful cloud forests of Polipoli Spring State Recreation Area, where rugged mountain biking and hiking trails await the intrepid.

Farther up, the Kula Hwy passes the tiny towns of Waiakoa and Keokea and, after a long stretch of ranchlands, becomes the Piilani Hwy (Hwy 31), which circles the island all the way to Hana.

Highlights

- Cheering on *paniolo*, Hawaii's expert cowboys, at the annual Fourth of July rodeo

- Sampling the bounty of Kula, Maui's verdant garden land

- Kicking back in rustic Makawao town and winding up the heights of Olinda Rd

- Single-track mountain biking through the redwood forests of Polipoli Spring

- Refreshing yourself at a peaceful B&B around Haiku village

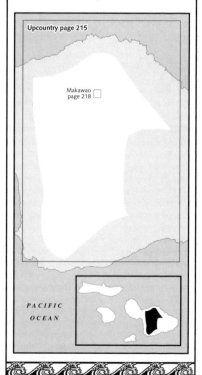

Upcountry page 215

Makawao page 218

PACIFIC OCEAN

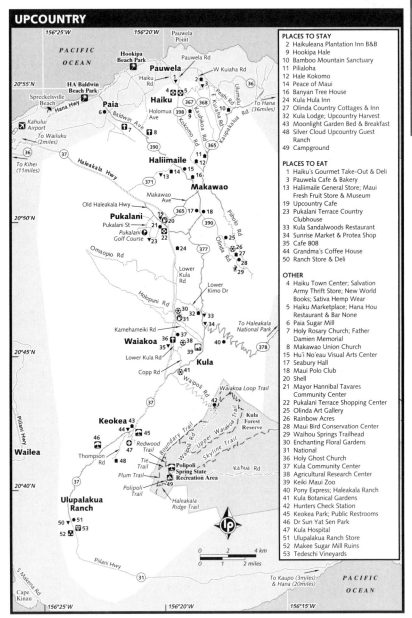

UPCOUNTRY

Map labels

PACIFIC OCEAN

156°25'W   156°20'W   Pauwela Point

Hookipa Beach Park
Pauwela Rd
Pauwela
W Kuiaha Rd

Haiku Rd
20°55'N   HA Baldwin Beach Park
Spreckelsville Beach
Hana Hwy
Haiku
Kahului Airport
To Wailuku (2miles)
Paia
Baldwin Ave
Holomua Ave
To Hana (36miles)

36   37
To Kihei (11miles)
Haleakala Hwy

Haliimaile

Makawao
Makawao Ave
Old Haleakala Hwy
20°50'N
Pukalani
Pukalani St
Pukalani Golf Course
Omaopio Rd

Lower Kula Rd
Lower Kimo Dr

Holopuni Rd
Kamehameiki Rd
To Haleakala National Park
20°45'N
Waiakoa
Lower Kula Rd
Kula
Copp Rd
Waipoli Rd
Waiakoa Loop Trail

Piilani Hwy
Keokea
Wailea
Redwood Trail
Thompson Rd
Tie Trail
Plum Trail
20°40'N
Ulupalakua Ranch
Polipoli Trail
Polipoli Spring State Recreation Area
Kahua Rd
Haleakala Ridge Trail

Kula Forest Reserve
Upper Waiakoa Trail
Skyline Trail
Boundary Trail
Waipoli Rd

0   2   4 km
0   1   2 miles

S Makena Rd
Piilani Hwy
Cape Kinau
To Kaupo (3miles) & Hana (20miles)

PACIFIC OCEAN

156°25'W   156°20'W   156°15'W

For information on Paia, see the Eastern Maui chapter.

PAIA TO MAKAWAO
Baldwin Avenue

Baldwin Ave (Hwy 390) slowly rolls from Paia to Makawao. The road starts out among the sugarcane fields near the old Paia Mill and passes two historic churches. The first is **Holy Rosary Church & Father Damien Memorial** (☎ *579-9951, 945 Baldwin Rd)*. Built in 1989, the simple garden memorial honors the priest who first went to work among the lepers on Molokai island.

Just before the road begins to really twist and turn, look for a solid stone building framed by palm trees, **Makawao Union Church** (☎ *579-9261, 1445 Baldwin Ave)*. The church's architect was the influential CW Dickey (see Architecture in the Facts about Maui chapter earlier), and inside koa wood pews and high-beamed ceilings make way for a vintage pipe organ. Perhaps its most beautiful aspect are the abstract stained-glass windows.

Past the 5-mile marker, Baldwin Ave rises to Kaluanui, the former plantation home of Harry and Ethel Baldwin. Another CW Dickey design, this house shows many of the well-known traits of early 20th-century Hawaiian Regional style that he pioneered. Now fully restored, the building belongs to **Hu'i No'eau Visual Arts Center** (☎ *572-6560,* W *www.huinoeau.com, 2841 Baldwin Ave; admission free; open 10am-4pm Mon-Sat)*, which takes its name (literally meaning 'an arts or skills club') from the group founded here by Ethel Baldwin in the 1930s. The center offers classes in printmaking, Hawaiian feather art, pottery, woodcarving and a dozen other arts. In the main house are now two galleries, a solarium and a small gift shop. Pick up a self-guided tour booklet of the grounds from the front desk.

Haliimaile

Haliimaile is a little pineapple town in the middle of plantation fields. Its nearly unpronounceable name means 'fragrant twining shrub' after the *maile* plants that once covered the area. They were coveted by Hawaiians for making horseshoe-shaped green lei. To get here, turn right (north) from Baldwin Ave onto Haliimaile Rd, a pastoral byway that winds slowly toward Pukalani and the Haleakala Hwy.

Although there is no town center per se, that's part of the charm. The old general store, built circa 1925, has been converted into one of the best restaurants on this side of Maui.

Next door is **Maui Fresh Fruit Store & Museum** (☎ *573-5129, 870 Haliimaile Rd; admission free; open 10am-6pm Mon-Sat)*, selling pineapples, local produce and gourmet food stuffs. At the back of this homey shop are a few photo exhibits and antique objects from the Maui Pineapple Company's century-long history on the island, providing a short, but sweet introduction to an era that has almost totally passed in Hawaii.

Places to Stay & Eat Haliimaile is *the* place to get away from it all. Consequently there is only one place to stay and another to eat.

Peace Of Maui (☎ *572-5045, 888-475-5045,* W *www.peaceofmaui.com, 1290 Haliimaile Rd)* Singles/doubles $40/45, 1-bedroom cottage with private bath & kitchen $75. Close to Baldwin Rd, this is a down-to-earth B&B with astounding sunsets across the open fields. The stand-alone cottage has a kitchen and sun deck with a distant ocean view. Guests in the main house share a full kitchen, barbecue grill, telephone and a place to store surfboards. Breakfast is not includedin the price, but the friendly owners provide complimentary homegrown fruit. Discount car rental and airport pick-ups are available.

Haliimaile General Store (☎ *572-2666, fax 572-7128,* W *www.haliimailegeneralstore.com, 900 Haliimaile Rd)* Lunch $9-12, dinner entrées $18-28. Entrées 50% off Mon. Open 11am-2:30pm Mon-Fri & 5:30pm-9:30pm daily. Just stepping through the gracious lanai and into the peach-colored general store feels like spring, with dramatic flower arrangements and artwork all around. Accompanied by a California-heavy wine list, the exuberant cooking of executive chef Bev Gannon fuses Hawaiian and Asian styles, for example ahi sashimi napoleon layered with smoked salmon and wontons. Lunch plays it safe with meatloaf sandwiches, onion rings and Kula garden salads.

MAKAWAO

In the 19th century ranching around Makawao got a real boost when voracious whalers docking in Lahaina clamored for fresh, red meat. Today the town is still bordered by working ranches. Every year on the Fourth of July, before the big rodeo kicks off, paniolo in their *palaka* (checkered shirts) and festive lei parade on horseback down the main street, which is lined with old-fashioned false-front buildings.

In the past decade, a health food store has set up down the street from Makawao Feed & Garden, and the gun shops have partly given way to storefronts specializing in Chinese herbs and yoga. Check the bulletin board at the health food store if you want to know what's happening in the alternative community.

So far Makawao remains more redneck than Rastafarian, and it's a very local scene. Everything is within a few minutes' walk of the main intersection of Baldwin Ave (Hwy 390) and Hwy 365, which cuts over from Pukalani. The Makawao Library (☎ 573-8786), 1159 Makawao Ave, is open noon to 8pm on Monday and Wednesday, 9:30am to 5pm on Tuesday, Thursday and Saturday.

Places to Stay

The bulletin board at the health food store often has ads for rooms and studios that can be rented on a daily, weekly or monthly basis. See Places to Stay under the following Olinda Rd section as well.

*Hale Hookipa Inn (☎ 572-6698, **W** www .maui-bed-and-breakfast.com, 32 Pakani Place)* Rooms $85-105, 2-bedroom suite $140-155. Hale Hookipa is in a richly historic 1920s Craftsman-style house near town. Rooms are furnished with antiques

and art, and the most expensive has its own lanai entrance and private bath with a claw-foot tub. The Kona Wing suite sleeps up to four people and has its own country kitchen. A continental buffet breakfast is served under the big Cook Island pine tree.

*Banyan Tree House (☎ 572-9021, fax 573-5052, **W** www.banyantreehouse.com, 3265 Baldwin Ave)* Cottages $85-110, 3-bedroom house $300. Banyan and monkeypod trees cover the grounds of an estate known as 'Sunnyside,' just north of downtown. Beyond the bamboo gates is a former plantation manager's home and four romantic cottages complete with private bath and lanai, some of which have cooking facilities, hammocks and ocean views. There's also a swimming pool.

Places to Eat

Makawao has some funky options you won't find anywhere else: a true steak house, a swanky Italian super club and famous local eats.

Down to Earth Natural Foods (☎ 572-1488, 1169 Makawao Ave) Open 8am-8pm daily. This healthy grocery store has organic produce, bulk and packaged foods, a dairy section, juices, sandwiches and a good salad bar with hot takeout items sold by the pound.

Rodeo General Store (☎ 572-1868, 3661 Baldwin Ave) Open 6:30am-10pm daily. It's your basic Hawaiian general store, good for groceries and supplies. Lest anyone accuse Makawao of not really being the Wild West anymore, note that this place was robbed at knifepoint in 1998.

Budget *Kitada's Kau Kau Corner (☎ 572-7241, Baldwin Ave)* Dishes under $6, combo plates $8. Open 6:30am-1:30pm Mon-Sat. Kitada's, in a funky old building opposite The Courtyard galleries, has been making saimin for generations. You can slurp down a generous-sized bowl for just $3.

Komoda Store & Bakery (☎ 572-7261, 3674 Baldwin Ave) Items $2-6. Open 6am-1:30pm Mon-Sat. Just south of Makawao's main intersection, family-run Komoda bakes tempting cream puffs, cinnamon rolls,

UPCOUNTRY

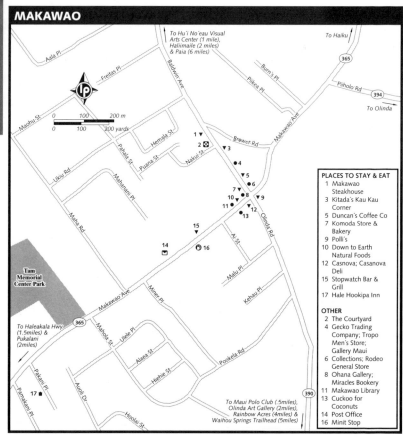

MAKAWAO

To Hu'i No'eau Visual Arts Center (1 mile), Haliimaile (2 miles) & Paia (6 miles)

To Haiku

To Olinda

Tam Memorial Center Park

To Haleakala Hwy (1.5miles) & Pukalani (2miles)

To Maui Polo Club (.5miles), Olinda Art Gallery (2miles), Rainbow Acres (4miles) & Waihou Springs Trailhead (5miles)

PLACES TO STAY & EAT
1 Makawao Steakhouse
3 Kitada's Kau Kau Corner
5 Duncan's Coffee Co
7 Komoda Store & Bakery
9 Polli's
10 Down to Earth Natural Foods
12 Casnova; Casanova Deli
15 Stopwatch Bar & Grill
17 Hale Hookipa Inn

OTHER
2 The Courtyard
4 Gecko Trading Company; Tropo Men's Store; Gallery Maui
6 Collections; Rodeo General Store
8 Ohana Gallery; Miracles Bookery
11 Makawao Library
13 Cuckoo for Coconuts
14 Post Office
16 Minit Stop

malasadas and other pastries. In fact, they're so famous they typically sell out by noon.

Casanova Deli (☎ 572-0220, *1188 Makawao Ave*) Dishes around $6. Open 7:30am-6pm Mon-Sat, 8:30am-5pm Sun. Casanova is the epicenter of hip, where fresh-faced locals dunk their biscotti and make gossipy mincemeat of passersby. Never mind, since the Italian delicatessen indoors is great for full country breakfasts and giant sandwiches (lemon chicken pesto or vegetable primavera, perhaps?). Strong coffee and tiramisu are prerequisites for lingering at chess tables.

There's also ***Duncan's Coffee Co*** (☎ 573-9075, *3647 Baldwin Ave*) for coffee without any attitude, plus all sorts of soups, sandwiches and baked goods made on-site.

Stopwatch Bar & Grill (☎ 572-1380, *1127 Makawao Ave*) Sandwiches $5-7, entrées $7-12. Open 11am-midnight daily; food served 11am-9pm (8pm Sunday). This sports bar is a favorite with those looking to fill their stomachs on the cheap; the two-for-one meal specials on some weeknights make fried food taste even better. Some more unusual entrées like Thai-style fish make their way onto the dinner menu, but it's the fruit and cream pies that win people over.

Mid-Range & Top End *Polli's* (☎ 572-7808, 1202 Makawao Ave) Breakfast & lunch dishes $6-10, dinner combination plates from $12. New York steak Mon $10. Keiki menu Tues $2. Open 7am-10pm Mon-Sat, 8am-10pm Sun. A sign over this Tex-Mex cantina says bluntly, 'Come in and eat, or we'll both starve.' The small bar can barely hold all those who are just waiting for tables to order huevos rancheros, baby back ribs or 'Makawowie' tacos. Vegetarians can substitute tofu or herb-simmered veggie taco mix.

Casanova (☎ 572-0220, 1188 Makawao Ave) Open for lunch 11:30am-2:30pm Mon-Sat, dinner 5:30pm-9:30pm daily. Lunch $8-12, dinner entrées from $20. It's a decidedly posh place to sup. Hot Italian sandwiches and pastas, plus crisp pizza baked in a kiawe-fired brick oven ($10 to $16), make way for at dinner island-fresh versions of calamari fritti or rigatoni Beverly Hills in vodka-tomato sauce.

Makawao Steakhouse (☎ 572-8711, 3612 Baldwin Ave) Mains $20-30. When all the dust settles on this cowboy town, you knew there had to be at least one steak house still standing. Here even the surroundings look old-fashioned, courtesy of pine paneling and paniolo photographs. Surf-and-turf specials and $20 all-you-can-eat nights make it a classic.

Entertainment

Casanova (☎ 572-0220, W www.casanova maui.com, 1188 Makawao Ave) Admission local/big name bands $5-10/20-25. Entertainment Wed-Sun. This is East Maui's hottest music spot, bringing in mainland performers as well as some of Hawaii's top musicians. DJs typically spin on 'Wild Wahine' midweek, followed by live bands – anything from salsa or blues to Jawaiian and Cuban jazz – on weekends. Casanova is an upscale scene, even if it is Upcountry (so leave your rubbah slippah at home).

Stopwatch Bar & Grill (☎ 572-1380, 1127 Makawao Ave) Makawao's only sports

bar has live music and DJs on some weekends, usually with no cover charge.

Shopping

In **The Courtyard** (3620 Baldwin Ave), there are a few gallery shops, notably **Hot Island Glass** (☎ 572-4527), where glassblowers are at work until 4:30pm daily, and **Designing Wahine** (☎ 573-0990) for local crafts.

Ohana Gallery (☎ 573-4749, 3682 Baldwin Ave) Real artwork by Upcountry artists, particularly innovative pottery and koa wood carvings, is sold here. Prices are just a tad higher than you're probably willing to pay, but look for sales.

Gallery Maui (☎ 572-8092, 1156 Makawao Ave) Down a leafy side lane off Baldwin Ave is the realm of bold and beautiful art, where free-form sculptures and enormous stained-glass pieces framed with bamboo are on display.

Gecko Trading Company (☎ 572-0249, 3621 Baldwin Ave) Claiming fans as far away as Honolulu, this feminine harbor of breezy skirts and tea blouses almost seems out of place on Makawao's muddy streets.

Tropo Men's Store (☎ 573-0356, 3643 Baldwin Ave) At last a serious place for hip aloha shirts, island hats and ties.

Cuckoo for Coconuts (☎ 573-6887, 1158 Makawao Ave) Get your vintage Hawaiian wear, Halloween costumes for Lahaina's Mardi Gras and all sorts of kitsch at Cuckoo's.

Miracles Bookery (☎ 572-2317, 3682 Baldwin Ave) Every alternative practitioner worth their weight in herbs or incense can be found here browsing the soulful tomes on Buddhism or stopping in to have their tarot read.

OLINDA ROAD

Scenic back roads head out in all directions from Makawao, and almost any you choose to explore will make an excellent country drive. If you're the kind of person who needs some kind of destination, choose Olinda Rd high on the slopes of Haleakala.

Olinda Rd picks up where Baldwin Ave leaves off and drifts up past the Oskie Rice

Arena, where rodeos take place. On autumn Sunday afternoons the **Maui Polo Club** (☎ 572-4915, W www.mauipolo.com; adult $3) plays its games at the polo fields here. On the opposite side of the road is **Seabury Hall** (☎ 572-7235), a prestigious college prep school, which hosts an annual craft fair in May.

Most of the folks living in rural Olinda are either farmers or artists. Soon you'll pass **Olinda Art Gallery** (1711 Olinda Rd; open 1pm-4pm Tues-Sat) and **Rainbow Acres** (☎ 573-8318, 2233 Olinda Rd; open 9am-4pm Tues & Thur), a garden of cactus and succulents for sale. From here, the road continues its close series of switchbacks, rising through forest past a few dramatic scenic turnouts.

Past the 11-mile marker is the **Maui Bird Conservation Center**. It is currently closed to the public, but its efforts to breed and release native Hawaiian bird life, including a few of the last native Hawaiian crows, are ongoing. Another minute farther along on the right-hand side of the road you'll see the signposted **Waihou Springs trailhead** (see

Don't Say Giddyup, Say Awiwi!

The history of *paniolo,* or Hawaiian cowboys, dates back at least fifty years before the Wild West cowboys on the mainland climbed into their stirrups after Custer's last stand.

It all started with Captain Vancouver, who landed the first cattle on the Big Island of Hawaii in 1793. The herd flourished, thanks to Kamehameha the Great placing a *kapu* on their slaughter. A decade later another foreigner by the name of Richard Cleveland brought horses to the Big Island and Maui. By the time Kamehameha III took over, both horses and cows were running rampant on the islands. So the king invited vaqueros from Spanish California to show the first Big Island cowboys the ropes in 1832. In fact, the word paniolo is likely a corruption of *español,* meaning Spaniard.

Soon there were working cowboys on every island, rounding up cattle and driving them down the mountainside, then swimming them out past sharks to the cattle boats headed for Honolulu markets. A whole paniolo culture developed, of slack-key guitar music, *palaka* (checkered shirts), *lauhala* hats and lei that told where each cowboy was from: pink roses for Maui, orange flowers from Lanai and kukui nuts on Molokai. Interestingly, Hawaiian women never rode sidesaddle, but instead draped themselves with yards of fabric and rode astride.

It was Ikua Purdy who brought the paniolo lasting fame in 1908 when he won the world championship for rodeo steer-roping at Frontier Days in Cheyenne, Wyoming. Even today his record of two steers in 56 seconds has never been bested. For 25 years Purdy worked as the foreman of Ulupalakua Ranch, where he was buried in 1945. A few dozen paniolo still follow in his footsteps on the national rodeo circuit, and in 1999 he was inducted into the National Cowboy Hall of Fame.

If you want to know more, *Aloha Cowboy* by Virginia Cowan-Smith and Bonnie Domrose Stone is a captivating account of 200 years of paniolo life. Or you could go out on a trail ride and experience the life for yourself.

Paniolo Talk:

pipi	cattle
kamalii or *keik*	calves
laho	bull
oni	time to move out, start work
hemo ka pua	open the gate
awiwi	hurry up
malia	slow down

the Hiking special section at the end of the Activities chapter). At the top of Olinda Rd, you can turn left onto Piiholo Rd and wind back down into Makawao.

Places to Stay

Olinda Country Cottages & Inn *(☎ 572-1453, 800-932-3435, fax 573-5326, ⓦ www .mauibnbcottages.com, 2660 Olinda Rd)* Room/suite $120/130, cottages $195-220. Two-night minimum stay. This stately Upcountry home and protea farm perches at the edge of the road and looks out over all of West Maui toward the ocean. The Pineapple Sweet in the main house has a cheery kitchen and panoramic windows. The luxury 'Hidden Cottage' has its own kitchen, washer/dryer and French doors leading onto an ocean-view deck with a bathtub built for two. Credit cards are not accepted.

Aloha Cottage *(☎ 573-8500, 888-328-3330, fax 573-8555, ⓦ www.alohacottage.com)* Cottage $195. Also called Lotus Blossom or The Thai Treehouse, the Aloha Cottage is built from imported Asian teak and set among groves of rainbow eucalyptus and bamboo. It is a faithful replica of a traditional Thai house, yet with all the modern extras. An open-air tub on a partly screened deck is perfect for midnight star-gazing. Private yoga classes and gourmet meals can be arranged.

HAIKU

Alexander & Baldwin grew their first 12 acres of sugarcane in 1869 near Haiku, and the village once had both a busy sugar mill and a pineapple cannery. Today Haiku, a scattered community stretching from Makawao north down the slopes to the coastal Hana Hwy, is seeing a bit of a revival. It's primarily a small-scale farming community, but its rural charm and alternative vibes have also drawn windsurfers, artists and other new residents.

The intersection of Haiku and Kokomo Rds is all that marks the center of Haiku. Across from the old cannery, a string of shops testifies to the village's alternative culture: an herbalist's pharmacy, a Salvation Army thrift store, **Sativa Hemp Wear** *(☎ 575-9988)* factory outlet and **New World Books** *(☎ 575-2200)* for essential oils, Zen alarm clocks and feng shui supplies.

For mundane photocopy, fax and shipping services, visit 1-Stop Postal Plus Shop *(☎ 575-2049)*, 800 Haiku Rd, in the Haiku Town Center.

Places to Stay

In Haiku combining a rural getaway with easy access to both the coast and mountains is easy. Although Haiku feels like the middle of nowhere, from Kahului airport, it's only around a 30-minute drive to most of these B&Bs. Most are small family-run operations, so make your reservations well in advance. The minimum stay is usually at least three days. Some places are available through booking agencies in Paia (see the East Maui chapter earlier), or a simple Web search will turn up handfuls more.

Hookipa Hale *(☎ 575-9357, fax 575-9482, ⓦ www.hookipahale.com, 1350 Kauhikoa Rd)* Rooms/luxury suite/1-bedroom apartment/2-bedroom cottage from $40/50/70/90. Almost too good to be true, this private country home is fully equipped with anything guests might need: full kitchen, refrigerator, barbecue grills, an open-air sitting area with twinkling white lights and most importantly, gracious hosts. Each spacious room has its own TV and shared telephone line, while the suite has an enormous private bathroom. A security deposit is required, and all types of travelers are welcome.

Hale Kokomo *(☎ 572-5613, ⓔ iej@ maui.net, ⓦ www.bbonline.com/hi/kokomo, 2719 Kokomo Rd)* Rooms $50-60, suites $80. Both lush and secluded, Hale Kokomo is a sprightly Victorian-style house with palm ferns in front. It's only ten minutes from the beach, too. Basic, cozy rooms share a bathroom and fridge, while suites have their own bathroom (not necessarily attached). All rates include breakfast.

Bamboo Mountain Sanctuary *(☎ 572-4897, fax 572-8848, ⓔ bamboomt@maui.net, ⓦ www.maui.net/~bamboomt, 1111 Kaupakalua Rd)* Singles/doubles $55/75, 2-bedroom oceanview cottage $150. In the mid-20th century this was a Japanese plantation house, which was later converted into the famed Maui Zendo by Robert Aitken Roshi's Diamond Sangha. Needless to say, if you're looking for a meditative experience, this is it. The organic setting is serene, on the edge of a forest preserve with ocean and mountain views all around. Rooms are simple and spare, but guests share access to a kitchen and living room with a video library. All guests are invited to attend morning *zazen*.

Lanikai Farm (☎ 572-1111, 800-572-1111, fax 572-3498, e lanibb@maui.net, w www.maui.net/~lanibb) Singles/doubles $65/70, 1-/2-bedroom cottage $80/105. Lanikai Farm is a modern place, set far back in the woods. Most rooms have a shared bath, and the cottages have a kitchen, fireplace and lanai. Breakfast includes homemade muffins and roasted macadamia nuts from the farm. Ask about discounts for families and extended stays.

Pilialoha (☎ 572-1440, fax 572-4612, e cottage@pilialoha.com, w www.pili aloha.com, 2512 Kaupakalua Rd) Cottage $110/130/150 per single/double/triple. This modest, split-level cottage set in a small eucalyptus grove has oak floors, sliding glass doors and a full kitchen, plus all the modern amenities. Hawaiiana reference books and fresh-cut flowers are scattered about, and Kona coffee, fruit and homemade breads are found on the breakfast table.

Haikuleana Plantation Inn B&B (☎ 575-2890, fax 575-9177, w www.haikuleana.com, 555 Haiku Rd) Suites $100-200. Located on a jungly private drive near Pauwela Cafe, this 1870s plantation doctor's home is furnished with antiques and vintage Hawaiian maps and art. Skip the more modern rooms in favor of the cedar-paneled Sandwich Islands suite, which comes with its own 18th-century captain's desk. An even more antique Buddha sits in the garden sanctuary.

Places to Eat & Drink

Pauwela Cafe & Bakery (☎ 575-9242, 375 W Kuiaha Rd) Items $2-7. Open 6am-2pm daily. This cafe is worth a detour off the Hana Hwy any time for all-day breakfasts,

banana bread, kalua pork sandwiches and strong coffee or fresh juice. Look for the collection of colored glass bottles in the window.

Haiku's Gourmet Take-Out & Deli (☎ 575-5404, 771 Haiku Rd) Mains $6-12. Open 6am-8pm daily. In a little house downhill from the old cannery, this is another good bakery serving deli lunches, salads and plates of chicken or ribs.

Veg Out (☎ 575-5320, Haiku Town Center, 810 Kokomo Rd) Most items $3-7. Open 10:30am-7:30pm Mon-Fri, 11:30am-6pm Sat & Sun. As you can see, healthy food just doesn't go out of style in Haiku. This vegetarian café has a long menu of burritos, salads and sandwiches, with fresh produce supplied by the same Upcountry truck farmers who eat here.

Colleen's Bake Shop & Cannery Pizza (☎ 575-9211, Haiku Town Center, 810 Kokomo Rd) Sandwiches & salads $5-11, whole pizza $13-21. Bake shop open 6am-9pm daily; pizzeria after 4:45pm only. The baked goods and sandwiches here are healthy, if not always the most tasty. However, some swear that the whole-wheat crust pizza is the best ever, as long as it's hot out of the oven. House specialties include the 'Virtually Vegan' and 'Sweet Pea' with pesto, ricotta, roasted peppers and, yes, green peas.

Hana Hou Restaurant & Bar None (☎ 575-2661, 810 Haiku Rd) Most dishes $5-15. Open 10am-10pm daily. In Hawaiian pidgin, the name means 'do it again.' Who are we to disagree? For some local grinds, pupus or burgers and beer, visit these friendly folks at the back of the old cannery parking lot.

PUKALANI

Pukalani, or 'hole in the heavens,' is the last major town before Haleakala National Park. It's a sunny, residential area of about 6000 residents, but there's nothing here to see.

If you need gas or supplies, take Hwy 37 into town. The Pukalani Terrace Shopping Center, located south of the intersection of Hwys 365 and 37, has a coin laundry, a bank with an ATM and the Pukalani post office (☎ 572-0019), which is open from 9am to

4pm weekdays and 10am to noon on Saturday morning.

Pukalani Golf Course (☎ 572-1314, ⓦ www.pukalanigolf.com, 360 Pukalani St; Green fees & cart for morning/afternoon tee-off $63/42) Among Maui's country clubs, Pukalani has sweeping Upcountry views and a very local feel.

Places to Eat
There's a ***Foodland*** supermarket and a few local eateries on Pukalani Terrace. Up the road next to McDonald's is a ***convenience store*** selling fried chicken and giant steak fries by the piece. It's legendary among locals.

Cow Country Cafe (Upcountry Cafe; ☎ 572-2395, 7 Aewa Place) Open 7am-3pm & 5:30pm-9pm Mon-Sat, Sun brunch 7am-1pm. If you're headed downhill from Haleakala after sunrise, skip the pricey Kula restaurants and make your way here instead. Although it's hidden in a little strip mall, and also confusingly called the Upcountry Cafe, the cow signs are easy to spot from the highway. Count on magnificent breakfast muffins and pancakes, guava shakes and sandwiches on home-baked bread later in the day.

Pukalani Terrace Country Clubhouse (☎ 572-1325, 360 Pukalani St) Buffet $9.50. Breakfast 7:30am-10:30am Mon-Fri, 6:30am-10:30am Sat & Sun, lunch 10:30am-2pm & dinner 5pm-9pm daily. The Pukalani golf club restaurant boasts grand ocean views. Either take the all-you-can-eat lunch buffet option or order a complete Hawaiian plate (around $10) with kalua pig, lomi salmon, poi and haupia for dessert. Don't expect great things, but it's an experience worth having if you haven't yet tried local Hawaiian food.

KULA
The Kula region, perched at an average elevation of 3000 feet, is the agricultural heartland of Maui. Crops such as lettuce, tomatoes, carrots, cauliflower and cabbage thrive in Kula's warm days, cool nights and rich volcanic soil. No gourmet cook in Hawaii would be anywhere without sweet Kula onions.

In the 19th century many of the Portuguese and Chinese sugarcane workers who saved enough money to move off the plantations came up to Kula and set up farms. During the California gold rush, Kula farmers shipped so many potatoes off to the miners that the area became known as 'Nu Kaleponi,' the Hawaiian pronunciation of New California.

Kula also grows most of Hawaii's protea, large bright flowers with an unusual flair. Some, like the pincushion varieties, are very delicate, and others have spinelike petals. Almost 90% of the carnations used in lei throughout Hawaii are grown in Kula, as are many of the chrysanthemums. In spring, you'll see bursts of color right along the roadside, as the purple blossoms of the jacaranda tree and the yellow flowers of gold oak bloom in profusion.

Gardens
All of Kula is a garden. But if you want to take a closer look, you can visit one of the many public walk-through gardens. They do begin to look alike and outside of winter can be quite dry, so unless you're an avid gardener, a quick stop at one should suffice.

The University of Hawaii maintains a 20-acre **Agricultural Research Center** (☎ 878-1213, Mauna Place; admission free; garden open 7am-3:30pm Mon-Thur) above Waiakoa Village. It's here that Hawaii's first protea were established in 1965, and dozens of new hybrids are under development. Hybrid cuttings are distributed to protea farms across Hawaii, which supply fresh flowers to the US, Japan and Europe. Some sections of the garden are used for experiments in plant pathology, but the rest is open to the public from Monday to Thursday (Friday is set aside for pesticide spraying). If you call ahead, you may get a personally guided tour. To get here, turn off Hwy 37 between the 12- and 13-mile markers and follow Copp Rd for a half mile and turn left onto Mauna Place.

Of all the commercial gardens, the **Enchanting Floral Gardens** is the most sunny, open and orderly, and has both tropical and cool-weather flowers (☎ 878-2531; adult/

child $5/1; open 9am-5pm daily). It's on Hwy 37 around the 10-mile marker. The **Kula Botanical Gardens** *(☎ 878-1715; adult/ child $5/1; open 9am-4pm daily)* is far less appealing, but they do have a Taboo Garden of poisonous plants.

There are many more shops that sell and ship protea, as well as other exotic flowers. **Sunrise Market & Protea Shop** *(☎ 878-1600, 876-0200, 800-222-2797, Crater Rd)* has a

---

Protea

It's a flower that only a mother could love. The protea family, which is named after the Greek god Proteus who could change shapes at will, comes in more than 1500 different varieties, from macadamia nuts to the showy King Protea, South Africa's national flower.

Originally all protea were native to South Africa. Their flowers vary from spiky carnations to stalks of tiny flowers held by brightly-colored bracts to artichoke blossoms, and they can be as small as a few millimeters or up to 12 inches in diameter. There are also protea evergreens, shrubs and herbs. Currently the Protea Atlas project in South Africa locates unique strands that are on the brink of eradication and stops them from dying out.

Hawaiian protea (pronounced 'PRO-teeah') account for 90% of the world market, with 85 species alone situated solely on the slopes of Haleakala. Protea thrive on sandy, acidic soil, and the cool nights following warm days in the Upcountry are ideal. There are only 27 protea farms left in the state, mostly family-run fields of under 10 acres. Upcountry nurseries can advise you on how to ship protea or take them home legally through customs. Often people along the island's rural highways will set out pots of protea that you can drive by and pick up, leaving money for them on the honor system. Fresh flowers can last up to three weeks after being cut and some arrangements dry quite well, but only the humble little macadamia nut protea can be eaten.

---

free roadside garden. The store sells dried and fresh flower arrangements and is located a quarter mile up from the intersection of Hwys 378 and 377 past the Haleakala National Park sign. Next to the Kula Lodge, **Upcountry Harvest** *(☎ 878-2824, 800-575-6470)* sells protea and also orchids.

Octagonal Church

The octagonal **Holy Ghost Church** *(☎ 878-1261, Lower Kula Rd; admission by donation; open daily)* is a hillside landmark in Waiakoa village. Built in the 1890s by former Portuguese plantation workers, the church has a beautifully ornate interior that put it on the National Register of Historic Places. The wooden altar and stations of the cross were done by an Austrian master carver and shipped to Hawaii.

Why an octagonal church? Some suggest it pays homage to Lisbon's Church of the Holy Ghost, which was built by Queen Isabella as thanksgiving for divine salvation from a plague that was spreading across Europe. Others attribute the design to Father James Biessel's having grown up near the octagonal chapel built by Charlemagne in Aachen, Germany. If you want to know more, open up the history binder shelved near the guest registry. Services are held at 5pm on Saturday and 9:30am on Sunday.

Keiki Maui Zoo

Run by the Maui Zoological Society, this small petting zoo *(☎ 878-2189, Kekaulike Ave)* harbors, of all things, a giraffe, as well as other wild beasties. It opens to the public for special zoo events usually on the first Saturday of the month from noon to 3pm ($5 per person). Guided tours can be arranged by prior appointment.

Haleakala Ranch

With vast holdings that once included even the grand volcano crater itself, the historic **Haleakala Ranch** *(HQ ☎ 572-7236, ⓦ www .haleakalaranch.com, Crater Rd)* is still in operation after 110 years. Qualifying rounds for the national rodeo circuit take place

Haleakala volcano looks across to the Big Island in the distance.

ANDREW SALLMON

What planet are you on? Haleakala NP

ANN CECIL

A well-deserved rest on Haleakala's rim

ANN CECIL

It's easy on the way down. Haleakala NP

ANN CECIL

Puu Pehe (Sweetheart Rock), Manele Bay, Lanai

Morning! Hulopoe Beach, Lanai

'X' marks the spot. Shipwreck Beach, Lanai

Rugged beauty and tangled history, Kalaupapa Peninsula, Molokai

Church Row, Molokai

here, as do roping practice sessions and keiki rodeo events a few times per month. They are also the only outfit that leads horseback tours inside Haleakala crater.

Pony Express (☎ 667-2200, fax 878-3581, ⓦ *www.ponyexpresstours.com*) Half-/full-day Haleakala volcano ride to crater floor/ Kapalaoa cabin with lunch $155/190, ranch rides $60-105. These stables are set in a eucalyptus grove off Crater Rd, about 2½ miles up from Hwy 377. Reservations are required and be sure to wear long pants and close-toed footwear (no sandals).

Places to Stay

Camp Kula (☎/fax 876-0000, ⓔ *camper@ maui.net, PO Box 111, Kula, HI 96790*) Rooms $35-80. Camp Kula is a gay-friendly bed and breakfast on seven secluded acres with pretty views of central Maui. There are five guest rooms, all wheelchair-accessible, ranging from a single bed with shared bath to a full suite with lanai. Rates include a breakfast of herbal teas, homegrown fruits and baked goodies. Guests also have access to a full kitchen and free Internet use.

Kula Hula Inn (☎ 572-9351, 888-485-2466, fax 572-1132, ⓦ *www.maui.net/~kula hula, 112 Hoopalua Dr*) Room $90, suites $110-125, cottage $145. For a taste of country living, try this modern home set on a private estate enjoying ocean and mountain views. Accommodations choices start with the New England-style room, move into the tropical Plumeria suite with waterbed and Jacuzzi, and finish at the fully outfitted Hula Moon cottage. Families are welcome, and breakfast is served daily except Sunday. Ask about discounts for extended stays.

Kula Lodge (☎ 878-2517, 800-233-1535, fax 878-2518, ⓦ *www.kulalodge.com, RR1 Box 475, Kula, HI 96790*) Studio $100, cottages with lofts $135, larger cottages $175. Kula Lodge, on Hwy 377, has five cottages in the same complex as its restaurant. All have private sundecks but are not notably special for the money. The cheapest accommodations are in a studio without a view. There are no TVs or phones, and breakfast is not included in the rates.

Places to Eat

If you're coming downhill from Haleakala during daylight hours and aren't too hungry to wait just a little bit longer, bypass the Kula restaurants and head straight for Cow Country Cafe (see Places to Eat in the Pukalani section, earlier).

Sunrise Market & Protea Shop (☎ 878-1600, 876-0200, 800-222-2797, *Crater Rd*) Open 7:30am-4pm daily. Get your post-sunrise java here along with bakery items, wrapped sandwiches or fresh and dried fruits.

Kula Lodge (☎ 878-2517, 800-233-1535, fax 878-2518, ⓦ *www.kulalodge.com*) Breakfast $7-10, lunch $11-18, dinner entrées $18-28. Open daily for breakfast 6:30am-11:15am, lunch 11:45am-4:15pm, dinner 4:45pm-9pm, Sun brunch 6:30am-1pm. This rustic lodge, on Hwy 377 less than a mile north of Haleakala Crater Rd, has wraparound windows with fine views of the central plains and the ocean beyond. Alas, the food is less than inspiring. Miso oysters Rockefeller or stuffed chicken diablo sound enticing, but they aren't tasty and prices are high.

Kula Sandalwoods Restaurant (☎ 878-3523, *Kula Hwy*) Dishes $7-12. Open 6:30am-2pm Mon-Sat, 6:30am-noon Sun. You'll find a similar view and better food at this family-run restaurant just before the Kula Lodge on the mauka side of Hwy 377. Breakfast includes waffles, signature omelettes and a superb eggs Benedict, while lunch features hearty sandwiches and fresh salads.

Cafe 808 (☎ 878-6874, *Lower Kula Rd*) Dishes $3-10. Open 6am-8pm daily. This local café is a quarter mile south of the Octagonal Church in Waiakoa. Its menu is as long and wide as its kitchen. Show up before 11am for banana pancakes, omelettes with home fries or a classic *loco moco*. Sandwiches and burgers compete with mixed lunch plates all the way through dinnertime.

POLIPOLI SPRING STATE RECREATION AREA

Polipoli Spring is high up in the Kula Forest Reserve on the western slope of Haleakala. Access is via Waipoli Rd, a switchbacking, narrow one-lane road through groves of eucalyptus and open rangeland (watch for cattle on the road). Layers of clouds often drift in and out, and when they lift you'll get panoramic views across green rolling hills to the islands of Lanai and Kahoolawe.

The whole area was planted during the 1930s by the Civilian Conservation Corp (CCC), a Depression-era work program. Several of the trails pass through old CCC camps and stands of redwood, ash, cypress, cedar and pines. In fact it all looks a lot like the Northern California coast. For some visitors from the mainland, this is a reason why *not* to go. But Polipoli still makes for a refreshing change from Hawaiian rain forest. Few people venture up this way, and except for the symphony of bird calls, everything is still. The park has a few picnic tables, a spookily deserted campground and a network of largely unused hiking and mountain-biking trails.

It's not usually possible to get all the way to the park without a 4WD vehicle, although you can usually reach a few trailheads. When conditions are cloudy, road visibility is measured in inches. The first six miles are paved, but have some soft shoulders. After that the road reverts to dirt (or possibly mud) as it enters the forest reserve.

It's another four grinding miles of potholes to the campground. It's really not worth even trying this last section in a standard car. Either content yourself with trailheads closer to the entrance or, better yet, bring a mountain bike with you and cycle it.

Both hiking trails described here are also open to mountain bikers, as are all park trails above the access road. For hikes farther inside the park, and the single-track Skyline Trail running downhill from Haleakala National Park, see the Hiking special section at the end of the Activities chapter.

Waiakoa Loop Trail

The trailhead for the Waiakoa Loop starts at the hunter check station 5 miles up Waipoli Rd, all paved. Walk three-quarters of a mile down the grassy spur road on the left to a gate marking the trail and be sure to close the gate behind you. The hike, which starts out in pine trees, makes a 3-mile loop. You can also connect with the Upper Waiakoa Trail at a junction about a half mile up the right side of the loop.

Upper Waiakoa Trail

The Upper Waiakoa Trail is a strenuous 7-mile trail that has been reconstructed in recent years by the Na Ala Hele group. The trail begins off Waiakoa Loop at an elevation of 6000 feet, climbs 1800 feet, switches back and then drops back down again. It's stony terrain, but it's high and open, with good views and stands of eucalyptus and native scrub. Bring plenty of water.

On the way down the trail passes the Mamane Trail spur, which connects to the Skyline Trail from the national park. This trail, however, ends on Waipoli Rd between the hunter check station and the campground. If you want to start at this end of the trail, keep an eye out for the trail marker for Waiohuli Trail, as the Upper Waiakoa Trail begins across the road.

Places to Stay

Come properly prepared, as this is cold country; winter temperatures frequently drop below freezing at night. For free camping permits or cabin reservations, see Accommodations in the Facts for the Visitor chapter earlier.

The basic *campground* at Polipoli has rest rooms, but no showers or drinking water. Fellow campers are likely to be pig hunters, and it's a desolate, damp place to pitch a tent; solo travelers may want to head elsewhere.

From the campground, which is about 10 minutes downhill from the Unit E 'Archery Only' sign at the end of the road, it's another half-mile walk down a forest trail to the *housekeeping cabin*. Unlike the other state cabins, this one has gas lanterns and a wood-burning stove but no electricity.

KEOKEA

Around the beginning of the 20th century, Keokea was home to mainly Hakka Chinese immigrants who farmed the remote Kula region. 'St John's House of Worship' is still written in Chinese above the door to the village's green-and-white **St John's Episcopal Church** (1907). Farther down the highway toward the Ulupalakua Ranch at the 18-mile marker, a few picnic tables and statuary mark the abandoned **Dr Sun Yat Sen Park**.

Although there's not much to it, Keokea is the last real town before Hana if you're swinging around the southern part of the island. It has a coffee shop, gas pump and a few small stores. On a clear day, you'll enjoy good views of West Maui and Lanai from the church and from elsewhere along the roadside.

For morning horseback rides, contact the *Thompson Ranch* (☎ 878-1910, Thompson Rd; 2-hr trail ride $60).

Places to Stay

Silver Cloud Upcountry Guest Ranch (☎ 878-6101, 800-532-1111, fax 878-2132, e slvrcld@maui.net, w www.maui.net/~ slvrcld, Thompson Rd) Rooms $85-125, studios $105-145, cottage $150. This former ranch turned B&B is on rural Thompson Rd, just over a mile from central Keokea. An atmospheric plantation house with hardwood floors, a fireplace and lounge

seats has six guest rooms, all with private baths. The converted bunkhouse out back has five rustic studios, which can sleep up to four people, and each has its own kitchenette. Also on the property is a honeymoon cottage with a kitchen, claw-foot bathtub and a wood-burning stove. Full breakfast is complimentary, and guests are free to use the common kitchen and living areas, as well as chess sets and hammocks.

Moonlight Garden Bed & Breakfast (☎ 878-6297, 878-6977, w www.maui.net/~ mauimoon, 213 Kula Hwy) 1-/2-bedroom cottage $115/125. Adjacent to a family home and working farm, this friendly place is secluded despite being within walking distance of the Keokea village center. The garden-like grounds are filled with fruit trees, whose goodness appears at breakfast along with muffins, granola and Kona coffee. The spacious one-bedroom cottage has a fireplace, hammock and stargazing deck, while the two-bedroom cottage has ikebana floral arrangements and is set next to a clump of Japanese bamboo. Both cottages have full kitchens, TVs, phones, washer/dryers and splendid sunset views clear out to the sea. There is a two-night minimum stay; and note, credit cards are not accepted.

Bloom Cottage (RR2 Box 229, Kula, HI 96790) 2-bedroom cottage $115/125/135 per double/triple/quad. This freestanding saltbox cottage sits beside the three-bedroom home originally built for a 1900s Kula priest. Both are available for rent through Hookipa Haven in Paia (see the East Maui chapter earlier). The cottage has its own kitchen, TV/VCR and a fireplace to ward off evening chills. Laundry facilities are shared by all guests. There's a three-night minimum stay.

Places to Eat

You can pick up a few simple grocery items a few doors down at *Fong Store* (and stop to browse for artwork at the small *Keokea Gallery*).

Grandma's Coffee House (☎ 878-2140, Hwy 37) Dishes $6-8. Open 7am-5pm daily. The Italian family that owns Grandma's has been growing coffee beans on the slopes of Haleakala since 1918. If you want to see what coffee trees look like, just walk out to the side porch. Local folks gravitate here for the homemade pastries and Kula vegetable salads and sandwiches. They all make for a good picnic if you're headed around the Piilani Hwy to Hana.

ULUPALAKUA RANCH

From Keokea, Hwy 37 winds south through ranch country with good views of Kahoolawe and the islet of Molokini. Even on overcast days, you can often see below the clouds to sunny Kihei on the coast. All of the open land on the slopes of the volcano above and below belongs to the Ulupalakua Ranch.

In the mid-19th century, there was a sugar plantation here owned by whaling ship captain James Makee. Originally it was called 'Rose Ranch' for the formal rose gardens he and his wife planted around their house and along the dirt trails. Isobel Fields, the stepdaughter of Robert Louis Stevenson, wrote about her visit in *This Life I've Loved,* in which she mentions Makee's infamous daughters, all six of whom rode horses astride, smoked and drank cocktails. Another famous visitor was King David Kalakaua, the 'Merrie Monarch,' who loved nothing better than late-night rounds of poker and champagne.

Since 1963 the ranch has been owned by the family of Pardee Erdman, a petroleum geologist from California. It's a 25,000-acre working ranch with about 6000 head of cattle, 600 Merino sheep and 150 head of Rocky Mountain elk. **Tedeschi Vineyards**, in the middle of Ulupalakua Ranch, is about 5½ miles south of Keokea. Unfortunately the wines are only worth tasting for novelty's sake. Ask for a free tasting of Maui Blanc, a pineapple dessert wine that is surprisingly light and dry, at the wine tasting room (☎ 878-6058, ⓦ *www.mauiwine.com; open 9am-5pm daily*). Other vintages are disappointing, but free tours of the winery are given at 10:30am and 1pm daily. The tasting room is attached to a small cottage built especially for royal visits. It now houses a small **museum** *(admission free)* of ranch history. Hawaiiana books, macadamia nut honey and Maui Onion cookbooks are on sale nearby.

Opposite the winery is ***Ulupalakua Ranch Store*** *(☎ 878-2561)* Open 9am to 5pm daily. It sells cowboy hats, T-shirts, souvenirs and snacks (try the huge $1 muffins). Remember that it's your last chance for food and drinks before Kaupo, which is around 25 lonely, dusty miles farther down the Piilani Hwy (see Beyond Hana in the East Maui chapter earlier for details on this spectacular route). Also be sure to check out the wooden cowboys on the store's front porch; they were carved by the late artist Reems Mitchell, who lived on the ranch.

A little farther down the road on the makai side you can see the remains of the three stacks of the **Makee Sugar Mill**, built in 1878.

Haleakala National Park

Haleakala National Park, one of Hawaii's two national parks, stretches from the summit of Haleakala volcano down to the waterfall pools of Oheo Gulch. There are separate entrances to both sections of the park, but no passage between them. This chapter concentrates on the volcano summit region, while Oheo Gulch is covered under Beyond Hana in the East Maui chapter, earlier.

In the Hawaiian language, *Haleakala* means 'House of the Sun.' Atop this very volcano the trickster demigod Maui lassoed the sun with ropes braided from his sister's hair, refusing to let go even as the sun begged for mercy. Not until the sun agreed to slow down its daily race across the sky, and thereby bathe the Hawaiian islands in more hours of glorious sunlight, did Maui release his Herculean hold.

Haleakala has long been thought of as the island's soul. In ancient times the volcano served as both a spiritual retreat and battleground for *kahuna* (priests). Other ancient Hawaiians quarried lava rock for tool-making and hid the bones of their ancestors or the umbilical cords of newborns deep inside the crater. Some people still believe it is a natural power point for magnetic and cosmic forces.

Whether it's the lingering *mana* (power) of the gods who once made their home here or the geological forces of the earth, which still release an occasional tremor, Haleakala does emanate a sense of awesome power. Jack London, who sailed to Hawaii in the early 1900s and wrote about it in *The Cruise of the Snark*, said that Haleakala had 'a message of beauty and wonder for the human soul that cannot be delivered by proxy.'

Prince Jonah Kalanianaole, the man who could've been king if the Hawaiian monarchy hadn't been overthrown, but instead became Hawaii's first congressional delegate, proposed Haleakala as a national park. When the bill was signed into law in

Highlights

- Watching the sunrise finger-paint the clouds above 10,000 feet at Haleakala summit

- Hiking between Pele's kaleidoscopic cinder cones in the crater desert

- Encountering endangered species, especially the *nene* (Hawaiian goose) and flowering silversword

- Taking lush ridge walks along the Paliku crater rim and peering down through Kaupo Gap

- Horseback rambling down the Sliding Sands trail

- Stargazing into the Milky Way and other electrifying moonlit crater adventures

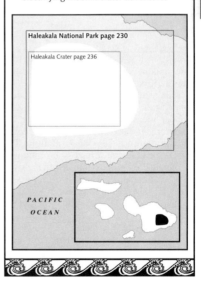

Haleakala National Park page 230

Haleakala Crater page 236

PACIFIC OCEAN

1916, Hawaii National Park joined Haleakala with its Big Island siblings, Mauna Loa and Kilauea. It wasn't until the 1960s that Haleakala National Park became an

HALEAKALA NP

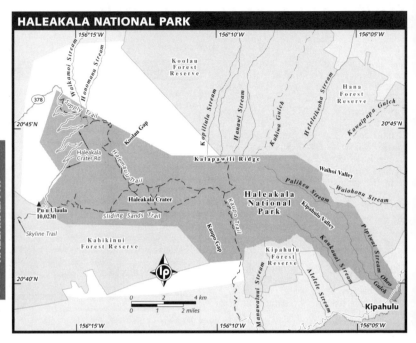

HALEAKALA NATIONAL PARK

independent entity and was expanded down into the Kipahulu Valley.

Today the park revolves around Haleakala volcano crater, an awesome geological wonder measuring 7½ miles wide by 2½ miles long and 3000 feet deep, which could enclose the entire isle of Manhattan. The crater resembles the surface of the moon, its seemingly lifeless floor dotted with high majestic cinder cones. There are impressive views from several points along the crater rim and remarkable hikes trailing across the basin floor.

The requisite pilgrimage to witness the sunrise from the rim of the crater is an experience that no one should pass up (see the boxed text). The early morning is usually the best time for viewing the crater. Later in the day, warm air forces clouds higher and higher until they pour through the two gaps in the crater's rim and into the crater itself. Sometimes there's a striking palette of colors at sunset reflected over a high, thin layer of cirrus clouds and a lower layer of fatter clouds that can be nearly as impressive as sunrise.

INFORMATION

Haleakala National Park (W www.nps.gov/hale/; 7-day admission pass $10 per car, $5 per person on foot, bicycle or motorcycle) never closes. The pay booth at the park entrance, however, only opens before dawn and is usually open until sunset. Sometimes you can drive through earlier for free, but don't count on it.

An annual Haleakala park pass costs $20. If you're going to Volcanoes National Park on the Big Island, consider buying a national parks pass ($50). It's good for unlimited entry to all US national parks for one year from the month of issue, and is nonrefundable and nonreplaceable. Seniors aged 62 and over who are US citizens or permanent residents qualify for the Golden Passport ($10), which grants unlimited free entry to all national parks and 50% off camping and activity fees.

Haleakala National Park headquarters (☎ 572-4400, 572-9306, open 7:30am-4pm daily) is less than a mile up from the pay booth. You can call ahead for recorded information on activities, camping permits and general park conditions or to request a park brochure. The office also stocks brochures, provides camping permits and sells books on geology, natural history, flora and fauna. A few silversword plants grow in front of the building, and occasionally a pair of nene wander around the parking lot.

There's another visitor center near the summit (see Haleakala Visitor Center, later). However, no food is sold anywhere inside the park, so bring plenty to eat, particularly if you're going up for the sunrise. You don't want a growling stomach to rush you back down the mountain before you've had a chance to explore. Hunting, firearms, roller blades, skateboards and any other activity that might disturb the fragile ecosystem are strictly prohibited. Bicycles are allowed only on paved roads and in parking lots.

Health

At high altitudes any inch of your skin can get scorched, even the backs of your ears, and even with cooling crater winds the sunlight is stronger than it feels here. On the other hand, hikers and campers who come unprepared for rain and freezing overnight temperatures inside the crater put themselves at risk of hypothermia.

Visitors rarely experience altitude sickness, or Acute Mountain Sickness (AMS), at Haleakala summit. An exception is those who have been scuba diving in the past 24 hours, so plan to do your Haleakala trip *before* any dives. Children, pregnant women and those in generally poor health are also susceptible. If you experience difficulty breathing, sudden headaches and dizziness, or more serious symptoms such as confusion and lack of motor coordination, descend immediately. Sometimes driving down the crater road just a few hundred feet will alleviate the problem. Panicking or hyperventilating will only makes things worse.

Haleakala, Dead or Alive?

Hawaii tourist publications tend to go overboard on the superlatives. Mauna Kea on the Big Island is labeled 'the world's tallest mountain,' which is true only if you cheat and measure starting from the ocean floor. Haleakala has often been proclaimed 'the largest dormant volcano crater in the world.' As impressive as that sounds, the volcano is neither dormant nor a crater, and probably not even the biggest of its kind.

Like all the Hawaiian islands, Haleakala is a shield volcano. Lava flows upwards from a hot spot in the earth's mantle as a tectonic plate moves over it. Melting of the upper mantle causes magma to rise up through the ocean floor, slowly accruing over time until at last a volcanic island emerges from the sea.

Similar to icebergs, these volcanoes show only a small part of their total mass above water, leaving 95% below on an ocean seamount. In its prime, Haleakala may have reached a height of 15,000 feet before water and wind erosion, and possibly glaciers, began to carve two large river valleys out of the rim. Eventually these valleys formed gaps that merged at the volcano summit to create a crater-like basin.

A true crater, on the other hand, can only be formed by explosions of viscous magma from a composite (or strata) volcano, which happens where tectonic plates converge, for example at Mt Fuji in Japan or Mt St Helens in Washington State. The numerous cinder cones inside 'Haleakala Crater' were actually formed by fountaining eruptions of volcanic vents, with yellow hues caused by sulfur and reds by iron oxide.

All shield volcanoes tend to go through a stage of renewed volcanism after their initial formation, and Haleakala has erupted ten times in the last millennium. The last eruption, over 200 years ago, sent a flow of lava towards Makena and La Perouse Bay. It's likely that many centuries in the future, lava will once again flow before Haleakala slips into eternal sleep.

HALEAKALA NP

ACTIVITIES

All park programs and guided hikes are free of charge.

Natural or cultural history talks that last around 20 to 30 minutes are held at the summit building at 9:30am, 10:30am and 11:30am daily.

Park rangers lead a moderately strenuous two-hour, 2-mile hike that goes partway down Sliding Sands Trail into the crater; meet at the trailhead at 9am on Tuesday or Friday.

Guided 3-mile, three-hour 'Walk on the Wet Side' hikes into the Waikamoi Preserve leave from Hosmer Grove campground at 9am on Monday and Thursday and last about three hours. Occasionally these hikes are canceled due to weather, so call ahead.

Other activities take place less frequently, or not at all in winter. Guided hikes along the 12-mile Sliding Sands–Halemau'u Trail are led once or twice a month. Evening stargazing programs and full moon hikes are offered between June and September when the weather is warm enough.

HALEAKALA CRATER ROAD

Haleakala Crater Rd (Hwy 378) twists and turns for 11 miles from Hwy 377 near Kula up to the park entrance, and then another 10 miles to the summit.

It's a fine paved road, but it's steep and winding and curiously lacking in guardrails to keep drivers from falling off the volcano. Take it easy, especially when pre-dawn conditions are dark and foggy. Cattle wander freely across the road at any time of day.

Allow about 1½ hours to reach the summit from Paia or Kahului, plus another 30 minutes from Kihei or 45 minutes from Lahaina. If you need gas, fill up the night before if you plan to get here for sunrise. There are no services on the crater road. Also loosen the cap on your gas tank about a quarter-turn before starting your ascent or when leaving your vehicle parked at a trailhead overnight to guard against vapor lock.

On your return from the summit, you'll see Maui unfolding below, with sugarcane fields creating a patchwork on the valley floor. The highway snakes back and forth, and sometimes as many as four or five switchbacks are in view all at once. Put your car in low gear to prevent brake failure and save gas. If you have the misfortune to end up trapped behind a downhill cycling tour group, be patient. Eventually they will pull over to the side and allow you to pass.

Although Lonely Planet does not recommend it, many people do successfully hitch the crater road. It's fairly easy, for example, to get short lifts between overlooks and trailheads. Make sure you do this during daylight hours, because standing on the side of this dangerous road after dark is dumb. If you can't find your own transport for the sunrise experience, see Organized Tours in the Getting Around chapter.

Hosmer Grove

Hosmer Grove, three-quarters of a mile before park headquarters, has a pleasant half-mile nature loop trail that begins in the campground. It starts in a forest of introduced trees and then passes into native Hawaiian shrubland. A trail guide to all the numbered posts and plaques is available at park headquarters.

The exotics in Hosmer Grove were introduced by Ralph Hosmer in 1910 in an effort to develop a lumber industry in Hawaii, one that could supply building materials and fuel for the sugar mills. Of the 86 experimental species planted here, only about 20 survived. Today you can see incense cedar, Norway spruce, Douglas fir, eucalyptus and various pines. Although the trees adapted well enough to grow, they didn't grow fast enough at these elevations to make tree harvesting practical. Thanks to this failure, today there's a park here instead.

Native plants you might see include *akala* (Hawaiian raspberry), *mamane, pilo, kilau* ferns and sandalwood. The *ohelo,* a berry sacred to Pele, and red and white berries of the *pukiawe,* which has evergreen leaves, both help feed the endangered nene.

There are wonderful scents and birdcalls along the trail. Fairly common are the native *iiwi* and *apapane,* both sparrow-size birds with bright red feathers. The iiwi has a very loud squeaking call, orange legs and a curved salmon- or yellow-colored bill. The apapane is a fast-moving bird with a black bill, black legs and a white undertail. It feeds on the nectar of ohia flowers, and its wings make a distinctive whirring sound.

Waikamoi Preserve Waikamoi Preserve is a 5230-acre reserve adjoining Hosmer Grove. In 1983, Haleakala Ranch conveyed the land's management rights to the Nature Conservancy. The area contains native koa and ohia rain forest and is a habitat for Hawaiian forest birds, including a number of rare and endangered species. The yellow-green Maui creeper and the crested honey-creeper, while both endangered, are more common than some of the others. The crested honeycreeper is a beautiful but aggressive bird that quite often dive-bombs apapane and chases them off branches.

The Nature Conservancy (☎ 572-7849) offers guided hikes on the second Saturday of each month for $25 ($15 for members). Advance reservations and a deposit are required. The National Park Service also offers free hikes in Waikamoi Preserve (see the Activities section, earlier).

Leleiwi Overlook

Leleiwi Overlook, at an elevation of 8840 feet, is just over midway between park headquarters and the summit visitor center. From the parking lot, it's a short walk out to the overlook, from where you can see the West Maui Mountains and both sides of the valley isthmus. You also get another angle on Haleakala Crater.

In the afternoon, if weather conditions are right, you might see the Brocken specter, an optical phenomenon that occurs at high elevations. Essentially, by standing between the sun and the clouds, your image is projected onto the clouds below. The light reflects off tiny droplets of water in the clouds, creating a circular rainbow around your shadow.

Kalahaku Overlook

Kalahaku Overlook, elevation 9324 feet, is about a mile above Leleiwi Overlook. The lower section has a fenced enclosure containing lots of silversword, from seedlings to mature plants.

The upper section has an observation deck looking down into Haleakala Crater. With the help of the deck's information plaque, you can clearly identify cinder cones on the crater floor below.

For photography, afternoon light is best. In the early morning, you can get more favorable light by walking a few minutes down an unmarked path to the left of the observation deck.

Haleakala Visitor Center

Before the summit, the visitor center at 9745 feet on the rim of the crater is the main sunrise-viewing spot. It is open 6am to 3pm daily in summer, from 6:30am in winter. The center has displays on geological and volcanic evolution and a recording explaining what you see on the crater floor 3000 feet below. Postcards and nature books are for sale here, and a ranger is usually on duty. There are washrooms and a pay phone, the only one inside the park.

Before dawn this parking lot fills up with tour vans, mountain bikers, horse trailers and all the regular folks coming to see the show. You can escape some of the crowds by scrambling up the path immediately beside the viewing area to White Hill Overlook (9778 feet). For more solitude, hike a short distance down Sliding Sands Trail, which begins at the back of the parking lot.

Summit

Pu'u Ulaula (Red Hill) Overlook, at 10,023 feet, is Maui's highest point. The gazebo building at the summit overlook has wrap-around windows, and on clear days you can see the Big Island, Lanai, Molokai and even Oahu. Off toward the crater is Magnetic Peak, which has an uncanny ability to mess with your compass.

The summit is about a half-mile drive uphill from the visitor center. Look around the parking lot for 'lava bombs,' pieces of molten lava that hardened after being expelled from volcanic vents.

The 37-mile drive from sea level to the summit of Haleakala is said to be the highest

Sunrise in the House of the Sun

Sunrise at Haleakala is an unforgettable experience, one that Mark Twain called 'the sublimest spectacle' he'd ever seen. About an hour before dawn, the night sky begins to pale and turn violet, and the stars fade away. Ethereal silhouettes of the mountain ridges appear as you drive up the twisting crater road.

Plan to arrive early at the summit, where first light hits about 30 minutes before the actual sunrise. The gentlest colors show up in the moments just before dawn. The bellies of the clouds lighten first, accenting the night sky with pale silvery slivers and streaks of pink. Then the light intensifies on the horizon in streaks of brilliant orange and reds. Don't forget to turn around for a look at Science City, whose domes turn a blazing pink. The best photo opportunities occur before the sun rises, because once the sun is up, the silvery lines and subtleties disappear.

Everyone comes out for the grand finale. The moment the disk of the sun appears, everything awakens and glows. Every morning is different, but it's often heard that partly cloudy skies put on the best show. Of course nothing compares to being right inside the heart of the volcano; crater sunrises are most spectacular at Holua campground, where it looks as though you could walk right out onto the clouds into the sun's fiery rays.

Before sunrise, temperatures hover around freezing and cold winds blow. There's often a frosty ice in the top layer of cinders, which crunch underfoot. If you don't have a sleeping bag or winter jacket to wrap yourself in, bring a warm blanket from your hotel. Then you can sit outside in a peaceful spot to take it all in, instead of huddling together inside the visitor center or gazebo building at the summit.

Check sunrise times and general weather conditions by calling ☎ 877-5111 before driving up. It's not uncommon for it to be cloudy and rainy at Haleakala when it's clear on the coast, because the volcano creates its own weather. A drizzly sunrise is a particularly disappointing nonevent after getting out of bed around 3am. If you wake up late, and you find yourself speeding up the crater road, pull over at one of the lower crater overlooks before first light erupts and you won't be disappointed by the view.

elevation gain in the shortest distance anywhere in the world. Every year endurance runners and sometimes mountain bikers race each other to the top (see Special Events in the Facts for the Visitor chapter).

Science City On the Big Island's Mauna Kea, scientists study the moon and stars. Here at Haleakala, appropriately enough considering its name, they study the sun.

Science City, just beyond the summit, is outside park headquarters and off-limits to visitors. It's under the jurisdiction of the University of Hawaii, which owns some of the domes and leases other land for a variety of private and government research projects. In addition to UH's solar observatory, the university's Institute of Astronomy operates a lunar ranging facility. Most recently the institute has joined hands with a UK-based educational foundation and broken ground for the Faulkes Telescope, which after completion will be the largest in the world dedicated to public outreach and remote classroom use.

Department of Defense–related projects include laser technology related to the 'Star Wars' project, satellite tracking and identification and a deep-space surveillance system. The newest military telescope, which became operational in 1997 and cost $123 million to build, is capable of identifying a basketball-size object flying in space 20,000 miles away.

HIKING THE CRATER

Hiking the crater floor offers a completely different angle on Haleakala's lunar landscape. Instead of peering down from the rim, you're looking up at the walls and towering cinder cones. It looks so much like a moonscape that US astronauts trained here before going to the moon. Speaking of which, these hikes are even more magical on full moon nights.

The sound of cinders crunching underfoot is often the only noise to reach your ears, except perhaps for the muffled bark of a *pueo* (Hawaiian owl). Ring-necked pheasants are also likely to be startled by your approach and swiftly dart up from the crater floor. The *uau* (dark-rumped petrel), which is an endangered species along with the nene and silversword, nests in the lava rocks after feeding down near the ocean. In fact these seabirds were thought to be extinct until seen again in the crater during the 1970s. Many insects also get blown here, and a few species of happy-face and wolf spiders crawl around the crater.

Around 27 miles of trails intersect at reliable junctions, almost all of which are marked with accurate hiking distances. To protect the fragile ecosystem, always keep to established trails and do not take advantage of even apparently well-trodden shortcuts through switchbacks. Walking single file down the very center of the trail will help protect the border habitat. When you encounter horses or mules, speak quietly and move your group to the downhill side of the trail if possible.

The weather at Haleakala can suddenly change from dry, hot desert-like conditions to cold, windy rain. Although the general rule is sunny in the morning and cloudy in the afternoon, fog and clouds can blow in at any time. No matter what the weather is like at the start of a hike, be prepared for temperatures that can drop into the 50s (°F) during the day and the 30s overnight at any time of year. The climate also changes radically as you walk across the crater floor. In the almost 4 miles between the Kapalaoa and Paliku cabins, rainfall varies from an annual average of 12 inches to 300 inches. December to May is the wet season.

With the average elevation on the crater floor at 6700 feet, the relatively thin air means that hiking can be tiring. The higher elevation also means that sunburn is more likely. Take sunscreen, rain gear, a few layers of clothing, a first-aid kit and plenty of food and water. You'll see high-altitude endurance runners jogging through the crater with nothing but a small hip pack and one-liter water bottle, but unless you're a dynamite world-class athlete, come fully prepared.

Other short nature trails to outlooks at Hosmer Grove are described earlier under the appropriate sections.

See the Hiking special section at the end of the Activities chapter if you're up for the challenging, if little-used **Skyline Trail** (also used by mountain bikers) down into Polipoli Spring State Recreation Area (see the Upcountry chapter). From near the summit in Haleakala National Park, take the road to the left of Science City to the iron gate and posted trailhead.

Sliding Sands Trail

Sliding Sands, the summit trail into the crater, starts at the south side of the visitor center parking lot. Most hikers enter the crater this way, and the soft, easy descent is accompanied by volcanic landscapes that overpower the senses. What hard-core hikers want to know is, how difficult is it to hike this trail *uphill*? Over time its loose cinder sands have become a bit more hard-packed, so it is nothing to fear, although it will still be slow going for most people.

Sliding Sands starts at 9740 feet and descends steeply over loose cinders down to the crater floor. The trail takes 9½ miles to Paliku campground and cabin, passing Kapalaoa cabin at 5¾ miles. This first 6-mile segment of the trail follows the south wall of the crater, winding down through what look like sand dunes. If you hike down immediately after catching the sunrise, you'll walk into the warming rays of the sun. There are great views on the way down, but except for a few shrubs, there's no vegetation in sight.

HALEAKALA NP

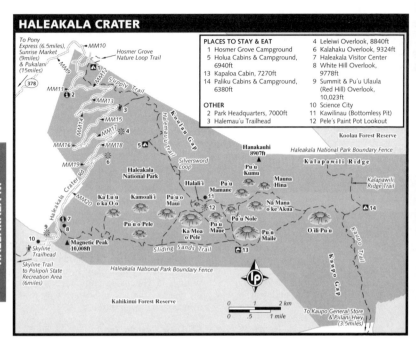

HALEAKALA CRATER

To Pony
Express (6.5miles),
Sunrise Market
(9miles)
& Pukalani
(15miles)

378

MM10

MM11

MM9

MM12

Hosmer Grove
Nature Loop Trail

Supply Trail

MM13

MM14

MM15

MM16

MM17

MM18

MM19

Koolau Gap

Halemauʻu Trail

Silversword
Loop

Hanakauhi
8907ft

Koolau Forest Reserve

Haleakala National Park Boundary Fence

PLACES TO STAY & EAT
1 Hosmer Grove Campground
5 Holua Cabins & Campground,
  6940ft
13 Kapaloa Cabin, 7270ft
14 Paliku Cabins & Campground,
  6380ft

OTHER
2 Park Headquarters, 7000ft
3 Halemauʻu Trailhead

4 Leleiwi Overlook, 8840ft
6 Kalahaku Overlook, 9324ft
7 Haleakala Visitor Center
8 White Hill Overlook,
  9778ft
9 Summit & Puʻu Ulaula
  (Red Hill) Overlook,
  10,023ft
10 Science City
11 Kawilinau (Bottomless Pit)
12 Pele's Paint Pot Lookout

Kalapawili Ridge

Puʻu
Kumu

Mauna
Hina

Kalapawili
Ridge Trail

Haleakala
National Park

Halaliʻi

Puʻu
Mamane

Puʻu
ʻo
Maui

Na Mana
o ke Akua

Kaʻu Luʻu
o ka Oʻo

Kamoaliʻi

Ka Moa
o Pele

Puʻu
Maue

Puʻu Nole

Oʻili Puʻu

Puʻu o Pele

Puʻu
Maile

Haleakala Crater Rd

MM20

Skyline
Trailhead

Magnetic Peak
10,008ft

Sliding Sands Trail

Skyline Trail
to Polipoli State
Recreation Area
(6miles)

Haleakala National Park Boundary Fence

Kahikinui Forest Reserve

Kaupo Trail

Kaupo Gap

0   1   2 km
0   .5   1 mile

To Kaupo General Store
& Piilani Hwy
(3.5miles)

About 2 miles down the Sliding Sands Trail (a descent of 1400 feet), a spur trail leads steeply down and then up the **Ka Luʻu o ka Oʻo** cinder cone, about half a mile to the north. Midway along this spur trail are some silversword plants. From the visitor center to the cinder cone and back, it's a strenuous three-hour hike. Because of the uphill return climb, this is a good hike to do early in the morning so as to avoid the midday heat.

After nearly four miles the trail hits the crater floor and intersects with the first of three trailheads leading off to the left into the center of the cinder desert. As you strike out across the crater floor for the mellow 2-mile walk to Kapalaoa (7270 ft), increasingly verdant ridges rise on your right, and grass begins to grow beneath your feet, giving way to ropy *pahoehoe* lava. Just before reaching Kapalaoa cabin, the other two trailheads into the center of the crater appear (see Exploring the Cinder Desert, later).

After about four hours, you should reach Kapalaoa cabin. Many hikers break here to refill their water bottles (remember to treat or filter the water first) or snack at the picnic tables and converse with nene. In the final 4 miles from Kapalaoa to Paliku cabin and campground, the trail gently rises and falls as lush vegetation increases. Paliku (6380 feet) sits beneath a sheer cliff at the eastern end of the crater. In contrast to the crater's barren western side, this area receives heavy rainfall that makes for grassy campsites, with ohia forests climbing the slopes. Somehow the final steps from Kapalaoa to Paliku seem to take an eternity, especially in a downpour.

Supply Trail

This little-known trail follows the old mule path used to get supplies down to the cabins on the crater floor. Unless you are camping at Hosmer Grove and looking for a shortcut over to the crater rim, however, you can safely skip this one. The trail starts from opposite the radio facility access road, which lies closer to Hosmer Grove on the campground turnoff road than the highway. The trail slowly ascends to run back alongside the highway for the first 1½ miles, then opens up for sweeping views down the volcano's rain forest slopes and out to sea; that is if the clouds haven't already rolled in. After one more mile, the Supply Trail intersects with the more popular Halemau'u Trail down into the crater.

Halemau'u Trail

Halemau'u Trailhead, 3½ miles above park headquarters, is marked. There's a fair chance you'll find nene in the parking lot, but many of these endangered creatures have been backed over by careless motorists. Be careful.

If you're not up for a long hike, you might try doing just part of the Halemau'u Trail. Even hiking the first mile to the crater rim gives a fine view of the crater, with Koolau Gap to the east. It's fairly level up to this point, sloping gently downward through grassy pastureland to the national park boundary fence.

After passing through the gate, the trail descends 1400 feet through 2 miles of well-cut switchbacks, and once it hits the floor of the crater, it's just over a mile to Holua cabin and campground. At 6940 feet, this is one of the lowest areas along this hike, and you'll see impressive views of the crater walls rising a few thousand feet to the west.

HALEAKALA NP

Honkin' Far from Canada, Eh?

The native *nene*, Hawaii's state bird, is a long-lost cousin of the Canada goose. Thanks to a captive breeding and release program on the Big Island and in England, it has slowly been brought back from the verge of extinction. In 1946 only 50 nene remained alive anywhere in the world. In fact there were no birds left inside Haleakala National Park at all until Boy Scouts carried junior birds back into the crater inside their backpacks! Currently the park's nene population is holding steady at about 250.

Nene generally nest in high cliffs from 6000 to 8000 feet, surrounded by rugged lava flows with sparse vegetation. Their feet have gradually adapted by losing most of their webbing. The birds are extremely friendly and love to hang out where people do, anywhere from cabins on the crater floor to park headquarters. Their curiosity and fearlessness has contributed to their undoing. Many nene have been backed over by careless drivers in parking lots or run over along the crater road. Others have been tamed by too much human contact, so no matter how much they beg for your banana and peanut butter sandwich, do not feed the nene. It only interferes with their successful return to the wild.

The Friends of Haleakala National Park (FHNP) (**w** *www.philipt.com/fohnp, PO Box 322, Makawao HI 86768*) is a nonprofit society that helps protect the park's habitats and wildlife, including the nene. Their Adopt-a-Nene program costs just $30 per adult ($20 for students and seniors), or you can contact them about volunteer service projects.

KEEP THEM *WILD*

DO NOT FEED THE NENE

NED FRIARY

A few large **lava tubes** around here are worth exploring. One is up a short steep trail behind the cabin, and the other is a 15-minute detour off the trail past the cabin.

If you were to hike down the switchbacks to the Holua cabin and back from the parking lot, the 8-mile roundtrip would be a good workout. But you'd miss out on the colorful cinder cones (see Exploring the Cinder Desert, later), which are an easy mile-long walk farther down the trail. Before reaching them, the **Silversword Loop** passes by silversword plants in various stages of growth and adds only an extra 0.1 miles to your trip. If you're here in summer, you should be able to see plants in bloom.

If you've started this hike too late in the morning, or the weather turns sour, you're not going to see much once the clouds roll in. From Holua, it's 6¼ miles to Paliku cabin, the trail's end, or 4 miles back up the switchbacks to the Halemau'u parking lot. One hint about the latter: every time you think you've reached the top, you'll discover that you're not actually there yet. Allow about two hours at a steady pace.

Sliding Sands–Halemau'u Trail

One of the most popular day hikes for people in good condition is this 11½ mile journey. Because of its steep descent, Sliding Sands Trail makes a better entry trail into the crater and Halemau'u Trailhead, at a lower elevation of 8000 feet, is an easier exit. Although this hike is a strenuous full-day outing, it's more than manageable if you're reasonably fit and start out early (ideally just after sunrise). Then you can take your time poking around in the crater without worrying about darkness falling before you finish your hike.

About 4 miles down Sliding Sands, after an elevation drop of 2500 feet, is the most direct spur to the Halemau'u Trail. This spur trail takes in many of the crater's most kaleidoscopic cinder cones, including **Pele's Paint Pot Lookout**. Then it's another 2 miles from the lookout to Holua cabin, and another 4 miles up through switchbacks to the Halemau'u parking lot. The trailhead parking lot is off Hwy 378, located about 6 miles below the summit visitor center and Sliding Sands trailhead. If you haven't arranged to be picked up, hitching a ride back up to the summit is fairly easy in the daylight.

Exploring the Cinder Desert

Almost all hiking trails lead to the belly of the beast, Haleakala's cinder desert. Still there is no easy way to see the whole area without backtracking at least once. As the spur trails are not very long, you may even have time to do them all.

Three major spur trails connect Sliding Sands Trail near Kapalaoa with the Halemau'u Trail between Paliku and Holua. The one farthest west takes about 40 minutes to meander between all the swirling colors of the cinder cones, and the angle of view changes with every step. If you prefer stark, black and barren, the other spur trails take you through *a'a* and *pahoehoe* lava fields; the one farthest east is also splattered with rust-red cinders.

All three trails end up on the north side of the cinder desert near the **Kawilinau**, also known as the Bottomless Pit. Legends say the pit leads down to the sea, though the Park Service says it's just 65 feet deep. You can't really get a good look down the narrow shaft, however, but you can easily imagine all of the ancestor bones that are probably lying at the bottom. Even if you have limited time, take the short loop trail around Pu'u Halāli'i cinder cone and sit for a while in the saddle of **Pele's Paint Pot Lookout**, arguably the most jaw-dropping vantage point in the entire crater. The two western spur trails intercept this loop at their northern end, and the third spur finishes nearby.

Five minutes east of the Bottomless Pit along the Halemau'u Trail, an unmaintained but well-marked spur trail wanders off for about ten minutes north into a lunar world colored only with a hundred shades of gray. When the trail peters out, turn back to avoid causing erosion damage.

Kalapawili Ridge Trail

OK, we know this is not an official trail anymore, but it still shows up on old maps.

Camel of the Plant World

The striking silversword, or *'āhinahina,* is a distant relative of the sunflower. Each plant can grow for three years up to half a century, but blooms only once in a lifetime. Even when the plants are not flowering, their elegant silver spikes waving in the crater winds is an otherwordly sight.

In its final year, a silversword shoots up a flowering stalk that sometimes reaches a height of over 6 feet. In summer the stalk flowers with hundreds of maroon and yellow blossoms; when the flowers go to seed in late autumn, the plant dies. It's as heart-rending as any operatic aria, especially when you realize these plants are endangered.

LEE FOSTER

The silversword, which is found only in Hawaii, was nearly wiped out in the early 20th century by grazing feral goats, pigs or cattle, as well as people who cut them down for souvenirs or to decorate parade floats.

Yet the silversword has always been a survivor. After all, it was able to adapt to the barren conditions of its endemic habitats, Haleakala on Maui and volcanoes on the Big Island. Its shiny leaves have evolved fine silver hairs to reflect the sun's ultraviolet radiation away from the plant, and the inward curl of these leaves further prevents dehydration. Its shallow expansive root system collects moisture hiding in the loose volcanic cinders, while longer taproots anchor the plants in the wind. Interestingly, the silversword has a few cousins with which it can produce a hybrid, including the *naenae,* a fragrant green perennial once used by Hawaiians to perfume *tapa* (bark cloth).

Today the silversword's survival depends on the protection of its fragile natural environment. National Park staff spent years painstakingly building a multimillion dollar, 32-mile-long fence to create a barrier against feral animals. They also monitor the populations of native insects responsible for cross-pollinating the plants.

Picking or otherwise disturbing a silversword is now illegal. Trespassers can be slapped with major fines, not to mention the wrath of Pele (see the Responsible Tourism boxed text in the Facts for the Visitor chapter). Half of all silverswords get trampled to death as seedlings, mostly by hikers who wander off-trail. If you want to see them up close, just walk the short Silversword Loop that veers off the Halemau'u Trail.

The trouble is finding the trailhead, which is tucked behind the Paliku campground and cabins. From there just keep heading uphill; after an hour or two, the trail empties out onto the high-flying Kalapawili Ridge, which affords great views of Hana and out to sea. Since this trail is not well maintained,

hike at your own risk. Allow five or six hours at least for the roundtrip.

Kaupo Trail

From the Paliku campground on the eastern edge of the crater floor, it's possible to continue another 8½ miles down to Kaupo

HALEAKALA NP

on the southern coast. The first 4 miles of the trail drop 2500 feet in elevation before reaching the park boundary fence. It's a steep rocky trail through rough lava and brushland, but worth coming this far just for the views.

The last 4½ miles pass through Kaupo Ranch property on a rough jeep trail descending to the bottom of Kaupo Gap, exiting at the east side of the Kaupo General Store (see Beyond Hana in the East Maui chapter). There are coastal views along the way but no water or shade cover. The steep angle of descent is a killer on your knees, too. At the very end the trail cuts through forests where trail markers become vague and feral pigs snuffle about. Your chances of getting lost are pretty good if you attempt to do this hike in the reverse direction uphill, which is just no fun at all (trust us, we've done it).

From the trailhead at the bottom of the mountain, it's another 1½ miles out to Kaupo General Store and the highway. Don't start dreaming about a bottle of cold water just yet, because Kaupo General Store seems to be shut more often than not. The 'village' of Kaupo is also a long way from anywhere, with very little traffic along the highway except for stray tourists and a few locals in pickup trucks. If you don't have any luck hitchhiking and have to walk the final stretch, it's 8 miles to Oheo Gulch campground.

The Kaupo Trail is a strenuous hike, and because of the remoteness and the ankle-twisting conditions, it's not advisable to do it alone. According to legend, this is the same route taken by Maui when he made his way up the volcano, so if you succeed you can pride yourself on having walked in the footsteps of a demigod. The National Park Service publishes a Kaupo Trail brochure that people considering the hike should pick up in advance.

PLACES TO STAY

Accommodations in the park are kept primitive on purpose. Either rough it with a tent or get lucky and score a cabin.

If you're think about camping, remember that sleeping in the elements above 7000 feet is nothing like camping on the beach. If you don't have a waterproof tent and winter-rated sleeping bag, just forget about it (see Camping in the Facts for the Visitor chapter for more advice). Do a day hike instead.

People staying in cabins and at the campgrounds share the same pit toilets and limited nonpotable water supplies. All water needs to be filtered or treated chemically before drinking. As the water tanks occasionally run dry, conserve carefully and ask the rangers about water levels before starting out. No open fires are allowed, and you'll need to pack out all your trash. There is no food, gas, electricity, showers or other supplies available. In the event of an actual emergency, rangers sometimes stay at the ranger cabins at Holua or Paliku.

Camping and cabin stays are strictly limited to three nights in the crater each month, with no more than two consecutive nights at any one site. You can squeeze out three additional nights of camping per month at both Hosmer Grove and Oheo Gulch (see Beyond Hana in the East Maui chapter).

Camping

Free tenting is allowed at three campgrounds inside the Upcountry section of the park.

Hosmer Grove has a ***drive-up campground*** accessed by the road immediately after the park entrance sign, but before the pay booth. Located at the 6800-foot elevation, Hosmer Grove tends to be cloudy and a bit wet, not to mention cold at night. There are picnic tables, grills, toilets and drinking water. Permits are not required, though there's a three-day camping limit per month. It's busier in summer than winter and is often full on holiday weekends.

Permits are required for ***backcountry camping*** at Haleakala National Park. There are only two campgrounds inside the crater, both beneath steep cliffs. One is at Holua, 4 miles down the Halemau'u trail, while the other sits at Paliku near a lush rain forest ridge (so you know that your shoes will never dry out here). When the afternoon clouds roll in, even the sites at Holua can get quite damp, so make sure your tent is waterproof. Do not camp near the cabins, but instead use the designated grassy areas, at Paliku off to the west side or up on the hill at Holua.

Each backcountry campground is limited to 25 people. Permits are issued at park headquarters on a first-come, first-served basis between 8am and 3pm daily. Permits can go quickly if large groups show up, a situation that is more likely to occur in summer. Sometimes the rangers require you to watch an audiovisual presentation on backcountry etiquette before issuing the permit.

Cabins

Haleakala National Park cabins 1-6 people $40, 7-12 people $80. Three basic cabins – one each at Holua, Kapalaoa and Paliku – lie along trails in the crater. The cabins were built by the Civilian Conservation Corp (CCC) in the 1930s, and each has an old-fashioned wood-burning stove, propane gas tanks with rangetop burners, some cooking utensils, 12 bunks with sleeping pads (but no bedding) and a limited supply of nonpotable running water and firewood. As it's illegal to gather kindling within the park boundaries, you should bring fire starter (either fire sticks or dry newspaper). Try to conserve water and firewood and sweep out each cabin before leaving, making sure to pack out all your trash. Anything left behind just feeds the rats and cockroaches.

There's a three-day limit, with no more than two consecutive nights in any cabin. Each cabin is rented to only one party at a time. The driest conditions are usually found at Kapalaoa, in the middle of the cinder desert and closest to the Sliding Sands trailhead. Those craving rain forests and lush pastures will find Paliku quite serene. Holua is a mixture of wet and dry conditions, but has superior sunrise views.

Hiking distances from the crater rim range from 4 to 10 miles.

The problem here is demand, which is so high the park service actually holds a monthly lottery to award reservations. To enter, your reservation request must be received two months prior to the first day of the month of your proposed stay (for example, requests for cabins on any date in July must arrive before May 1). A separate request is needed for each month. Your chances increase if you list alternate dates within the same calendar month and choose weekdays rather than weekends.

The address for reservation requests is Haleakala National Park, PO Box 369, Makawao, HI 96768, ATTN: CABINS. Only written reservation requests are accepted (no phone or fax). Always mail your requests early since postal delivery to Hawaii can take a bit longer than to the mainland. You can send for a form or just submit the information on a regular sheet of paper; include your name, address, phone number, specific dates and cabins, and the number of people in your group.

Do not send money with your request form. If you are selected in the lottery, you will be notified, at which point the fees will have to be paid in full at least three weeks prior to the reservation date. Your permit will be mailed to you, unless you specifically ask to pick it up at the park headquarters. If you plan to do the latter, you will not be able to head down right after sunrise because the headquarters doesn't open until 7:30am. Either way you will need to call up to two days in advance or visit the park headquarters in person with your photo ID to find out the combinations for the ancient cabin locks.

Cancellations occasionally occur, creating last-minute vacancies, especially in winter. Calls regarding cancellations are accepted only between 1pm and 3pm daily, and you'll need to have a credit card available to secure the cabin if there is a vacancy. If you're in Maui for a month or longer, your chances of getting one this way are pretty good.

HALEAKALA NP

Excursions

If the plasticky tourism of Lahaina begins to break your heart, sneak down to Maui's public ferry slip. Step aboard the commuter ferry to old-school Molokai, an island where there isn't a single stoplight in sight. An even faster ferry zips you to Lanai, the former pineapple island turned adventure playground.

Lanai

Until recently, Lanai was a one-crop, one-company, one-town island. The latter two still hold true, and so does the first if you consider how wealthy tourists have been handily substituted for pineapples.

For over half a century, Castle & Cooke, the company run by billionaire David Murdock that owns 98% of Lanai, ran the island as its own private pineapple plantation. At one point nearly one-fifth of the world's pineapples were grown here, but competition from more cheaply produced pineapples overseas eroded the profitability of the Lanai crop. There are still 100 acres of high-profile 'show fields' that grow pineapples destined for the local market, but the last commercial harvest was in 1992.

Until the early 1990s, Lanai had only one little hotel with just 10 rooms. The few visitors who came this way were largely hunters, hikers and independent travelers trying to avoid the tourist scene on the other islands. In the past decade, Castle & Cooke has opened two luxury resorts, both with 18-hole golf courses, and built some of the island's first million-dollar vacation homes.

On the surface, things haven't altered all that radically. The center of Lanai remains Lanai City – not a city at all, but merely a little plantation town of tin-roofed houses and shops. It's still home to all but a few dozen of Lanai's 3200 residents. Approximately a third of the people living on Lanai were born in the Philippines; Filipino immigrants first came to the island to work on

Highlights

- Riding across the channels on Hawaii's only interisland ferries
- Adventuring on Lanai's 4WD roads to shipwrecks and petroglyphs
- Snorkeling in Manele Bay and diving in the grottos of the Cathedrals
- Ambling along Molokai's wild, windswept beaches and camping out
- Following the mule trail down to the historic settlement of Kalaupapa
- Mountain biking on ranch trails above the world's highest sea cliffs

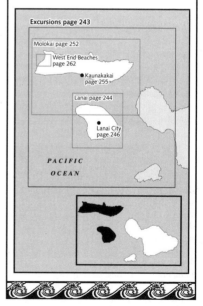

Excursions page 243

Molokai page 252

West End Beaches page 262

Kaunakakai page 255

Lanai page 244

Lanai City page 246

PACIFIC OCEAN

Dole's pineapple plantation in the mid-20th century.

Not surprisingly, Lanai can be quite expensive to visit. One of the easiest ways to get a glimpse of it is to take the ferry over

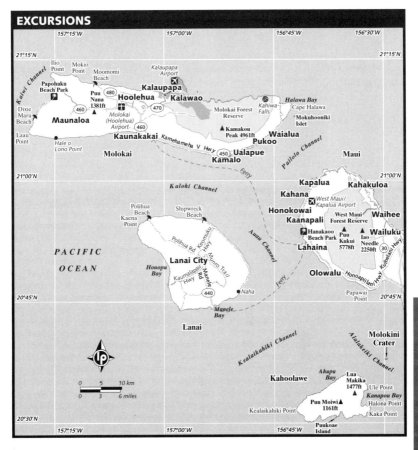

EXCURSIONS

from Maui in the morning, snorkel at Hulopoe Bay, which has the island's finest beach, and then take the boat back in the afternoon. If you camp overnight at Manele Bay or take your ease at one of the resorts, make time to explore some of Lanai's obscure archeological and geological sites, which lie along rutted dirt roads and require renting a 4WD vehicle, or at least a mountain bike.

Geography & Geology

Lanai is the sixth-largest Hawaiian island. It's 18 miles long, 13 miles wide and has an area of 140 sq miles. The vaguely fin-shaped island was formed by a single volcano, Palawai, now long extinct. Today, the large flat basin of Palawai crater contains most of Lanai's arable land.

The island's terrain and climate are dominated by a ridge running from the northwest to the southeast. From there a series of gulches radiates down to the east coast, while on the other side lies a cool central plateau with Lanai City perched at around 1600 feet.

The remote southwest coast has sheer cliffs, some higher than 1000 feet. The island has white-sand beaches, bright red earth blowing in dry, dusty gullies, forested ravines and cool, foggy uplands. It also has the last native dryland forest in the whole state.

Flora & Fauna

The island of Lanai has suffered the greatest loss of native forests, plants and birds of any of the main Hawaiian Islands, thanks to drastic overgrazing. After a long period of decline, green sea turtles have been making a comeback along Lanai's remote northeastern shore.

Keep your eyes open for wild animals – sightings of mouflon sheep on the inland hills are not uncommon. Axis deer are even more prolific here than on Molokai, the only other Hawaiian island where they roam free. Because Lanai has no mongooses, introduced game birds such as ring-necked pheasants, quails, doves and wild turkeys are all common.

Activities

The public recreation complex in Lanai City, which includes **Lanai Gym**, has a 75-foot-long pool, a basketball court and a

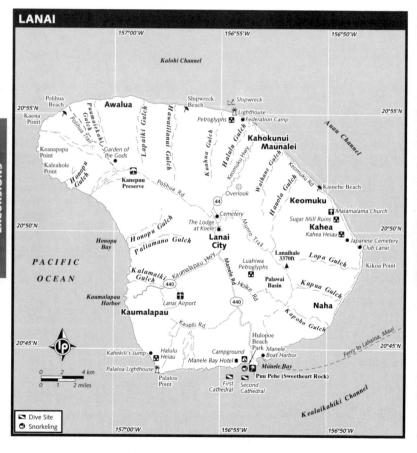

couple of lighted tennis courts. On the north side of Lanai City, the nine-hole **Cavendish Golf Course** is the only free golf course in Hawaii. Anyone can play; simply bring your clubs and begin! Off-islanders should drop a few bills in the donation box.

For day trips, dive and snorkel operators are listed in the Activities chapter. The ***Club Lanai*** (☎ *871-0626,* W *www.clublanai.com; adults $75*) catamaran sails daily from Lahaina Harbor to a private beach on Lanai's east coast. ***Lanai Ecoadventure Centre*** (☎ *565-7737,* W *www.kayakhawaii.com, 338 8th St*) offers guided half-day kayak and snorkeling tours for $69. They also rent camping and outdoor sports gear, including mountain bikes.

Both resort hotels offer a variety of activities, including tennis, diving and horseback riding. Green fees at their designer golf courses top out at $200 for nonguests, cart included. The waterfront ***Challenge at Manele*** (☎ *565-2222*) was judged brutal but rewarding by Jack Nicklaus. Partly designed by Greg Norman, the ***Experience at Koele*** (☎ *565-4653*) sits below mountains and is equally challenging – it once took Nicklaus eight shots just to get off the 17th tee.

Getting There & Around

Almost everyone takes the ferry, but it is also possible to fly to Lanai. See Within Hawaii in the Getting There & Away chapter.

For car rental, Lanai City Service (☎ 565-7227, 800-533-7808, 1036 Lanai Ave) is an affiliate of Dollar. Compact cars cost $60 a day, 4WD Jeep Wranglers around $120. No additional insurance is available and discounts are rare. A one-day deposit is required for advance bookings, which are strongly advised. Lanai City Service provides limited taxi service and free transfers to its in-town office for vehicle rental customers.

The Lodge at Koele and the Manele Bay Hotel have a shuttle bus that meets guests at the ferry dock or airport. Half-hourly shuttles for guests between the two resorts stop at the Hotel Lanai.

All of Lanai's 4WD roads are conquerable by mountain bike, but be prepared to dodge 4WDs and choke on a bit of dust.

Muddy Lanai

Most roads on Lanai are dirt roads, many of them built to service the pineapple fields of yesteryear; their conditions vary from good to impassable, largely depending on the weather.

If you rent a 4WD vehicle and plan to travel these roads, ask the rental agency for the current best routes to out-of-the-way sights – often there are a few alternatives, and the agencies know which roads are washed out and which are passable. If you do go off the beaten path and get stuck, it can be a long walk back to town, and you can expect to pay a painful amount for the towing and repair fees.

Lanai Ecoadventure Centre (see Activities, earlier) rents mountain bikes for $25 to $30 per day.

LANAI CITY

Lanai City (we use the term 'city' lightly) is nestled among Norfolk pines on a cool central plateau beneath the slopes of Lanaihale (3370 feet). All of the tidy houses are brightly painted, and many have flowering front gardens. Yes, it's a 1950s kind of life.

On Sunday mornings, a stroll by the **Hawaiian Church** (*cnr 5th & Gay Sts*) will treat you to fine melodies of choir music. Or you can kick back in **Lanai City Community Park** and 'talk story' with the old-timers.

If it's overcast in Lanai City, chances are that Shipwreck Beach or Manele Bay will still be sunny.

There are two banks with 24-hour ATMs. The post office (☎ 565-6517, 620 Jacaranda St) is off the north side of the park. There are community notice boards here, as well as at the east end of the park and by the grocery stores and the launderette. Lanai's public library (☎ 565-6996) also doubles as the school library; call ahead to check hours and Internet access. Lanai Community Hospital (☎ 565-6411) offers 24-hour emergency services.

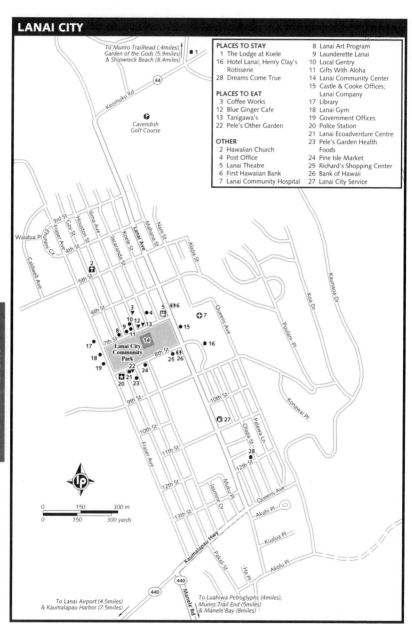

LANAI CITY

PLACES TO STAY
1 The Lodge at Koele
16 Hotel Lanai; Henry Clay's Rotisserie
28 Dreams Come True

PLACES TO EAT
3 Coffee Works
12 Blue Ginger Cafe
13 Tanigawa's
22 Pele's Other Garden

OTHER
2 Hawaiian Church
4 Post Office
5 Lanai Theatre
6 First Hawaiian Bank
7 Lanai Community Hospital
8 Lanai Art Program
9 Launderette Lanai
10 Local Gentry
11 Gifts With Aloha
14 Lanai Community Center
15 Castle & Cooke Offices; Lanai Company
17 Library
18 Lanai Gym
19 Government Offices
20 Police Station
21 Lanai Ecoadventure Centre
23 Pele's Garden Health Foods
24 Pine Isle Market
25 Richard's Shopping Center
26 Bank of Hawaii
27 Lanai City Service

To Munro Trailhead (.4miles), Garden of the Gods (5.9miles) & Shipwreck Beach (8.4miles)

Keomuku Rd

44

Cavendish Golf Course

Waialua Pl
3rd St
Fraser Ave
Gay St
Houston St
Ilima Ave
4th St
Caldwell Ave
Jacaranda St
Koele Ave
Lanai Ave
Mahana St
Nani St
5th St
6th St
7th St
8th St
9th St
10th St
11th St
12th St
13th St

Alapa St
Queens Ave
Koa Dr
Kaunaoa Dr
Puulani Pl
Konawai Pl
Palawai Ln
Olopua St
Mului Pl
Jasmine Dr
Kaumalapau Hwy
Manele Rd
Pakeli St
Ha Pl
Akahi Pl
Kualua Pl
Akolu Pl

Lanai City Community Park

EXCURSIONS

0   150   300 m
0   150   300 yards

To Lanai Airport (4.5miles) & Kaumalapau Harbor (7.5miles)

To Luahiwa Petroglyphs (4miles), Munro Trail End (5miles) & Manele Bay (8miles)

440
440

Places to Stay

Dreams Come True (☎ 565-6961, 800-566-6961, fax 565-7056, **e** hunters@aloha.net, 547 12th St) Rooms $99. This plantation-era B&B house is furnished with Asian antiques. Each room has its own bath – though it may be across the hall – and two have four-poster beds. Some travelers have reported it noisy and not such an excellent value, however. Continental breakfast includes homemade bread and fresh fruit. Ask about discount vehicle rental for guests.

Hotel Lanai (☎ 565-7211, 800-795-7211, fax 565-6450, **w** www.hotellanai.com, 828 Lanai Ave) Rooms $95-105, 1-room cottage $140. This quaint hotel was built by Dole in 1923 and has an engaging mountain-lodge ambiance that's a throwback to an earlier era. Fully restored rooms are hardly soundproof, but they have pedestal sinks, bleached pine furnishings and patchwork quilts. Rates include continental breakfast.

Lodge at Koele (☎ 565-7300, 800-321-4666, fax 565-4561, **w** www.lanai-resorts.com) Room/suite packages from $300/500. With the character of an overgrown plantation estate, this low-rise resort hotel north of town effects a genteel image of afternoon tea, lawn bowling and croquet. Its lobby, called the Great Hall, is stuffed with an eclectic collection of antiques, artwork and upholstered furnishings, plus Hawaii's two largest stone fireplaces.

Places to Eat

The island's largest grocery stores, *Richard's Shopping Center* and *Pine Isle Market*, both close early and at lunchtime. *Pele's Garden Health Foods* (☎ 565-9629) is an organic grocery store that sells cheeses, deli-style meats and fresh juices. Locals also hang out at *Coffee Works* (☎ 565-6962, 604 Ilima Ave) for homemade croissants, muffins and soups (as well as darn good Thai iced coffee).

Blue Ginger Cafe (☎ 565-6363, cnr 7th St & Ilima Ave) Breakfast or lunch $5-8, dinner mains $10-15. Open from 6am-9pm daily. This unpretentious little bakery-café with cement floors and plastic chairs dishes up three square meals a day. Next door

Tanigawa's (☎ 565-6537) has the most popular old-fashioned burgers on Lanai – you can get one with the works for a mere $3.

Pele's Other Garden (☎ 565-9628, cnr 8th & Houston Sts) Lunch $5-8, dinner mains $10-16. Open 9:30am-3pm & 5pm-9pm Mon-Sat. It offers deli sandwiches at lunch, when you can sit on the front porch and watch the Lanai City traffic trickle by, and a hearty Italian bistro menu at dinner.

Henry Clay's Rotisserie (☎ 565-4700) Entrées $19-29. Open 5:30pm-9pm daily. The most bustling dinner spot is at the Hotel Lanai (see Places to Stay, earlier), where the chef shows off his New Orleans roots. Main dishes include a memorable eggplant Creole angel-hair pasta, and his gourmet pizzas are available for takeout.

The *Lodge at Koele* (see Places to Stay, earlier) also has a few formal dining options.

Entertainment

People go to bed early in Lanai City, and there's no real nightlife. The *Lodge at Koele* (see Places to Stay, earlier) usually has mellow Hawaiian music nightly.

Lanai Theatre (☎ 565-7500) Adult/child $7/4.50. The island's cozy little movie theater shows first-run features a few nights per week.

Shopping

Most shops are not open Sunday.

Gifts With Aloha (☎ 565-6589, 363 7th St) The name fits! Drop by for handcrafted jewelry, island wear, photography and woodcarvings.

Local Gentry (☎ 565-9130, 363 7th St) A real find, this shop sells clothes handpicked from around the world – don't miss the $10 bargain treasure chest.

Lanai Art Program (☎ 565-7503, 339 7th St) Hours can be a bit irregular, but this community arts center shop is also worth a look.

MANELE BAY & HULOPOE BAY

Manele Harbor is a natural crescent-shaped harbor backed by sheer cliffs. In the early 20th century, cattle were herded down to Manele Bay for shipment to Honolulu, and you can still see the remains of a cattle chute if you walk around the point at the end of the parking lot. Inside Manele Bay, coral is abundant near the cliffsides, where the bottom of the bay quickly slopes off to about 40 feet. To the west is **Cathedrals**, a popular scuba diving site.

Both Manele and Hulopoe bays are part of a marine life conservation district, which prohibits the removal of coral and rocks and restricts many fishing activities. The two bays are parted by a volcanic cinder cone that's sharply eroded on its southerly seaward edge. There's a small sea arch below the point. Watch out for *kona* storms, when leeward winds produce strong currents and swells. Head to the left side of Hulopoe Bay, where there are lots of colorful coral and reef fish. Just beyond the sandy beach, there's a low lava shelf with tide pools worth exploring and a protected splash pool.

Generally, the most action occurs when the boats from Maui pull in with snorkelers. If you arrive by boat, it's a 10-minute walk from Manele Bay to **Hulopoe Beach Park**, with its gently curving white-sand beach. It's long and broad and protected by a rocky point to the south. The Manele Bay Hotel sits on a low seaside terrace.

Hulopoe Beach Campground Camping registration fee $5; site $5 per person per night. Surprisingly, even with the luxury hotel nearby, camping is still allowed just a short stroll from Hulopoe Beach. The public beach park has solar-heated showers, restrooms, picnic tables, pay phones and water fountains. Things get pretty busy, especially on weekends, so make reservations with Lanai Company (☎ 565-3978) and pick up permits at the Castle & Cooke offices in Lanai City (see earlier). If the six official sites are full, you could join local families who illegally pitch tents on the beach.

AROUND THE ISLAND
Lanai's adventures stem from its 4WD trails. If renting a 4WD looks pricey, then this is your lucky day for learning how to really mountain bike. Otherwise, a standard car will get you as far as the turnoff to Shipwreck Beach.

Northwest Lanai
From Lanai City, the section of Polihua Rd up to the Garden of the Gods is a fairly level, albeit dusty route that usually takes about 20 minutes to drive from town. To travel onward to Polihua Beach is another matter, however; the rocky and narrow descent is suitable only for those with 4WD experience. Depending on when the road was last graded, the trip could take anywhere from 20 minutes to an hour.

Follow Lanai Ave north of town past the Lodge at Koele, turning left between the tennis courts and the stables to head west. The first part of the trail is clearly marked by etched rocks reading 'Garden of the Gods.' After making a right turn, the dirt road passes through former pineapple fields and the Nature Conservancy's **Kanepuu Preserve**, a diverse native dryland forest, the last in Hawaii. Credit for saving this ecosystem goes to naturalist and former ranch manager George Munro, who fenced out feral goats and cattle in the 1920s. There's a quick self-guided tour with interpretive signs.

There's no garden at the dry **Garden of the Gods**, but rather a landscape of wind-sculpted rocks in rich shades of ocher, sienna and pink. How godly the garden appears depends on what you're looking for. Some people just see rocks, while others find the formations hauntingly beautiful. **Polihua Beach**, on the northwestern tip of the island, is a broad, 1½-mile-long white-sand beach. Although it's gorgeous, strong winds kick up the sand, insects often make it uncomfortable and water conditions are treacherous year-round.

Shipwreck Beach
From Lanai City, head north on Lanai Ave and bear right on Keomuku Rd (Hwy 44). This well-paved road heads into hills and pastures with grazing cattle before gently sloping down to the coast. Along the way you get vistas of the undeveloped southeast shore of Molokai and its tiny islet Mokuhooniki, in great contrast to Maui and its Kaanapali high-rises off to the right.

Where the pavement turns to dirt, head left for **Shipwreck Beach**. True to its name, there are a couple of shipwrecks, as well as a coastline that's good for beachcombing. A low rock shelf lines much of the shore, so the shallow, murky waters are not great for swimming or snorkeling. Lots of driftwood washes up on this windswept beach. Some of the pieces are identifiable as the sun-bleached timbers of shipwrecks – hulls, side planks, perhaps even a gangplank. There are also fishing nets, ropes and the occasional glass float from Japan.

Look for the old Federation Camp beach shacks on your right as you drive in. Park somewhere nearby before the sand gets too deep and then walk for about 10 minutes down to the site of a former **lighthouse**, set on a lava-rock point. From its cement foundations, vague trail markings lead directly inland to a cluster of boulder **petroglyphs**. The rocky path runs through ground cover of flowering golden ilima and pink and yellow lantana.

It's about 15 minutes farther up the beach to a rusting WWII **liberty ship** (cargo ship) that washed up on the reef. You can see the shipwreck clearly from the light-house foundations. It's possible to walk another 6 miles all the way to Awalua, where there's not much else to see besides another shipwreck. The hike is windy, hot and dry, although the farther down the beach you go, the prettier it gets.

Luahiwa Petroglyphs

Lanai's highest concentration of ancient petroglyphs are carved into dozens of boulders overlooking Palawai Basin. Unfortunately, many of the petroglyphs are quite weathered (though still superior to those found on Maui). Some misguided visitors have further damaged the petroglyphs by trying to re-engrave them with burning sticks or chalk.

It's a little challenging to get to the Luahiwa petroglyphs. Head south from Lanai City along Manele Rd and look for six taller pine trees on your left. Turn left onto that dirt road and head for the water tower on the ridge, taking a sharp left after the first mile. Stay on this upper road for at least a half mile until the first boulders are visible. Since the trail requires some tight maneuvering here, it might be a better option to park down below and walk to the petroglyphs.

Munro Trail

The Munro Trail is an exhilarating 8½-mile adventure that can be negotiated in a 4WD vehicle, by mountain bike or on foot. It is named for naturalist George Munro, who planted the trees along the trail and else-where around the island in order to provide a watershed.

The trail passes through sections planted with eucalyptus and Norfolk pine and is draped with ferns. It climbs up along the ridge of Lanaihale, which at 3370 feet is the highest point on Lanai. On a clear day, you can see almost all of the inhabited Hawaiian Islands from various points along the route. Do not stray off the main trail as it descends for six miles onto the central plateau. When you hit the cattle grate, you'll know that the paved highway is not far away.

Be forewarned that this dirt trail can become very muddy, particularly in winter or after rain. Although it was thoroughly overhauled in 2001, 4WDs still occasionally get stuck. Those making the journey under their own steam should be prepared for slippery, steep grades. To start, head north from Lanai City and turn right about a mile past the Lodge at Koele onto a paved cemetery road. From there just follow the signs.

Molokai

According to ancient chants, Molokai is a child of Hina, goddess of the moon and mother of Maui. Today the island is just about the last stronghold of rural Hawaii, with almost 50% of its population claiming native Hawaiian ancestry.

If you're looking for lots of action, this isn't the place. Molokai survives in a time warp: no packaged Hawaiiana, no high-rises and no stoplights. With so much small-town character, even newcomers find themselves waving the shaka sign out on the road to virtual strangers. At times it seems more

The Off-Limits Island of Kahoolawe

Kahoolawe, the smallest of the main Hawaiian islands, appears like a low wall on the horizon. When viewed from Maui, it often has a rosy glow because of all the red dust in the air, particularly during the afternoon breezes. At night, it's pitch black, devoid of any light.

In 1981, Kahoolawe was added to the National Register of Historic Places as a significant archaeological area. For nearly a decade, this devastated island had the ironic distinction of being the only such historic place that was being used by its government for bombing target practice.

In many ways, the island's story mirrors the journey of the Hawaiian people, from wayfinders of ancient Polynesia through US annexation to the native sovereignty movement of today.

Origins

In ancient times this was the place where kahuna and navigators were trained, and it played an important role in early Pacific migrations. The channel between Lanai and Kahoolawe, as well as the westernmost point of island itself, is named Kealaikahiki, meaning 'pathway to Tahiti.' When early Polynesian voyagers made the journey between Hawaii and Tahiti, they lined up their canoes at this departure point.

More than 500 archaeological sites have been identified on Kahoolawe. Puu Moiwi, a large cinder cone in the center of the island, contains one of Hawaii's largest ancient adze quarries. Other sites include heiau and many stone and wood fishing shrines. There is a stone called the Navigator's Chair atop Puu Moaulaiki, the island's second-highest peak.

Prisoners, Opium & Ranches

Kahoolawe was always an arid island. Over time its native dryland forest was denuded by Hawaiian villagers, and by the time of Western contact it was largely uninhabited and barren.

From 1830, Kaulana Bay, on the island's northern side, served as a place of exile for Maui men accused of petty crimes. But Kahoolawe proved to be less of a 'prison isle' than intended. In 1841, some of the prisoners managed to swim to Molokini and then on to Maui, where they stole both food and canoes and paddled back with their booty (including a few female prisoners they sprang from the penal colony on Lanai). For decades, Kahoolawe's secluded southwestern side was also used by smugglers importing Chinese opium.

Ranchers, who brought the first cattle over around 1880, tried to tame Kahoolawe. Land mismanagement was the order of the day. By the early 1900s, feral goats, pigs and sheep had dug up, rooted out and chewed off so much of Kahoolawe's vegetation that the island was largely a dust bowl.

When Angus MacPhee got his lease from the territorial government in 1918, Kahoolawe was overrun with goats and looked like a wasteland. MacPhee rounded up the goats, stored rainwater in redwood tanks and planted grasses and ground cover. Once again the land was green, but not for too long.

Target Kahoolawe

After the Pearl Harbor attack in 1941, the US military took control of Kahoolawe and began bombing practice over the entire island. Ranch buildings and water cisterns were used as targets

like some forgotten outpost of the South Pacific than a modern island squeezed between the high-rises of Oahu and Maui.

Here you can sit on the edge of an 800-year-old fishpond and watch the sun rise over Haleakala on distant Maui. Later, you can walk along Hawaii's largest beach with barely another soul in sight. In the evening, you can watch the sun set behind rustling palms in Molokai's royal coconut grove.

Although the island has garnered a reputation for being wary of outsiders, any trav-

The Off-Limits Island of Kahoolawe

and reduced to rubble. After the war, civilians were forbidden from returning to Kahoolawe; MacPhee was never compensated for his losses.

In 1953, a presidential decree gave the US Navy official jurisdiction over the island, with the stipulation that when Kahoolawe was no longer 'needed,' the live ammunition would be removed and the island would be returned to the territory of Hawaii in a 'habitable condition.'

Kahoolawe Movement

By the 1970s, Hawaiian politicians were petitioning the federal government to cease its military activities and return Kahoolawe to the state.

Then in 1976, a small group of Hawaiian activists set out in boats for Kahoolawe to attract attention to the bombings. There were a series of occupations, some lasting more than a month and many activists were jailed.

During one of the 1977 crossings, group members George Helm and Kimo Mitchell mysteriously disappeared in the waters off Kahoolawe. Helm had been an inspirational Hawaiian-rights activist, and with his death the Protect Kahoolawe Ohana (PKO) movement sprang up. Helm's vision of turning Kahoolawe into a sanctuary of Hawaiian culture and identity quickly became widespread among islanders.

In 1980, in a court-sanctioned consent decree, the Navy reached an agreement that allowed the PKO regular access for religious, cultural, scientific and educational purposes. Although the bombing continued, the decree restricted the Navy from using live munitions on part of the island and from bombing archaeological sites (isn't precision bombing wonderful?).

In October 1990, as Hawaii's two US senators, Daniel Inouye and Daniel Akaka, were preparing a congressional bill to stop the bombing, President Bush issued an order to halt military activities.

On May 7, 1994, in a ceremony marked by Hawaiian rituals, chants and prayers, the US Navy signed over control of the island of Kahoolawe to the state and Hawaii's first native Hawaiian governor, John Waihee.

Kahoolawe Today

One enormous obstacle that remains is the cleaning up of live munitions from the island. The federal government has established a fund of up to $400 million for that purpose, but the cleanup now slowly underway will still take years to complete. Meanwhile, two million tons of soil are still lost to erosion each year.

Proposals for the island's future range from establishing a marine sanctuary to protect coral and potential nesting grounds for monk seals and sea turtles to making the island the center for a new Hawaiian nation.

There's no general public access to the island. If you're interested in becoming a working volunteer for the PKO, who make regular trips to the island to plant vegetation, clean up cultural sites and rebuild ancient trails, click to ⓦ www.kahoolawe.org or write to Protect Kahoolawe Ohana, PO Box 152, Honolulu, HI 96810.

eler who shows genuine *aloha aina* (love of the land) will always be welcome.

History

For centuries, the battling armies of Maui and Oahu were careful to bypass Molokai and its powerful *kahuna* – priests, healers, sorcerers and wise people. Molokai's kahuna kept potential invaders at bay through carvings of poisonwood idols and other elaborate rituals; they were said to be able to simply pray their enemies to death.

EXCURSIONS

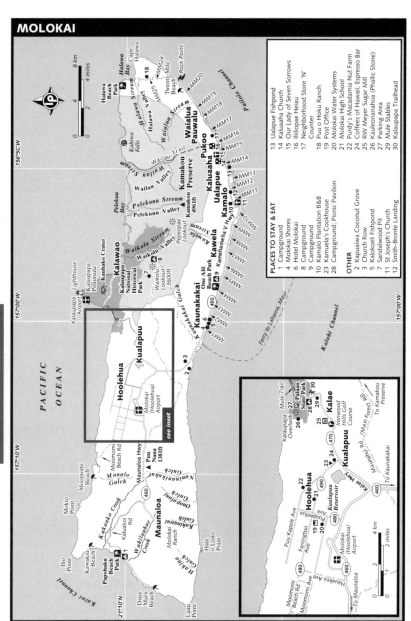

MOLOKAI

PLACES TO STAY & EAT
1 Campground
4 Molokai Shores
6 Hotel Molokai
8 Campground
9 Campground
10 Kamalo Plantation B&B
23 Kamuela's Cookhouse
28 Campground; Picnic Pavilion

OTHER
2 Kapuaiwa Coconut Grove
3 Church Row
5 Kalokoeli Fishpond
7 Sandalwood Pit
11 St Joseph's Church
12 Smith-Bronte Landing

13 Ualapue Fishpond
14 Kaluaaha Church
15 Our Lady of Seven Sorrows
16 Ililiopae Heiau
17 Neighborhood Store 'N'
   Counter
18 Puu o Hoku Ranch
19 Post Office
20 Molokai Water Systems
21 Molokai High School
22 Coffees of Hawaii; Espresso Bar
24 Purdy's Macadamia Nut Farm
25 RW Meyer Sugar Mill
26 Kauleonanahoa (Phallic Stone)
27 Parking Area
29 Mule Stables
30 Kalaupapa Trailhead

By the 18th century, their *mana* (spiritual power) wasn't enough to protect the island. Internal dissent among the *ali'i* (chiefs) led Molokai's rulers to align themselves with chiefs from other islands. Oahu, Maui and the Big Island all got involved in the ensuing power struggle. Although Oahu ruled for a time, Kamehameha the Great ultimately took over Molokai when he conquered and unified all of the islands in 1795.

In the 1850s, Kamehameha V acquired the bulk of Molokai's arable land, forming Molokai Ranch. Overgrazing by cattle and sheep led to the destruction of native vegetation. After the king's death, the ranch was sold off to Honolulu business interests. Sugar was planted, but crops quickly failed. Later, the island became the world's largest honey exporter, only to have an epidemic wipe out the hives and the industry in the mid-1930s.

In the meantime, Molokai Ranch continued its efforts to find '*the* crop for Molokai.' Cotton, rice and numerous grain crops all took their turn biting Molokai's red dust. Finally, pineapple took root as the crop most suitable and plantation-scale production began in Hoolehua in the 1920s.

Despite an influx of immigrant plantation laborers, the island's native Hawaiian community stayed strong. This was in part because of the Hawaiian Homes Act of 1921, which awarded 40-acre tracts of land starting on Molokai. The purpose of the act was to encourage homesteading among native Hawaiians, who had become the most landless ethnic group in Hawaii.

In the 1970s, overseas competition brought an end to the pineapple's reign on Molokai. Since then Molokai Ranch, which still owns about one-third of Molokai, or more than half of the island's privately held lands, has tried several schemes over the years to draw money from tourism.

In the 1990s, the ranch operated a small safari wildlife park where tourists were carted around in vans to snap pictures of exotic animals. Some of the animals also served as targets for trophy hunters willing to pay $1500 to shoot an African eland or blackbuck antelope. Local activists have long rejected the kind of tourist-oriented development that has all but consumed Maui. As a consequence, Molokai now has the highest unemployment levels in the state.

Geography & Geology

With a total land area of 260 sq miles, Molokai lies midway in the Hawaiian chain, equally close to both Maui and Lanai.

Geologically speaking, Molokai is a union of two separate shield volcanoes. An afterthought of Madam Pele created the Kalaupapa Peninsula long after the rest of the island was formed.

Molokai's North Shore, from Kalaupapa to Halawa, is an impenetrable wilderness of deeply cut valleys and coastal mountains. Here the world's highest sea cliffs (the *Guinness Book of Records* says so) reach heights of 3300 feet with an average gradient of more than 55 degrees.

Flora & Fauna

Molokai has rich soil, and some optimists feel the island has the potential to be Hawaii's 'breadbasket.' Significant crops include watermelons, dryland taro, macadamia nuts, sweet potatoes, string beans and onions.

Feral pigs roam the upper wetland forests, and wild goats inhabit the steep canyons and valley rims. The axis deer are descendants of a small herd sent as a gift to Kamehameha V from India in 1868. All three wreak havoc on the environment and are hunted game animals.

Accommodations

Only a few of Molokai's many B&Bs are listed in this chapter. To find more, check with the B&B booking agencies listed in the Facts for the Visitor chapter, or click to W www.molokai.com, W www.visitmolokai.com or W www.molokai-aloha.com.

Camping By far the most popular place to pitch a tent is Papohaku Beach (see West End, later). One Alii Beach Park is closer to Kaunakakai, but it's not very private (think floodlights and carousing locals). Up near the Kalaupapa Overlook and trailhead,

EXCURSIONS

Palaau State Park offers camping in a grassy field next to a picnic pavilion. It often rains here and at the primitive camping ground at Waikolu Lookout in Kamakou Preserve. Both of the latter sites are described under Central Molokai, later.

Permits for Palaau State Park and Waikolu Lookout cost $5 per person per night. There's a five-day maximum stay at either. Apply for permits at the Department of Land & Natural Resources office (☎ 567-6923) in the Molokai Water Systems building, which is just south of the post office in Hoolehua. The office is open 7:30am to 4pm Monday to Friday. On Maui you can pick up permits in advance from the Division of State Parks office in Wailuku (see Camping in the Facts for the Visitor chapter).

Permits for Papohaku and One Alii Beaches cost $3/50¢ adult/child per night. They are issued by the Department of Parks & Recreation (☎ 553-3204) at the Mitchell Pauole Center in Kaunakakai. The office is open 8am to 4pm Monday to Friday. Permits are limited to three consecutive days. If you want to camp longer, you should return here for a new permit.

Getting There & Around

Taking the ferry may not be cheaper or faster than commuter flights, but it is indubitably more fun. See Interisland Ferries in the Getting There & Away chapter.

Molokai Airport, also called Hoolehua Airport, has car rental booths, a snack bar, a liquor lounge, a lei (garland) stand, pay phones and a visitor information booth that is occasionally staffed. The first thing you see as you drive out of the airport is a sign reading, 'Aloha! Slow Down – This is Molokai.' Hallelujah.

Renting a car on Molokai is just about essential. Every car on the island can get booked over weekends, especially during festivals. Budget (☎ 567-6877) and Dollar (☎ 567-6156) base their operations at Molokai Airport. At Island Kine Auto Rental (☎ 553-5242, ☎ 866-527-7368, fax 553-3880, w www.molokai-car-rental.com), shiny new compacts go for around $30 per day, all inclusive. Trucks and 4WDs are also available.

If you're up for long hauls and steady uphill climbs, it is possible to cycle around Molokai. Molokai Bicycle (☎ 553-3931, 800-709-2453, w www.bikehawaii.com/molokai bicycle, 80 Mohala St, Kaunakakai) is a small operation that rents mountain (rigid or full-suspension) and road bikes for $15 to $25 per day. Ask about pick-up and drop-off services and weekly discounts.

KAUNAKAKAI

Kaunakakai, Molokai's only real town, takes much of its character from what it doesn't have. There's no neon, no elevators, no strip malls and almost no fast-food chains. There's not much standard evening entertainment in Kaunakakai.

The Molokai Visitors Association (☎ 553-3876, 800-800-6367, fax 553-5288, w www.molokai-hawaii.com, Kamoi Professional Bldg, suite 700, Kamoi St) can give you the lowdown on what's happening around the island. The office is open 8:30am to 4:30pm Monday to Friday.

Banks with 24-hour ATMs are one of the few concessions to the modern world. Since Molokai doesn't have a daily newspaper, bulletin boards are the prime source of news and announcements. Molokai's two free and entertaining weeklies are *The Dispatch* and the *Molokai Advertiser-News*.

On or around Ala Malama Ave, the town's broad main street, there is a post office, a library, a couple of restaurants, a bakery, a coin laundry and just about everything else a small town needs. All of the shops have aging wooden false fronts, giving the illusion of an old Wild West town. Molokai General Hospital (☎ 808-553-5331, 280 Puali St) is 400 yards to the north.

Things to See & Do

Gone are the days when pineapple was loaded from **Kaunakakai Wharf**, but an interisland barge still pulls into the harbor with supplies a couple of times a week. On the west side of the wharf road, near the canoe shed, are the stone foundations of the **Kamehameha V House**, now overgrown.

As Molokai was his favorite island playground, Kamehameha V also planted the

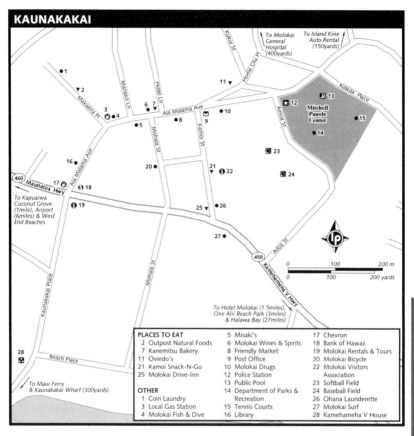

KAUNAKAKAI

To Molokai
General
Hospital
(400yards)

To Island Kine
Auto Rental
(150yards)

Mitchell
Pauole
Center

To Kapuaiwa
Coconut Grove
(1mile), Airport
(6miles) & West
End Beaches

To Hotel Molokai (1.5miles),
One Alii Beach Park (3miles)
& Halawa Bay (27miles)

To Maui Ferry
& Kaunakakai Wharf (300yards)

PLACES TO EAT	5 Misaki's	17 Chevron
2 Outpost Natural Foods	6 Molokai Wines & Spirits	18 Bank of Hawaii
7 Kanemitsu Bakery	8 Friendly Market	19 Molokai Rentals & Tours
11 Oviedo's	9 Post Office	20 Molokai Bicycle
21 Kamoi Snack-N-Go	10 Molokai Drugs	22 Molokai Visitors
25 Molokai Drive-Inn	12 Police Station	Association
	13 Public Pool	23 Softball Field
OTHER	14 Department of Parks &	24 Baseball Field
1 Coin Laundry	Recreation	26 Ohana Launderette
3 Local Gas Station	15 Tennis Courts	27 Molokai Surf
4 Molokai Fish & Dive	16 Library	28 Kamehameha V House

Kapuaiwa Coconut Grove, farther west, in the 1860s. The grove is under the management of Hawaiian Home Lands today. Watch out for falling coconuts! Across the road is **Church Row**, where any denomination that attracts even a handful of Hawaiian members receives its own little tract of land. In effect, a quaint white church with green trim sits next to a quaint green church with white trim, and so on down the line.

Activities

In terms of swimming, the Kaunakakai area is a dud, with a coastline of silty, shallow waters. A few miles east of town, **One Alii**

Beach Park is used mainly for picnics, parties and camping. In town, the **Mitchell Pauole Center** has an indoor public swimming pool and two lighted tennis courts.

To buy or rent boogie boards, snorkel gear and other sports equipment, call Molokai Fish & Dive (☎ 553-5926, Ala Malama Ave), Molokai Surf (☎ 553-5093, Kamehameha V Hwy) or Molokai Bicycle (see Getting There & Around, earlier).

Places to Stay

If you want to camp at *One Alii Beach Park* or check out other B&Bs and condos, see the Accommodations section earlier.

Ka Hale Mala (☎/fax 553-9009, ⓦ www
.molokai-bnb.com, PO Box 1582, Kaunakakai, HI 96748) 4-room apartment $80,
each additional person $15. Occupying the
ground level of a modern home east of Kaunakakai, this spotless 900-sq-ft B&B rental
has a full kitchen and garden lanai. Guests
can borrow snorkeling gear and street bikes.
If you're lucky, the full gourmet breakfast
may include taro pancakes or banana frit-
ters. Credit cards are not accepted.

Hotel Molokai (☎ 553-5347, 800-367-5004,
fax 553-5047, ⓦ www.hotelmolokai.com,
Kamehameha V Hwy) Standard/oceanfront
rooms $80/130, kitchenette units $135. This
Polynesian-style hotel has a laid-back aloha
atmosphere that's perfect for Molokai.
Rooms set in clusters of two-story buildings
have private baths, ceiling fans, telephones
and cable TVs. There's an oceanfront pool,
plus top-notch sunsets and stargazing from
the reefside beach. The waterfront tiki bar
occasionally has mellow Hawaiian music,
especially on Aloha Friday afternoon.

Places to Eat

Misaki's and **Friendly Market** are the
island's two major grocery stores. **Molokai
Wines & Spirits** also sells snacks, imported
beer and Hawaiian microbrews.

Outpost Natural Foods (☎ 553-3377, 70
Makaena Pl) This health food store stocks
bulk granola, dried fruit, yogurt and fresh
produce, some of it organic. It sells fresh
juices, deli items and a daily takeout special,
such as tofu quiche with salad, for under $5.

Kanemitsu Bakery (☎ 553-5855, Ala
Malama Ave) Open 5:30am-6:30pm Wed-
Mon. Kanemitsu makes the Molokai bread
that is famous around the islands, but you
can skip the attached restaurant. For night
owls, there's the time-honored tradition of
going down the alley behind the bakery to
knock on the door and persuade the night-
shift baker to sell you a hot loaf.

Kamoi Snack-N-Go (☎ 553-3742, Molokai Professional Plaza) Open until 9pm daily.
This combination convenience store and ice
cream shop sells about 30 different flavors
of gourmet, Honolulu-made Dave's Ice
Cream. A giant one-scoop cone costs $1.60.

Molokai Drive-Inn (☎ 553-5655, Kamehameha V Hwy) Open 6:30am-10pm daily.
This landmark used to be a Dairy Queen,
but Molokai wasn't quite ready for that so
the sign came down. Nowadays, its takeout
window serves 100% local Hawaiian food.
There are plastic tables inside where you
can chow down.

Most of Kaunakakai's other daytime
eateries are old-fashioned lunch counters.
At Filipino-style **Oviedo's** (Ala Malama
Ave) you can fill up for $5.

Hotel Molokai (see Places to Stay, earlier)
Breakfast or lunch $5-10, dinner mains
$12.50-17.50, early-bird or buffet dinner $10.
Open 7am-10am, 11:30am-1pm & 6pm-9pm
daily. This is the best breakfast spot in town,
and the wait staff are – well, absolutely fabulous. At lunch, you can order burgers, teri-
yaki chicken or mahimahi sandwiches, while
fresh fish, barbecue and steaks come out at
dinner. The open-air restaurant and bar sit
right on the beach, with waves lapping at
the shore and even your table legs.

Shopping

Molokai Fish & Dive (see Activities, earlier)
Although just about every shop in Kaunakakai has an assortment of T-shirts pro-
claiming Molokai's rural pride, with slogans
such as 'Keep Hawaiian Lands in Hawaiian
Hands' and 'Molokai Mo Bettah,' this place
has the best selection.

Kamakana Fine Arts Gallery (☎ 553-
8520, Ala Malama Ave) This upstairs art
gallery represents over 80 Molokai artists
by displaying woodcarvings, handcrafted
jewelry and lei, woven bags and more.

EAST MOLOKAI

The pastoral drive from Kaunakakai to
Halawa Valley takes about 1½ hours to
cover 27 miles. It's a good paved road that
hugs the ocean for much of the drive, with
the mountains of East Molokai rising up to
the north.

Kamalo, a small roadside village 10 miles
east of Kaunakakai, holds **St Joseph's
Church**. Built by Father Damien in 1876, this
simple, one-room wooden church has some
of its original wavy glass panes.

Three-quarters of a mile past the 11-mile marker, look for a small hanging sign on the makai side of the road pointing out the **Smith-Bronte Landing**. A little memorial plaque set among the kiawe trees commemorates the first civilian flight from the US mainland to Hawaii. Oahu was the intended destination, but the two pilots instead safely crash-landed on Molokai in 1927.

About a half mile past the 13-mile marker, impressive **Ualapue Fishpond** lies on the seaward side of the road. After the 14-mile marker, look for the defunct Ah Ping Store and its gas pump dating from the 1930s.

The ruins of Molokai's first church are next at **Kaluaaha**. They are a bit off the road and inland but (barely) visible if you keep an eye out. A quarter of a mile later is **Our Lady of Seven Sorrows Church**, a 1966 reconstruction of a Father Damien original. Nearby another ancient fishpond has the high-rise-studded shores of West Maui as an incongruous backdrop.

Quiet **Iliiliopae Heiau** is Molokai's biggest and best-known temple and is thought to be the oldest as well. Once used for human sacrifices, its stones still seem to emanate vibrations of the past. Visiting the *heiau* (temple) is usually straightforward, but since it is on private property, act respectfully. Start by walking inland along a dirt road 0.6 miles past the 15-mile marker, or immediately after Mapulehu Bridge. After 10 minutes, cut left across a streambed where handwritten signs point you deeper into the jungle.

The sleepy backwater of **Pukoo** was once the seat of local government – complete with a courthouse, jail, wharf and post office – until the plantation folks built Kaunakakai. The ***Neighborhood Store 'N' Counter*** (☎ 558-8498), near the 16-mile marker, is the only place to get a meal (under $8) on the east side.

Twenty-Mile Beach is a stretch of white sand that pops up right along the roadside. When the tide is low, the water can be too shallow for swimming. Snorkeling is much better beyond the reef, but unless it's very calm, the currents are dangerous. As the

Fishponds

Along the road to Halawa Valley, look makai every so often, for Molokai's southeast coast is strung with the largest concentration of ancient fishponds in Hawaii.

These giant fishponds are evidence that the early Hawaiians had a highly developed system of aquaculture. One type of pond was inshore and totally closed off from the sea. The other was a shoreline fishpond, created by a stone wall parallel to the beach, and scalloped back toward shore on both ends to form an enclosure. According to legend, fishponds were said to be the work of the *menehune*, Hawaii's mythical race of little people, who made them appear virtually overnight. In reality, it took hard labor.

Molokai once had more than 60 productive shoreline fishponds, constructed from the 13th century onward. Built of lava rock upon the reefs, their slatted sluice gates were set into place and prayed over by kahuna. The gates allowed small fish into the pond, where they were hand-fed with breadfruit and sweet potatoes. Fattened fish that couldn't pass back through the narrow slats were easily scooped up with a net.

Many fishponds were strictly for the ali'i, and commoners were not allowed to eat the fish raised in them. Grazing by cattle and sheep introduced in the mid-1800s resulted in widespread erosion, and the clay that washed down from the mountains choked out the ponds. Over the years, efforts have been made to restock a few of the fishponds, mostly with mullet and milkfish. One of the most impressive and easily visited is the Kalokoeli Fishpond behind Molokai Shores condos east of Kaunakakai.

road swings left before the 21-mile marker, **Rock Point** attracts local surfers.

Tall grasses just at the edge seem to be trying to reclaim the road, while ironwood trees and the spindly spikes of sisal plants punctuate the surrounding hills. Just before the 24-mile marker there's a view of the small island of **Mokuhooniki**, a seabird sanctuary. One more mile brings you to **Puu o Hoku Ranch**, where the bones of Lanikaula, a revered 16th-century kahuna, lie hidden in a grove of sacred kukui. Over the years, many islanders claim to have seen the night lanterns of ghost marchers bobbing along near the grove. Stop by the ranch store for organic produce or to ask about mountain-bike trails and horseback rides.

After passing the 25-mile marker, the jungle begins to close in, and the scent of eucalyptus fills the air. There are lots of beep-as-you-go hairpin bends. At the end of the road, **Halawa Beach** was a favored surfing spot for Molokai chiefs. The beach has double coves separated by a rocky outcrop. When the water is calm, there's good swimming, but both coves are subject to dangerous rip currents, especially in high surf or when Halawa Stream, which empties into the north cove, is flowing heavily.

Places to Stay

To find other B&Bs and condos, see Accommodations, earlier.

Kamalo Plantation Bed & Breakfast (☎/fax 558-8236, W *www.molokai.com/kamalo, Kamehameha V Hwy*) Cottage/beach house $85/140. This rural B&B is in a fruit orchard opposite St Joseph's Church, so naturally breakfast includes fresh fruit and homemade breads. The grounds have the stone foundation of an ancient heiau, and the genial owners can point out little-known hiking trails in the area.

Puu o Hoku Ranch (☎ 558-8109, fax 558-8100, W *www.puuohoku.com, PO Box 1889, Kaunakakai, HI 96748*) 2-bedroom cottage/lodge house $100/175. The name of this ranch started by Paul Fagan of Hana, Maui, fame means 'where hills and stars meet.' Jimmy Stewart, JFK and other famous folks have all visited here. The country cottage with its shady lanai, wicker furnishings and sunny kitchen makes for a memorable and romantic getaway.

CENTRAL MOLOKAI

Central Molokai takes in the Hoolehua Plains, which stretch from Kamakou Pre-

serve to windswept Moomomi Beach in the west. The most trodden route in central Molokai is the drive up to the Kalaupapa Overlook.

Turning north off Hwy 460 onto Hwy 470 (Kalae Hwy), the road starts in dry grasslands and climbs past a coffee plantation, the town of Kualapuu, a restored sugar mill, mule stables and the trail down to the Kalaupapa Peninsula. The road ends at Palaau State Park, site of the Kalaupapa Overlook.

Kamakou Preserve

The mountains that form the spine of Molokai's east side reach all the way up to Kamakou (4961 feet), the island's highest peak. Kamakou Preserve is a treasure, but its protected wilderness state exists in part because the rutted dirt road leading to it makes it a challenge to reach. During the rainy season, vehicles leave tracks and the road tends to get progressively more rutted until it's regraded in the summer.

The 10-mile drive up to **Waikolu Lookout** (3600 feet) takes about 45 minutes, depending on road conditions. A mile before the lookout is the 19th-century **Sandalwood Pit**, a grassy depression on the left. The pit was dug to the exact measurements of a 75-foot-long ship's hold. After being filled with fragrant sandalwood logs, the wood was strapped to the backs of laborers, who hauled it down to the harbor for shipment to China. The sea captains made out like bandits, while Hawaii lost its sandalwood forests.

The lookout, just before the preserve entrance, gives panoramic views of remote Waikolu Valley. If it's been raining recently, numerous waterfalls stream down the sheer cliffsides. Morning is the best time for views, as afternoon trade winds commonly carry clouds to the upper level of the canyon. Opposite the lookout is a primitive *campground* with pit toilets (see Accommodations, earlier). Bring along an ample supply of drinking water and rain gear.

The same goes for those who plan on hiking inside the preserve. The 1-mile boardwalk trail to spectacular **Pepeopae**

Overlook starts from the main 4WD trail about 2½ miles after the entrance. The trail passes through nearly undisturbed Hawaiian montane bog, a mysterious miniature forest with stunted trees and dwarfed plants. For guided and volunteer trips with the Nature Conservancy, see the Hiking special section at the end of the Activities chapter.

Kalaupapa Peninsula

Kalaupapa means 'Flat Leaf,' an accurate description of the lava slab peninsula that was created when a low shield volcano poked up out of the sea long after the rest of Molokai had been formed. The dormant Kauhako Crater, visible from the overlook, contains a little lake that's more than 800 feet deep.

At the base of majestic and formidable cliffs, Kalaupapa Peninsula was a leprosy colony for over a century. In 1835, doctors diagnosed Hawaii's first case of leprosy, one of many diseases introduced by foreign laborers. Alarmed by the spread of the disease by the 1860s, King Kamehameha V signed into law an act that banished people with leprosy to this peninsula. Once the afflicted arrived at Kalaupapa, there was no way out, not even in a casket.

Before modern medicine, leprosy manifested itself in dripping, foul-smelling sores. Eventually, patients experienced loss of sensation and tissue degeneration that could lead to extreme deformity or even loss of limbs. Some captains were so terrified of the disease that they would not land at Kalaupapa, but instead pushed patients overboard into rough, shark-infested waters. Those who could, swam to shore. Many others drowned.

Early conditions at the settlement were unspeakably horrible. Those who were relatively healthy stole rations from the weak. Many children were enslaved and women forced into prostitution. Not surprisingly, life spans were invariably short. Father Damien (Joseph de Veuster) arrived at Kalaupapa in 1873. He was a Belgian priest who devoted the latter part of his life to helping people with leprosy before contracting and dying of the disease himself.

He wasn't the first missionary to come, but he was the first to stay. Father Damien nursed the sick, wrapped bandages on oozing sores, hammered coffins and dug graves. A talented carpenter, he also built churches and decent housing for the sick, but mostly he gave them a sense of hope.

Even in Father Damien's day, it was one of the least contagious of all communicable diseases. Only 4% of humans are even susceptible to leprosy. The same year that Father Damien arrived on Kalaupapa, Norwegian Dr Gerhard Hansen discovered *Mycobacterium leprae,* the bacteria that causes leprosy, and proved that the disease was not hereditary. Since the 1940s sulfone antibiotics have been used successfully to control leprosy, but the isolation policies in Kalaupapa weren't abandoned until 1969.

Although no longer a 'colony,' Kalaupapa Peninsula is still home to around 100 people with the condition. Kalaupapa National Historical Park is jointly managed by the Hawaii Department of Health and the National Park Service. Residents are, of course, free to leave, but for many this is their only home and they've fiercely refused to be bought out by the state or federal governments over the years, residing on this wildly beautiful peninsula by choice.

While the state of Hawaii officially uses the term 'Hansen's Disease' for leprosy, many Kalaupapa residents consider that to be a euphemism that fails to reflect the stigma they have suffered and continue to use the old term. However, the degrading term 'leper' is universally offensive.

Organized Tours Only guests of Kalaupapa residents are allowed to stay overnight. Old state laws require everyone who enters the settlement to have a permit and to be at least 16 years old. These regulations are still enforced to protect the privacy of the patients. By law, you cannot wander around Kalaupapa Peninsula by yourself. Visitors must join a guided tour, offered Monday to Saturday, for which your reservation acts as your 'permit.'

On typical tours, the village looks nearly deserted. The main sights are cemeteries,

EXCURSIONS

Mail Home Some Aloha

The postmaster of the Hoolehua post office stocks baskets of unhusked coconuts that you can address and mail off as a unique (and perhaps edible!) 'postcard.' These coconuts, which the postmaster gathers on her own time, are free for this 'post-a-nut' purpose, and she keeps a few felt pens on hand so you can jot down a message on your chosen coconut. Priority mail postage for an average-size coconut to anywhere in the USA costs from $5. The Hoolehua post office is open 7:30am to 11:30am and 12:30pm to 4:30pm Monday to Friday.

churches and memorials. Places where residents go to 'talk story' – the post office, store and hospital – are pointed out, but no stops are made. Visitors are not allowed to photograph any of the residents. Kalaupapa is a tourist attraction but its people are not.

Kalaupapa has a little air strip at the edge of the peninsula and air service via small prop planes. Passengers must first book a tour with one of the following companies before buying air tickets.

Damien Tours *(☎ 567-6171)* Land tour $30. Tours of the peninsula in an old school bus are run by Richard Marks, a wry storyteller, an oral historian and the third generation of his family to live on Kalaupapa. Advance reservations are required (call between 4pm and 8pm) and bring your own lunch.

Molokai Mule Ride *(☎ 553-3876, 800-567-7550, fax 553-5288, W www.muleride.com)* Tours $150. The mules move none too quickly – actually, hiking down can be faster – but there's a certain thrill in trusting your life to these sure-footed beasts. The trip begins at the mule stables at 8am sharp with a short riding instruction by real *paniolo* (Hawaiian cowboys). Advance reservations are strongly advised.

The only land route is the 3-mile switchback mule trail down the *pali* (cliffs). The trail starts on the east side of Hwy 470 just north of the mule stables. You might see cars parked by the gate. Don't be intimidated by the 'Unauthorized Persons Keep Out' sign at the start of the path *if* you have tour reservations. The trail descends about 1600 feet on 26 narrow cliffside switchbacks, but it's not strenuous. Allow over an hour for the descent, and slightly more for the return trip.

Kualapuu

In 1991, coffee trees were planted on formerly fallow pineapple fields around here by **Coffees of Hawaii** *(☎ 567-9241, 800-709-2326)*. For free samples of rich Molokai brews, stop by the company shop just off the highway. The ***Espresso Bar*** also has bagels and sandwiches for noshing. If you're interested in mule-drawn wagon tours of the fields, call ahead.

To the west is **Purdy's Macadamia Nut Farm** *(admission free; usually open 9:30am-3:30pm Mon-Sat).* Unlike tours on the Big Island that focus on processing, Purdy takes you into his orchard and explains how the nuts grow. A single macadamia tree can simultaneously be in different stages of progression – with flowers in blossom, tiny nuts just beginning and clusters of mature nuts. Visitors can crack open nuts with a hammer and sample macadamia blossom honey with slices of fresh coconut.

EXCURSIONS

Kamuela's Cookhouse (☎ 567-9655) Breakfast or lunch $5-10, dinner mains $8-15. Open 6:30am-2:30pm & 5:30pm-8:30pm Tues-Fri, 8am-2pm Sat & Sun. The Cookhouse is a busy place for such a small town, but that's because it serves the best grinds on Molokai. Breakfasts are huge and homemade desserts are a specialty – try a slice of chocolate–macadamia nut pie or lilikoi-orange cheesecake.

RW Meyer Sugar Mill Museum

Rudolph Meyer, an industrious German farmer, was on his way to the California Gold Rush when he dropped by Hawaii, married a member of Hawaiian royalty and landed a tidy bit of property in the process. This restored sugar mill (☎ 567-6436; admission $2.50; open 10am-2pm Mon-Sat), which is the last of its kind, operated for only a decade. You can follow a self-guided tour.

Palaau State Park

Palaau State Park is at the northern end of Hwy 470. The **Kalaupapa Overlook** perches on the edge of a 1600-foot cliff. It's like an aerial view without the airplane. Interpretive plaques identify the landmarks below. In the opposite direction, a five-minute trail leads to Hawaii's premier phallic stone, **Kauleonanahoa**, poking up in an ironwood grove. Women hoping to become pregnant can sleep here overnight, and some also leave offerings of lei and dollar bills.

A quarter-mile back down the road farther south, there's a *campground* underneath a stand of eucalyptus and ironwood trees. This grassy field gets more than its fair share of rain, however, and fronts the highway. There are restrooms inside the cement picnic pavilion, but no potable water.

Moomomi Beach

Windswept Moomomi Beach, located on the western edge of the Hoolehua Plains, is ecologically unique. Some endangered native plant species found here exist nowhere else on earth. It is also one of the few spots in the populated Hawaiian Islands where green sea turtles still find a suitable breeding habitat.

Many archaeological finds have also been preserved over time by the aridity of Moomomi's expansive coastal sand dunes. **Moomomi Bay** has a tiny sandy beach that is part of the Hawaiian Home Lands. It is marked by a picnic pavilion with restrooms. The broad, white-sand beach that most people call Moomomi is at **Kawaaloa Bay**, a windy 20-minute walk to the west. High surf and rough currents should keep you out of the water at either place. Because of the fragile ecology of the dunes, visitors should stay along the beach and on trails only.

For guided hikes and volunteer work trips with the Nature Conservancy, refer to the Hiking special section at the end of the Activities chapter. Otherwise, good luck getting here through the maze of red dirt roads. Some are quite smooth and others deeply rutted. If it hasn't been raining heavily, standard cars might just make it (though the car rental agencies forbid drivers from trying). Unless the rougher Moomomi Ave has been regraded recently, take Farrington Ave west from the highway instead.

WEST END

The Maunaloa Hwy (Hwy 460) heads west from Kaunakakai, passes Molokai Airport, and climbs into the high, grassy rangeland of Molokai's arid western side. Molokai Ranch owns most of the land on this side of the island.

Maunaloa

The Molokai Ranch headquarters and lodge (see the following page) are in this little plantation-era town at the end of the road. Inside the 'logo' shop, the activity desk can book you on kayak tours, equestrian and mountain-bike trail rides, plus a wealth of other activities. Rates for nonguests are steep, but discounts may be negotiable if things are slow.

Farther down the street you'll find a rural post office, general store and gas station. The *Big Wind Kite Factory* (☎ 552-2364, 120 Maunaloa Hwy) sells kites of all shapes and styles. If you're lucky, you can watch them being made. An extension of the kite factory is a shop that sells, among other miscellany, Hawaiiana books.

The Lodge at Molokai Ranch (☎ *552-2741, 877-726-4656, fax 534-1606,* Ⓦ *www .molokairanch.com, Maunaloa Hwy)* Accommodations packages $250-500. Guests generally don't see much of Molokai outside the ranch gates – then again, the ranch does own 54,000 acres. It's a full-service experience, with free Internet access, free beach gear and generous discounts on outdoor adventures and even spa treatments. Guests stay either at the vintage lodge in Maunaloa or out in a deluxe canvas bungalow at Kaupoa Beach Village, where chefs prepare made-to-order barbecues in an outdoor pavilion. The lodge has an upscale, if somewhat unexciting restaurant and one of Molokai's only watering holes, the ***Paniolo Bar***.

If chicken is your thing, there's a ***KFC*** next to the modern, three-screen ***Maunaloa Town Cinemas*** (☎ *552-2707).*

West End Beaches

From Molokai's West End beaches, the twinkling lights of Oahu are just 26 miles away.

Off Hwy 460 at the 15-mile marker, a road leads down to the sprawling Kaluakoi Resort, now defunct due to environmental mismanagement by its Japanese owners. There are a few condominium complexes now, but the old golf course is slowly returning to the wild. The white sands of **Kepuhi Beach** front the old Kaluakoi Hotel, but swimming conditions are often dangerous. Condo guests use the hotel swimming pool instead. Local surfers head for the north end of the beach.

If you're looking for something quieter, head north along the coastal golf greens (now actually brown) and up over a rocky point to **Kawakiu Beach**, a white-sand crescent with bright turquoise waters and good swimming when seas are calm, most often in summer.

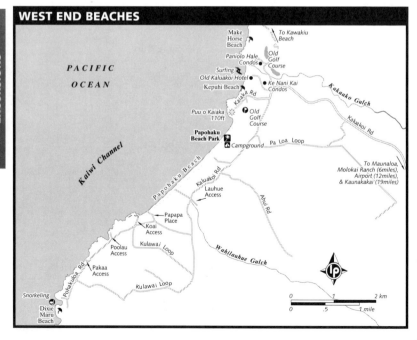

WEST END BEACHES

In the other direction, a short hike leads up to the top of **Puu o Kaiaka**, a 110-foot-high promontory at the south end of Kepuhi Beach, and rewards you with a nice view of Papohaku Beach. At the top, you'll find the remains of a pulley that was once used to carry cattle down to waiting barges for transport to Oahu slaughterhouses.

The highway turns south toward **Papohaku Beach**, which lays claim to being Hawaii's largest beach. It could hold the entire population of Molokai without getting crowded, although that would be an unlikely scenario. The main drawbacks are severe winds and the water itself, which is too treacherous for swimming.

Papohaku Beach Park is a choice site for camping – beautiful and quiet, with the surf lulling you to sleep and the birds waking you up – except, of course, when it gets busy with boisterous local families. Secure your tent carefully, as the wind sometimes blows with hardy gusts. There are picnic facilities, restrooms, outdoor *and* indoor showers, water fountains and some thorny kiawe trees. See the Accommodations section earlier for permit details.

A few miles south of Papohaku is **Dixie Maru Beach**, a popular family beach with a small, protected bay for swimming and snorkeling. The sand is an interesting confetti of waterworn coral bits and small shells.

EXCURSIONS

Glossary

a'a – rough, jagged lava

ae – yes

ahi – yellowfin tuna

ahu – stone cairns used to mark a trail; altar or shrine

ahupuaa – traditional land division, usually wedge-shaped and extending from the mountains to the sea

aikane – friend

aina – land

akamai – smart, clever

aku – bonito or skipjack tuna

akua – god, spirit, idol

akule – big-eyed scad

ala – road, path or trail

ali'i – chief, royalty

aloha – traditional greeting meaning love, welcome

aloha aina – love of the land

amakihi – small, yellow-green bird; one of the more common native birds

anaana – psycho-spiritual method of influencing or explaining events

anuenue – rainbow

aole – no

apapane – bright-red native Hawaiian honeycreeper

au – marlin

aumakua – ancestral spirit helper

awa – kava, made into an intoxicating brew

awapuhi – wild ginger

bento – Japanese boxed lunch or meal

crack seed – snack food, usually dried fruits or seeds; can be sour, salty or sweet

haku lei – crown of flowers worn on the head or around a hat

hala – pandanus plant or screw pine; leaves used in weaving mats and baskets

hale – grass-roofed house

hana – work; or bay, when used as a compound in place names

haole – Caucasian, literally 'without breath'

hapa – half; person of mixed blood

hapa haole – half white; used for a person, thing or idea

hau – indigenous lowland Hibiscus tree whose wood is often used for outrigger canoes

haupia – coconut tapioca pudding

Hauoli Makahiki Hou – Happy New Year

Hawaii nei – all the Hawaiian Islands, as distinguished from the Big Island

heiau – ancient Hawaiian temple

Hina – Polynesian goddess, wife of Ku and mother of Maui

holoholo – walk, drive, sail, visit or ramble around for pleasure

holoku – long dress similar to the *muumuu,* but more fitted and European in style

holua – ancient Hawaiian sled or sled course

honu – turtle

hooilo – winter

hookipa – hospitality, welcome; to visit

hoolaulea – celebration, party

hooponopono – new beginning; to correct; traditional Hawaiian reconciliation process

housekeeping cabin – self-catering cabin

huhu – angry

hui – social group, club, organization

hula – traditional Hawaiian dance

hula halau – hula school or group

humuhumunukunukuapuaa – rectangular triggerfish, Hawaii's unofficial state fish

ihi – respect

iiwi – bright-red native forest bird with a salmon-colored beak

iliahi – Hawaiian sandalwood

iliili – stones; Hawaiian hot stone therapy

imu – underground earthen oven used in traditional *luau* cooking to prepare things like *kalua* pig

issei – first generation of Japanese-Hawaiians

kahili – feathered standard, used as a symbol of royalty

kahuna – wise person in any field, commonly a priest, healer or sorcerer

kahuna nui – high priest

kai – saltwater

kalo – see *taro*

kalua – traditional method of baking in an underground oven *(imu)*

kamaaina – native-born Hawaiian or longtime resident; literally, 'child of the land'

kanaka – human being, man, person (usually of Hawaiian descent)

kane/Kane – man; one of the four main Hawaiian gods

kapa – see *tapa*

kapu – taboo, part of the strict ancient Hawaiian social system; often used on signs to mean 'Keep Out'

kau – summer

kaukau – food

kava – mildly narcotic drink made from the roots of *Piper methysticum,* a pepper shrub

keiki – child, children

kiawe – relative of the mesquite tree introduced to Hawaii in the 1820s and now very common; its branches are covered with thorns

kii – deity image, statue

kipuka – 'island' of land spared when lava flows around it; an oasis

ko – sugarcane

koa – native hardwood tree, often used in woodworking of furniture and native crafts; fishing shrines (different pronunciation)

kohola – whale

kokua – help, cooperation, please; 'Please Kokua' on a trash can is a gentle way of saying, 'Don't litter'

kona – leeward; leeward wind

koolau – windward

Ku – Polynesian god of many manifestations, including god of war, farming and fishing; husband of Hina

kukui – candlenut tree, Hawaii's official state tree; its oily nuts were once burned in lamps

kupuna – grandparent, respected elder

la – sun

Laka – goddess of the hula

lanai – verandah, porch

lani – sky, heaven

lauhala – leaves of the *hala* plant used in weaving

laulau – wrapped package; bundles of pork or beef with salted fish that are wrapped in leaves and steamed

lei – garland of flowers, leaves, shells, kukui nuts or feathers

lilikoi – passion fruit

limu – seaweed

lio – horse

lolo – stupid, crazy

lomi – to rub or soften; *lomi* salmon is raw, diced salmon marinated with tomatoes and onions

lomi lomi – traditional Hawaiian massage

Lono – Polynesian god of harvest, agriculture, fertility and peace

loulu – native fan palms

luakini – type of *heiau* dedicated to the war god Ku and used for human sacrifice

luau – traditional Hawaiian feast

mahalo – thank you

mahimahi – dolphin (the fish, not the mammal)

mahu – traditional Hawaiian transgender person; gay man

maile – native plant with twining habit and fragrant leaves; often used for lei

makaainana – commoners, literally 'people who tend the land'

makaha – sluice gate used to regulate the level of water in a traditional Hawaiian fishpond

makai – toward the sea

makaku – creative, artistic *mana*

makani – wind

malasada – Portuguese fried dough served warm, similar to a doughnut

malihini – newcomer, visitor

malo – loincloth

mana – supernatural or spiritual power

manini – convict tang (a reef fish); anything small or insignificant

mano – shark

Maui Nui – literally 'Big Maui,' referring to the ancient island group of Maui, Kahoolawe, Lanai and Molokai, which today comprise Maui County

mauka – toward the mountains, inland
mauna – mountain
mele – song, chant
menehune – 'the little people' who according to legend built many of Hawaii's fishponds, *heiau* and other stonework
moana – ocean, open sea
moku – island
mo'o – water spirit, water lizard
mu – body catcher who secured sacrificial victims for *luakini*
muumuu – long, loose-fitting dress introduced by the missionaries

nalu – wave
Neighbor Islands – main Hawaiian islands, outside of Oahu
nene – native goose, Hawaii's state bird
nisei – second generation of Japanese-Hawaiians
noni – Indian mulberry; a small tree with yellow, smelly fruit that is used medicinally
nuku puu – native honeycreeper with a bright-yellow underbelly

ohana – family, extended family
ohelo – low-growing native shrub with edible, red berries favored by *nene;* said to be sacred to the goddess Pele
ohia lehua – native Hawaiian tree with tufted, feathery flowers
olo – surfboards used by Hawaiian royalty
ono – delicious; the wahoo fish
opae – shrimp
opakapaka – pink snapper

pahoehoe – smooth, ropy lava that is quick-flowing
pahu – wood and sharkskin drum
pakalolo – marijuana; literally 'crazy smoke'
pali – cliff
palila – native honeycreeper
paniolo – Hawaiian cowboy
pau – finished, no more; *pau hana* means quitting time
Pele – goddess of fire and volcanoes
piko – navel, umbilical cord
pili – bunchgrass, commonly used for thatching houses
pipikaula – salted, dried beef that is served broiled

pohaku – rock
poi – gooey paste made from *taro* root, usually eaten as a side dish, a staple of the Hawaiian diet
poke – chopped raw fish commonly marinated in soy sauce, oil and chili pepper; anything prepared similarly
Poliahu – goddess of snow
pono – harmony
pueo – Hawaiian short-eared owl
puka – any kind of hole or opening
pule – prayer
pupu – snack food, hors d'oeuvre; shells
puu – hill, peak, cinder cone
puuhonua – place of refuge

saimin – Hawaiian version of Asian noodle soup (ramen)
shaka sign – hand gesture used as a greeting
shahkbait – very pale, untanned person

tabi – Japanese-style split-toed shoes, used for reef-walking
talk story – to chat, shoot the breeze, tell tales
tapa – cloth made from the beaten bark of the paper mulberry tree, used for early Hawaiian clothing *(kapa)*
taro – plant with green, heart-shaped leaves cultivated for its edible root, which is mashed to make *poi*
ti – common native plant; its long, shiny leaves are used for wrapping food and making hula skirts
tutu – aunt, respected older woman

ukulele – stringed musical instrument derived from the *braguinha,* which was introduced to Hawaii in the 1800s by Portuguese immigrants
ulu – breadfruit
ulu maika – ancient Hawaiian game, similar to bowling
unipihili – spirits of the dead

waa – canoe
wahine – woman
wai – freshwater
wailele – waterfall
wane – sea urchin
wikiwiki – hurry, quick

LONELY PLANET

You already know that Lonely Planet produces more than this one guidebook, but you might not be aware of the other products we have on this region. Here is a selection of titles which you may want to check out as well:

Hawaii
ISBN 1 86450 047 6
US$19.95 • UK£12.99

Hawaii The Big Island
ISBN 1 74059 345 6
US$16.99 • UK£9.99

Los Angeles
ISBN 1 74059 021 X
US$15.99 • UK£9.99

USA
ISBN 1 86450 308 4
US$24.99 • UK£14.99

South Pacific
ISBN 0 86442 717 4
US$24.95 • UK£15.99

South Pacific Phrasebook
ISBN 0 86442 595 3
US$6.95 • UK£4.99

Available wherever books are sold.

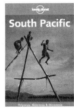

Lonely Planet Guides by Region

Lonely Planet is known worldwide for publishing practical, reliable and no-nonsense travel information in our guides and on our Web site. The Lonely Planet list covers just about every accessible part of the world. Currently there are 16 series: Travel guides, Shoestring guides, Condensed guides, Phrasebooks, Read This First, Healthy Travel, Walking guides, Cycling guides, Watching Wildlife guides, Pisces Diving & Snorkeling guides, City Maps, Road Atlases, Out to Eat, World Food, Journeys travel literature and Pictorials.

AFRICA Africa on a shoestring • Botswana • Cairo • Cairo City Map • Cape Town • Cape Town City Map • East Africa • Egypt • Egyptian Arabic phrasebook • Ethiopia, Eritrea & Djibouti • Ethiopian Amharic phrasebook • The Gambia & Senegal • Healthy Travel Africa • Kenya • Malawi • Morocco • Moroccan Arabic phrasebook • Mozambique • Namibia • Read This First: Africa • South Africa, Lesotho & Swaziland • Southern Africa • Southern Africa Road Atlas • Swahili phrasebook • Tanzania, Zanzibar & Pemba • Trekking in East Africa • Tunisia • Watching Wildlife East Africa • Watching Wildlife Southern Africa • West Africa • World Food Morocco • Zambia • Zimbabwe, Botswana & Namibia
Travel Literature: Mali Blues: Traveling to an African Beat • The Rainbird: A Central African Journey • Songs to an African Sunset: A Zimbabwean Story

AUSTRALIA & THE PACIFIC Aboriginal Australia & the Torres Strait Islands • Auckland • Australia • Australian phrasebook • Australia Road Atlas • Cycling Australia • Cycling New Zealand • Fiji • Fijian phrasebook • Healthy Travel Australia, NZ and the Pacific • Islands of Australia's Great Barrier Reef • Melbourne • Melbourne City Map • Micronesia • New Caledonia • New South Wales • New Zealand • Northern Territory • Outback Australia • Out to Eat – Melbourne • Out to Eat – Sydney • Papua New Guinea • Pidgin phrasebook • Queensland • Rarotonga & the Cook Islands • Samoa • Solomon Islands • South Australia • South Pacific • South Pacific phrasebook • Sydney • Sydney City Map • Sydney Condensed • Tahiti & French Polynesia • Tasmania • Tonga • Tramping in New Zealand • Vanuatu • Victoria • Walking in Australia • Watching Wildlife Australia • Western Australia
Travel Literature: Islands in the Clouds: Travel in the Highlands of New Guinea • Kiwi Tracks: A New Zealand Journey • Sean & David's Long Drive

CENTRAL AMERICA & THE CARIBBEAN Bahamas, Turks & Caicos • Baja California • Belize, Guatemala & Yucatán • Bermuda • Central America on a shoestring • Costa Rica • Costa Rica Spanish phrasebook • Cuba • Cycling Cuba • Dominican Republic & Haiti • Eastern Caribbean • Guatemala • Havana • Healthy Travel Central & South America • Jamaica • Mexico • Mexico City • Panama • Puerto Rico • Read This First: Central & South America • Virgin Islands • World Food Caribbean • World Food Mexico • Yucatán
Travel Literature: Green Dreams: Travels in Central America

EUROPE Amsterdam • Amsterdam City Map • Amsterdam Condensed • Andalucía • Athens • Austria • Baltic States phrasebook • Barcelona • Barcelona City Map • Belgium & Luxembourg • Berlin • Berlin City Map • Britain • British phrasebook • Brussels, Bruges & Antwerp • Brussels City Map • Budapest • Budapest City Map • Canary Islands • Catalunya & the Costa Brava • Central Europe • Central Europe phrasebook • Copenhagen • Corfu & the Ionians • Corsica • Crete • Crete Condensed • Croatia • Cycling Britain • Cycling France • Cyprus • Czech & Slovak Republics • Czech phrasebook • Denmark • Dublin • Dublin City Map • Dublin Condensed • Eastern Europe • Eastern Europe phrasebook • Edinburgh • Edinburgh City Map • England • Estonia, Latvia & Lithuania • Europe on a shoestring • Europe phrasebook • Finland • Florence • Florence City Map • France • Frankfurt City Map • Frankfurt Condensed • French phrasebook • Georgia, Armenia & Azerbaijan • Germany • German phrasebook • Greece • Greek Islands • Greek phrasebook • Hungary • Iceland • Iceland, Greenland & the Faroe Islands • Ireland • Italian phrasebook • Italy • Kraków • Lisbon • The Loire • London • London City Map • London Condensed • Madrid • Madrid City Map • Malta • Mediterranean Europe • Milan, Turin & Genoa • Moscow • Munich • Netherlands • Normandy • Norway • Out to Eat – London • Out to Eat – Paris • Paris • Paris City Map • Paris Condensed • Poland • Polish phrasebook • Portugal • Portuguese phrasebook • Prague • Prague City Map • Provence & the Côte d'Azur • Read This First: Europe • Rhodes & the Dodecanese • Romania & Moldova • Rome • Rome City Map • Rome Condensed • Russia, Ukraine & Belarus • Russian phrasebook • Scandinavian & Baltic Europe • Scandinavian phrasebook • Scotland • Sicily • Slovenia • South-West France • Spain • Spanish phrasebook • Stockholm • St Petersburg • St Petersburg City Map • Sweden • Switzerland • Tuscany • Ukrainian phrasebook • Venice • Vienna • Wales • Walking in Britain • Walking in France • Walking in Ireland • Walking in Italy • Walking in Scotland • Walking in Spain • Walking in Switzerland • Western Europe • World Food France • World Food Greece • World Food Ireland • World Food Italy • World Food Spain **Travel Literature:** After Yugoslavia • Love and War in the Apennines • The Olive Grove: Travels in Greece • On the Shores of the Mediterranean • Round Ireland in Low Gear • A Small Place in Italy

Lonely Planet Mail Order

Lonely Planet products are distributed worldwide. They are also available by mail order from Lonely Planet, so if you have difficulty finding a title, please write to us. North and South American residents should write to 150 Linden St, Oakland, CA 94607, USA; European and African residents should write to 10a Spring Place, London NW5 3BH, UK; and residents of other countries to Locked Bag 1, Footscray, Victoria 3011, Australia.

INDIAN SUBCONTINENT & THE INDIAN OCEAN Bangladesh • Bengali phrasebook • Bhutan • Delhi • Goa • Healthy Travel Asia & India • Hindi & Urdu phrasebook • India • India & Bangladesh City Map • Indian Himalaya • Karakoram Highway • Kathmandu City Map • Kerala • Madagascar • Maldives • Mauritius, Réunion & Seychelles • Mumbai (Bombay) • Nepal • Nepali phrasebook • North India • Pakistan • Rajasthan • Read This First: Asia & India • South India • Sri Lanka • Sri Lanka phrasebook • Tibet • Tibetan phrasebook • Trekking in the Indian Himalaya • Trekking in the Karakoram & Hindukush • Trekking in the Nepal Himalaya • World Food India **Travel Literature**: The Age of Kali: Indian Travels and Encounters • Hello Goodnight: A Life of Goa • In Rajasthan • Maverick in Madagascar • A Season in Heaven: True Tales from the Road to Kathmandu • Shopping for Buddhas • A Short Walk in the Hindu Kush • Slowly Down the Ganges

MIDDLE EAST & CENTRAL ASIA Bahrain, Kuwait & Qatar • Central Asia • Central Asia phrasebook • Dubai • Farsi (Persian) phrasebook • Hebrew phrasebook • Iran • Israel & the Palestinian Territories • Istanbul • Istanbul City Map • Istanbul to Cairo • Istanbul to Kathmandu • Jerusalem • Jerusalem City Map • Jordan • Lebanon • Middle East • Oman & the United Arab Emirates • Syria • Turkey • Turkish phrasebook • World Food Turkey • Yemen **Travel Literature**: Black on Black: Iran Revisited • Breaking Ranks: Turbulent Travels in the Promised Land • The Gates of Damascus • Kingdom of the Film Stars: Journey into Jordan

NORTH AMERICA Alaska • Boston • Boston City Map • Boston Condensed • British Columbia • California & Nevada • California Condensed • Canada • Chicago • Chicago City Map • Chicago Condensed • Florida • Georgia & the Carolinas • Great Lakes • Hawaii • Hiking in Alaska • Hiking in the USA • Honolulu & Oahu City Map • Las Vegas • Los Angeles • Los Angeles City Map • Louisiana & the Deep South • Miami • Miami City Map • Montréal • New England • New Orleans • New Orleans City Map • New York City • New York City City Map • New York City Condensed • New York, New Jersey & Pennsylvania • Oahu • Out to Eat – San Francisco • Pacific Northwest • Rocky Mountains • San Diego & Tijuana • San Francisco • San Francisco City Map • Seattle • Seattle City Map • Southwest • Texas • Toronto • USA • USA phrasebook • Vancouver • Vancouver City Map • Virginia & the Capital Region • Washington, DC • Washington, DC City Map • World Food New Orleans **Travel Literature**: Caught Inside: A Surfer's Year on the California Coast • Drive Thru America

NORTH-EAST ASIA Beijing • Beijing City Map • Cantonese phrasebook • China • Hiking in Japan • Hong Kong & Macau • Hong Kong City Map • Hong Kong Condensed • Japan • Japanese phrasebook • Korea • Korean phrasebook • Kyoto • Mandarin phrasebook • Mongolia • Mongolian phrasebook • Seoul • Shanghai • South-West China • Taiwan • Tokyo • World Food Hong Kong • World Food Japan **Travel Literature:** In Xanadu: A Quest • Lost Japan

SOUTH AMERICA Argentina, Uruguay & Paraguay • Bolivia • Brazil • Brazilian phrasebook • Buenos Aires • Buenos Aires City Map • Chile & Easter Island • Colombia • Ecuador & the Galápagos Islands • Healthy Travel Central & South America • Latin American Spanish phrasebook • Peru • Quechua phrasebook • Read This First: Central & South America • Rio de Janeiro • Rio de Janeiro City Map • Santiago de Chile • South America on a shoestring • Trekking in the Patagonian Andes • Venezuela **Travel Literature:** Full Circle: A South American Journey

SOUTH-EAST ASIA Bali & Lombok • Bangkok • Bangkok City Map • Burmese phrasebook • Cambodia • Cycling Vietnam, Laos & Cambodia • East Timor phrasebook • Hanoi • Healthy Travel Asia & India • Hill Tribes phrasebook • Ho Chi Minh City (Saigon) • Indonesia • Indonesian phrasebook • Indonesia's Eastern Islands • Java • Lao phrasebook • Laos • Malay phrasebook • Malaysia, Singapore & Brunei • Myanmar (Burma) • Philippines • Pilipino (Tagalog) phrasebook • Read This First: Asia & India • Singapore • Singapore City Map • South-East Asia on a shoestring • South-East Asia phrasebook • Thailand • Thailand's Islands & Beaches • Thailand, Vietnam, Laos & Cambodia Road Atlas • Thai phrasebook • Vietnam • Vietnamese phrasebook • World Food Indonesia • World Food Thailand • World Food Vietnam

ALSO AVAILABLE: Antarctica • The Arctic • The Blue Man: Tales of Travel, Love and Coffee • Brief Encounters: Stories of Love, Sex & Travel • Buddhist Stupas in Asia: The Shape of Perfection • Chasing Rickshaws • The Last Grain Race • Lonely Planet…On the Edge: Adventurous Escapades from Around the World • Lonely Planet Unpacked • Lonely Planet Unpacked Again • Not the Only Planet: Science Fiction Travel Stories • Ports of Call: A Journey by Sea • Sacred India • Travel Photography: A Guide to Taking Better Pictures • Travel with Children • Tuvalu: Portrait of an Island Nation

Index

Bold indicates maps.

Places to Stay

Places to Eat

Boxed Text

MAP LEGEND

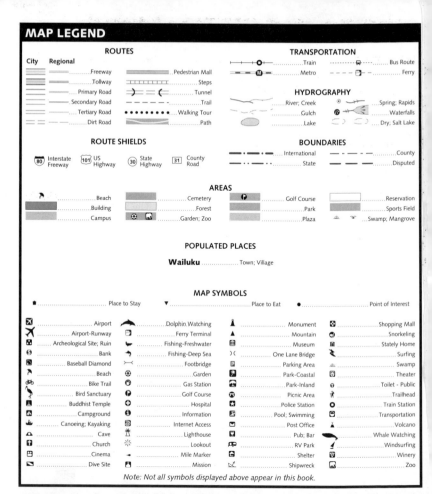

ROUTES

City | Regional

............Freeway
............Tollway
.... Primary Road
.... Secondary Road
.... Tertiary Road
.... Dirt Road

.... Pedestrian Mall
.... Steps
.... Tunnel
.... Trail
... Walking Tour
.... Path

ROUTE SHIELDS

Interstate Freeway — US Highway — State Highway — County Road

AREAS

.... Beach
..............Building
.... Campus

.... Cemetery
..............Forest
.... Garden; Zoo

TRANSPORTATION

................Train
.... Metro

.........Bus Route
.... Ferry

HYDROGRAPHY

...........River; Creek
.... Gulch
.... Lake

.... Spring; Rapids
............Waterfalls
.... Dry; Salt Lake

BOUNDARIES

.... International
.... State

............County
..........Disputed

.... Golf Course
..............Park
..............Plaza

............Reservation
.... Sports Field
...Swamp; Mangrove

POPULATED PLACES

Wailuku .... Town; Village

MAP SYMBOLS

.... Place to Stay
.... Place to Eat
.... Point of Interest

.... Airport
.... Airport-Runway
...... Archeological Site; Ruin
.... Bank
.... Baseball Diamond
.... Beach
.... Bike Trail
.... Bird Sanctuary
.... Buddhist Temple
.... Campground
.... Canoeing; Kayaking
.... Cave
.... Church
.... Cinema
.... Dive Site

.... Dolphin Watching
.... Ferry Terminal
.... Fishing-Freshwater
.... Fishing-Deep Sea
.... Footbridge
.... Garden
.... Gas Station
.... Golf Course
.... Hospital
.... Information
.... Internet Access
.... Lighthouse
.... Lookout
.... Mile Marker
.... Mission

.... Monument
.... Mountain
.... Museum
.... One Lane Bridge
.... Parking Area
.... Park-Coastal
.... Park-Inland
.... Picnic Area
.... Police Station
.... Pool; Swimming
.... Post Office
.... Pub; Bar
.... RV Park
.... Shelter
.... Shipwreck

.... Shopping Mall
.... Snorkeling
.... Stately Home
.... Surfing
.... Swamp
.... Theater
.... Toilet - Public
.... Trailhead
.... Train Station
.... Transportation
.... Volcano
.... Whale Watching
.... Windsurfing
.... Winery
.... Zoo

Note: Not all symbols displayed above appear in this book.

LONELY PLANET OFFICES

Australia
Locked Bag 1, Footscray, Victoria 3011
☎ 03 8379 8000 fax 03 8379 8111
email talk2us@lonelyplanet.com.au

USA
150 Linden Street, Oakland, CA 94607
☎ 510 893 8555, TOLL FREE 800 275 8555
fax 510 893 8572
email info@lonelyplanet.com

UK
10a Spring Place, London NW5 3BH
☎ 020 7428 4800 fax 020 7428 4828
email go@lonelyplanet.co.uk

France
1 rue du Dahomey, 75011 Paris
☎ 01 55 25 33 00 fax 01 55 25 33 01
email bip@lonelyplanet.fr
www.lonelyplanet.fr

World Wide Web: www.lonelyplanet.com *or* AOL keyword: lp
Lonely Planet Images: lpi@lonelyplanet.com.au